3

ORIGINAL STORY:
Mag Hsu

ART:
Nao Emoto

3

CONTENTS

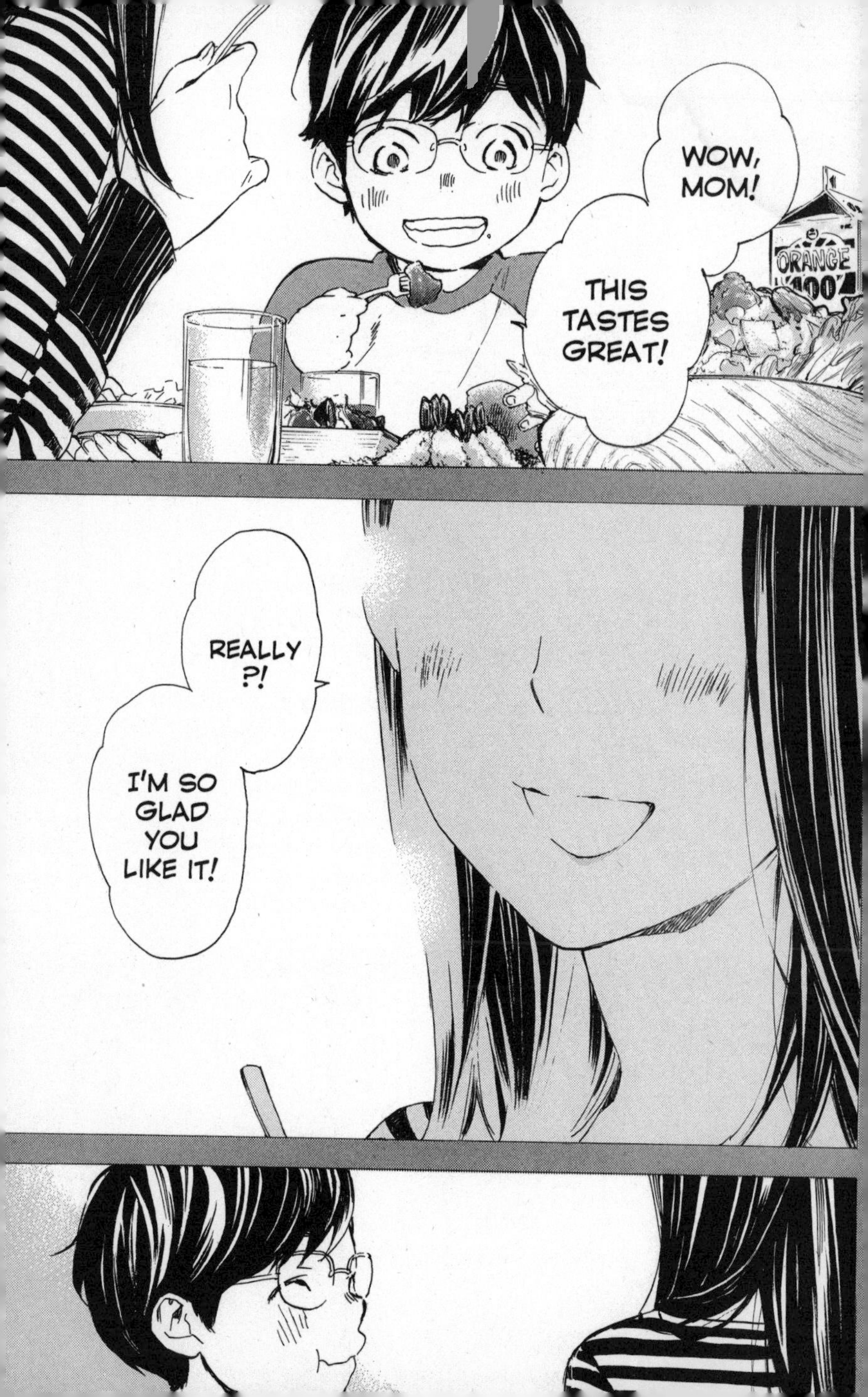
WOW, MOM!
THIS TASTES GREAT!
ORANGE 100
REALLY ?!
I'M SO GLAD YOU LIKE IT!

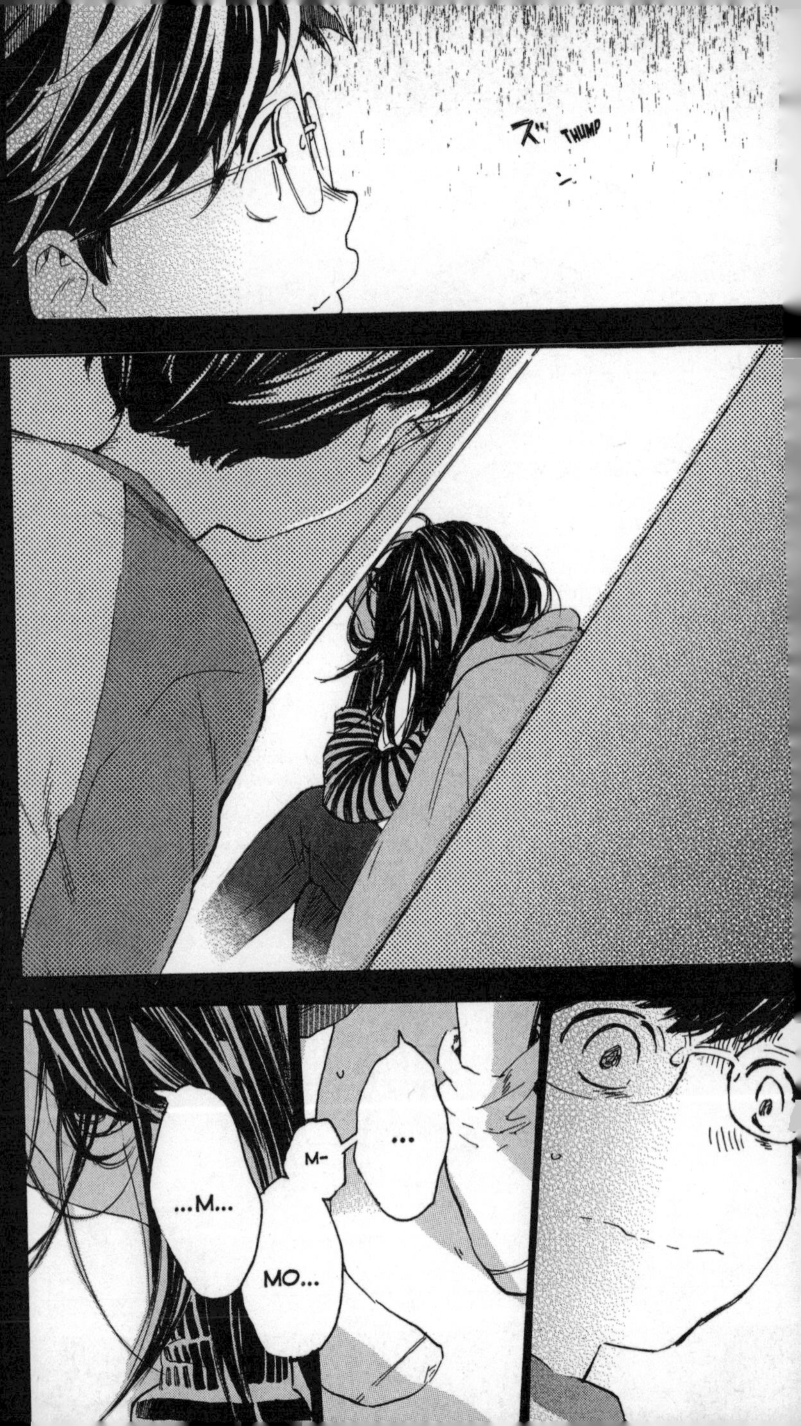
ズン
THUMP
...
M-
...M...
MO...

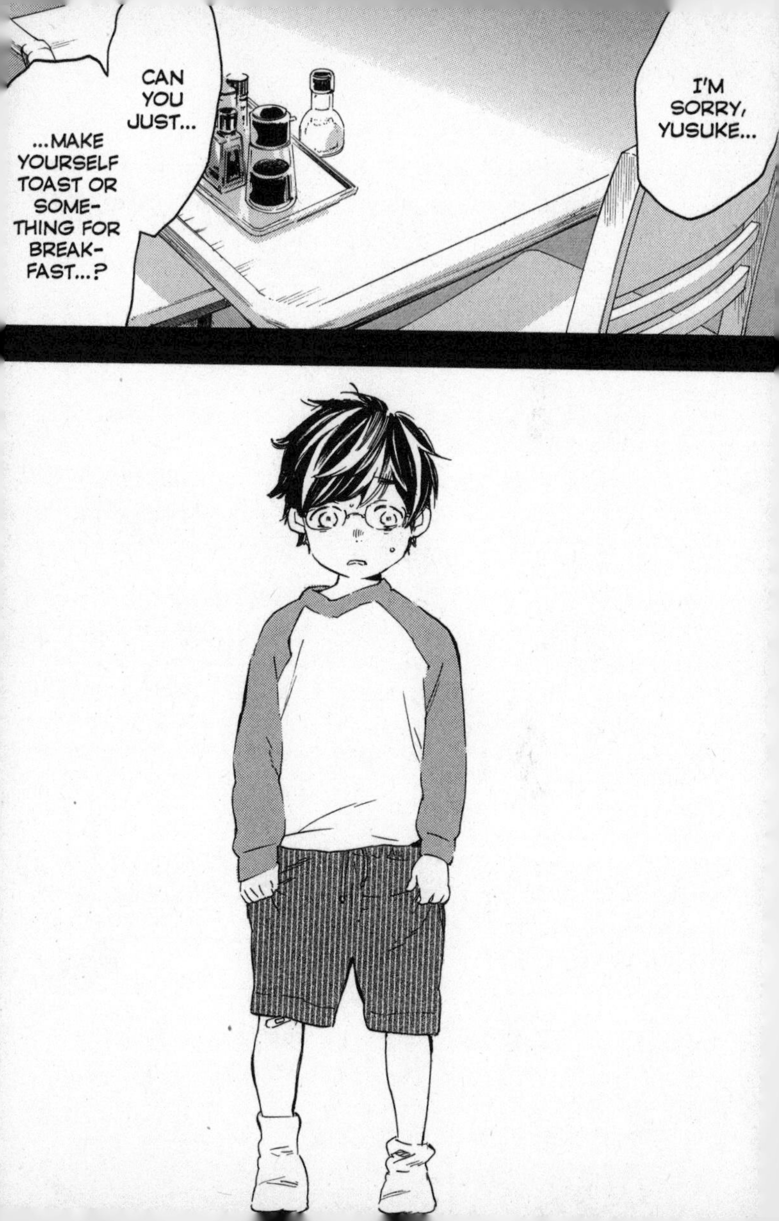
I'M SORRY, YUSUKE...
CAN YOU JUST...
...MAKE YOURSELF TOAST OR SOME-THING FOR BREAK-FAST...?

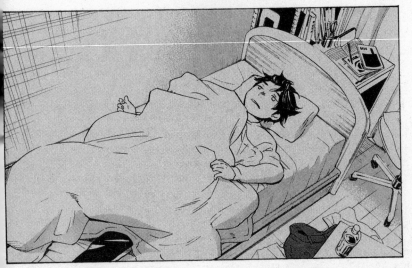

OH...

THAT DREAM AGAIN.

KREAK

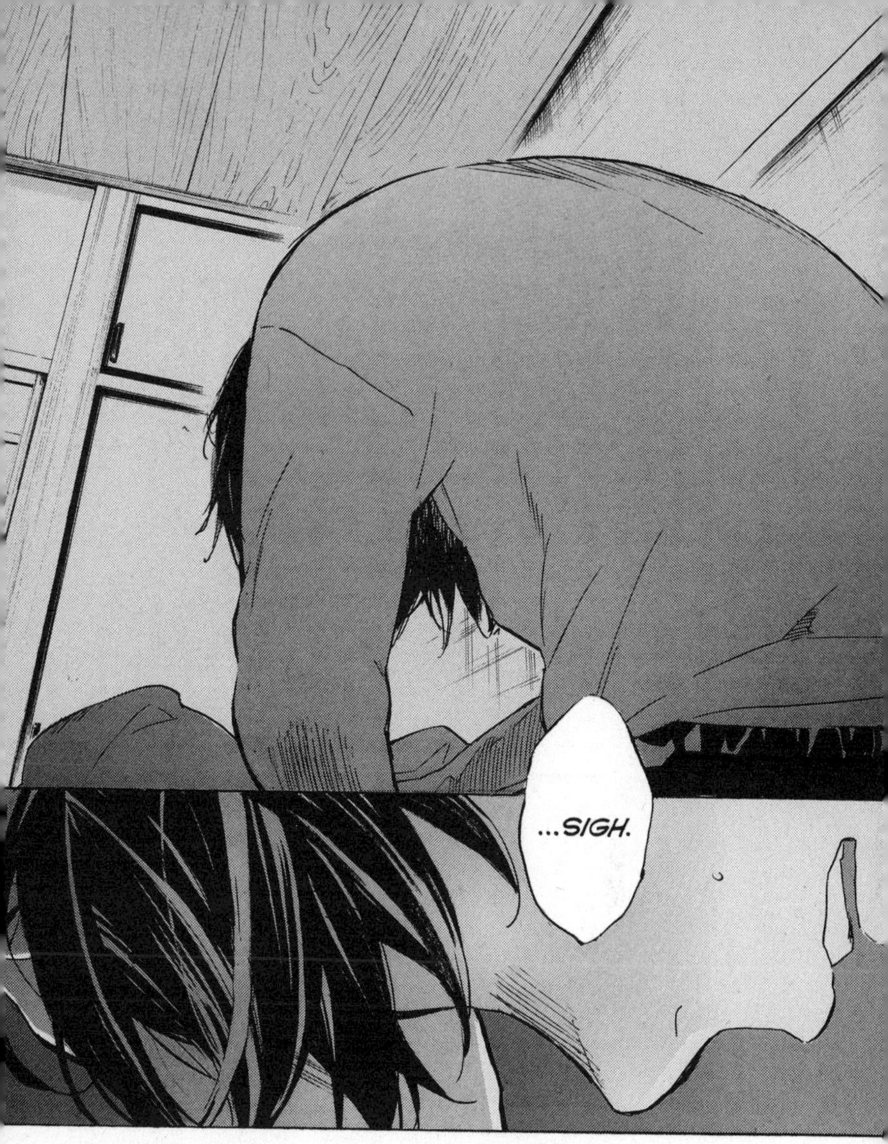
...SIGH.

CHAPTER 16:
Tsukushi Makino 5

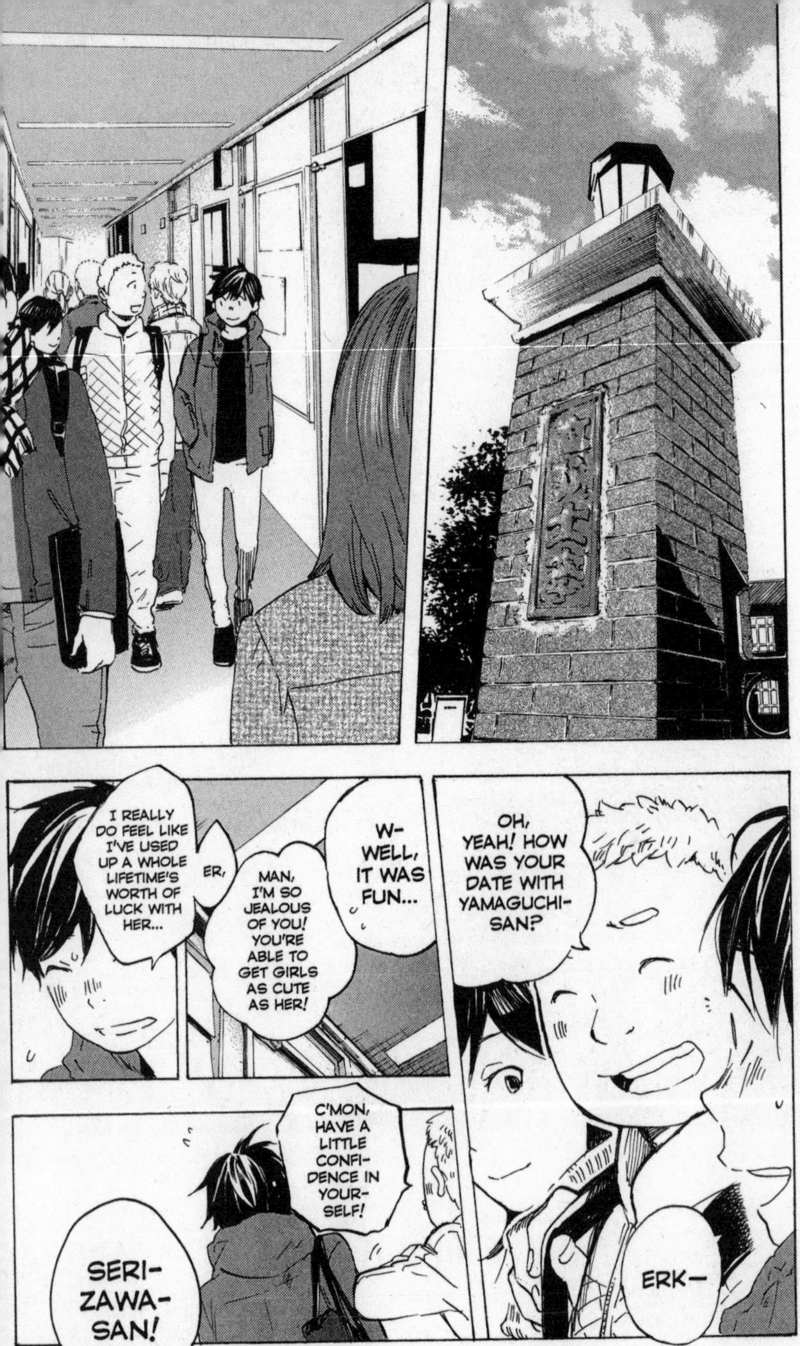
OH, YEAH! HOW WAS YOUR DATE WITH YAMAGUCHI-SAN?
ERK—
W-WELL, IT WAS FUN...
MAN, I'M SO JEALOUS OF YOU! YOU'RE ABLE TO GET GIRLS AS CUTE AS HER!
ER,
I REALLY DO FEEL LIKE I'VE USED UP A WHOLE LIFETIME'S WORTH OF LUCK WITH HER...
C'MON, HAVE A LITTLE CONFIDENCE IN YOURSELF!
SERI-ZAWA-SAN!

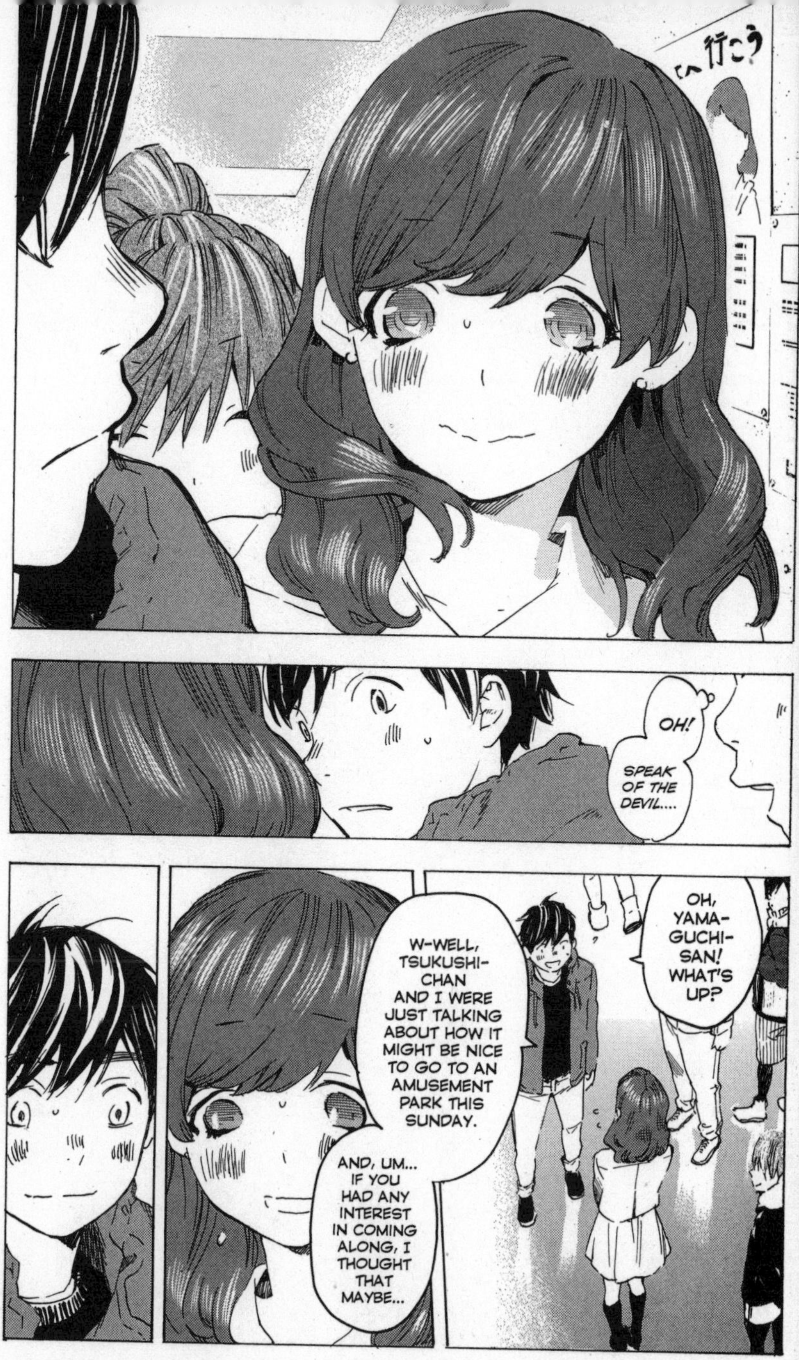
へ行こう
OH!
SPEAK OF THE DEVIL....
OH, YAMA-GUCHI-SAN! WHAT'S UP?
W-WELL, TSUKUSHI-CHAN AND I WERE JUST TALKING ABOUT HOW IT MIGHT BE NICE TO GO TO AN AMUSEMENT PARK THIS SUNDAY.
AND, UM... IF YOU HAD ANY INTEREST IN COMING ALONG, I THOUGHT THAT MAYBE...

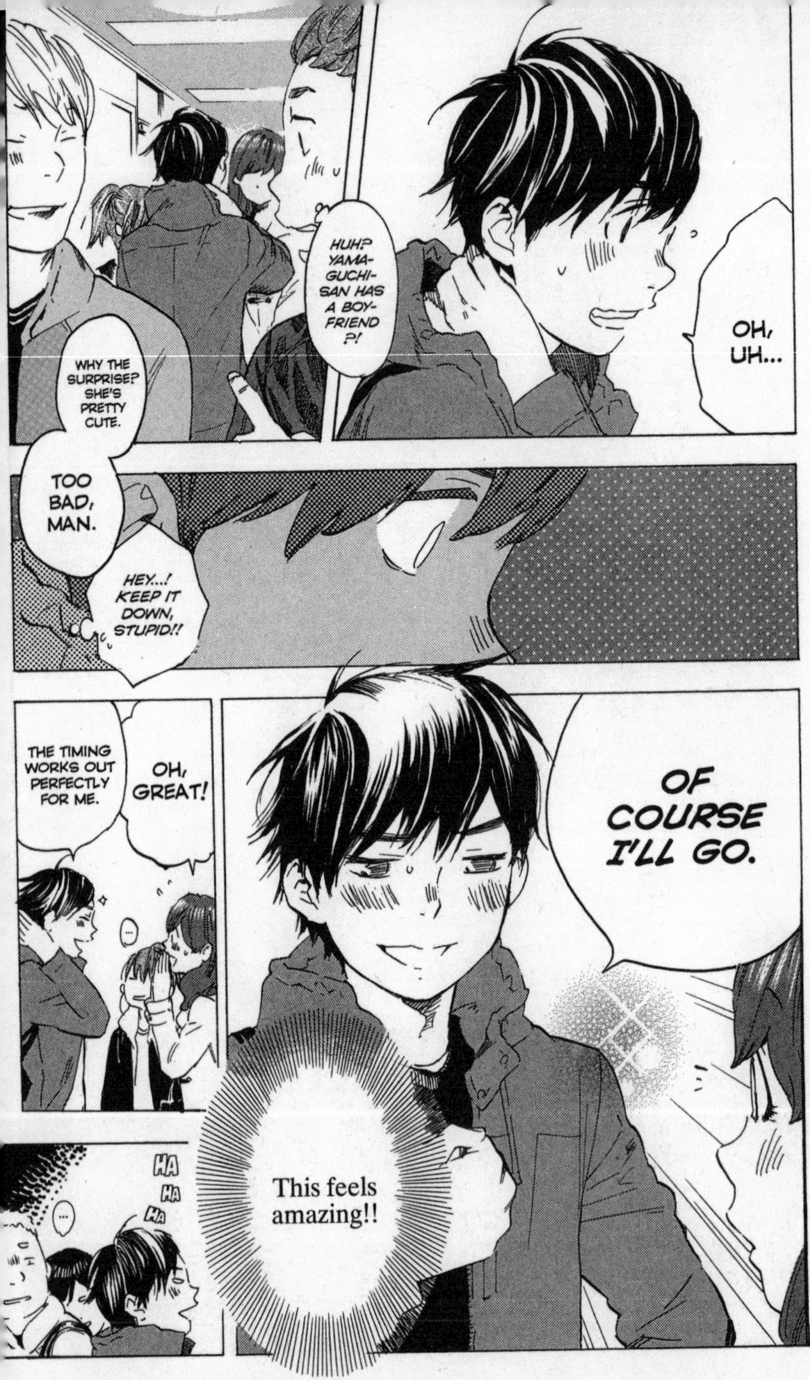
OH, UH...
HUH? YAMAGUCHI-SAN HAS A BOYFRIEND?!
WHY THE SURPRISE? SHE'S PRETTY CUTE.
TOO BAD, MAN.
HEY...! KEEP IT DOWN, STUPID!!
OF COURSE I'LL GO.
This feels amazing!!
OH, GREAT!
THE TIMING WORKS OUT PERFECTLY FOR ME.
...
HA HA HA
...

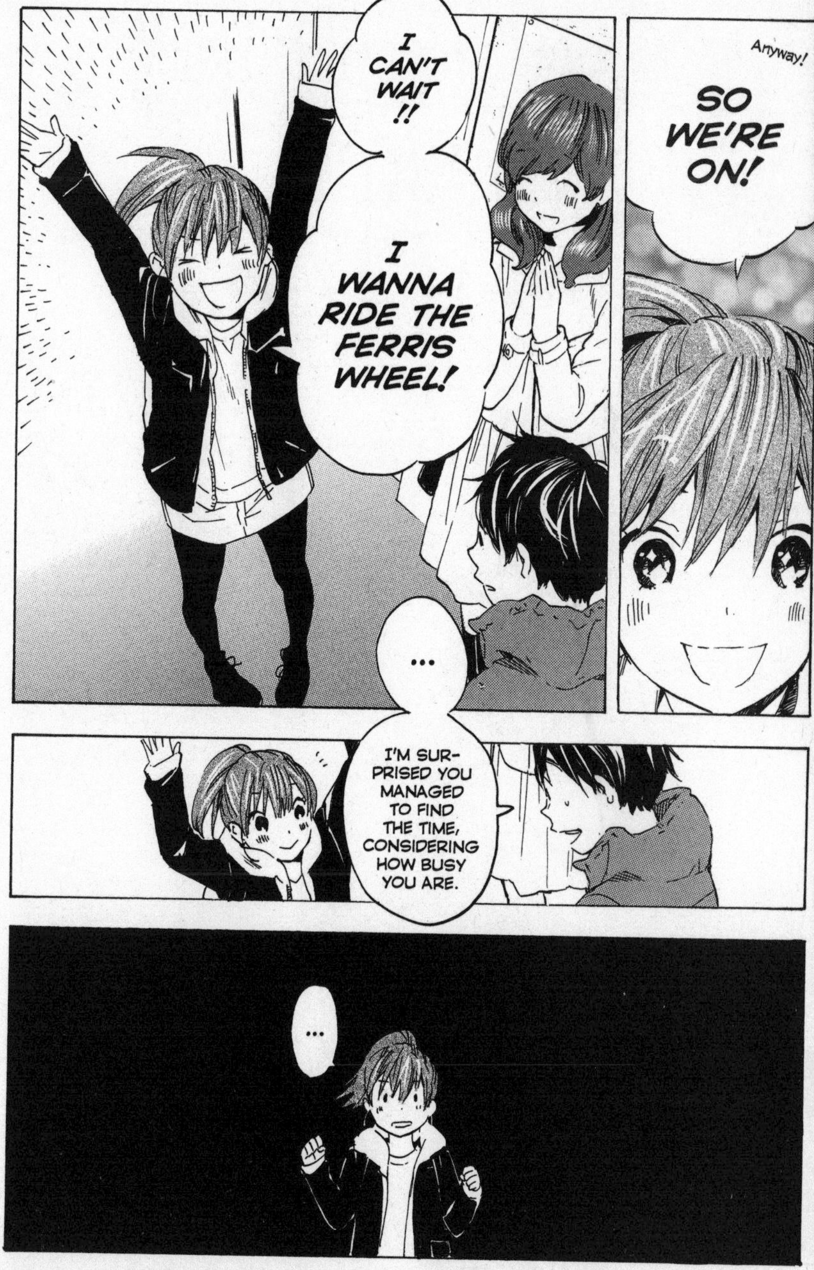
Anyway!
SO WE'RE ON!
I CAN'T WAIT!!
I WANNA RIDE THE FERRIS WHEEL!
...
I'M SURPRISED YOU MANAGED TO FIND THE TIME, CONSIDERING HOW BUSY YOU ARE.
...

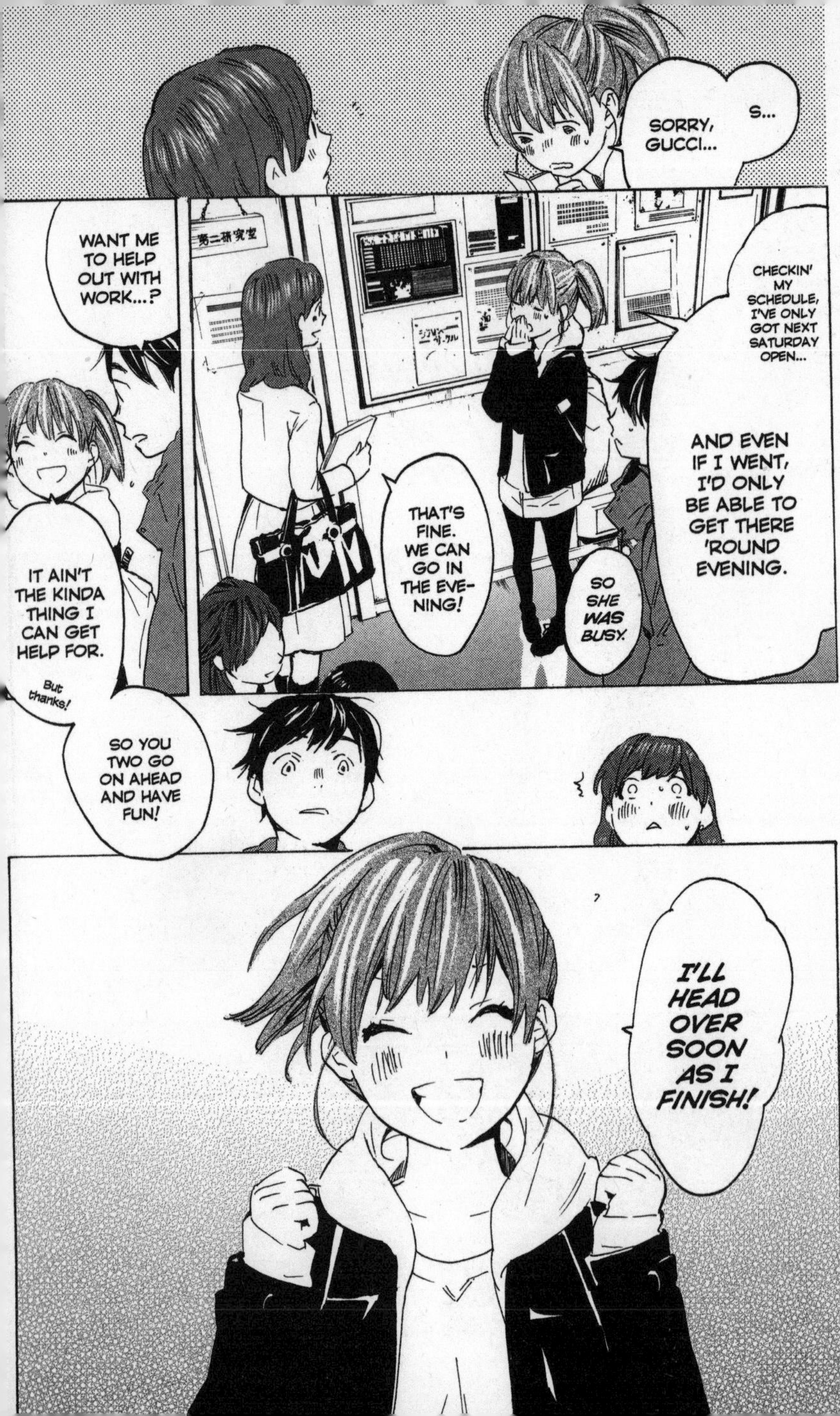

S...
SORRY, GUCCI...
CHECKIN' MY SCHEDULE, I'VE ONLY GOT NEXT SATURDAY OPEN...
AND EVEN IF I WENT, I'D ONLY BE ABLE TO GET THERE 'ROUND EVENING.
SO SHE WAS BUSY.
THAT'S FINE. WE CAN GO IN THE EVE- NING!
WANT ME TO HELP OUT WITH WORK...?
IT AIN'T THE KINDA THING I CAN GET HELP FOR.
But thanks!
SO YOU TWO GO ON AHEAD AND HAVE FUN!
I'LL HEAD OVER SOON AS I FINISH!

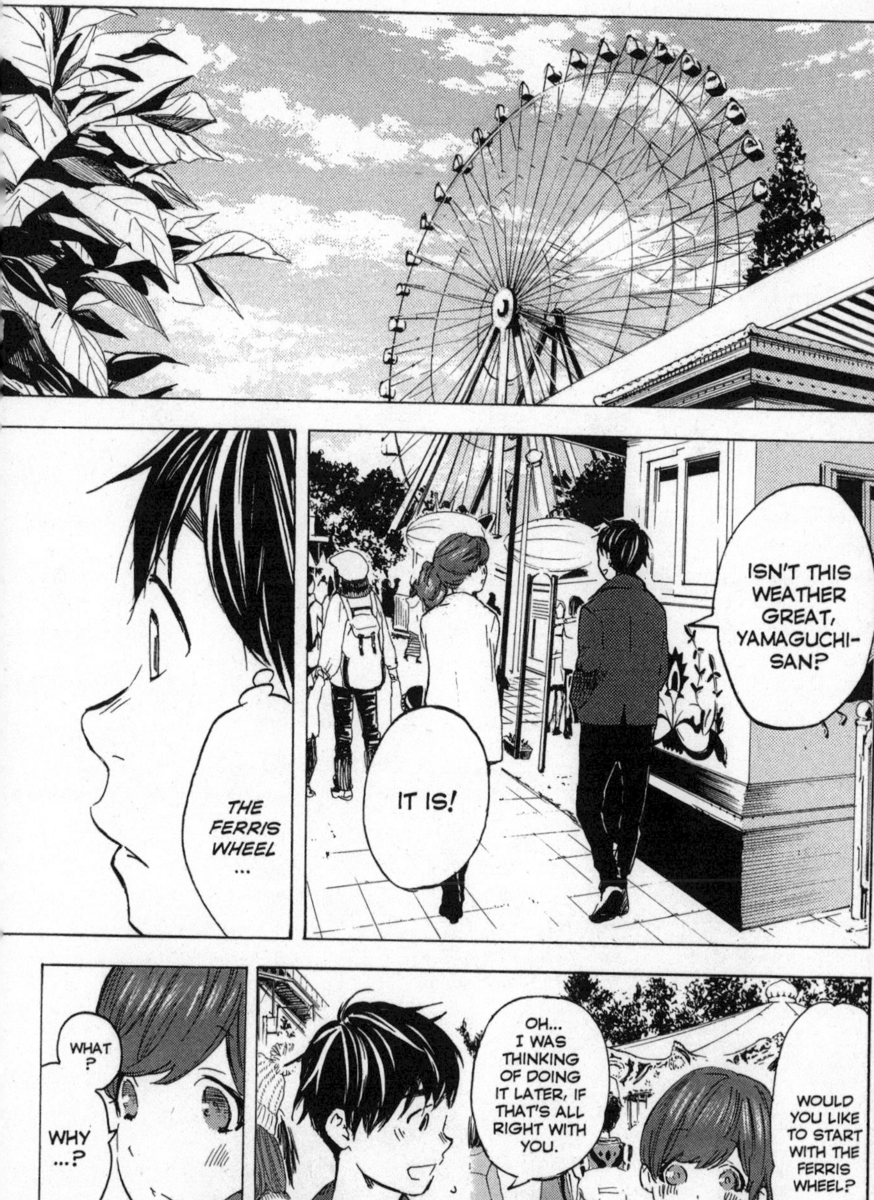
ISN'T THIS WEATHER GREAT, YAMAGUCHI-SAN?
IT IS!
THE FERRIS WHEEL ...
WOULD YOU LIKE TO START WITH THE FERRIS WHEEL?
OH... I WAS THINKING OF DOING IT LATER, IF THAT'S ALL RIGHT WITH YOU.
WHAT ?
WHY ...?

...OH! OKAY.

ALL RIGHT, THEN LET'S WAIT!

THANKS.

...

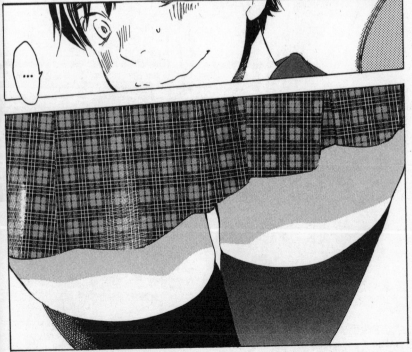

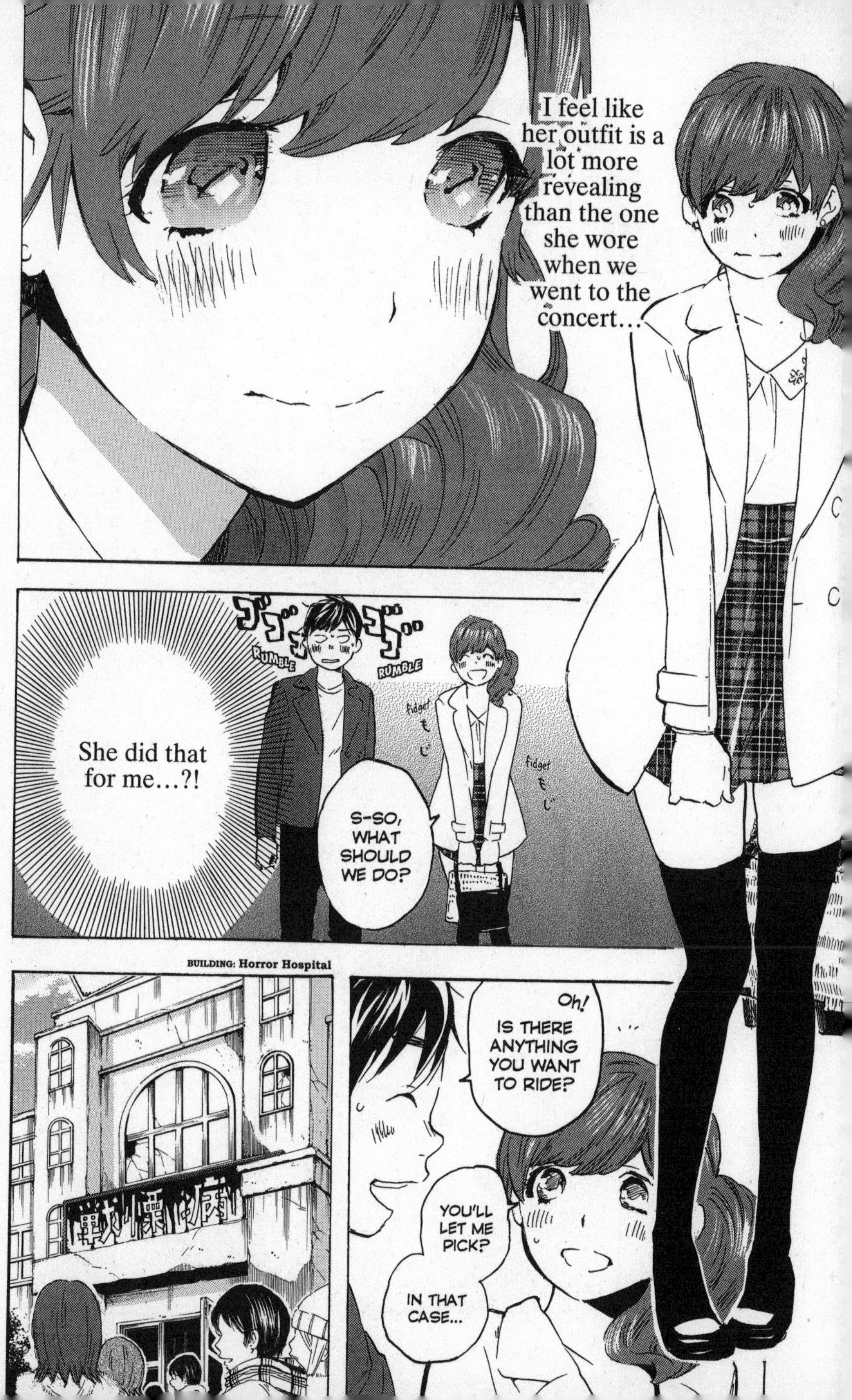

I feel like her outfit is a lot more revealing than the one she wore when we went to the concert…
RUMBLE
RUMBLE
fidget
fidget
S-SO, WHAT SHOULD WE DO?
She did that for me…?!
Oh! IS THERE ANYTHING YOU WANT TO RIDE?
…
YOU'LL LET ME PICK?
IN THAT CASE…
BUILDING: Horror Hospital

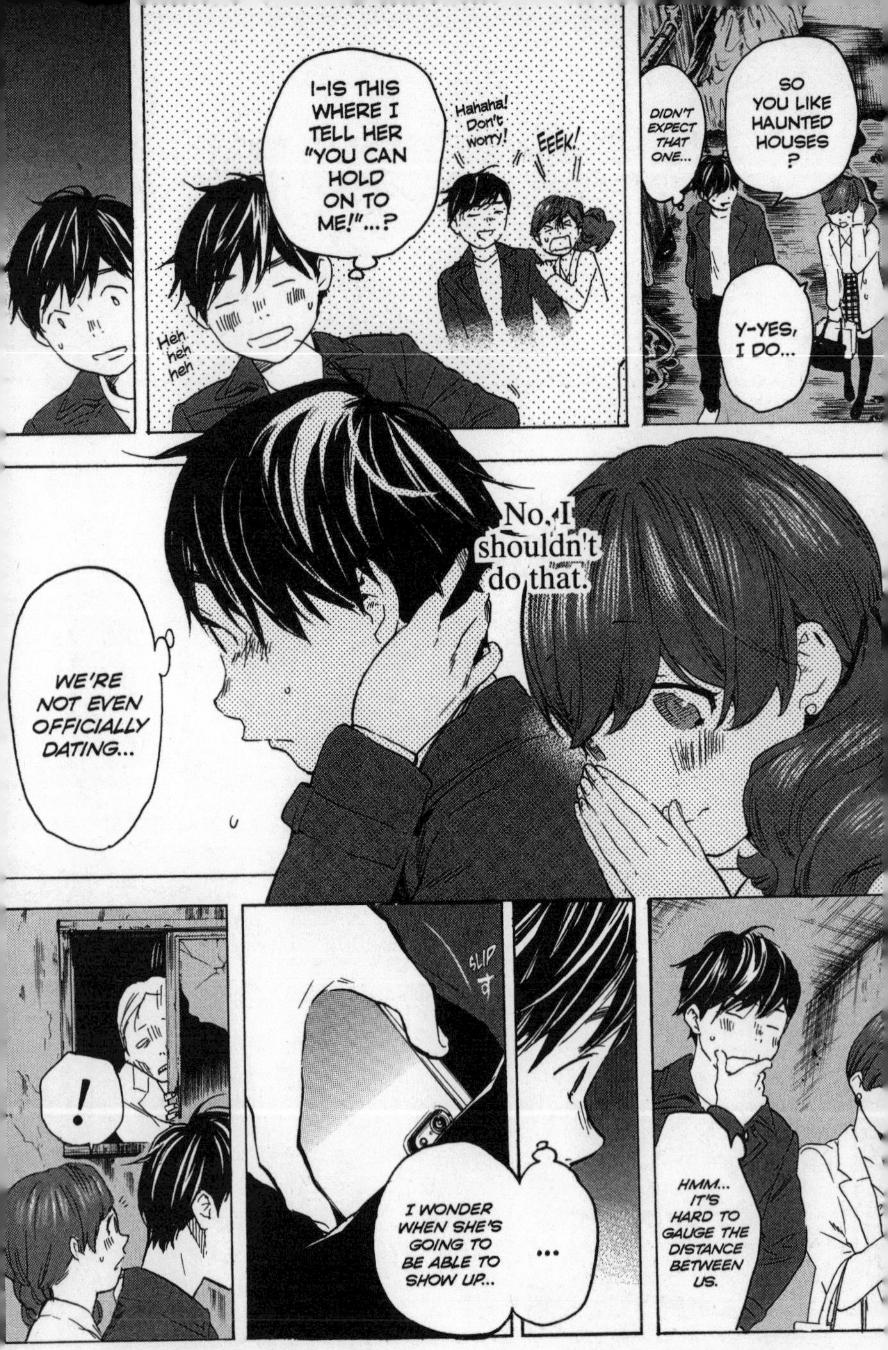
SO YOU LIKE HAUNTED HOUSES?
DIDN'T EXPECT THAT ONE...
Y-YES, I DO...
I-IS THIS WHERE I TELL HER "YOU CAN HOLD ON TO ME!"...?
Hahaha! Don't worry!
EEEK!
Heh heh heh
No, I shouldn't do that.
WE'RE NOT EVEN OFFICIALLY DATING...
HMM... IT'S HARD TO GAUGE THE DISTANCE BETWEEN US.
...
SLIP
す
I WONDER WHEN SHE'S GOING TO BE ABLE TO SHOW UP...
!

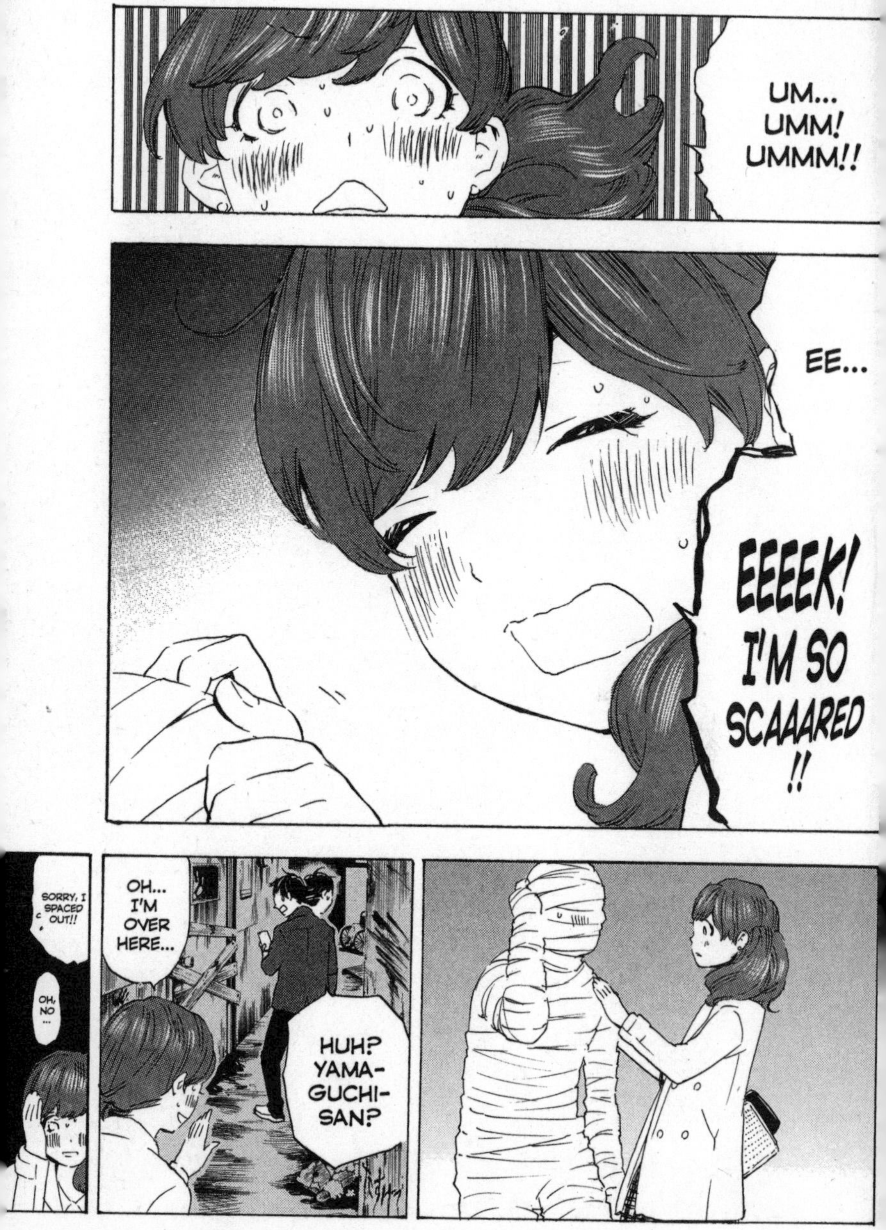
UM... UMM! UMMM!!
EE...
EEEEK! I'M SO SCAAARED !!
HUH? YAMA-GUCHI-SAN?
OH... I'M OVER HERE...
SORRY, I SPACED OUT!!
OH, NO ...

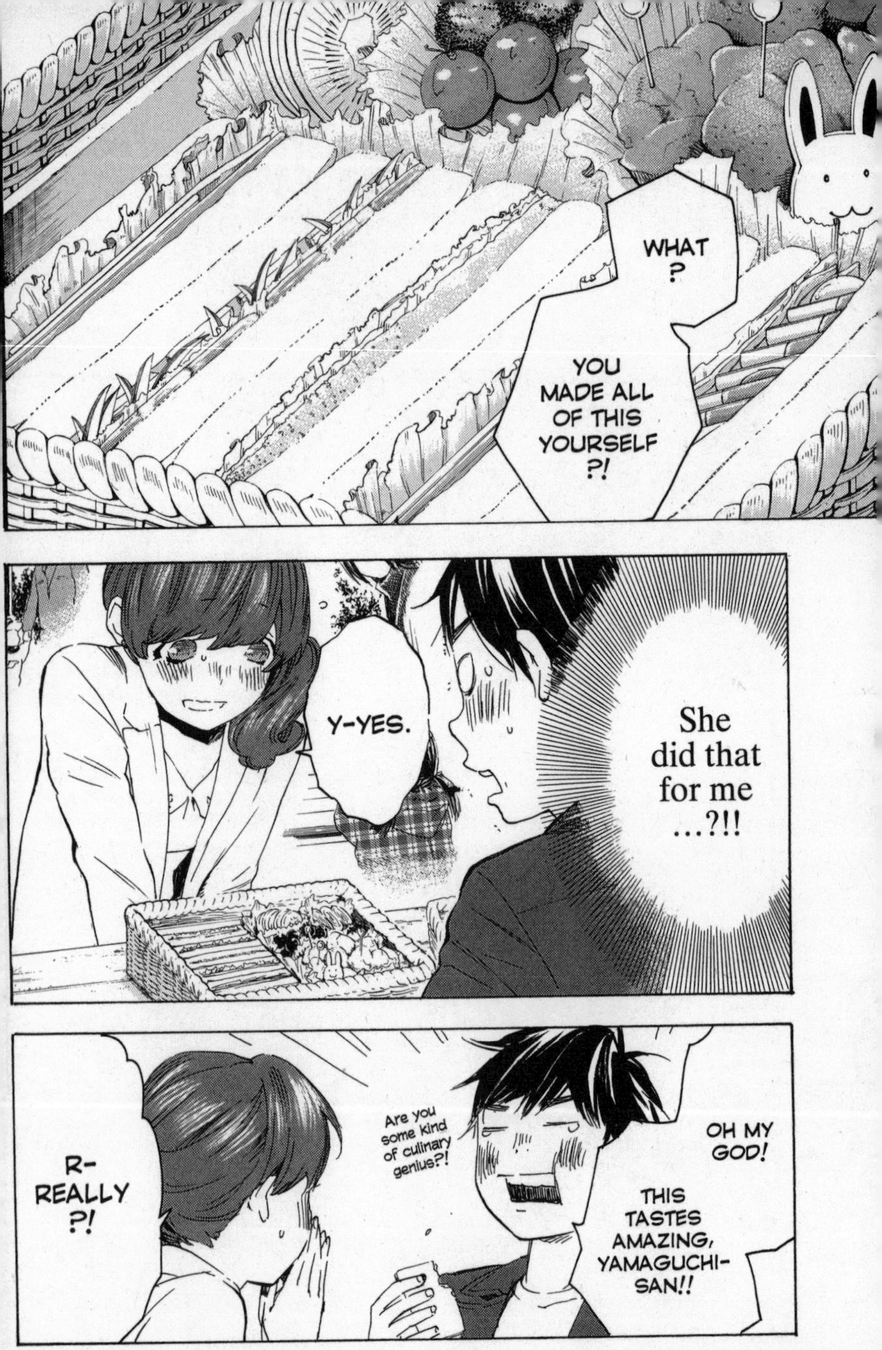
WHAT?
YOU MADE ALL OF THIS YOURSELF?!
She did that for me...?!!
Y-YES.
OH MY GOD!
THIS TASTES AMAZING, YAMAGUCHI-SAN!!
Are you some kind of culinary genius?!
R-REALLY?!

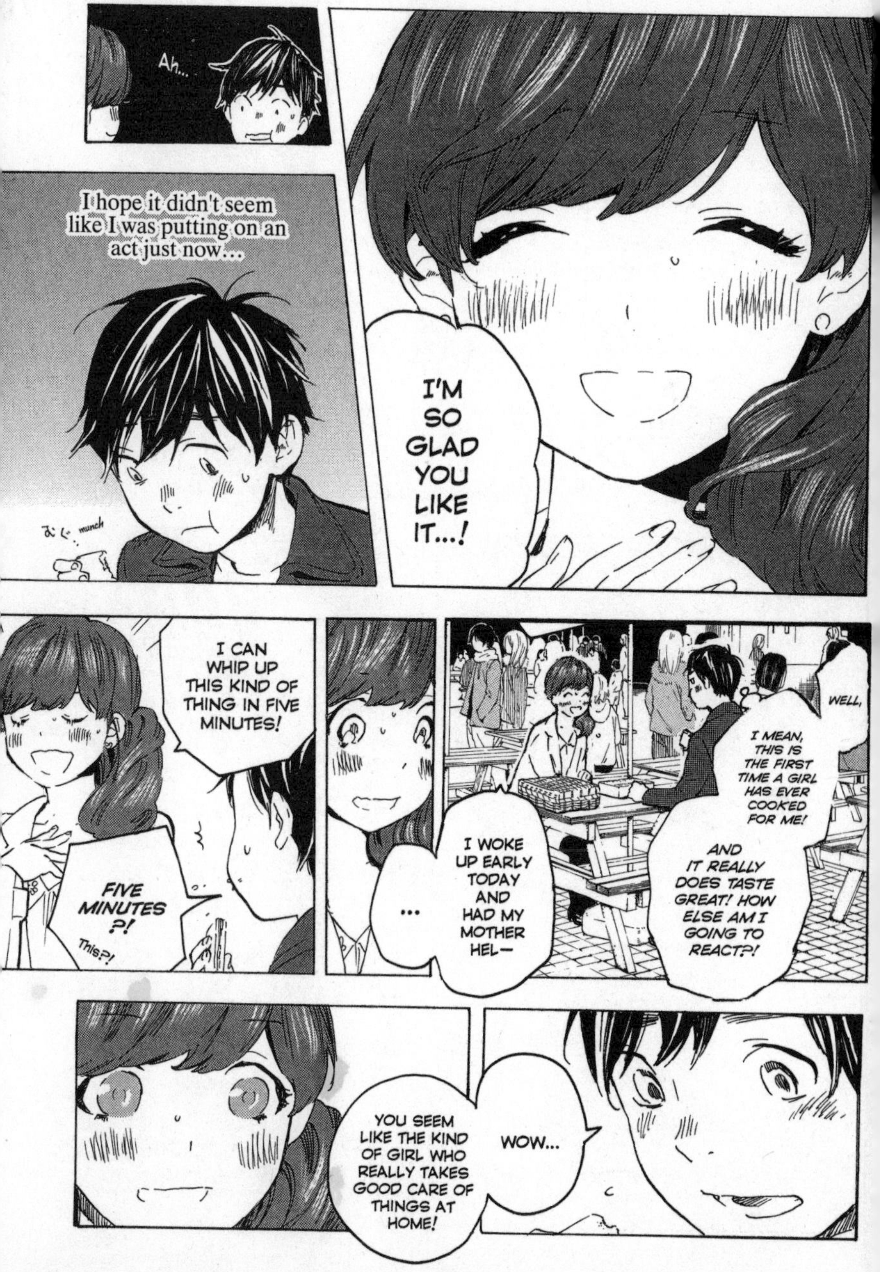
I'M SO GLAD YOU LIKE IT...!
Ah...
I hope it didn't seem like I was putting on an act just now...
むぐ… munch
WELL, I MEAN, THIS IS THE FIRST TIME A GIRL HAS EVER COOKED FOR ME!
AND IT REALLY DOES TASTE GREAT! HOW ELSE AM I GOING TO REACT?!
I WOKE UP EARLY TODAY AND HAD MY MOTHER HEL—
...
I CAN WHIP UP THIS KIND OF THING IN FIVE MINUTES!
FIVE MINUTES ?!
This?!
WOW...
YOU SEEM LIKE THE KIND OF GIRL WHO REALLY TAKES GOOD CARE OF THINGS AT HOME!

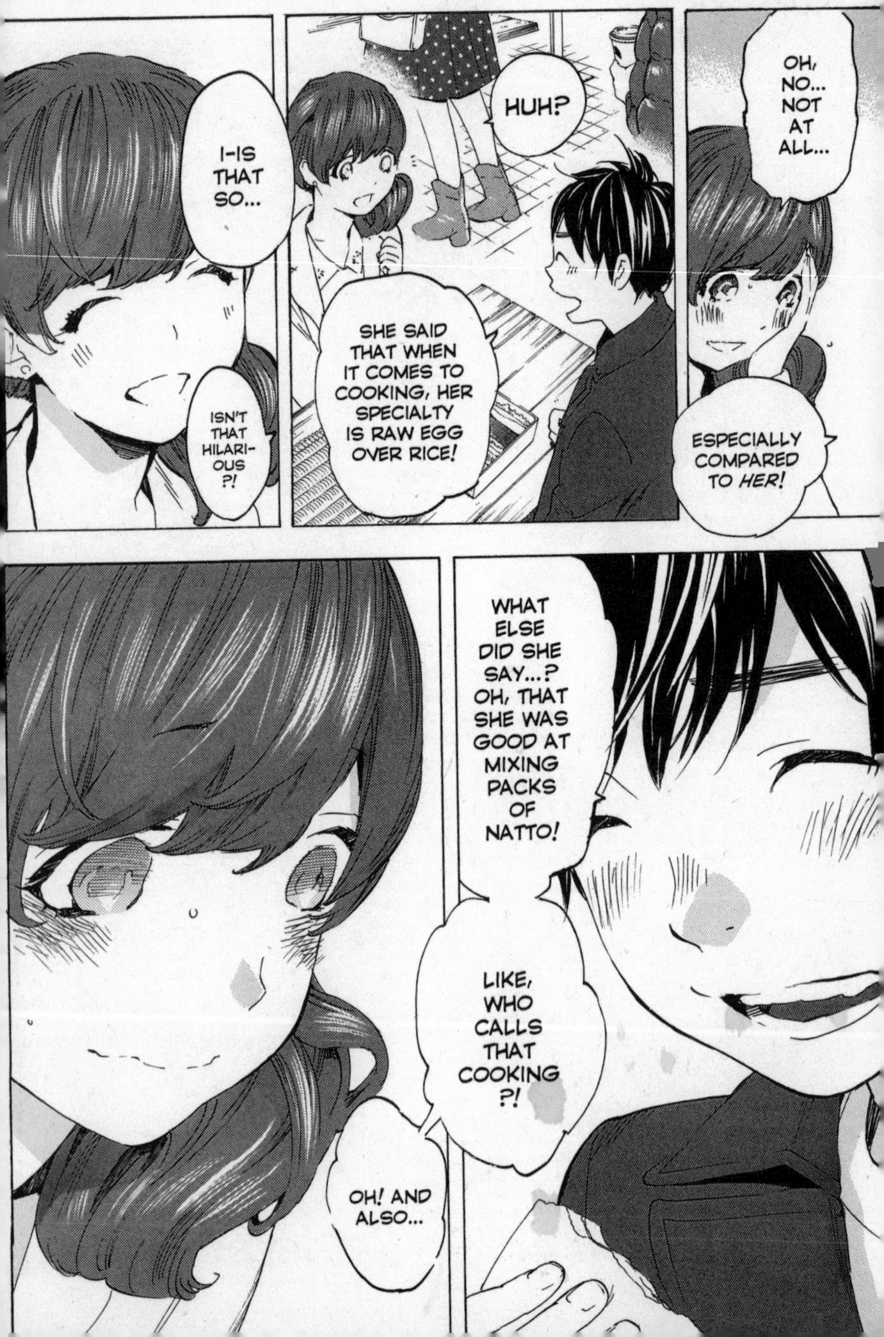
OH, NO... NOT AT ALL...
ESPECIALLY COMPARED TO *HER*!
HUH?
SHE SAID THAT WHEN IT COMES TO COOKING, HER SPECIALTY IS RAW EGG OVER RICE!
I-IS THAT SO...
ISN'T THAT HILARI-OUS?!
WHAT ELSE DID SHE SAY...? OH, THAT SHE WAS GOOD AT MIXING PACKS OF NATTO!
LIKE, WHO CALLS THAT COOKING?!
OH! AND ALSO...

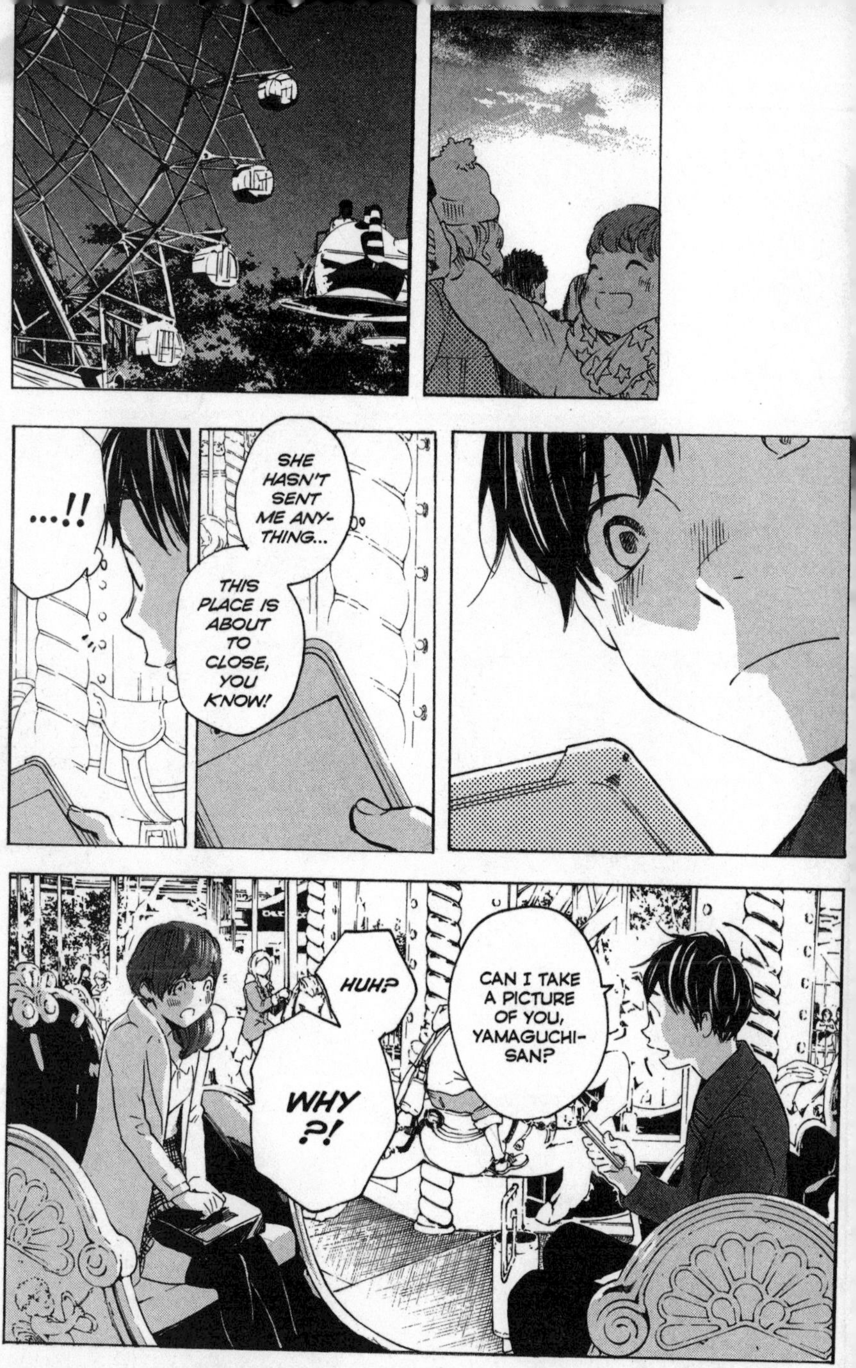
SHE HASN'T SENT ME ANY-THING...
THIS PLACE IS ABOUT TO CLOSE, YOU KNOW!
...!!
CAN I TAKE A PICTURE OF YOU, YAMAGUCHI-SAN?
HUH?
WHY?!

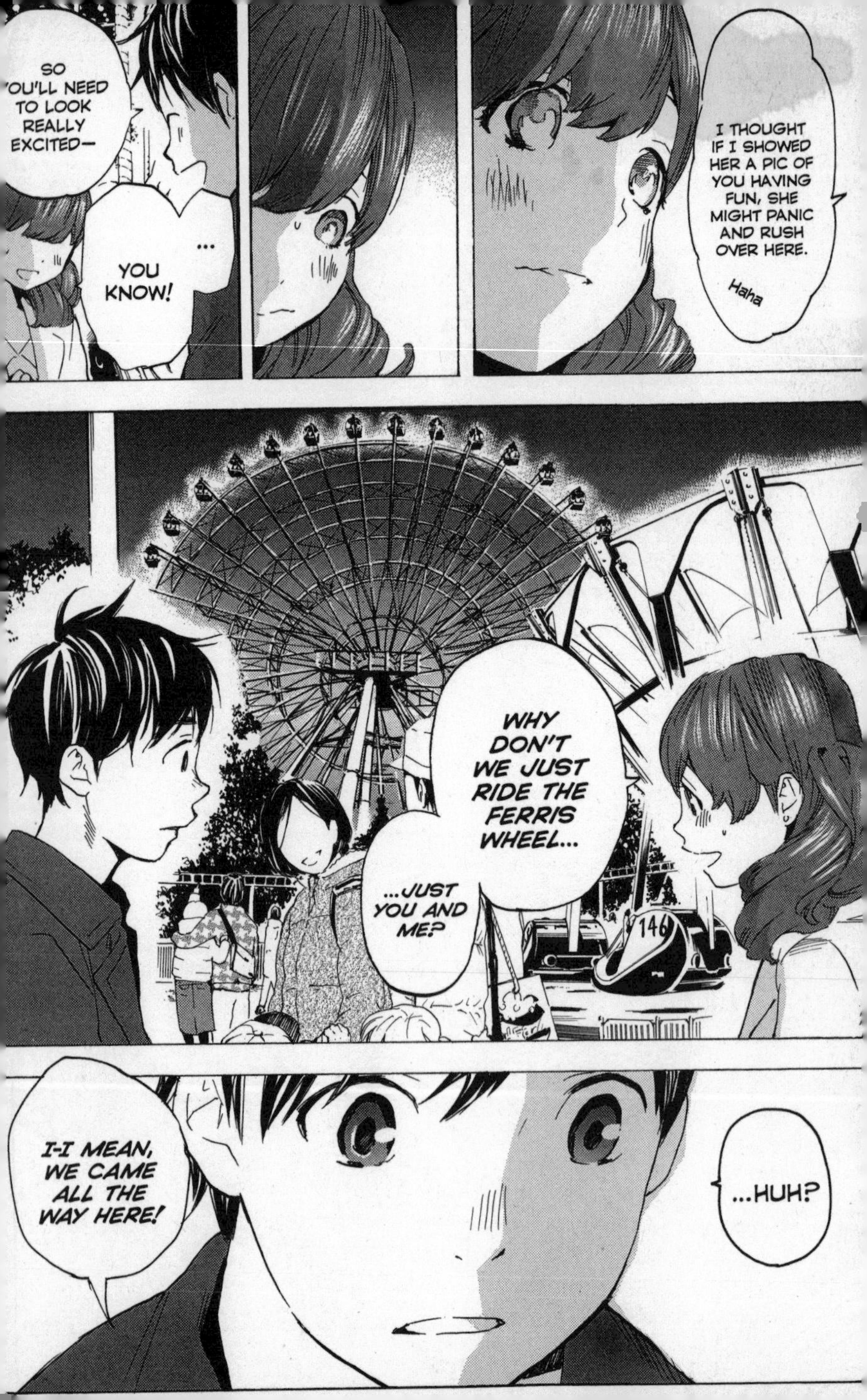
I THOUGHT IF I SHOWED HER A PIC OF YOU HAVING FUN, SHE MIGHT PANIC AND RUSH OVER HERE.
Haha
SO OU'LL NEED TO LOOK REALLY EXCITED—
... YOU KNOW!
WHY DON'T WE JUST RIDE THE FERRIS WHEEL...
...JUST YOU AND ME?
146
...HUH?
I-I MEAN, WE CAME ALL THE WAY HERE!

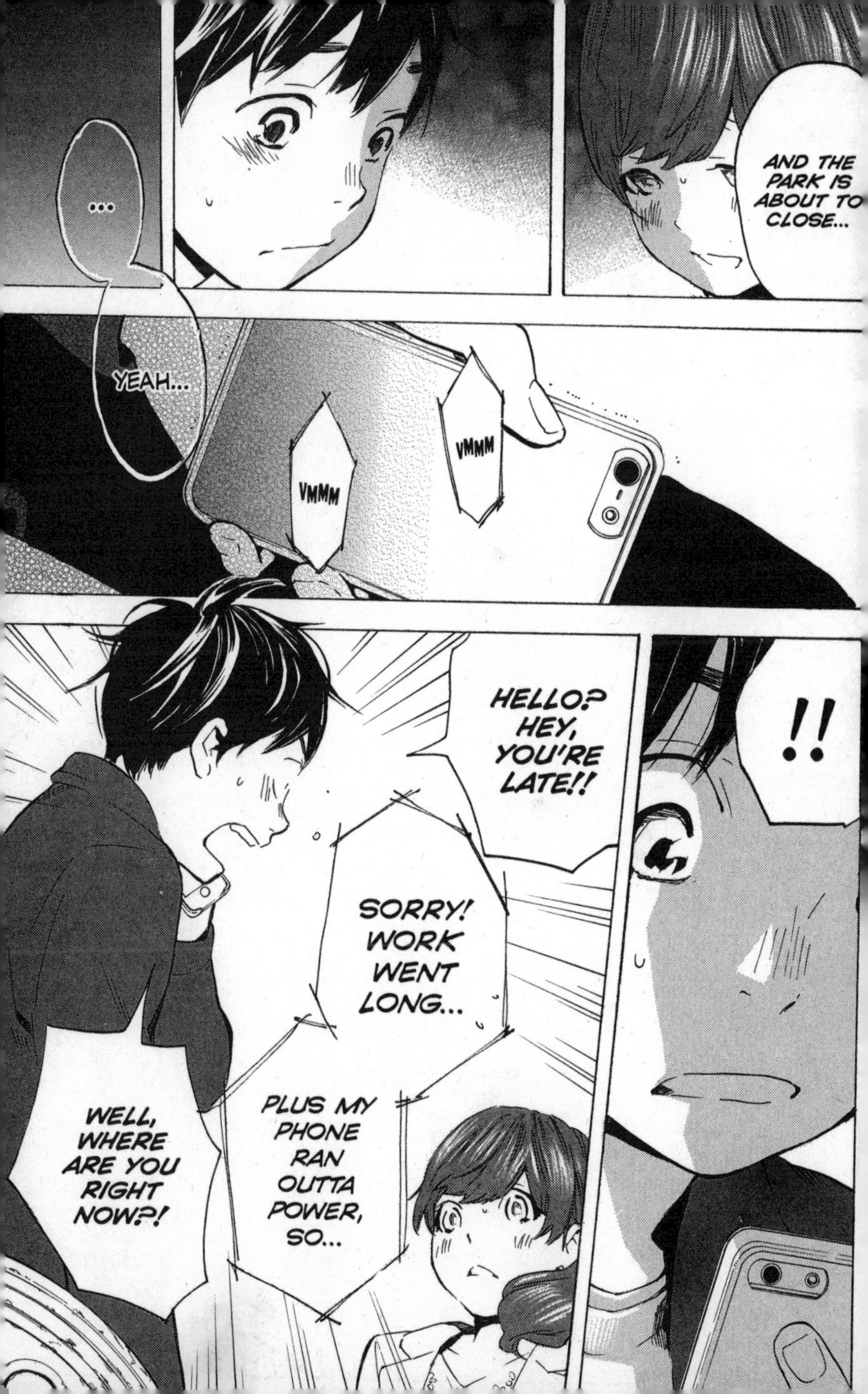
AND THE PARK IS ABOUT TO CLOSE...
...
YEAH...
VMMM
VMMM
!!
HELLO? HEY, YOU'RE LATE!!
SORRY! WORK WENT LONG...
PLUS MY PHONE RAN OUTTA POWER, SO...
WELL, WHERE ARE YOU RIGHT NOW?!

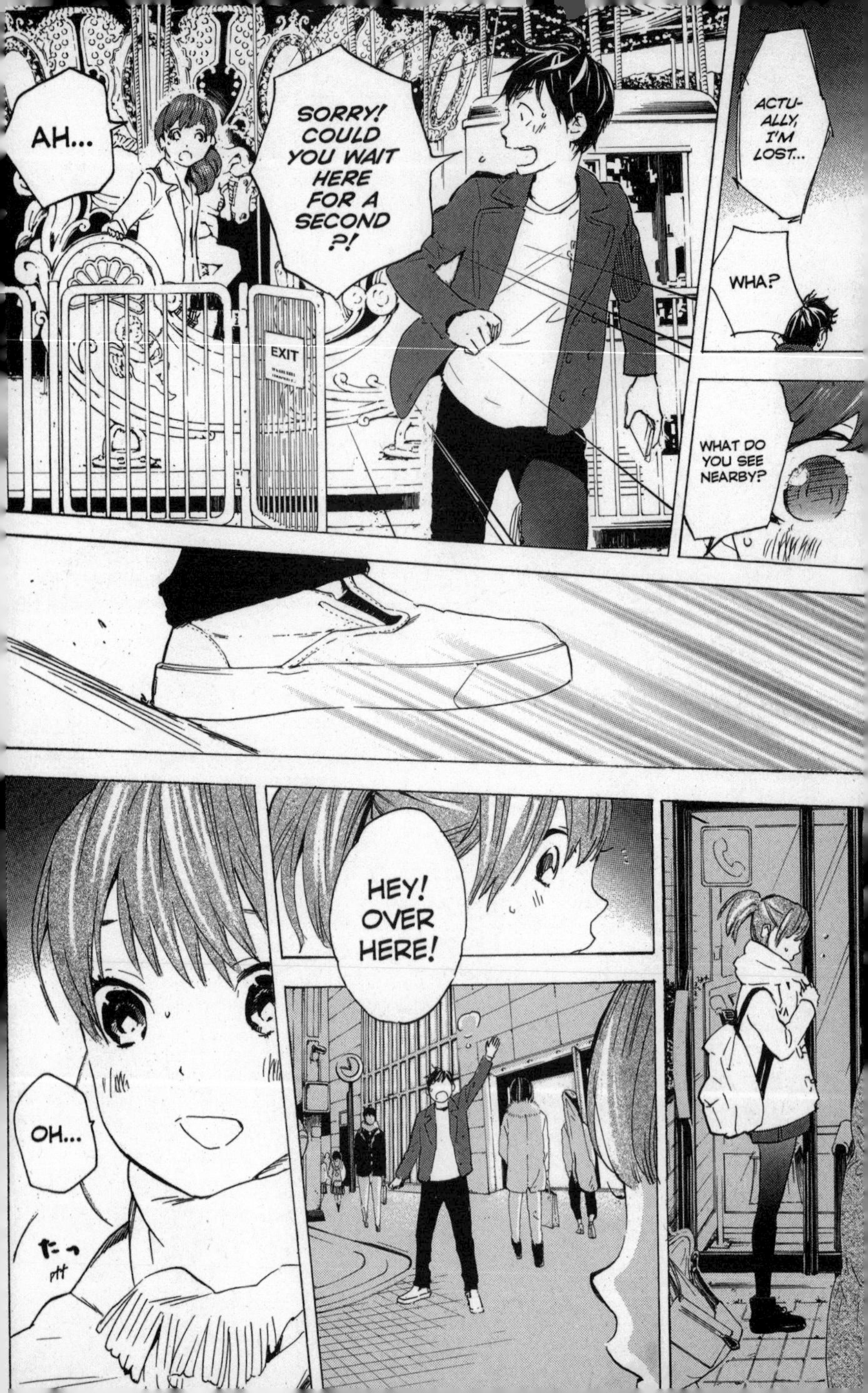
ACTU-ALLY, I'M LOST...
WHA?
WHAT DO YOU SEE NEARBY?
SORRY! COULD YOU WAIT HERE FOR A SECOND ?!
AH...
EXIT
HEY! OVER HERE!
OH...
たっ
pIH

PANT

PANT

PANT

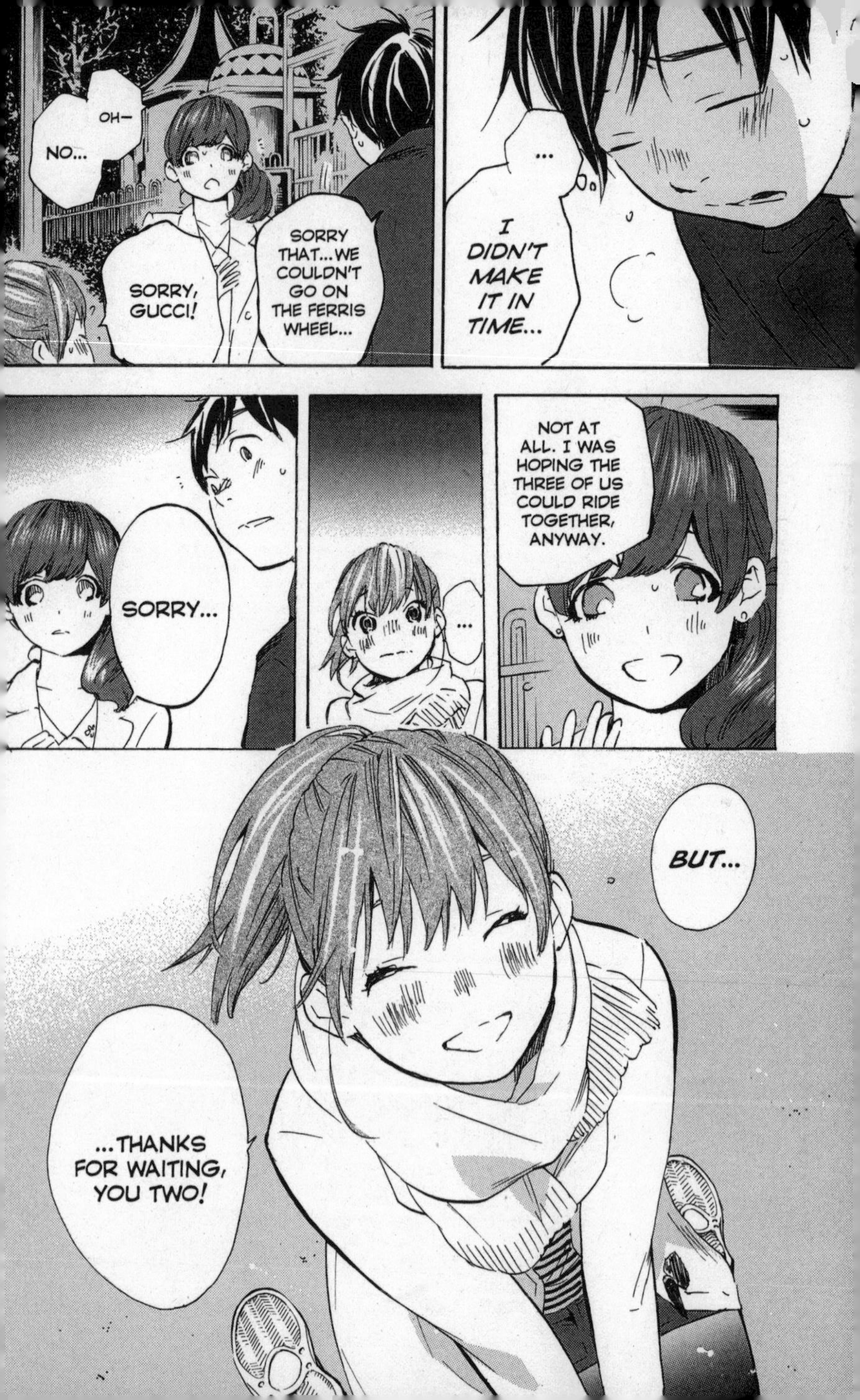
...
I DIDN'T MAKE IT IN TIME...
SORRY THAT...WE COULDN'T GO ON THE FERRIS WHEEL...
OH— NO...
SORRY, GUCCI!
NOT AT ALL. I WAS HOPING THE THREE OF US COULD RIDE TOGETHER, ANYWAY.
...
SORRY...
BUT...
...THANKS FOR WAITING, YOU TWO!

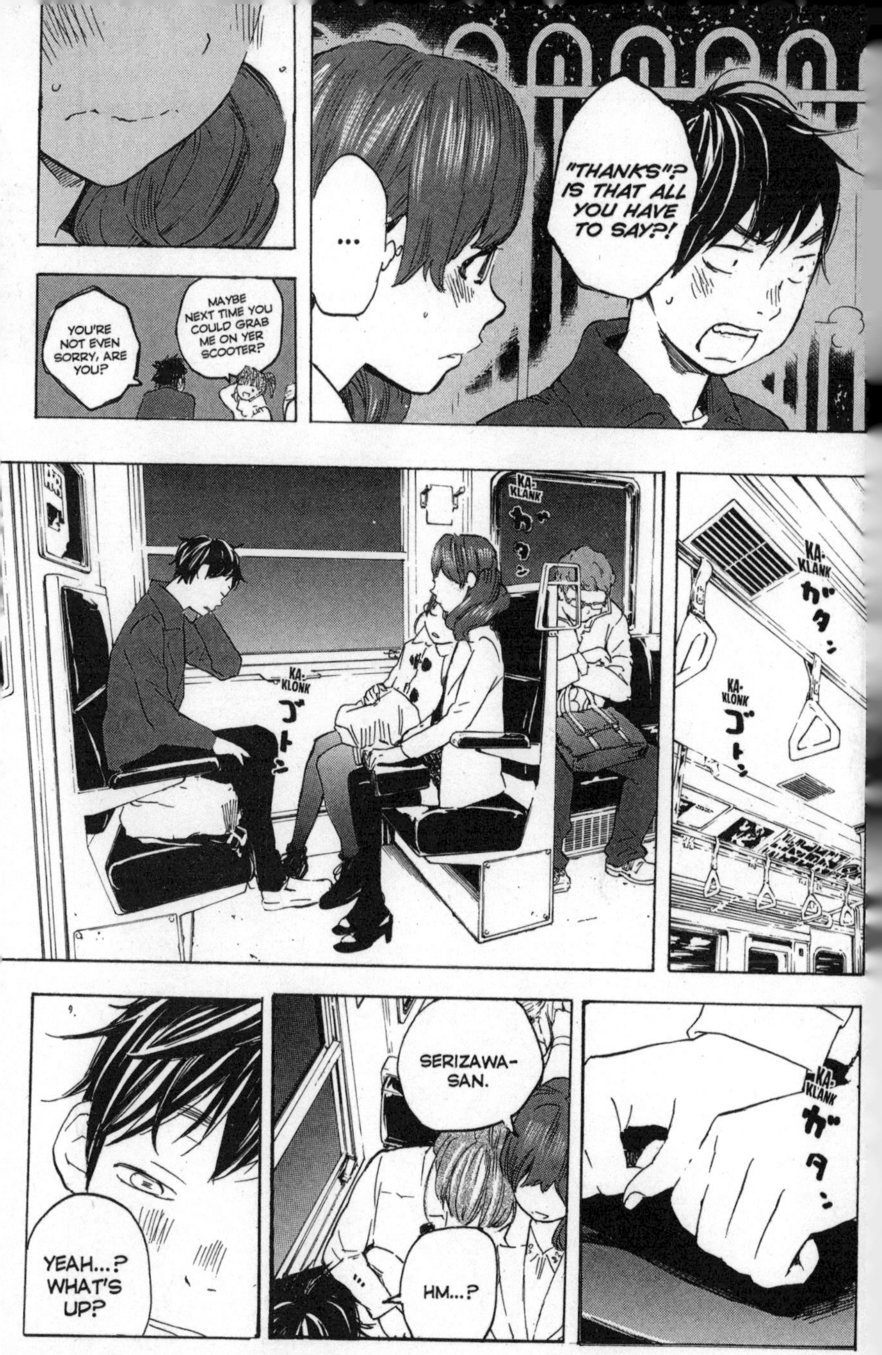
"THANKS"? IS THAT ALL YOU HAVE TO SAY?!
...
MAYBE NEXT TIME YOU COULD GRAB ME ON YER SCOOTER?
YOU'RE NOT EVEN SORRY, ARE YOU?
KA-KLANK
ガタン
KA-KLONK
ゴトン
KA-KLANK
ガタン
KA-KLONK
ゴトン
KA-KLANK
ガタン
SERIZAWA-SAN.
HM...?
YEAH...? WHAT'S UP?

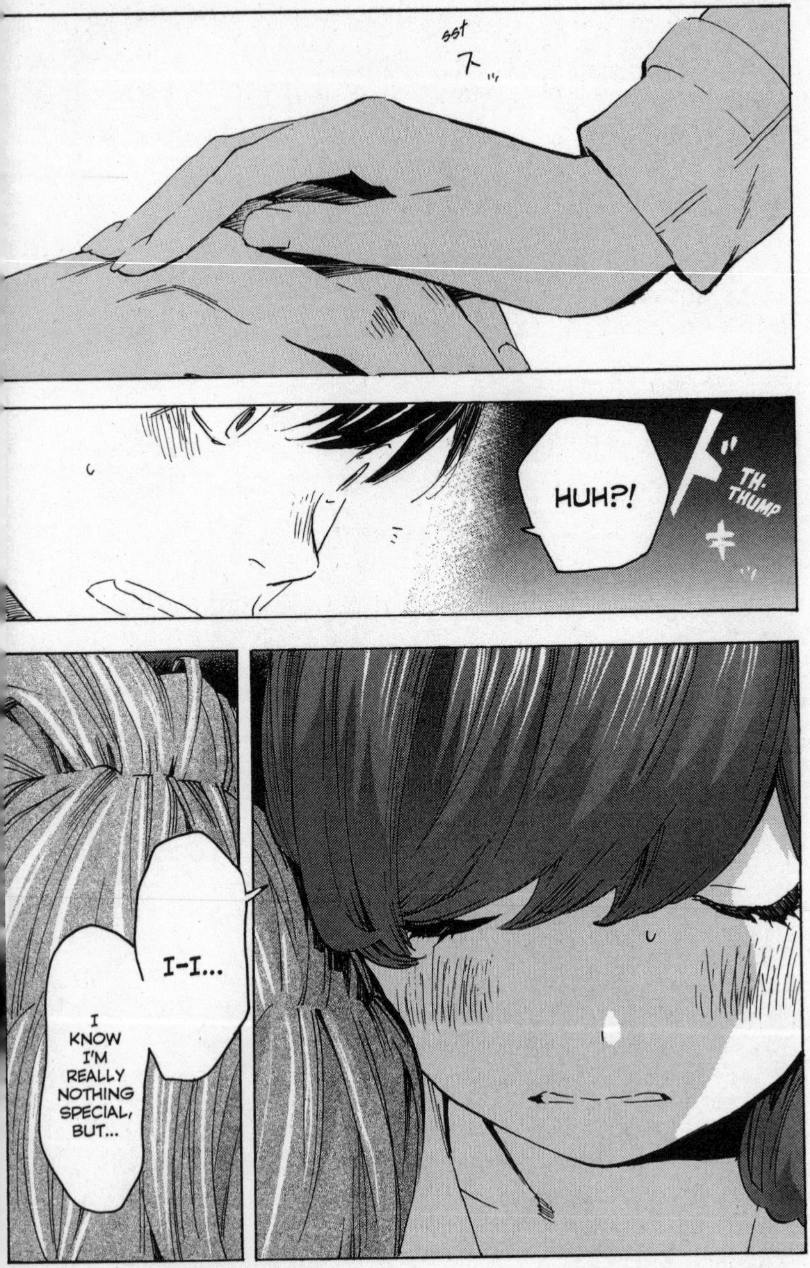
sst
ス
HUH?!
TH-THUMP
ド
キ
I-I...
I KNOW I'M REALLY NOTHING SPECIAL, BUT...

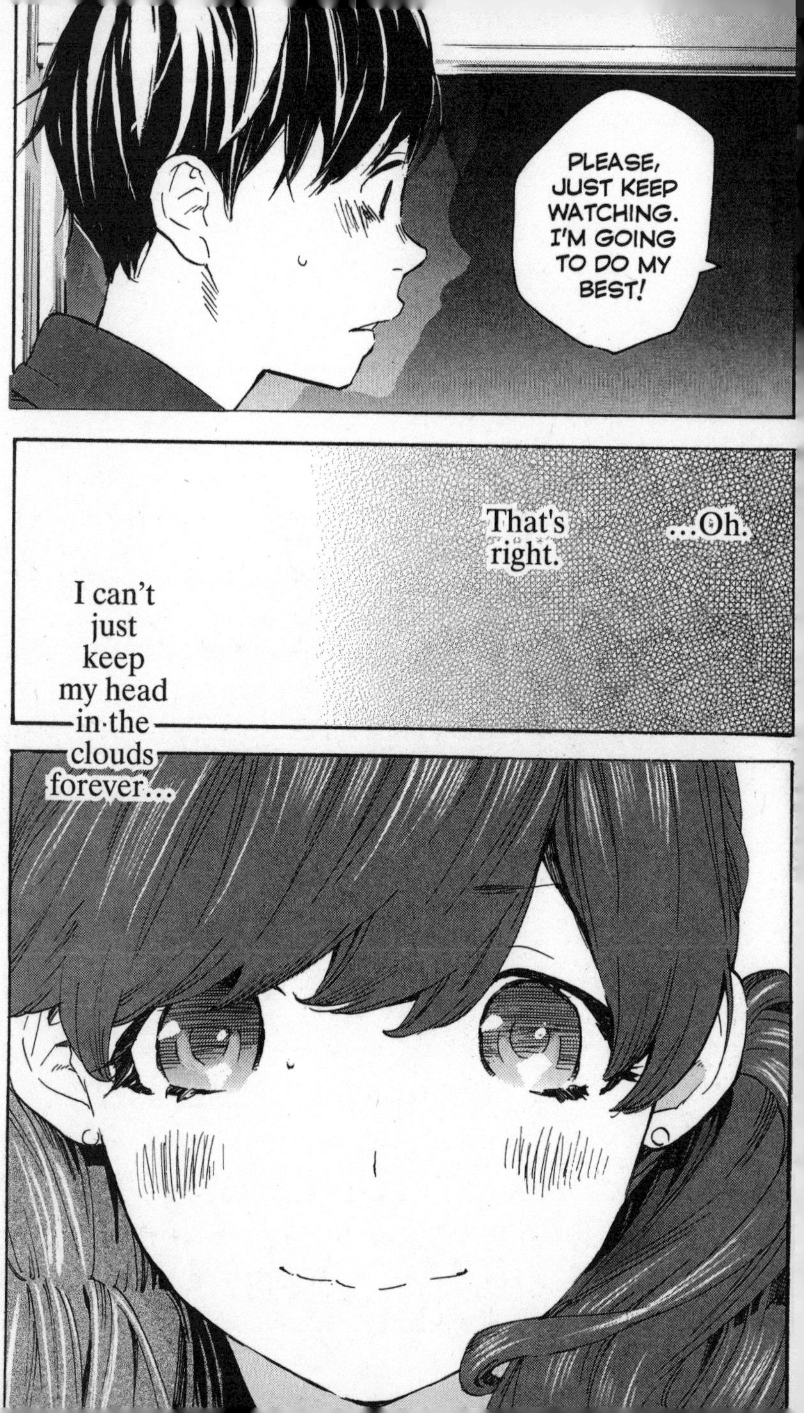
PLEASE, JUST KEEP WATCHING. I'M GOING TO DO MY BEST!
...Oh.
That's right.
I can't just keep my head in the clouds forever...

Forget Me Not

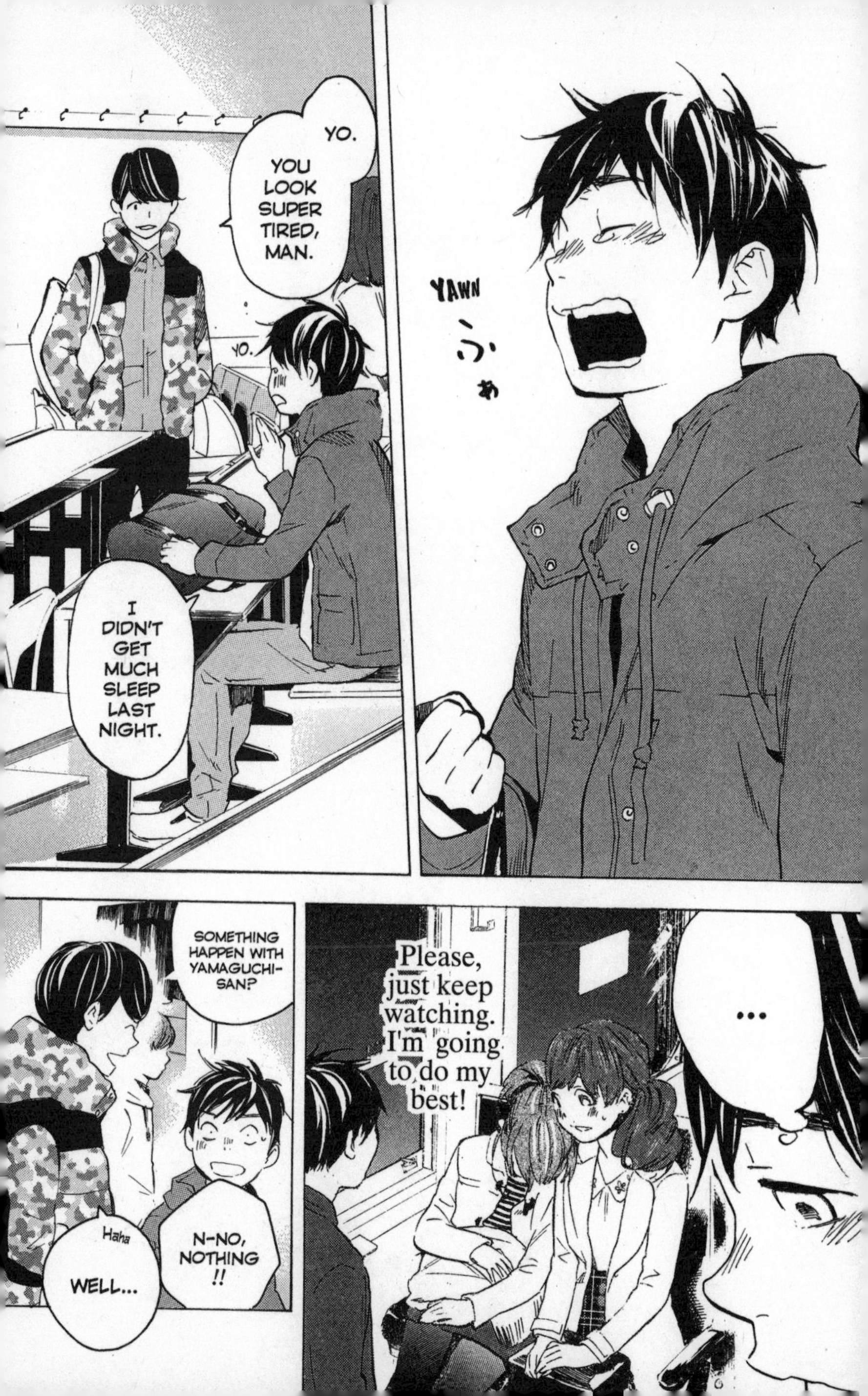
YAWN
ふぁ
YO.
YOU LOOK SUPER TIRED, MAN.
YO.
I DIDN'T GET MUCH SLEEP LAST NIGHT.
...
Please, just keep watching. I'm going to do my best!
SOMETHING HAPPEN WITH YAMAGUCHI-SAN?
N-NO, NOTHING!!
Haha
WELL...

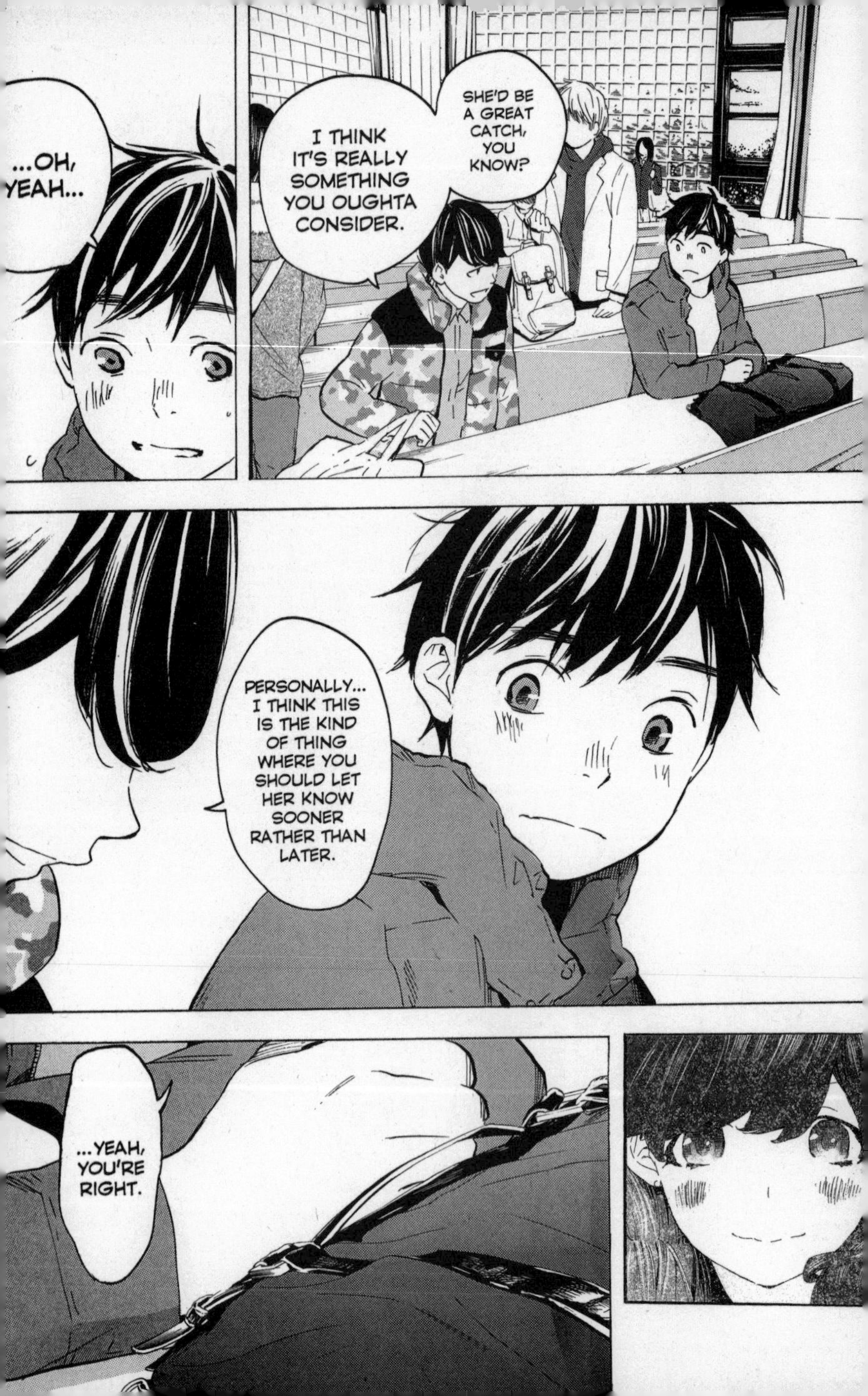
SHE'D BE A GREAT CATCH, YOU KNOW?
I THINK IT'S REALLY SOMETHING YOU OUGHTA CONSIDER.
...OH, YEAH...
PERSONALLY... I THINK THIS IS THE KIND OF THING WHERE YOU SHOULD LET HER KNOW SOONER RATHER THAN LATER.
...YEAH, YOU'RE RIGHT.

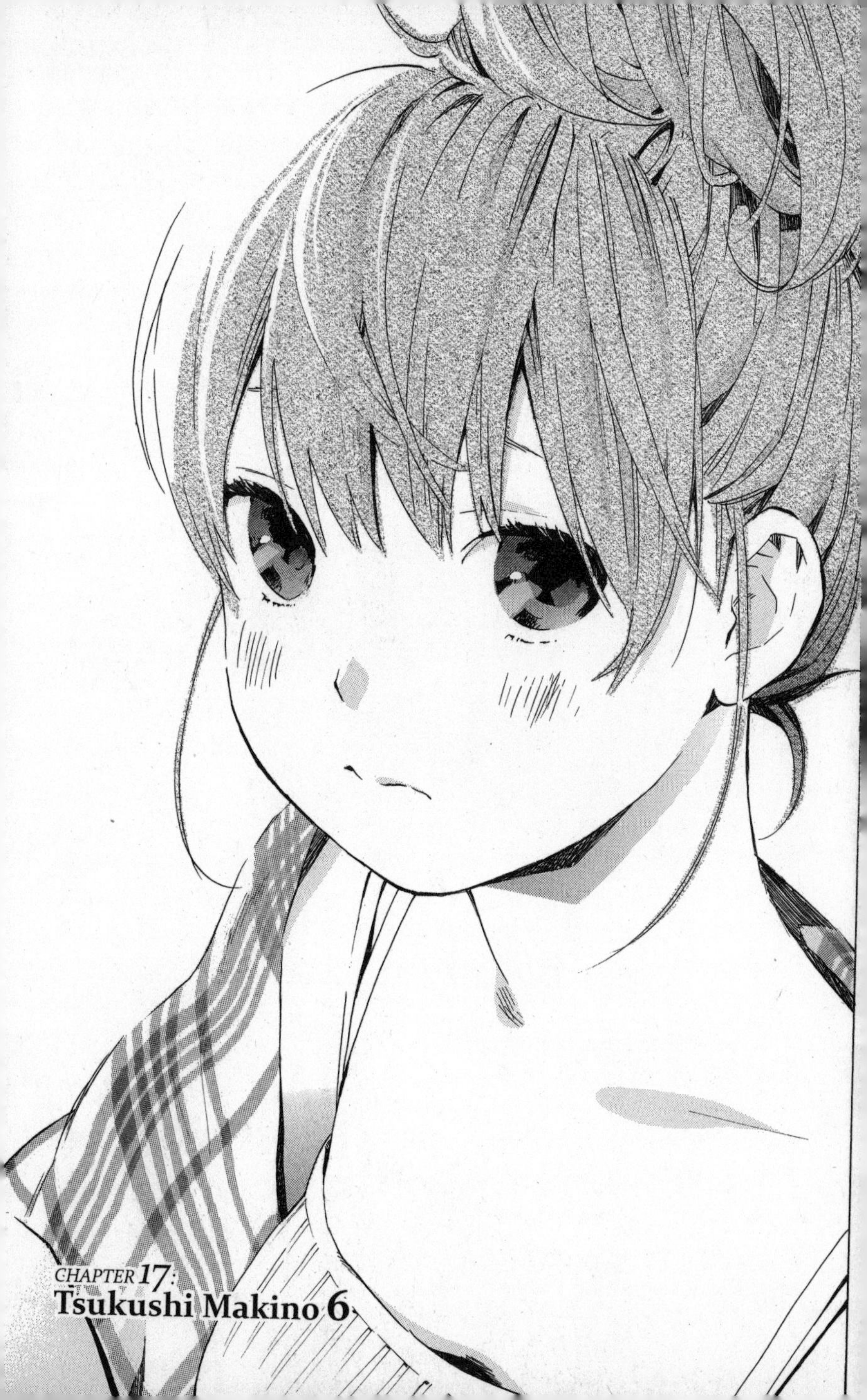

CHAPTER 17: Tsukushi Makino 6

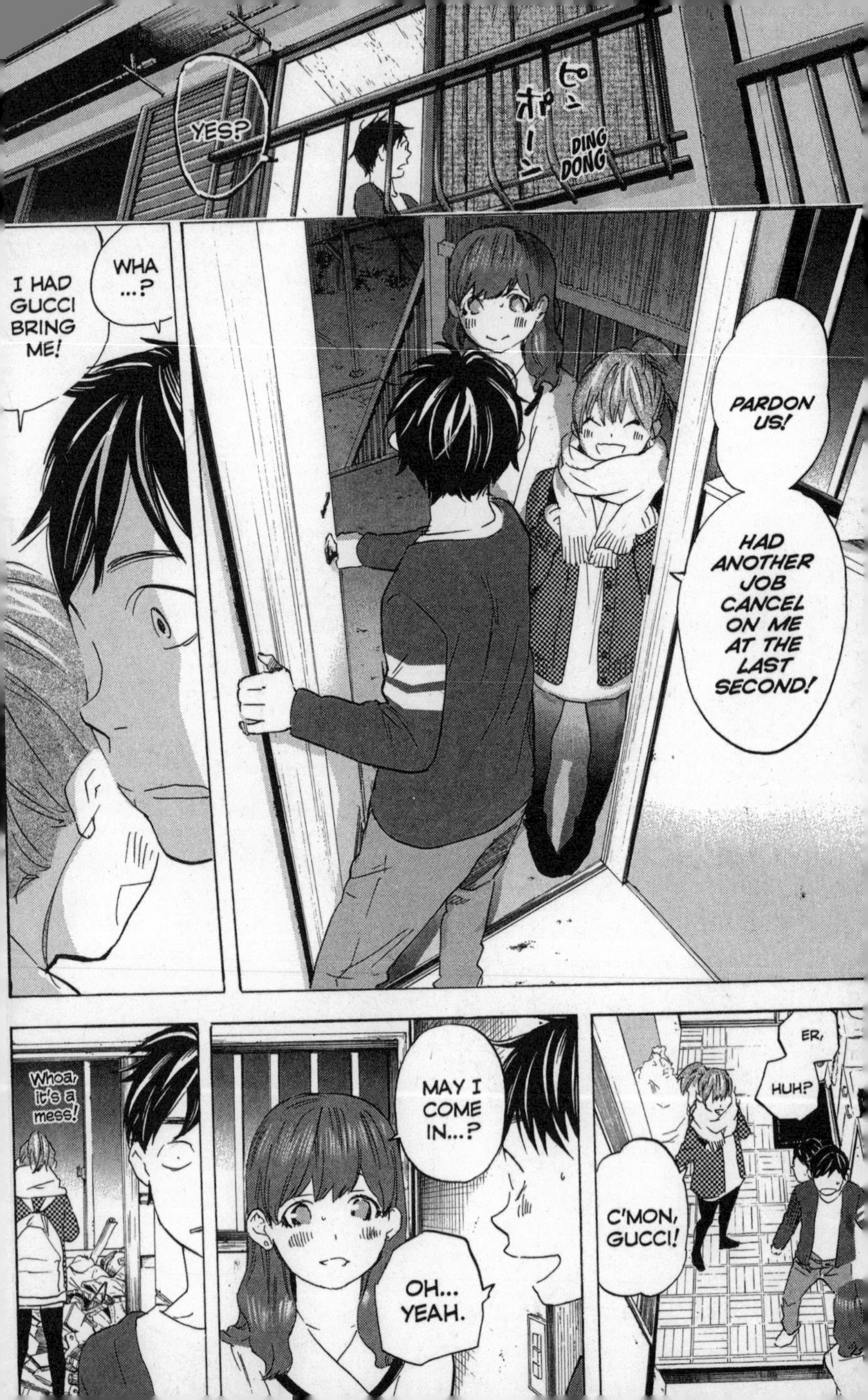
ピンポーン
DING DONG
YES?
PARDON US!
HAD ANOTHER JOB CANCEL ON ME AT THE LAST SECOND!
WHA ...?
I HAD GUCCI BRING ME!
ER, HUH?
C'MON, GUCCI!
MAY I COME IN...?
OH... YEAH.
Whoa, it's a mess!

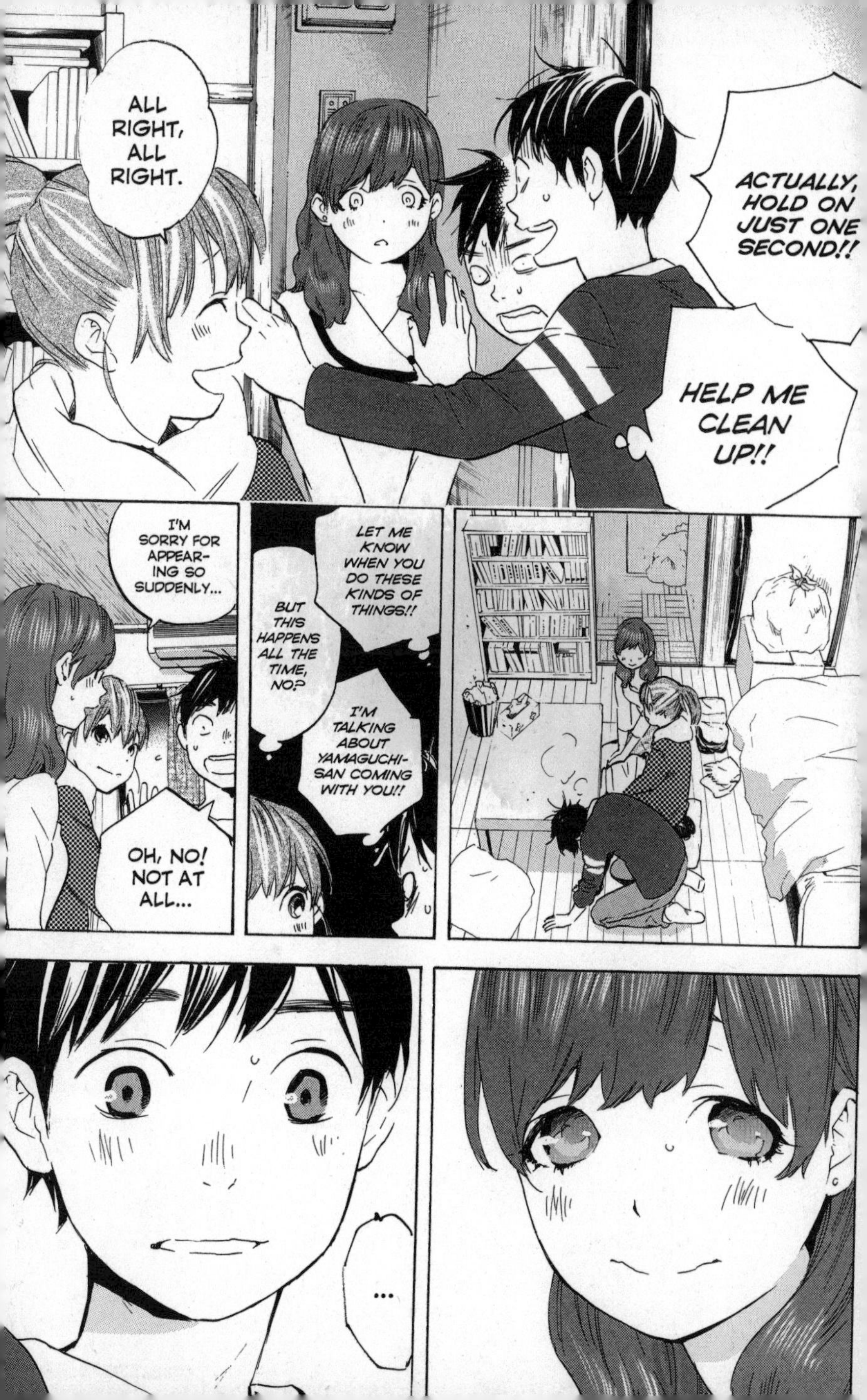
ACTUALLY, HOLD ON JUST ONE SECOND!!
HELP ME CLEAN UP!!
ALL RIGHT, ALL RIGHT.
LET ME KNOW WHEN YOU DO THESE KINDS OF THINGS!!
BUT THIS HAPPENS ALL THE TIME, NO?
I'M TALKING ABOUT YAMAGUCHI-SAN COMING WITH YOU!!
I'M SORRY FOR APPEARING SO SUDDENLY...
OH, NO! NOT AT ALL...
...

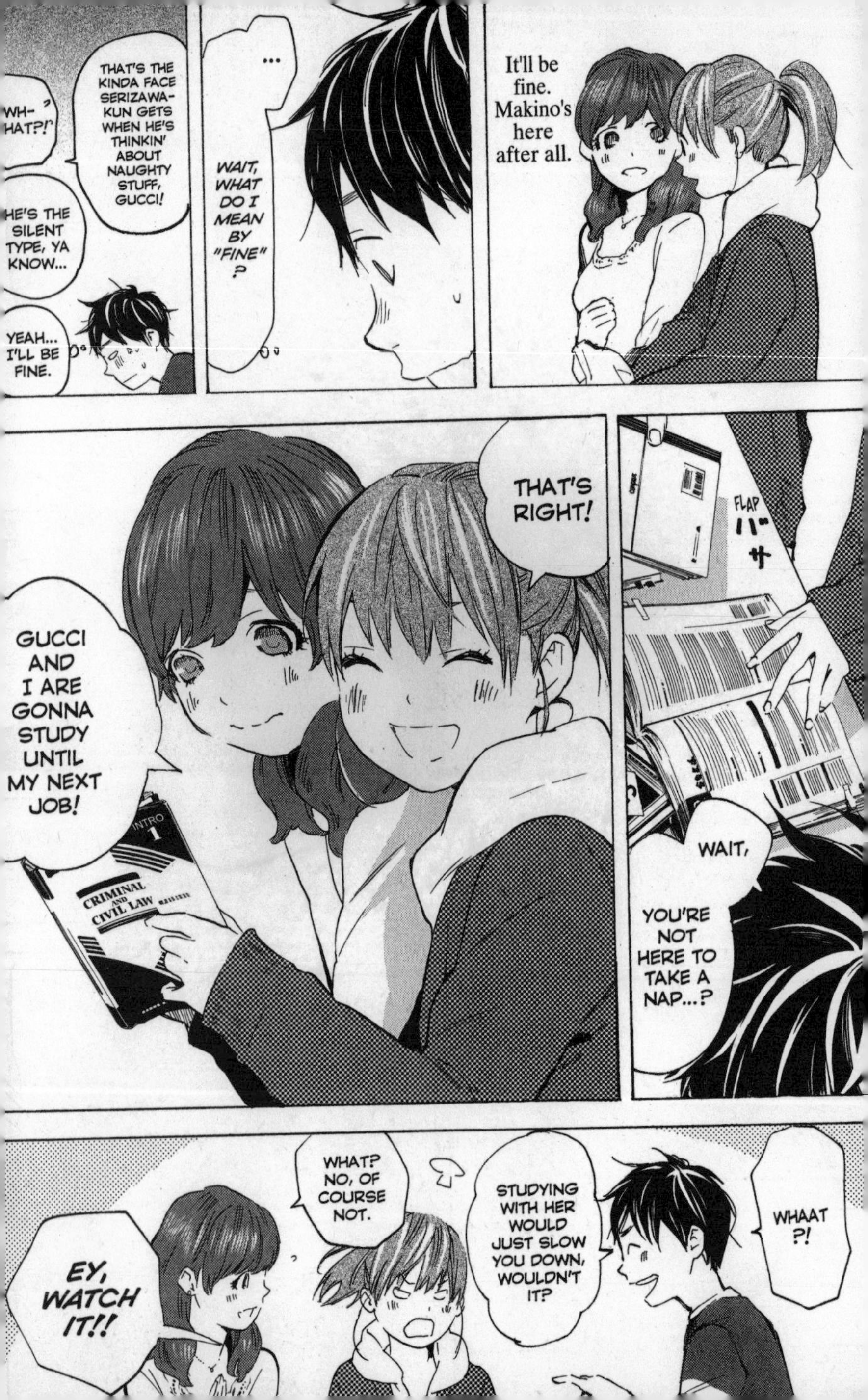
It'll be fine. Makino's here after all.
...
WAIT, WHAT DO I MEAN BY "FINE"?
THAT'S THE KINDA FACE SERIZAWA-KUN GETS WHEN HE'S THINKIN' ABOUT NAUGHTY STUFF, GUCCI!
WH-HAT?!
HE'S THE SILENT TYPE, YA KNOW...
YEAH... I'LL BE FINE.
FLAP
ハサ
WAIT,
YOU'RE NOT HERE TO TAKE A NAP...?
THAT'S RIGHT!
GUCCI AND I ARE GONNA STUDY UNTIL MY NEXT JOB!
INTRO 1
CRIMINAL AND CIVIL LAW
WHAAT?!
STUDYING WITH HER WOULD JUST SLOW YOU DOWN, WOULDN'T IT?
WHAT? NO, OF COURSE NOT.
EY, WATCH IT!!

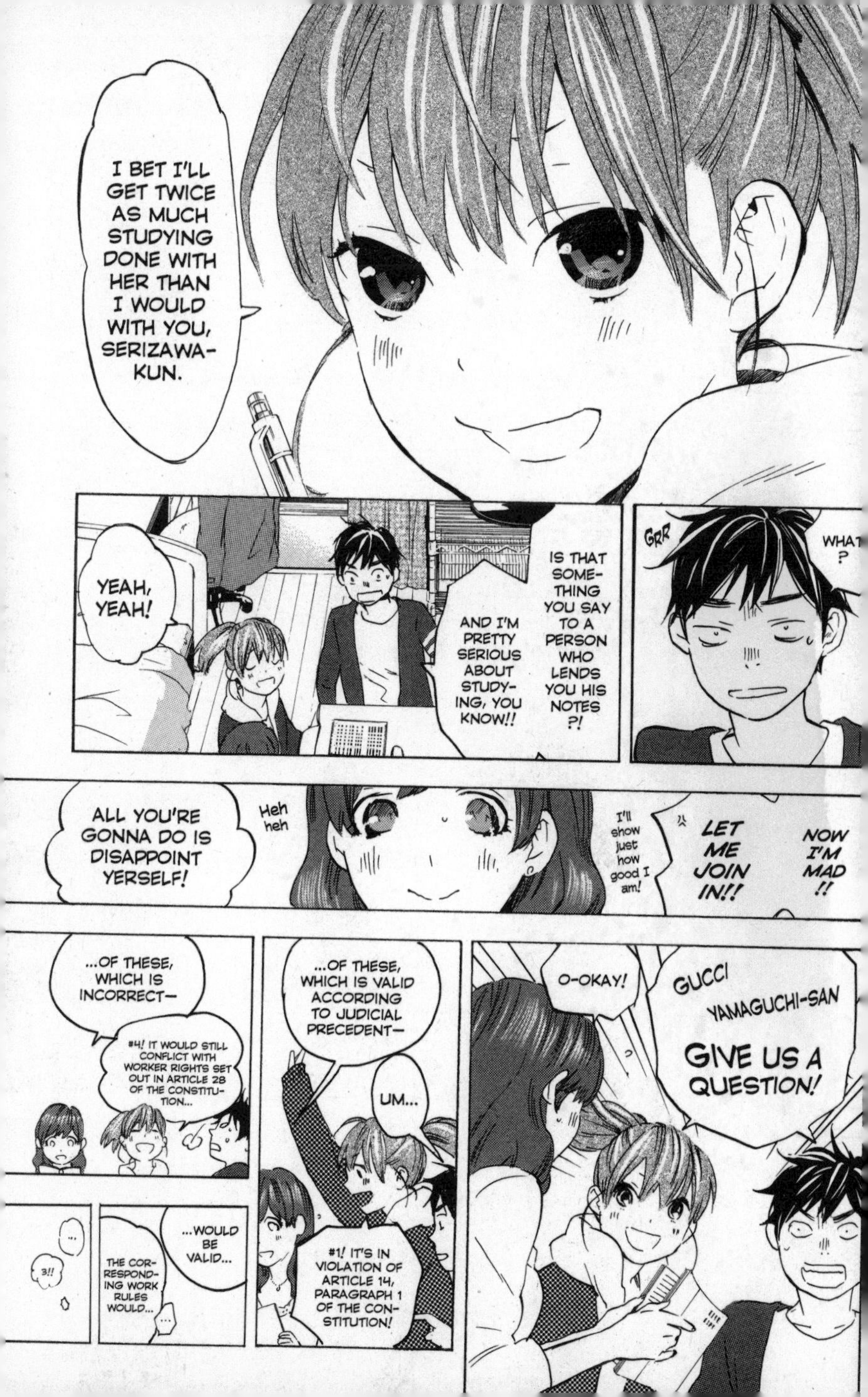
I BET I'LL GET TWICE AS MUCH STUDYING DONE WITH HER THAN I WOULD WITH YOU, SERIZAWA-KUN.
GRR
WHAT?
IS THAT SOMETHING YOU SAY TO A PERSON WHO LENDS YOU HIS NOTES?!
AND I'M PRETTY SERIOUS ABOUT STUDYING, YOU KNOW!!
YEAH, YEAH!
NOW I'M MAD!!
LET ME JOIN IN!!
I'll show just how good I am!
Heh heh
ALL YOU'RE GONNA DO IS DISAPPOINT YERSELF!
GUCCI
YAMAGUCHI-SAN
GIVE US A QUESTION!
O-OKAY!
...OF THESE, WHICH IS VALID ACCORDING TO JUDICIAL PRECEDENT—
UM...
#1! IT'S IN VIOLATION OF ARTICLE 14, PARAGRAPH 1 OF THE CONSTITUTION!
...OF THESE, WHICH IS INCORRECT—
#4! IT WOULD STILL CONFLICT WITH WORKER RIGHTS SET OUT IN ARTICLE 28 OF THE CONSTITUTION...
...WOULD BE VALID...
THE CORRESPONDING WORK RULES WOULD...
...
...
3!!

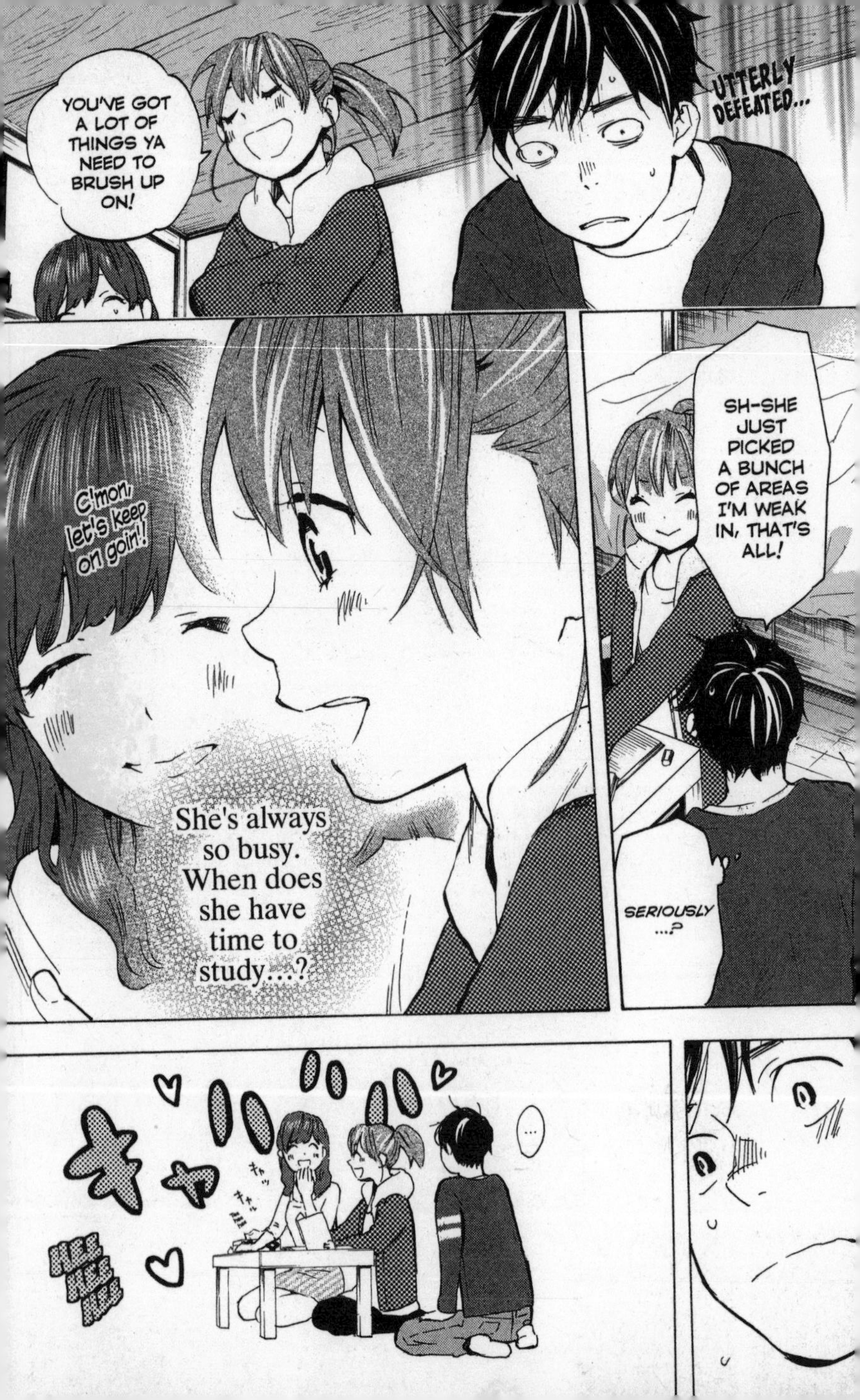
UTTERLY DEFEATED...
YOU'VE GOT A LOT OF THINGS YA NEED TO BRUSH UP ON!
SH-SHE JUST PICKED A BUNCH OF AREAS I'M WEAK IN, THAT'S ALL!
SERIOUSLY ...?
C'mon, let's keep on goin'!
She's always so busy. When does she have time to study...?
...

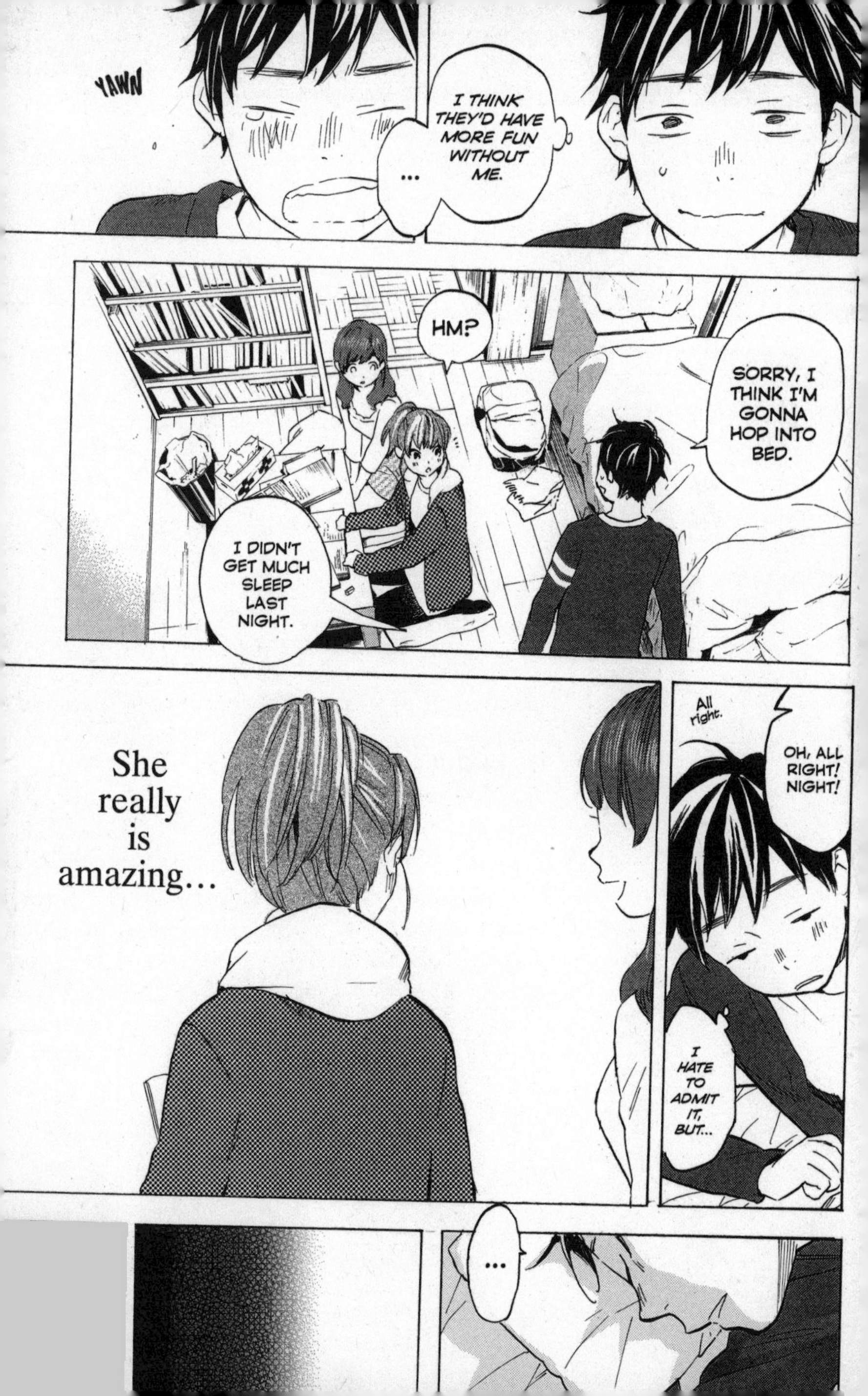
I THINK THEY'D HAVE MORE FUN WITHOUT ME.
...
YAWN
SORRY, I THINK I'M GONNA HOP INTO BED.
HM?
I DIDN'T GET MUCH SLEEP LAST NIGHT.
All right.
OH, ALL RIGHT! NIGHT!
I HATE TO ADMIT IT, BUT...
She really is amazing...
...

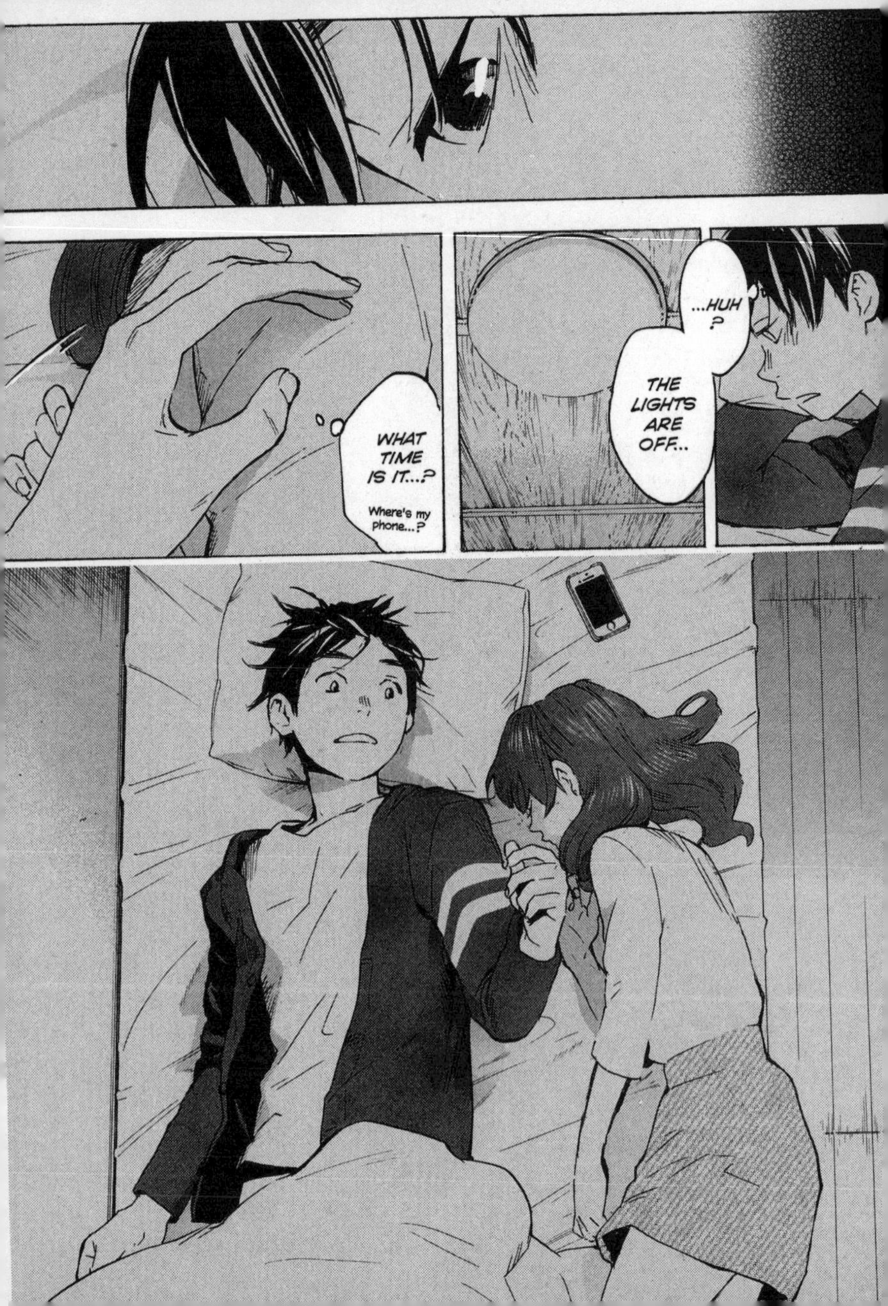
...HUH?
THE LIGHTS ARE OFF...
WHAT TIME IS IT...?
Where's my phone...?

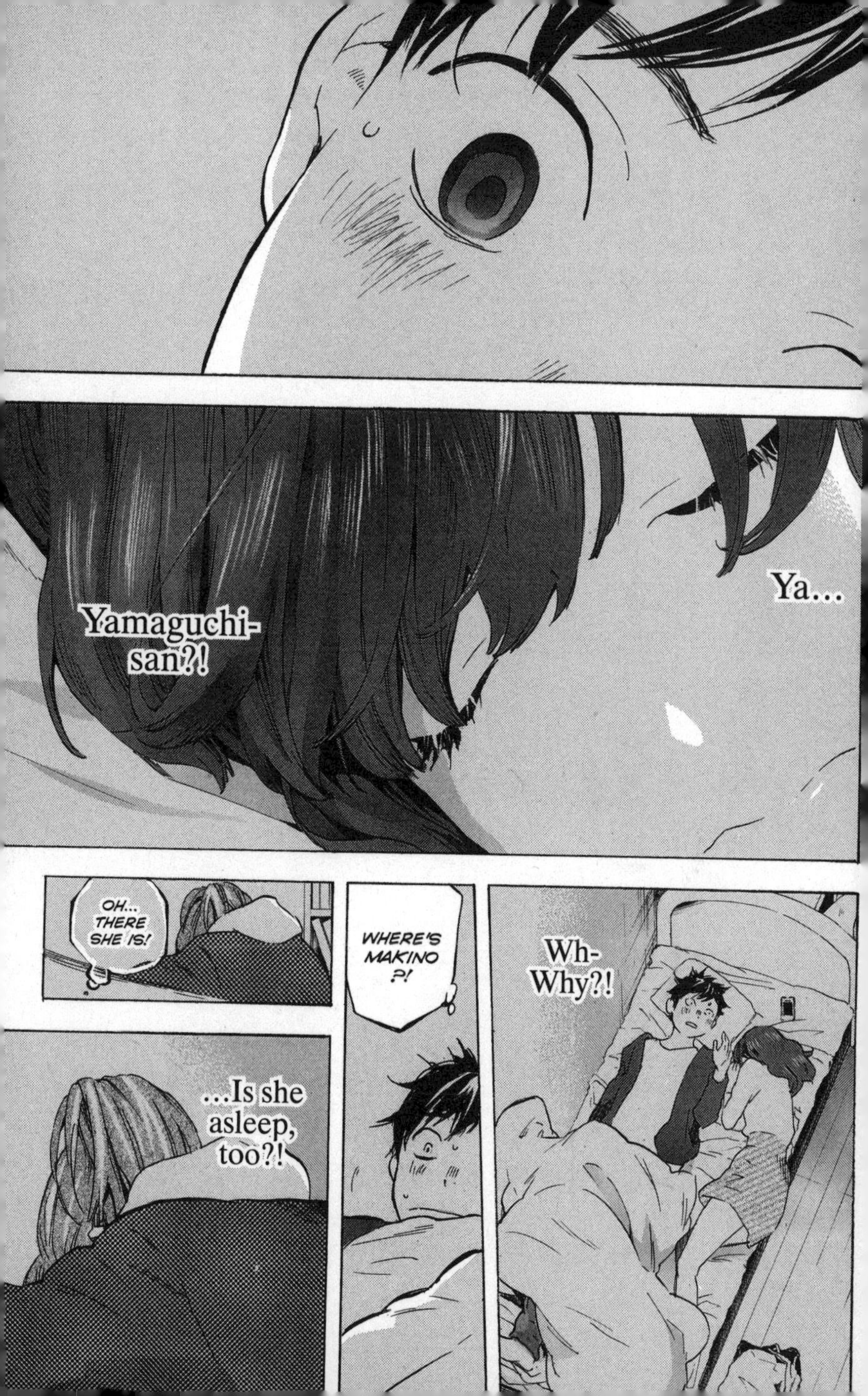
Ya...
Yamaguchi-san?!
Wh- Why?!
WHERE'S MAKINO?!
OH... THERE SHE IS!
...Is she asleep, too?!

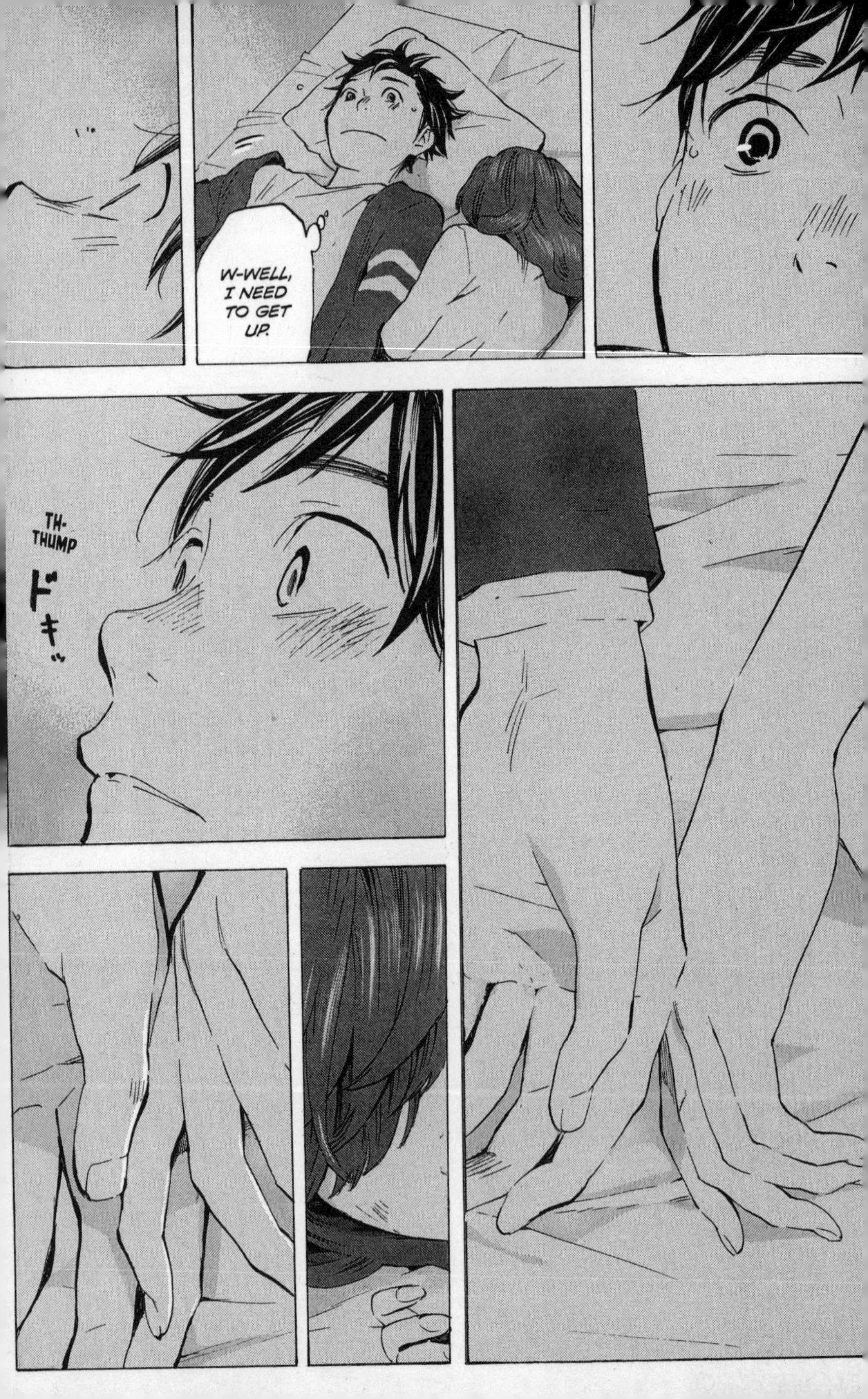
W-WELL, I NEED TO GET UP.
TH-THUMP
ドキッ

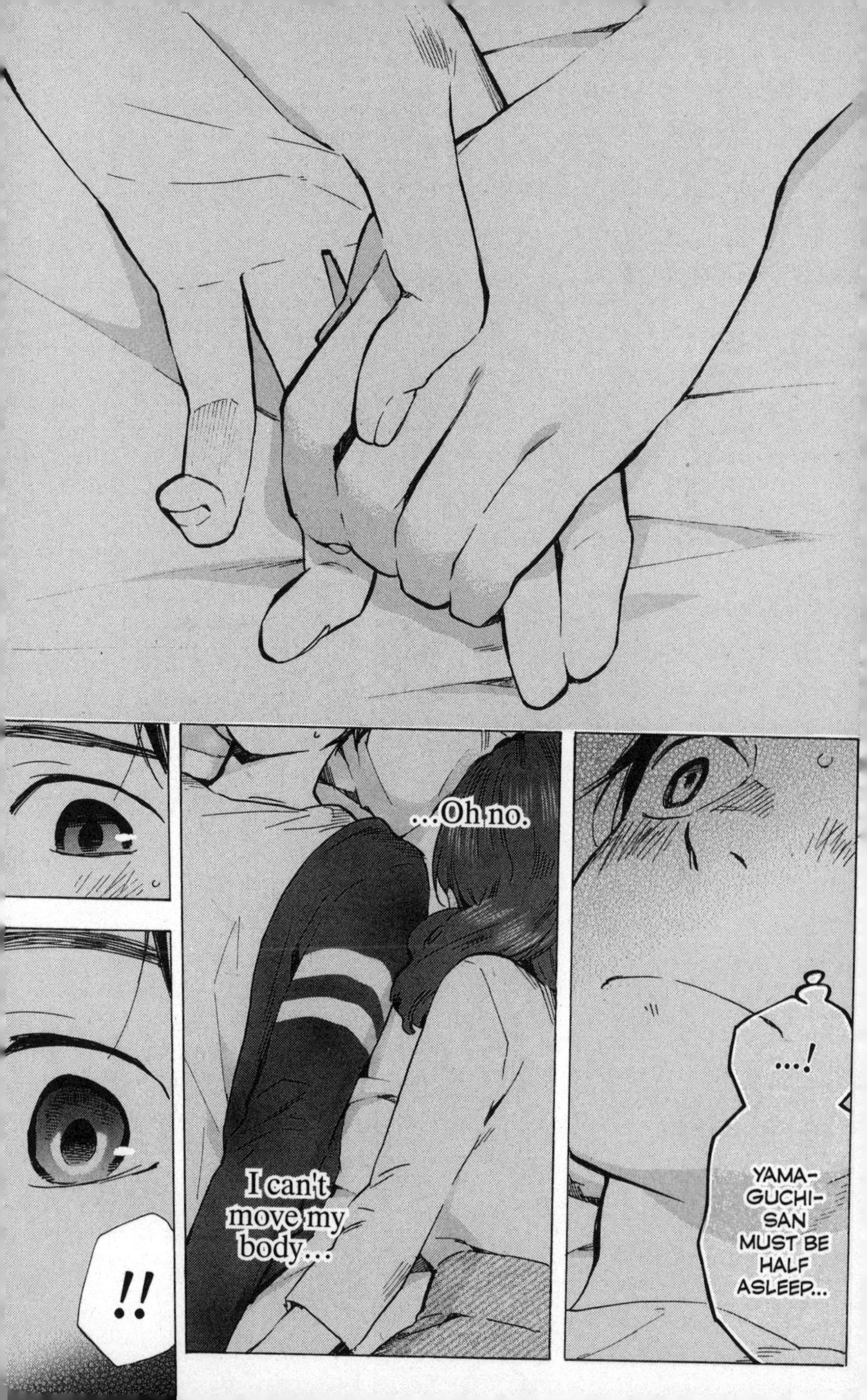
...!
YAMAGUCHI-SAN MUST BE HALF ASLEEP...
...Oh no.
I can't move my body...
!!

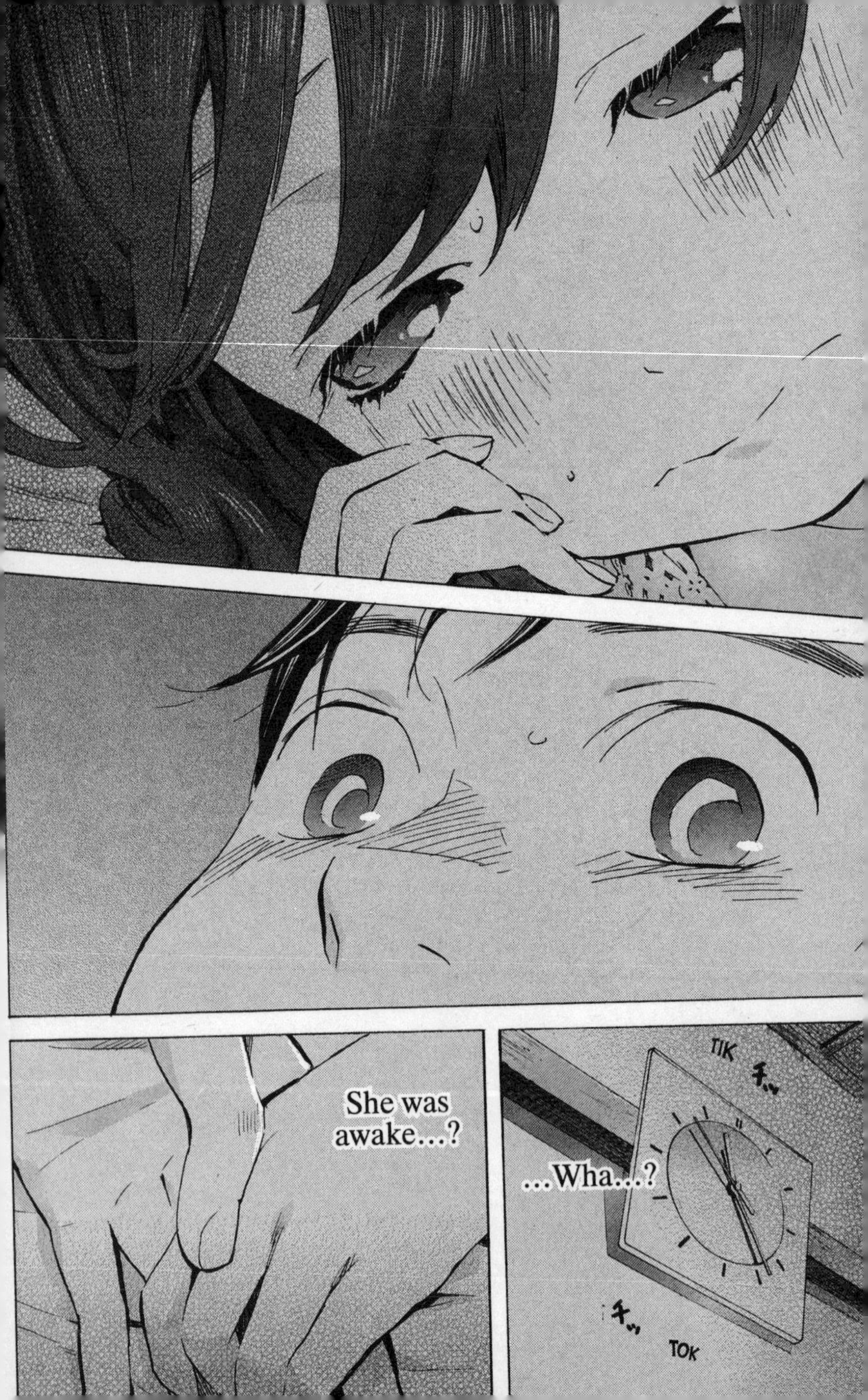
TIK
チッ
...Wha...?
チッ
TOK
She was awake...?

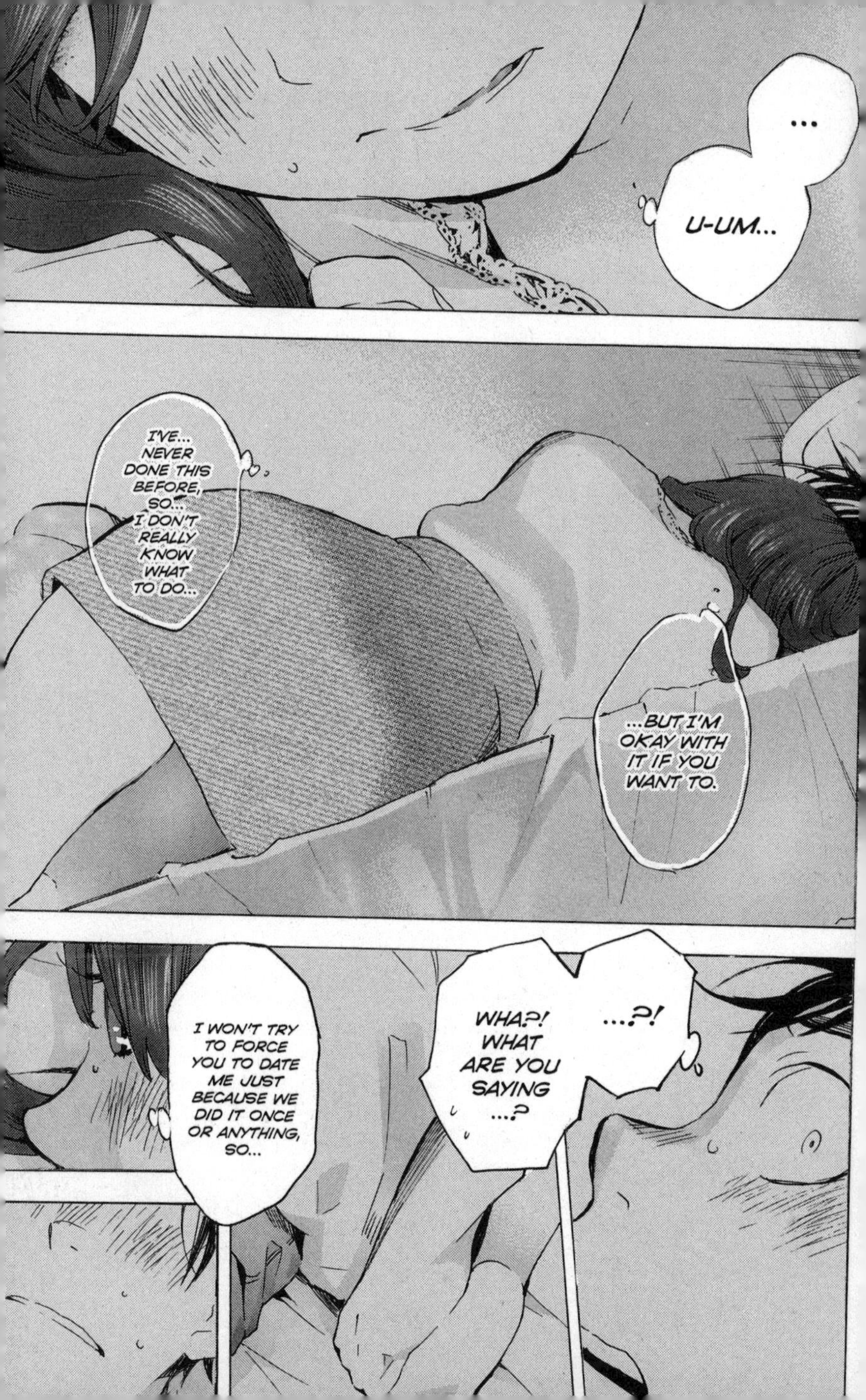
...
U-UM...
I'VE... NEVER DONE THIS BEFORE, SO... I DON'T REALLY KNOW WHAT TO DO...
...BUT I'M OKAY WITH IT IF YOU WANT TO.
...?!
WHA?! WHAT ARE YOU SAYING ...?
I WON'T TRY TO FORCE YOU TO DATE ME JUST BECAUSE WE DID IT ONCE OR ANYTHING, SO...

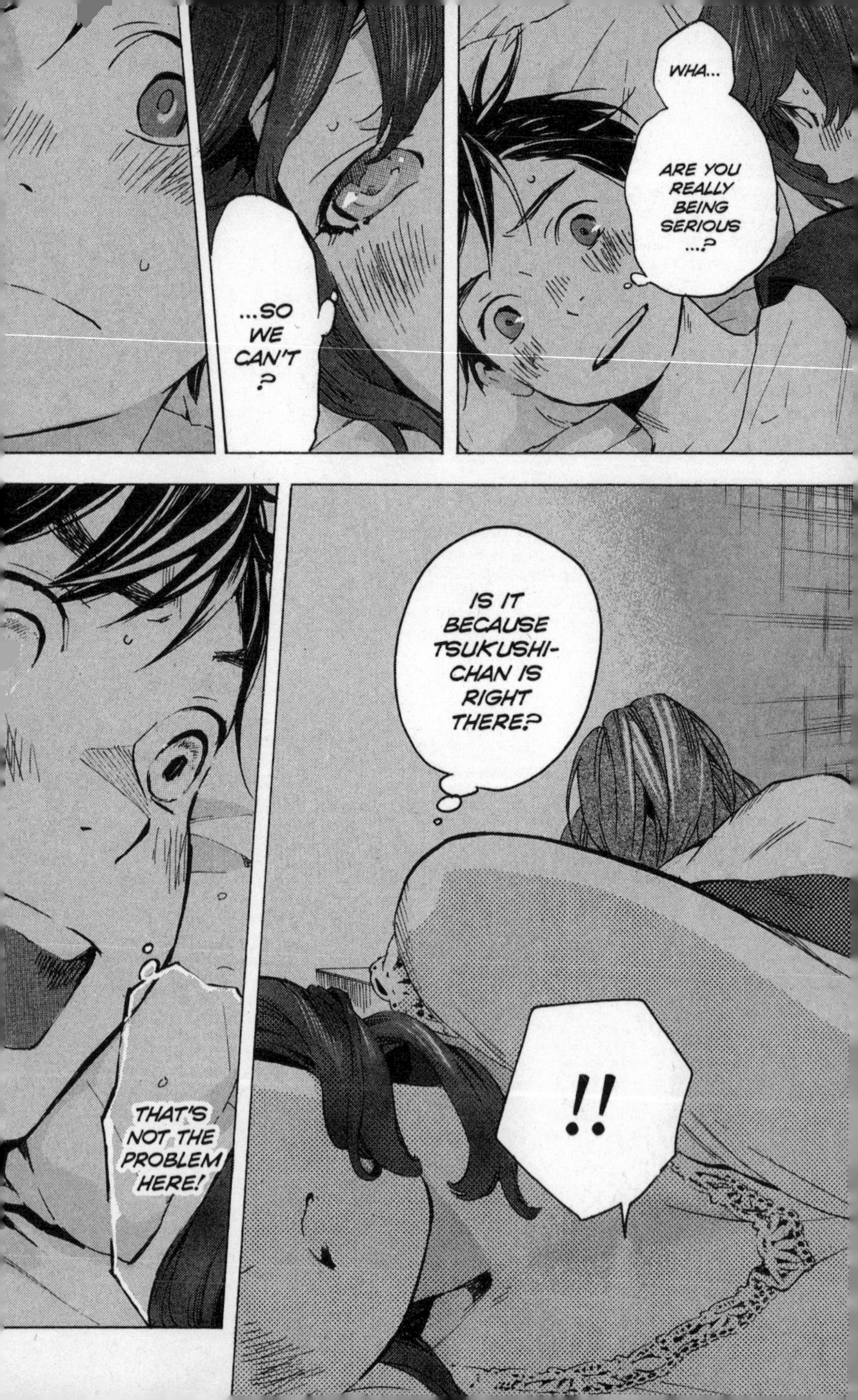
WHA...
ARE YOU REALLY BEING SERIOUS ...?
...SO WE CAN'T ?
IS IT BECAUSE TSUKUSHI-CHAN IS RIGHT THERE?
!!
THAT'S NOT THE PROBLEM HERE!

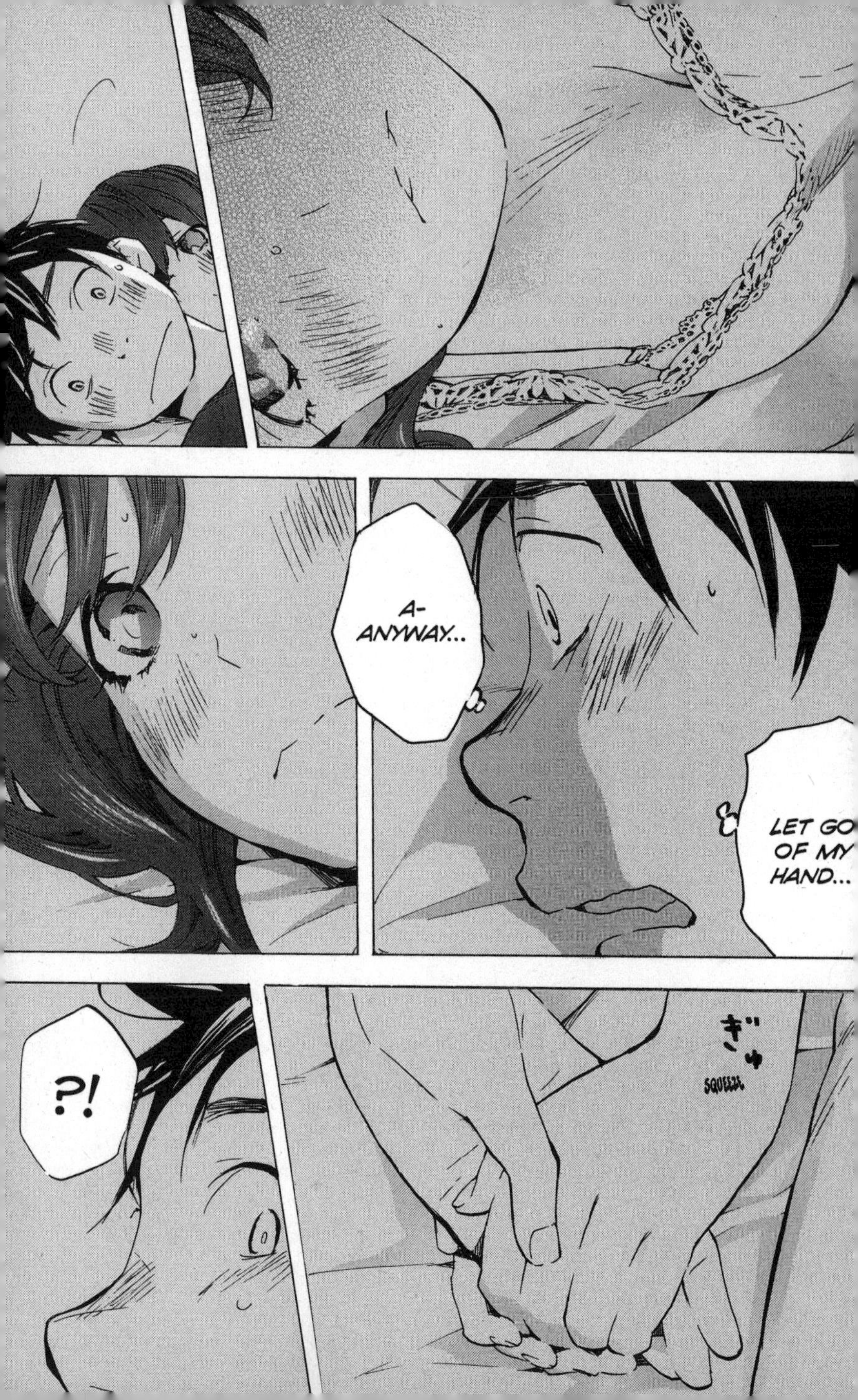
A-
ANYWAY...
LET GO OF MY HAND...
ぎゅ
SQUEEZE
?!

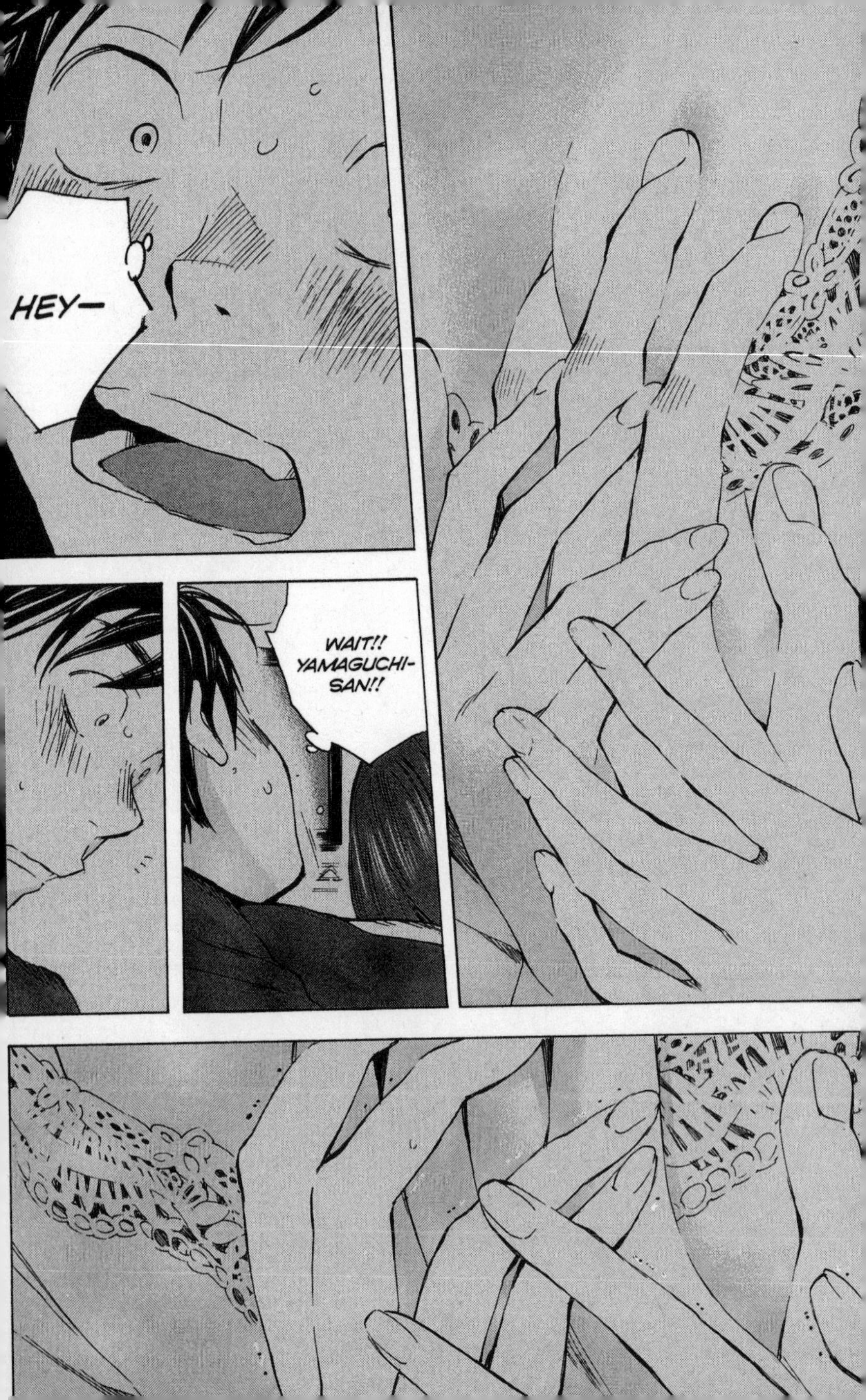
HEY—
WAIT!! YAMAGUCHI-SAN!!

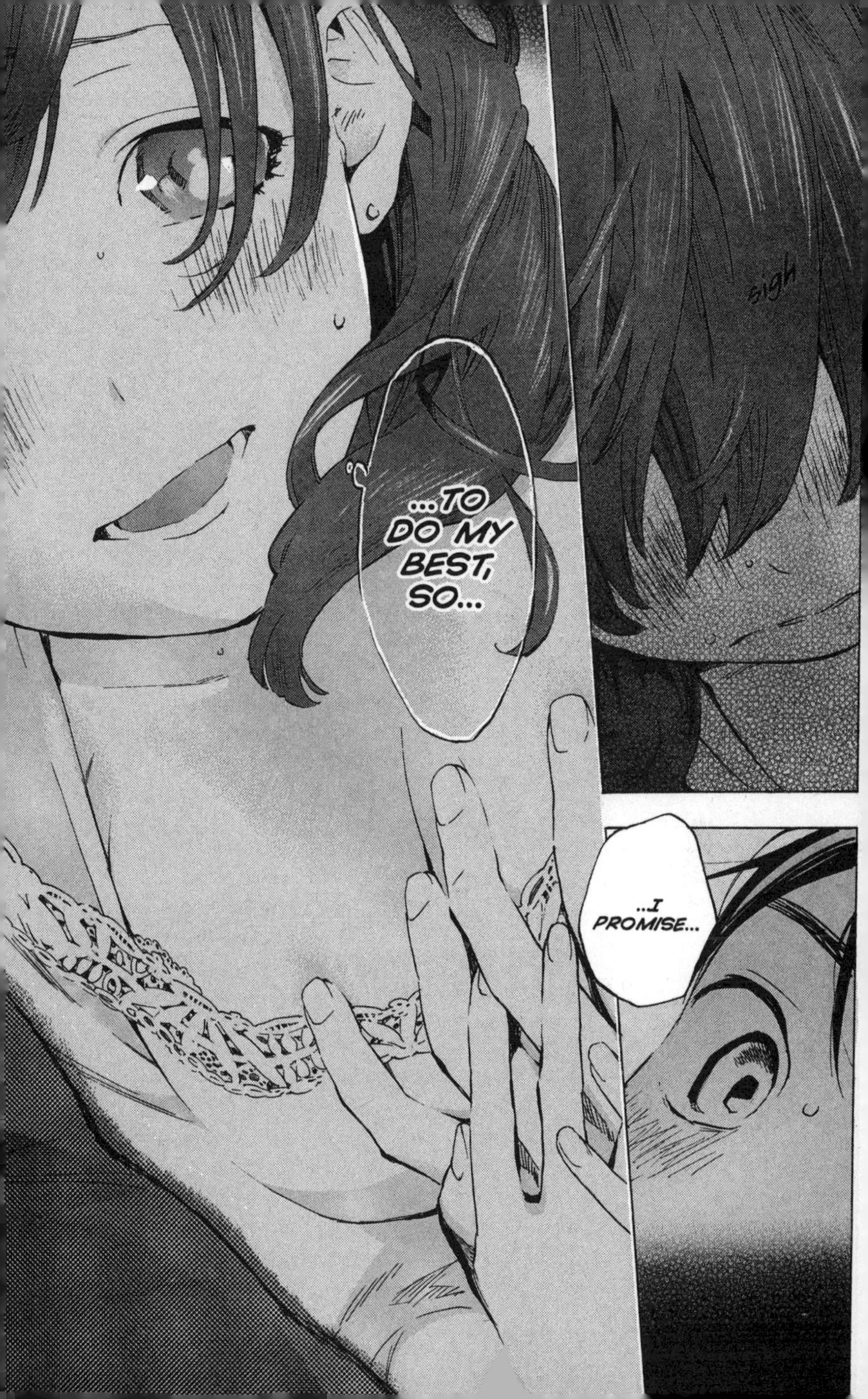
sigh
...I PROMISE...
...TO DO MY BEST, SO...

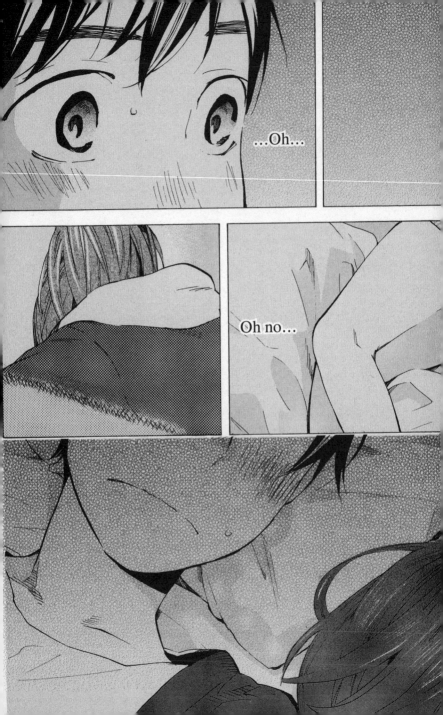

...Oh...

Oh no...

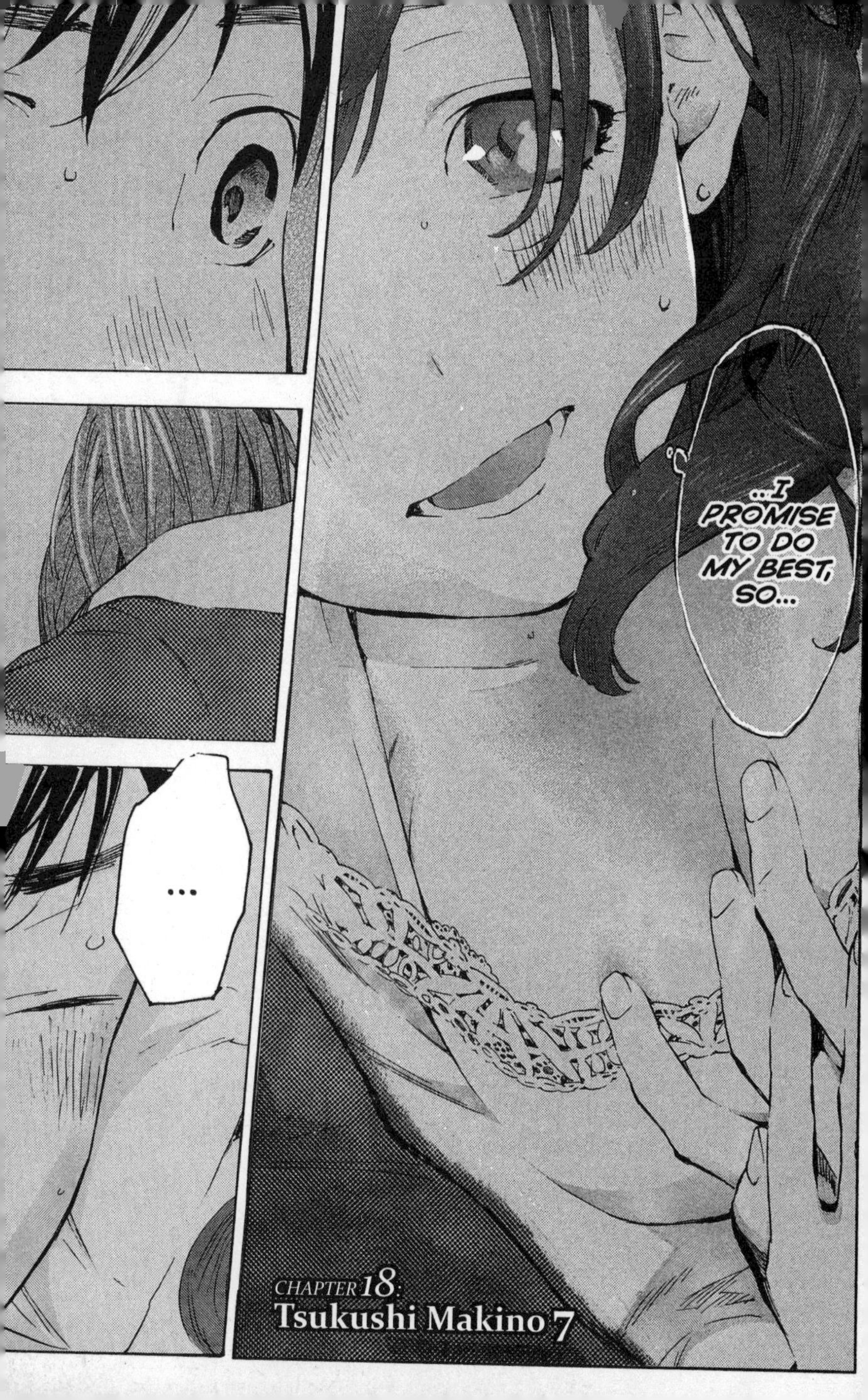
...I PROMISE TO DO MY BEST, SO...
CHAPTER 18: Tsukushi Makino 7
...

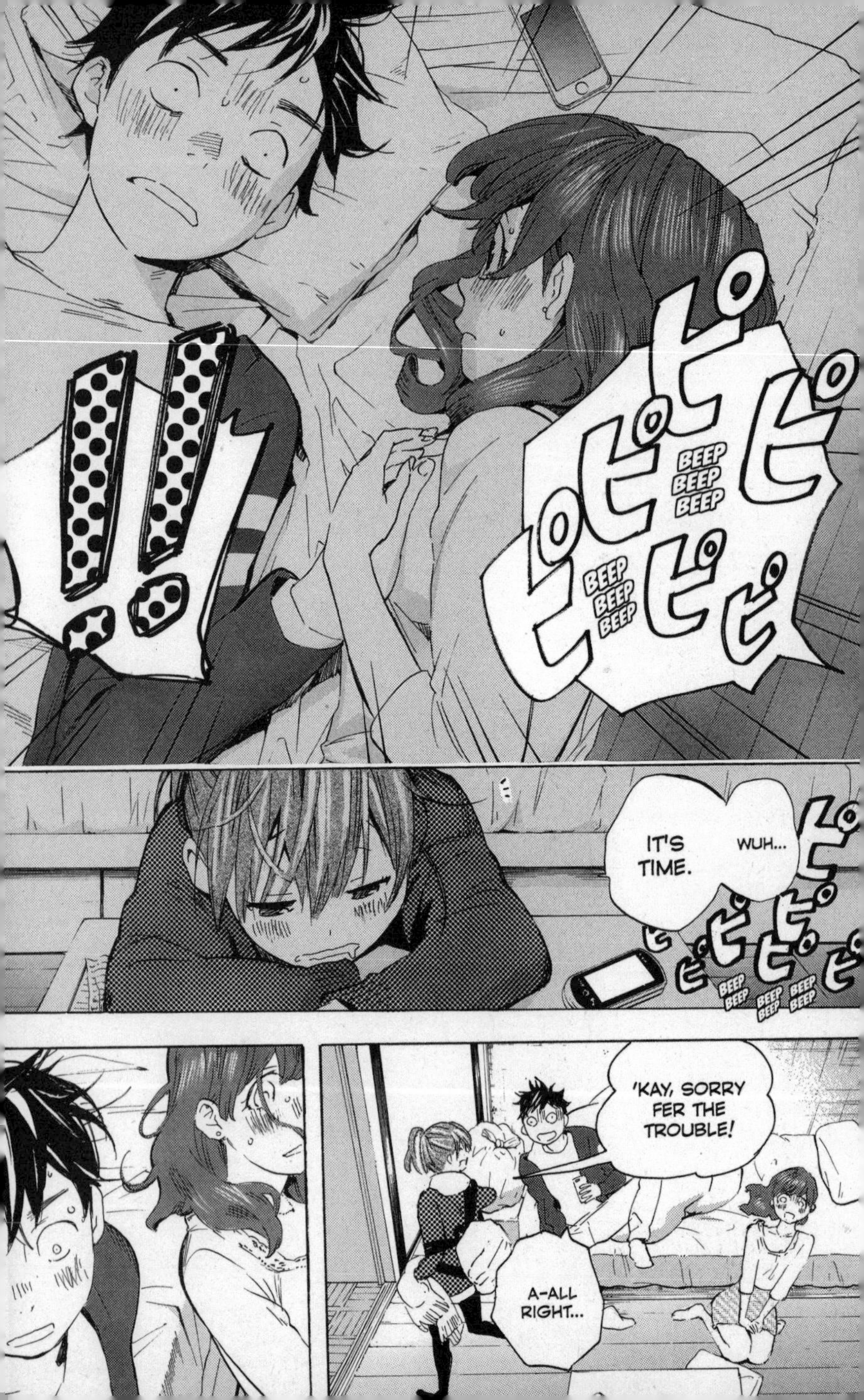
ピピピ
BEEP BEEP BEEP
ピピピ
BEEP BEEP BEEP
!!
WUH...
IT'S TIME.
ピピピピピ
BEEP BEEP BEEP BEEP BEEP BEEP
'KAY, SORRY FER THE TROUBLE!
A-ALL RIGHT...

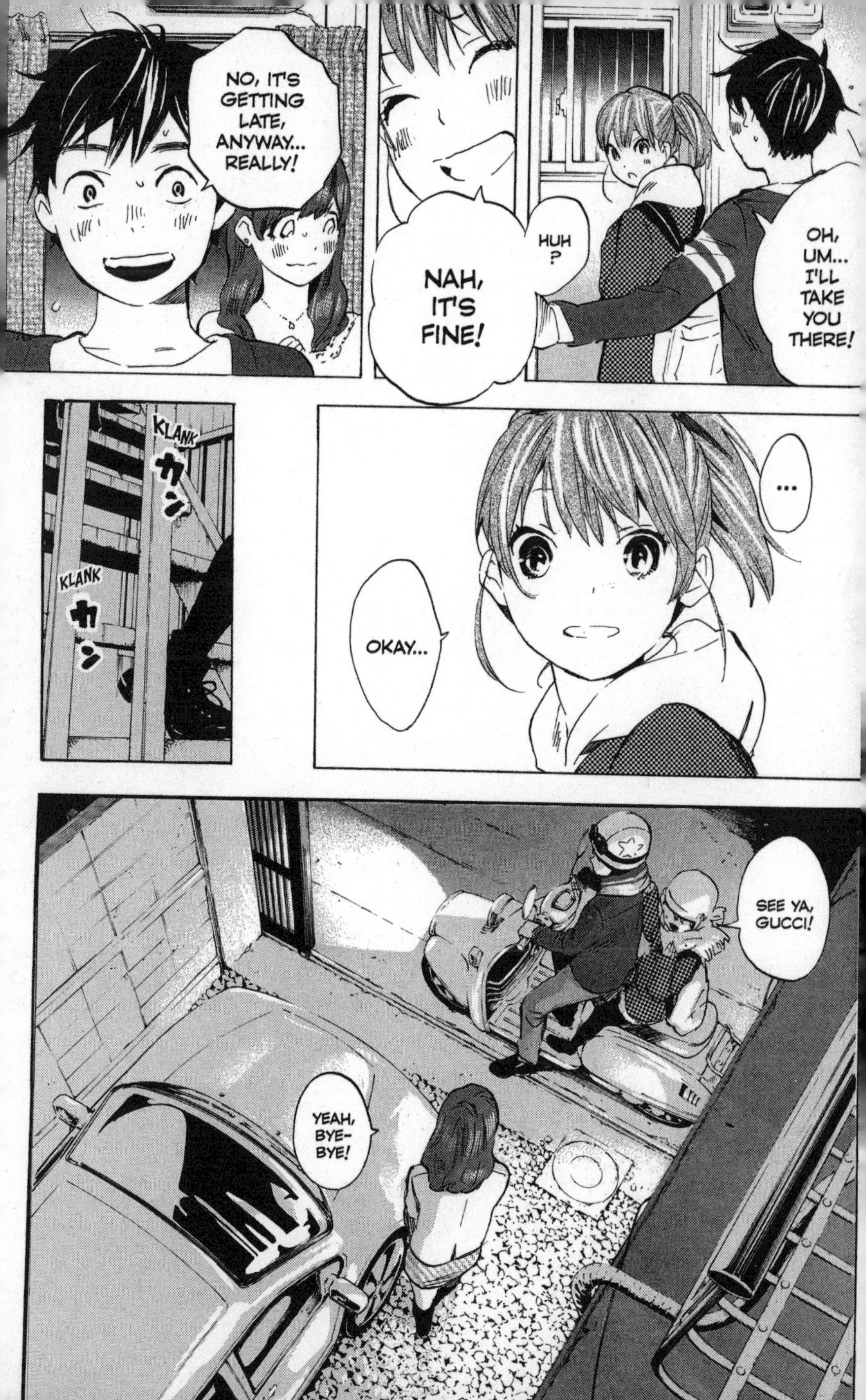
OH, UM... I'LL TAKE YOU THERE!
HUH?
NAH, IT'S FINE!
NO, IT'S GETTING LATE, ANYWAY... REALLY!
...
OKAY...
KLANK
カン
KLANK
カン
SEE YA, GUCCI!
YEAH, BYE-BYE!

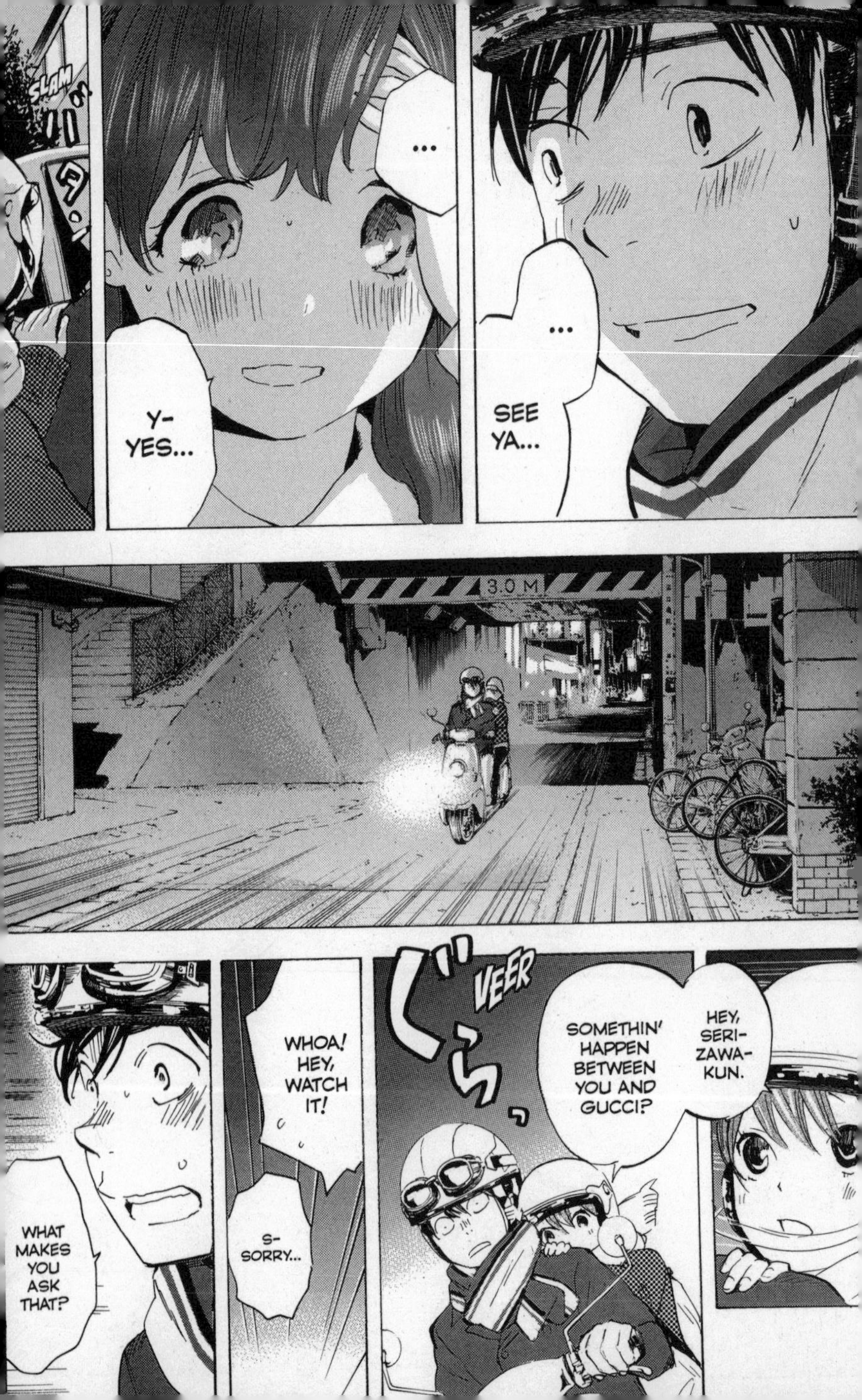
...
SEE YA...
...
Y-YES...
SLAM
3.0 M
HEY, SERI-ZAWA-KUN.
SOMETHIN' HAPPEN BETWEEN YOU AND GUCCI?
VEER
WHOA! HEY, WATCH IT!
S-SORRY...
WHAT MAKES YOU ASK THAT?

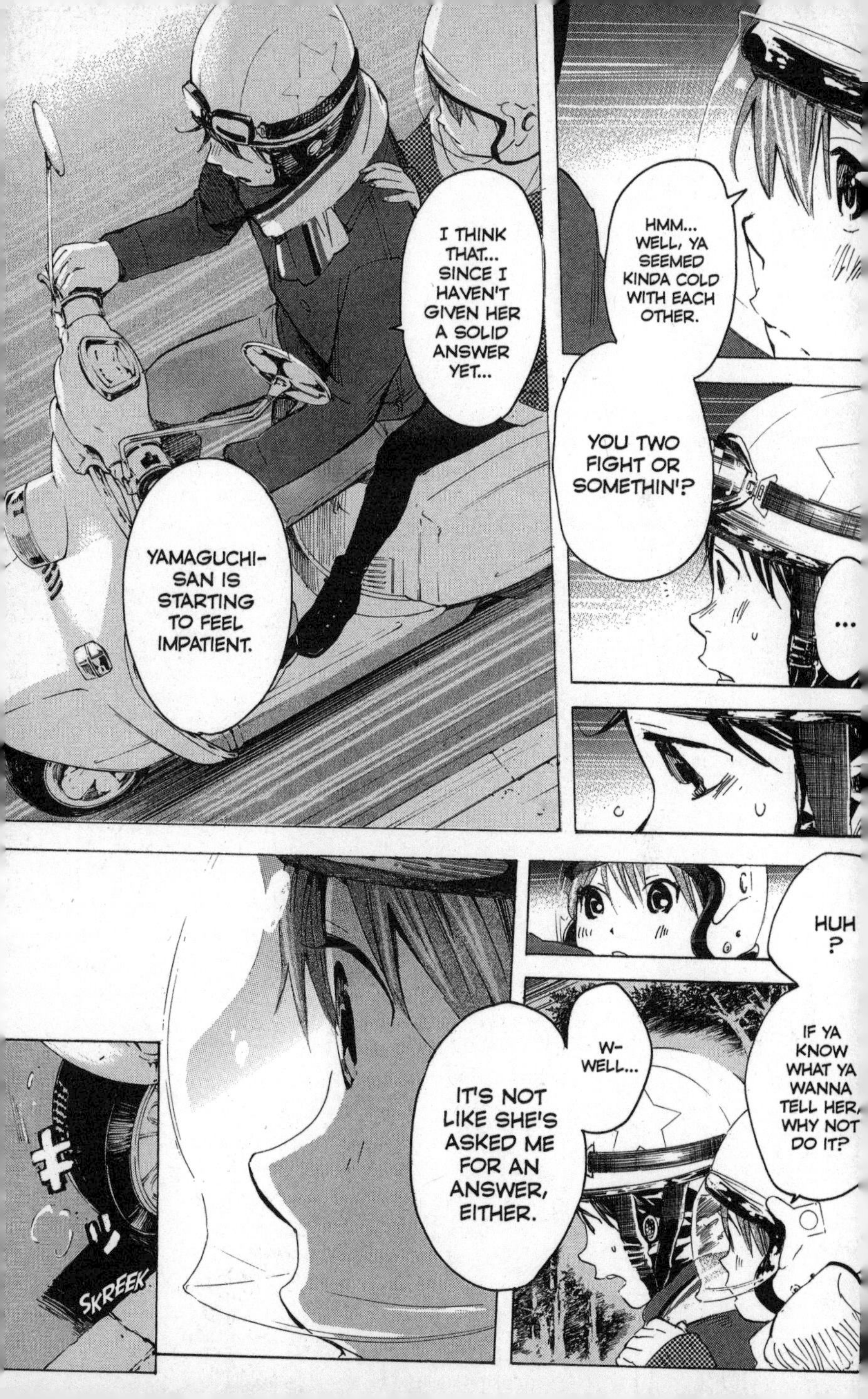
HMM... WELL, YA SEEMED KINDA COLD WITH EACH OTHER.
YOU TWO FIGHT OR SOMETHIN'?
...
I THINK THAT... SINCE I HAVEN'T GIVEN HER A SOLID ANSWER YET...
YAMAGUCHI-SAN IS STARTING TO FEEL IMPATIENT.
HUH?
IF YA KNOW WHAT YA WANNA TELL HER, WHY NOT DO IT?
W-WELL...
IT'S NOT LIKE SHE'S ASKED ME FOR AN ANSWER, EITHER.
SKREEK

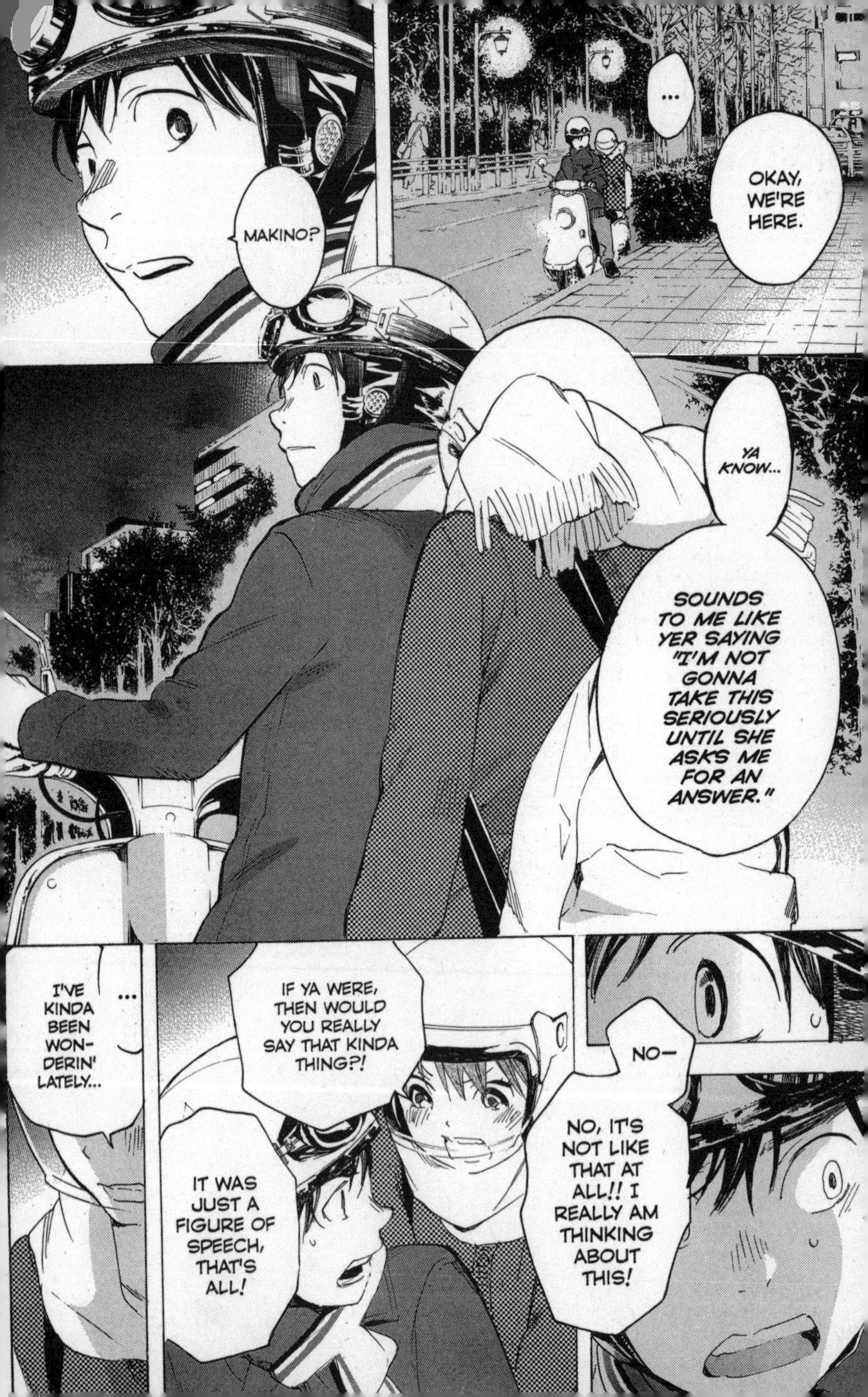
OKAY, WE'RE HERE.
...
MAKINO?
YA KNOW...
SOUNDS TO ME LIKE YER SAYING "I'M NOT GONNA TAKE THIS SERIOUSLY UNTIL SHE ASKS ME FOR AN ANSWER."
NO—
NO, IT'S NOT LIKE THAT AT ALL!! I REALLY AM THINKING ABOUT THIS!
IF YA WERE, THEN WOULD YOU REALLY SAY THAT KINDA THING?!
IT WAS JUST A FIGURE OF SPEECH, THAT'S ALL!
...
I'VE KINDA BEEN WON-DERIN' LATELY...

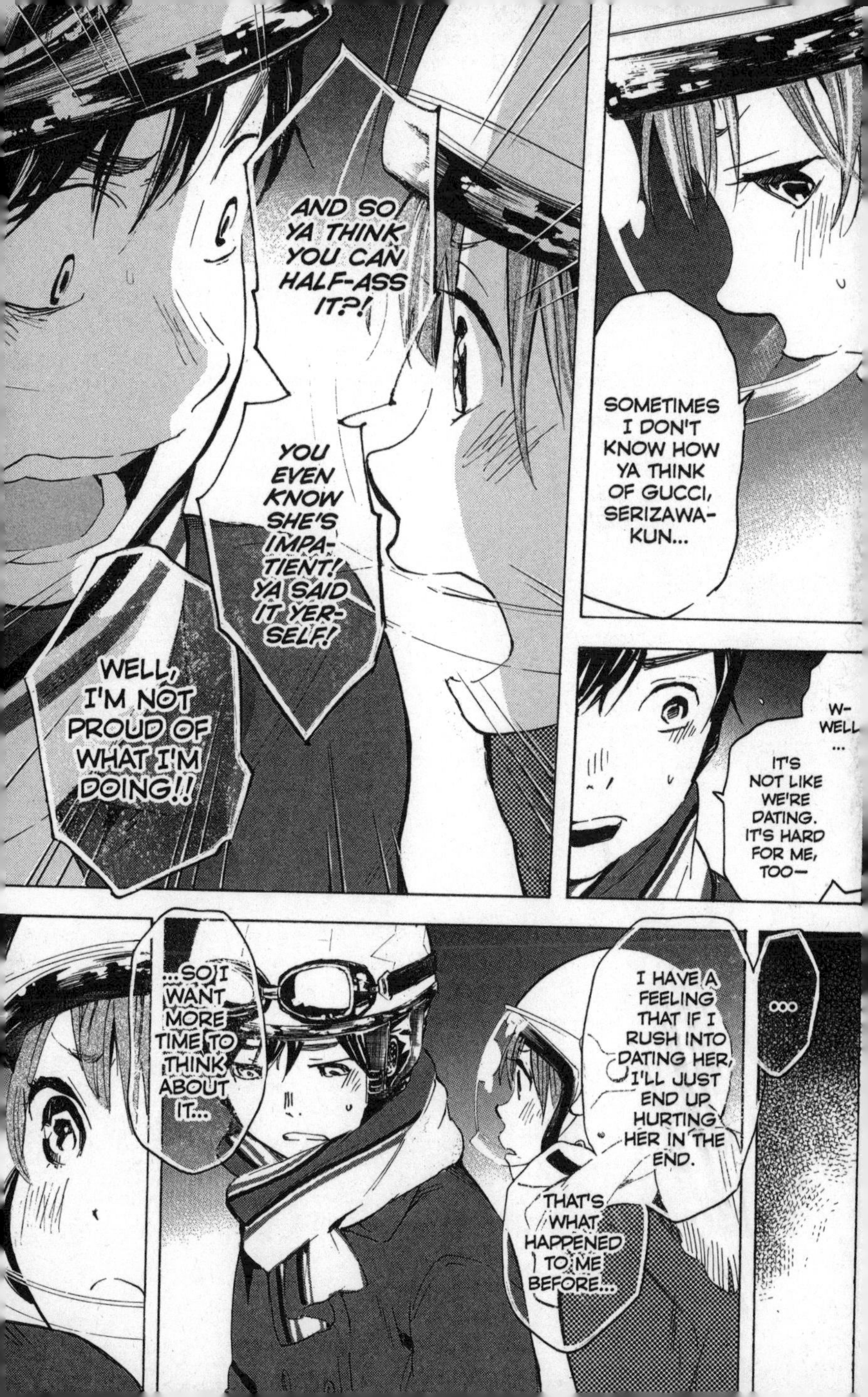
SOMETIMES I DON'T KNOW HOW YA THINK OF GUCCI, SERIZAWA-KUN...
W-WELL...
IT'S NOT LIKE WE'RE DATING. IT'S HARD FOR ME, TOO—
AND SO YA THINK YOU CAN HALF-ASS IT?!
YOU EVEN KNOW SHE'S IMPATIENT! YA SAID IT YERSELF!
WELL, I'M NOT PROUD OF WHAT I'M DOING!!
...
I HAVE A FEELING THAT IF I RUSH INTO DATING HER, I'LL JUST END UP HURTING HER IN THE END.
THAT'S WHAT HAPPENED TO ME BEFORE...
...SO I WANT MORE TIME TO THINK ABOUT IT...

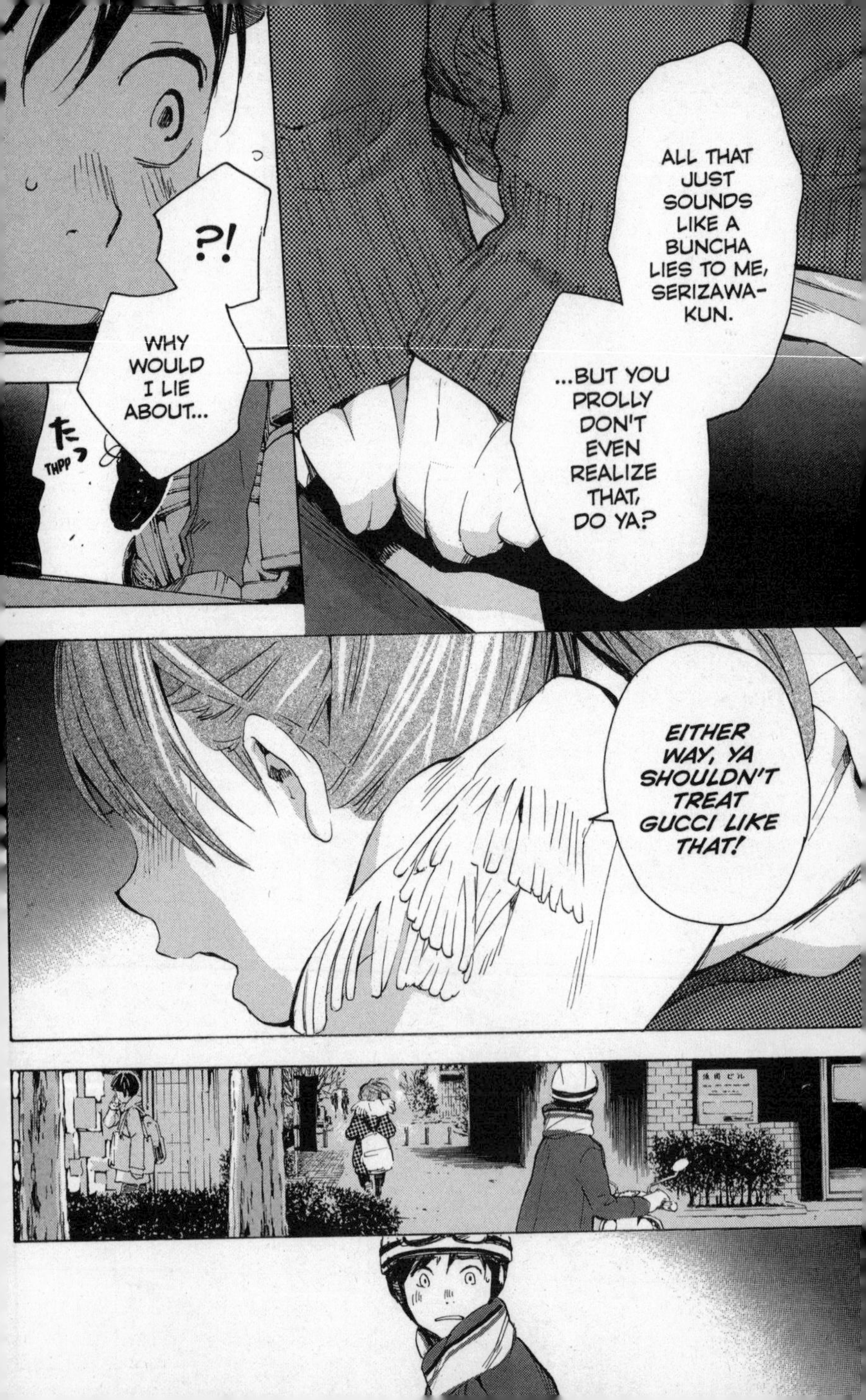
ALL THAT JUST SOUNDS LIKE A BUNCHA LIES TO ME, SERIZAWA-KUN.
...BUT YOU PROLLY DON'T EVEN REALIZE THAT, DO YA?
?!
WHY WOULD I LIE ABOUT...
たっ
THPP
EITHER WAY, YA SHOULDN'T TREAT GUCCI LIKE THAT!

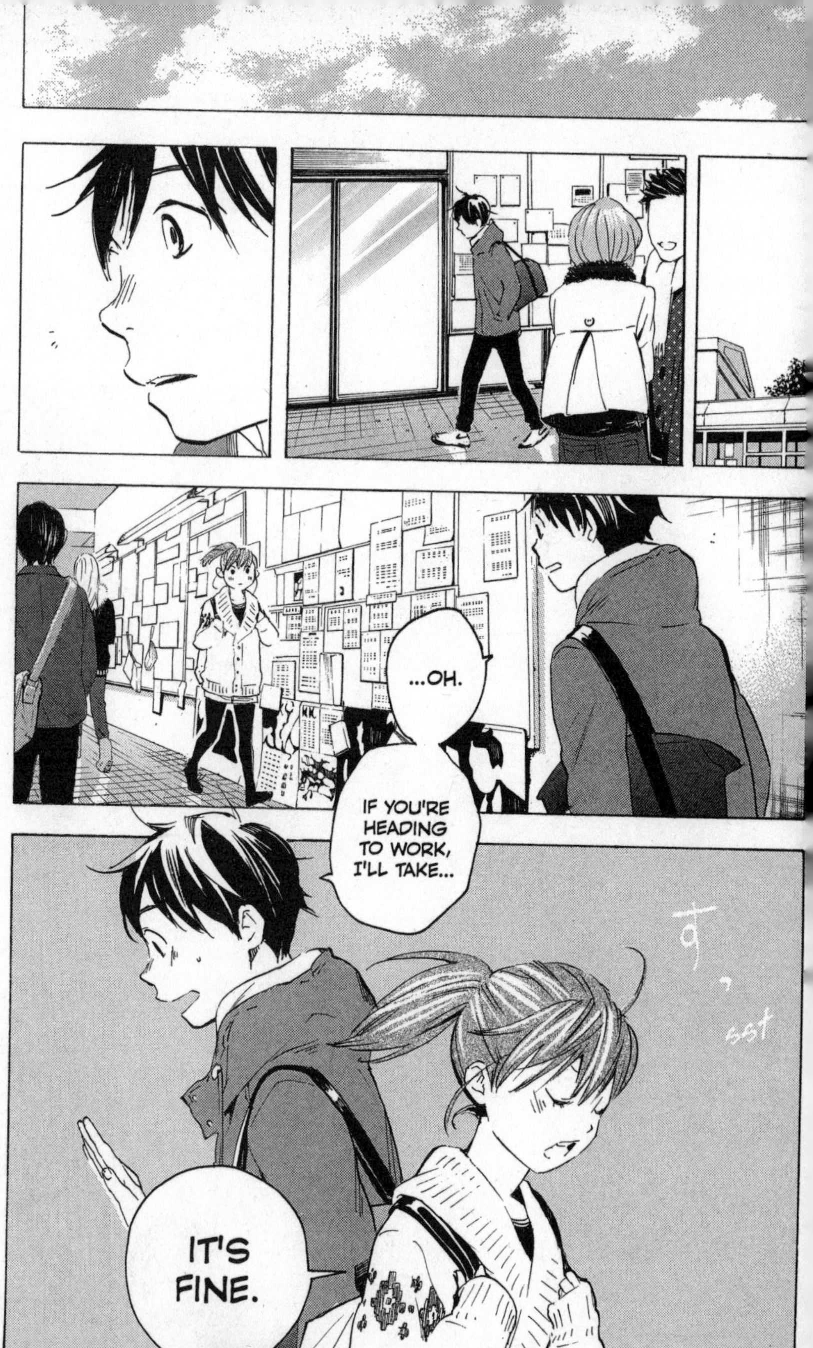
...OH.
IF YOU'RE HEADING TO WORK, I'LL TAKE...
す、
SST
IT'S FINE.

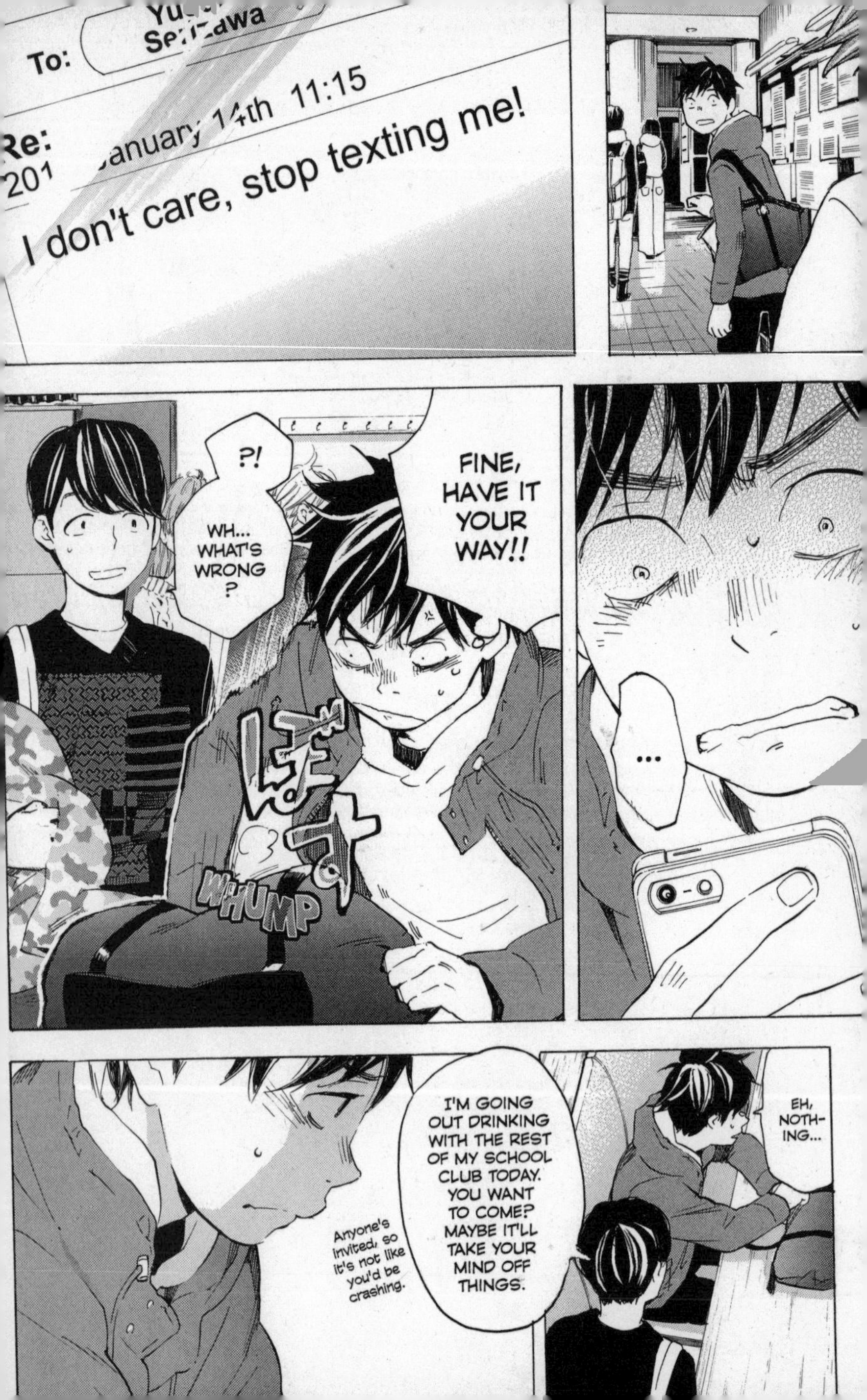
To:
Re:
January 14th 11:15
I don't care, stop texting me!
...
FINE, HAVE IT YOUR WAY!!
?!
WH... WHAT'S WRONG?
WHUMP
EH, NOTHING...
I'M GOING OUT DRINKING WITH THE REST OF MY SCHOOL CLUB TODAY. YOU WANT TO COME? MAYBE IT'LL TAKE YOUR MIND OFF THINGS.
Anyone's invited, so it's not like you'd be crashing.

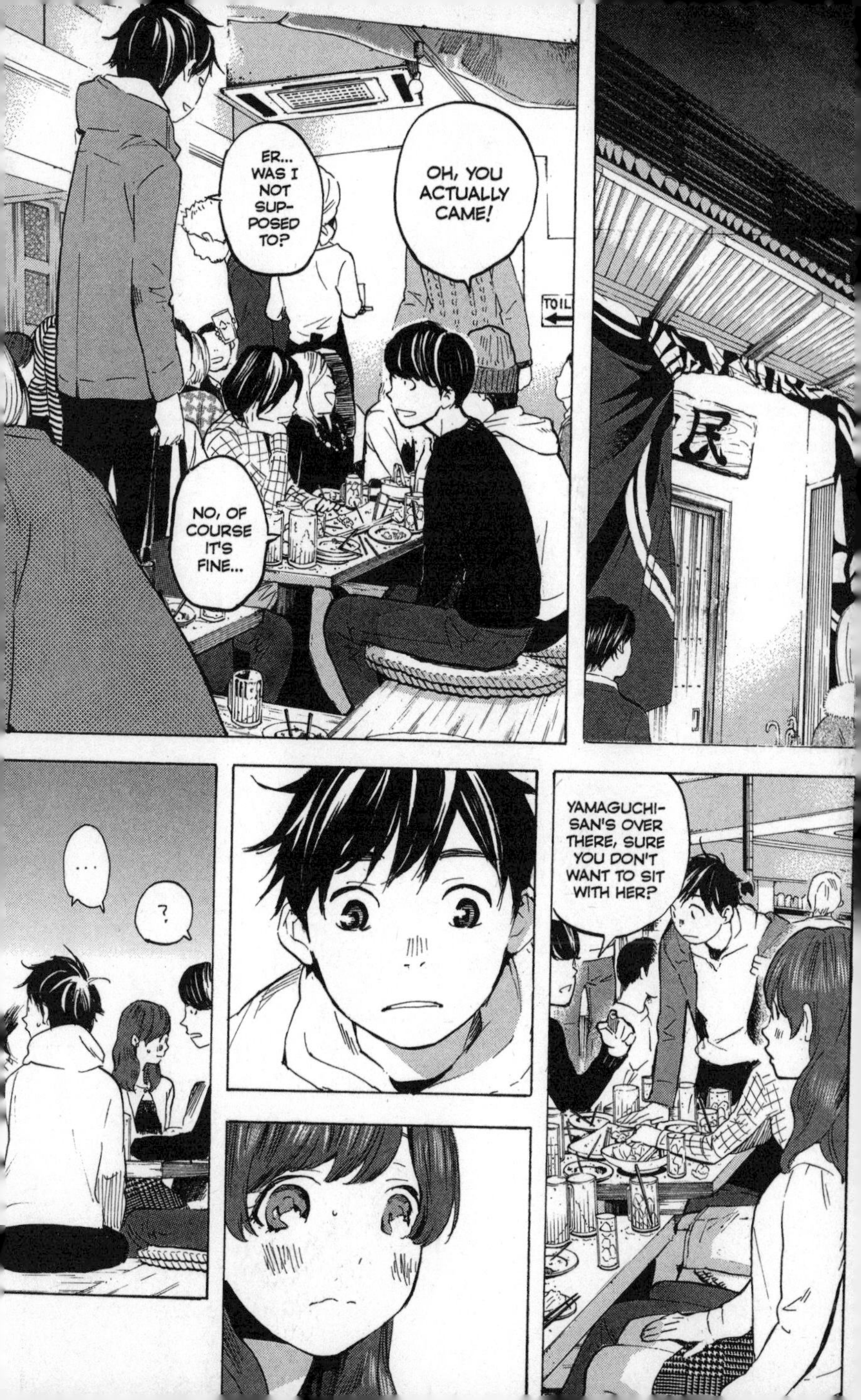
OH, YOU ACTUALLY CAME!
ER... WAS I NOT SUP-POSED TO?
TOIL
NO, OF COURSE IT'S FINE...
YAMAGUCHI-SAN'S OVER THERE, SURE YOU DON'T WANT TO SIT WITH HER?
...
?

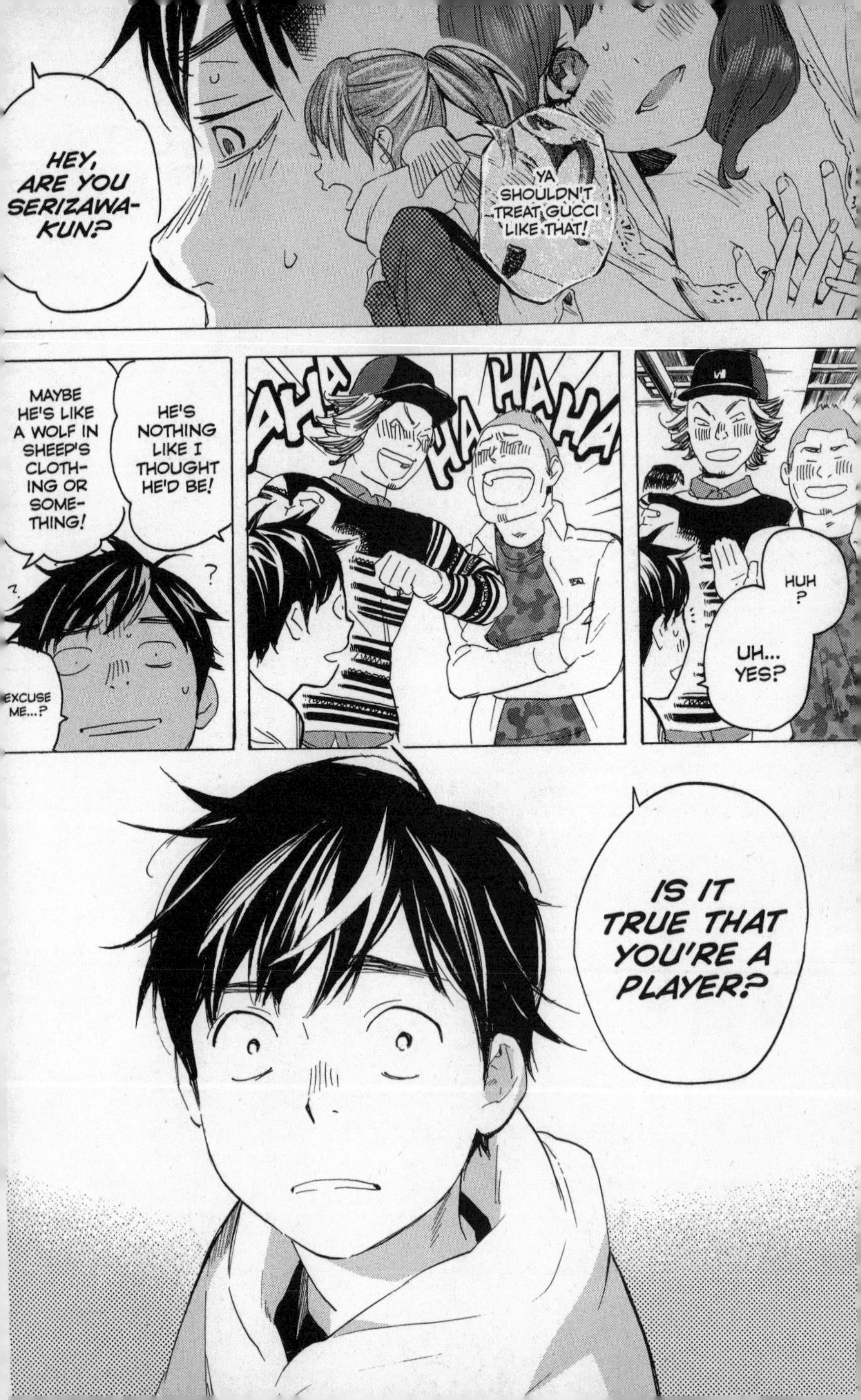
YA SHOULDN'T TREAT GUCCI LIKE THAT!
HEY, ARE YOU SERIZAWA-KUN?
HUH?
UH... YES?
AHA
HA HAHA
HE'S NOTHING LIKE I THOUGHT HE'D BE!
MAYBE HE'S LIKE A WOLF IN SHEEP'S CLOTHING OR SOMETHING!
?
EXCUSE ME...?
IS IT TRUE THAT YOU'RE A PLAYER?

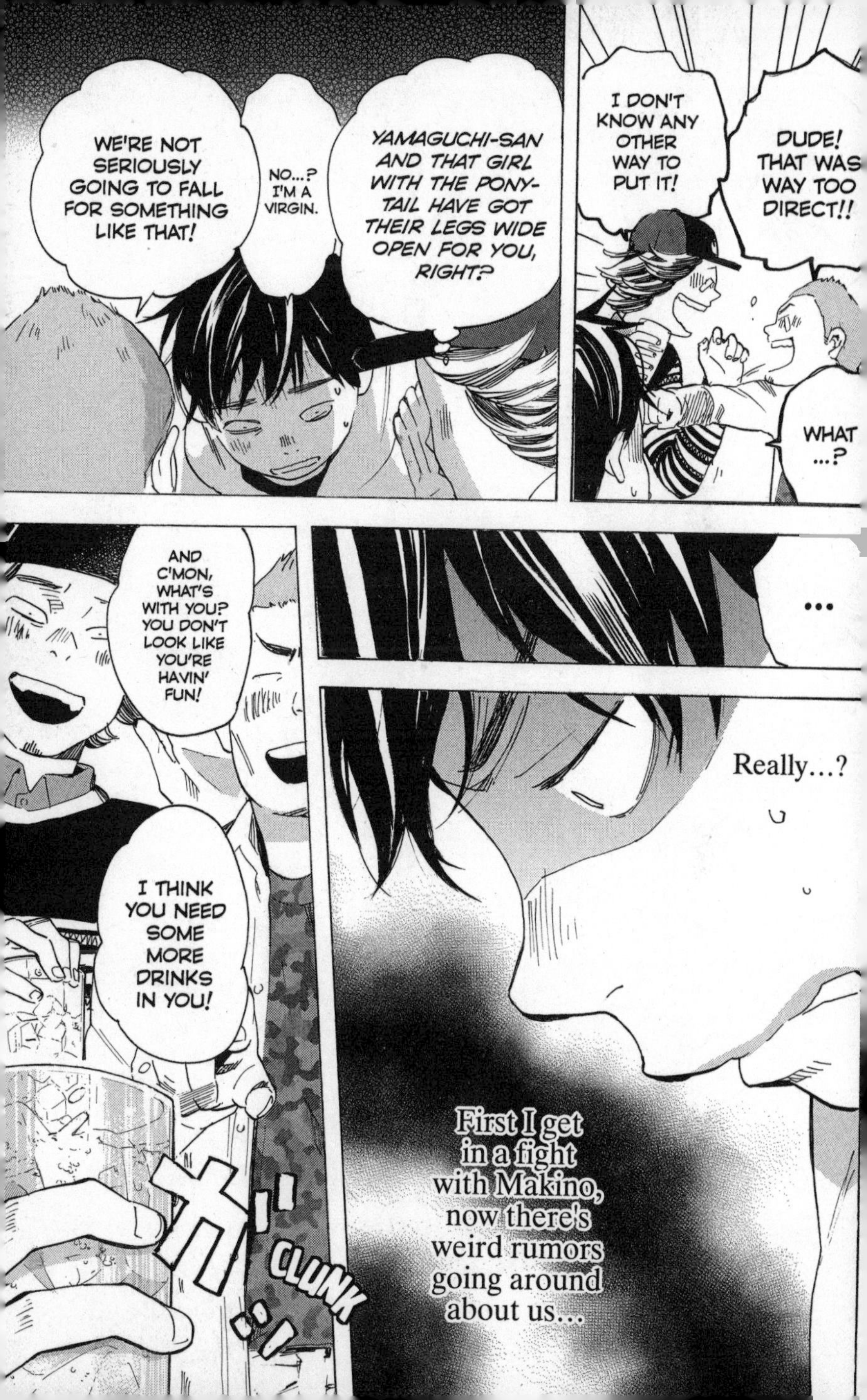
DUDE! THAT WAS WAY TOO DIRECT!!
I DON'T KNOW ANY OTHER WAY TO PUT IT!
WHAT ...?
YAMAGUCHI-SAN AND THAT GIRL WITH THE PONY-TAIL HAVE GOT THEIR LEGS WIDE OPEN FOR YOU, RIGHT?
NO...? I'M A VIRGIN.
WE'RE NOT SERIOUSLY GOING TO FALL FOR SOMETHING LIKE THAT!
...
Really...?
First I get in a fight with Makino, now there's weird rumors going around about us...
AND C'MON, WHAT'S WITH YOU? YOU DON'T LOOK LIKE YOU'RE HAVIN' FUN!
I THINK YOU NEED SOME MORE DRINKS IN YOU!
CLUNK

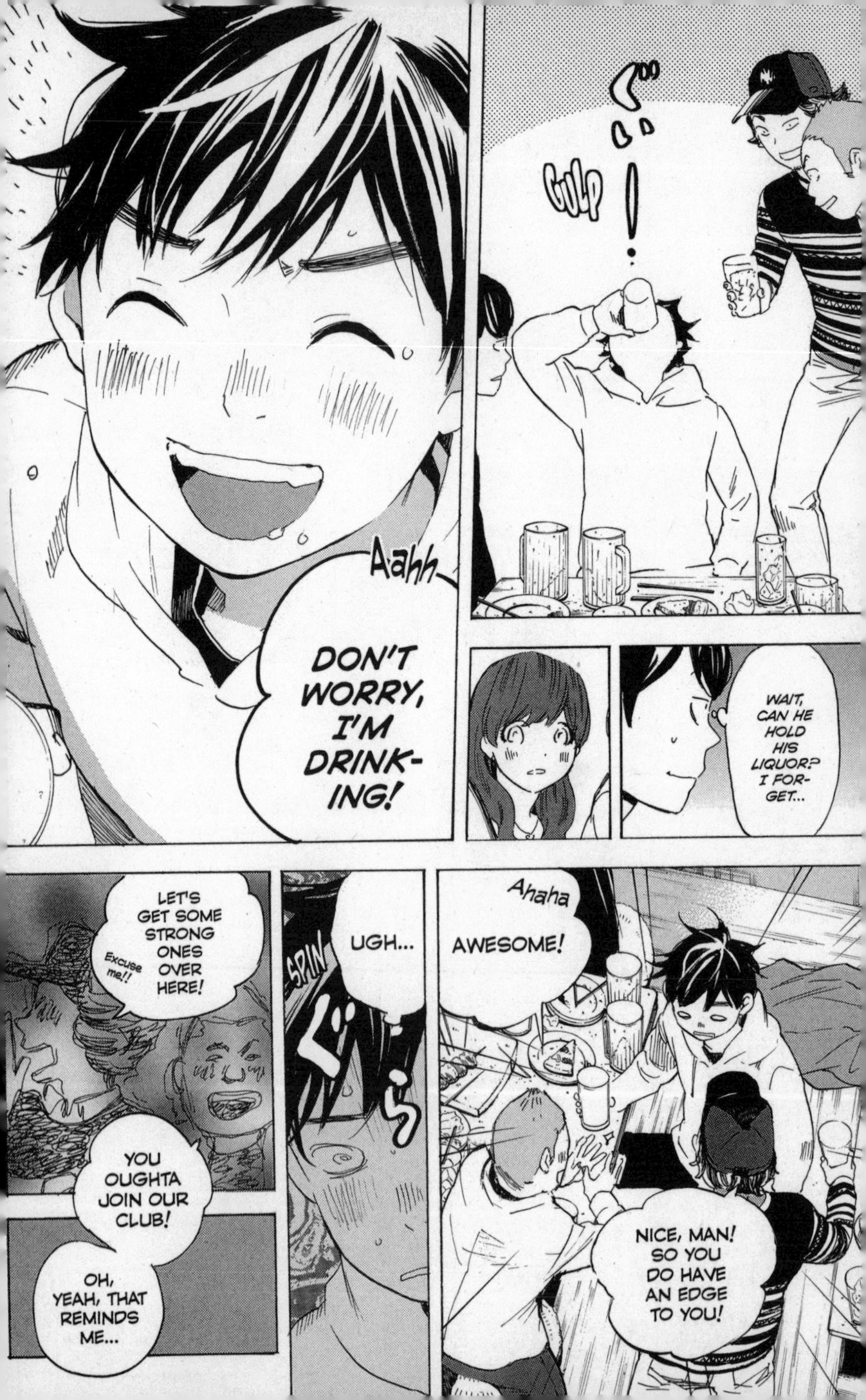
GULP
WAIT, CAN HE HOLD HIS LIQUOR? I FORGET...
Aahh
DON'T WORRY, I'M DRINKING!
Ahaha
AWESOME!
NICE, MAN! SO YOU DO HAVE AN EDGE TO YOU!
SPIN
UGH...
LET'S GET SOME STRONG ONES OVER HERE!
Excuse me!!
YOU OUGHTA JOIN OUR CLUB!
OH, YEAH, THAT REMINDS ME...

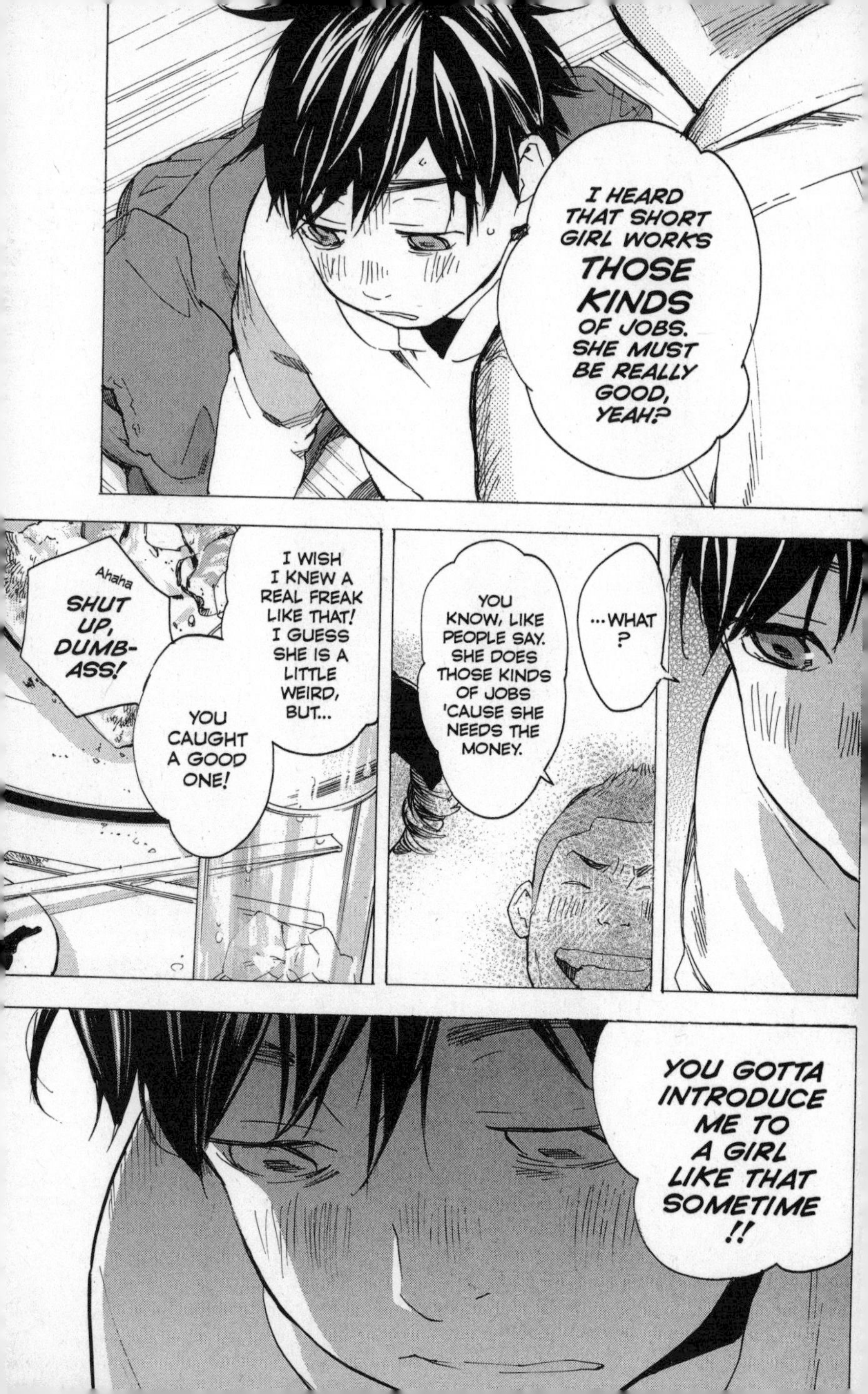

I HEARD THAT SHORT GIRL WORKS THOSE KINDS OF JOBS. SHE MUST BE REALLY GOOD, YEAH?
...WHAT ?
YOU KNOW, LIKE PEOPLE SAY. SHE DOES THOSE KINDS OF JOBS 'CAUSE SHE NEEDS THE MONEY.
I WISH I KNEW A REAL FREAK LIKE THAT! I GUESS SHE IS A LITTLE WEIRD, BUT...
Ahaha
SHUT UP, DUMB-ASS!
YOU CAUGHT A GOOD ONE!
YOU GOTTA INTRODUCE ME TO A GIRL LIKE THAT SOMETIME!!

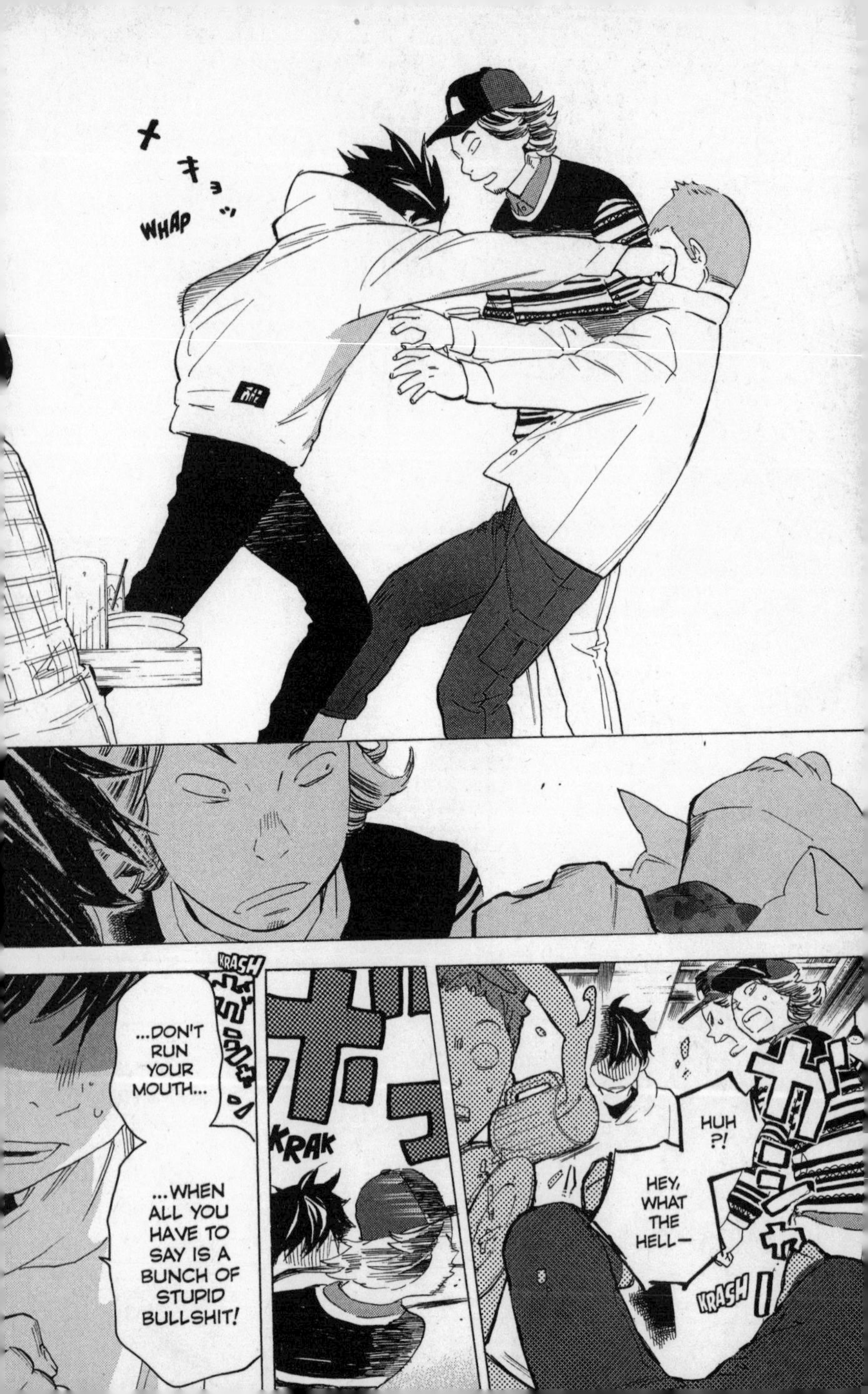

メキョッ
WHAP
HUH ?!
HEY, WHAT THE HELL—
KRASH
KRAK
KRASH
...DON'T RUN YOUR MOUTH...
...WHEN ALL YOU HAVE TO SAY IS A BUNCH OF STUPID BULLSHIT!

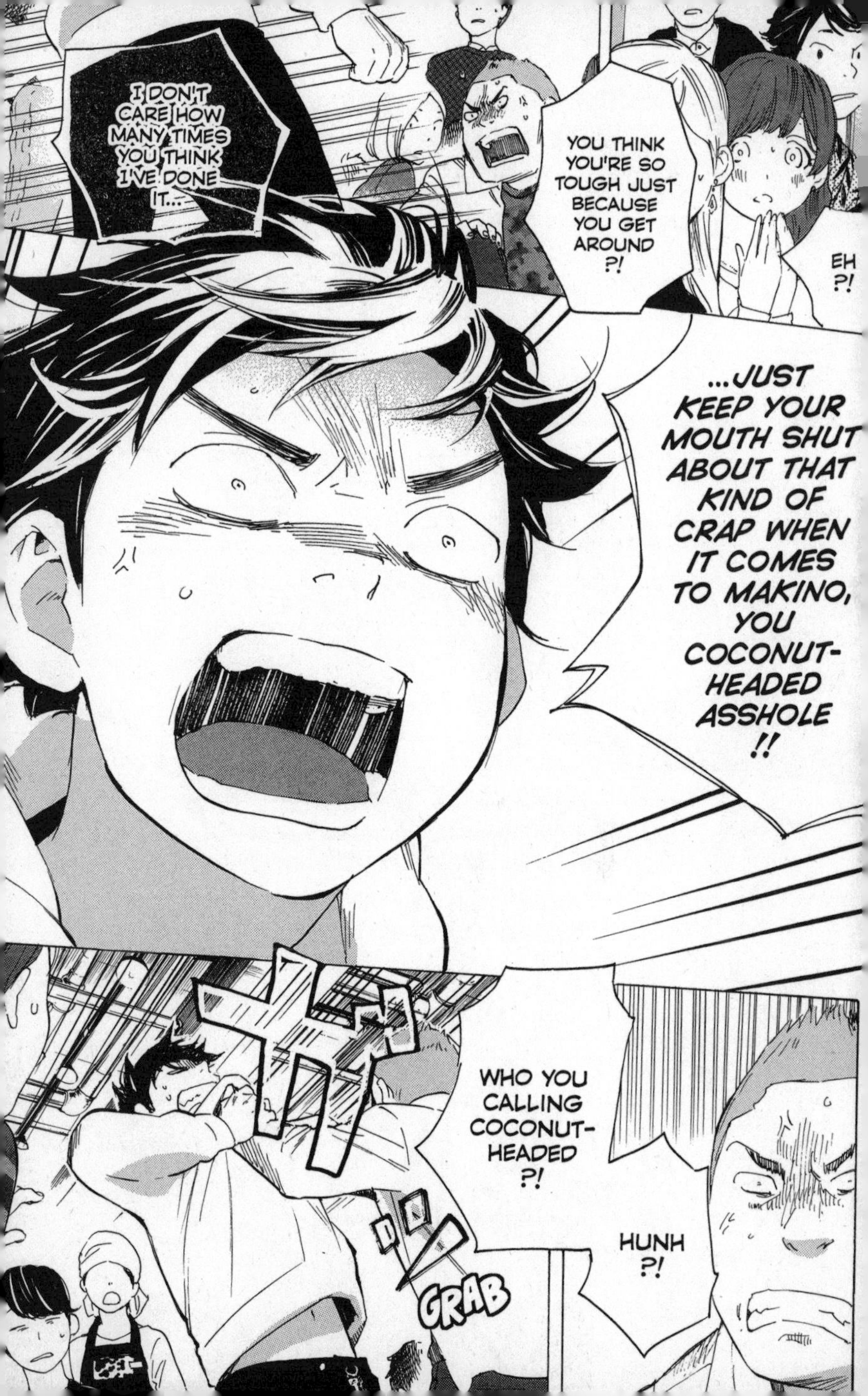
EH?!
YOU THINK YOU'RE SO TOUGH JUST BECAUSE YOU GET AROUND?!
I DON'T CARE HOW MANY TIMES YOU THINK I'VE DONE IT...
...JUST KEEP YOUR MOUTH SHUT ABOUT THAT KIND OF CRAP WHEN IT COMES TO MAKINO, YOU COCONUT-HEADED ASSHOLE!!
HUNH?!
WHO YOU CALLING COCONUT-HEADED?!
GRAB

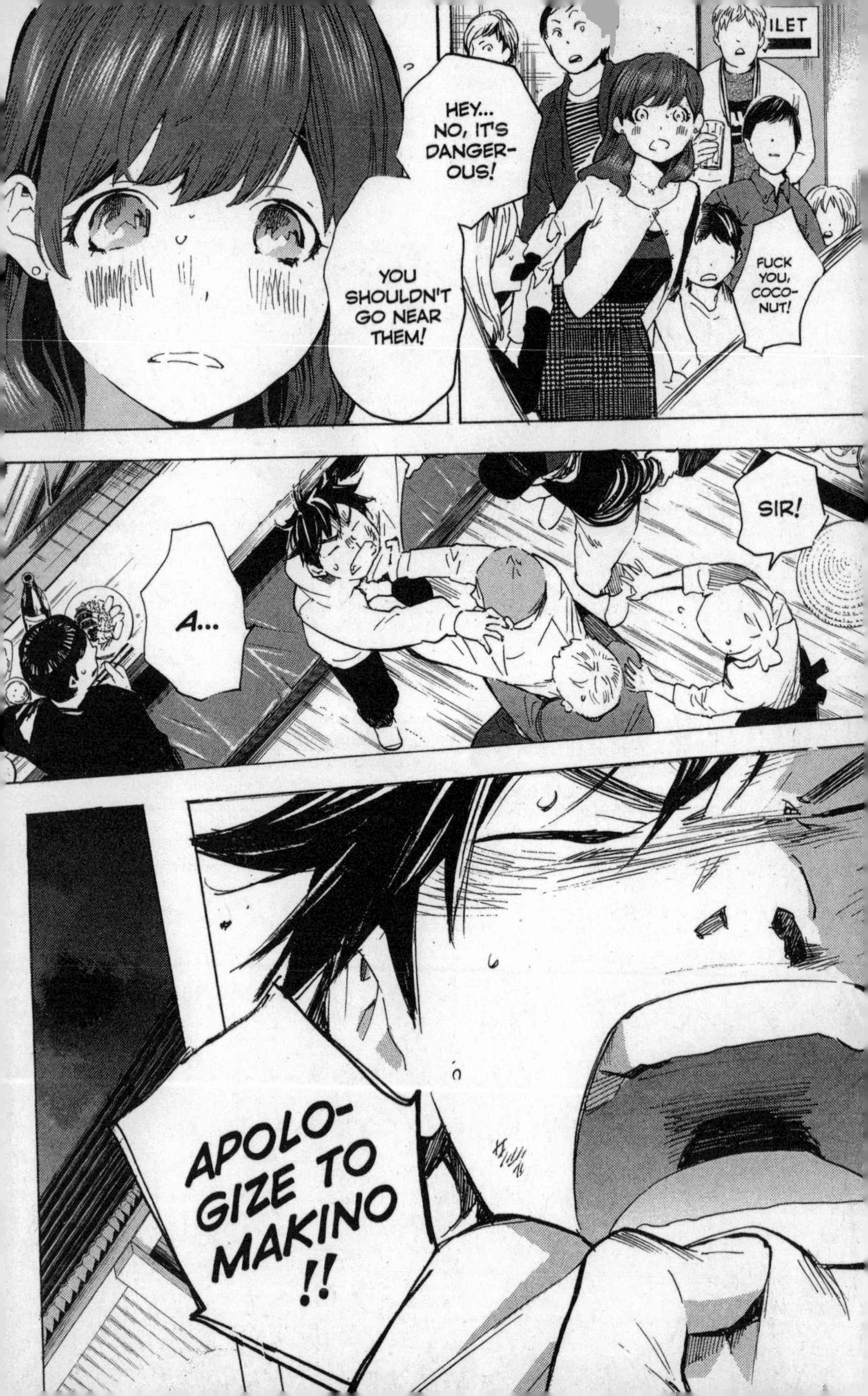
ILET
HEY... NO, IT'S DANGER-OUS!
FUCK YOU, COCO-NUT!
YOU SHOULDN'T GO NEAR THEM!
SIR!
A...
APOLO-GIZE TO MAKINO!!

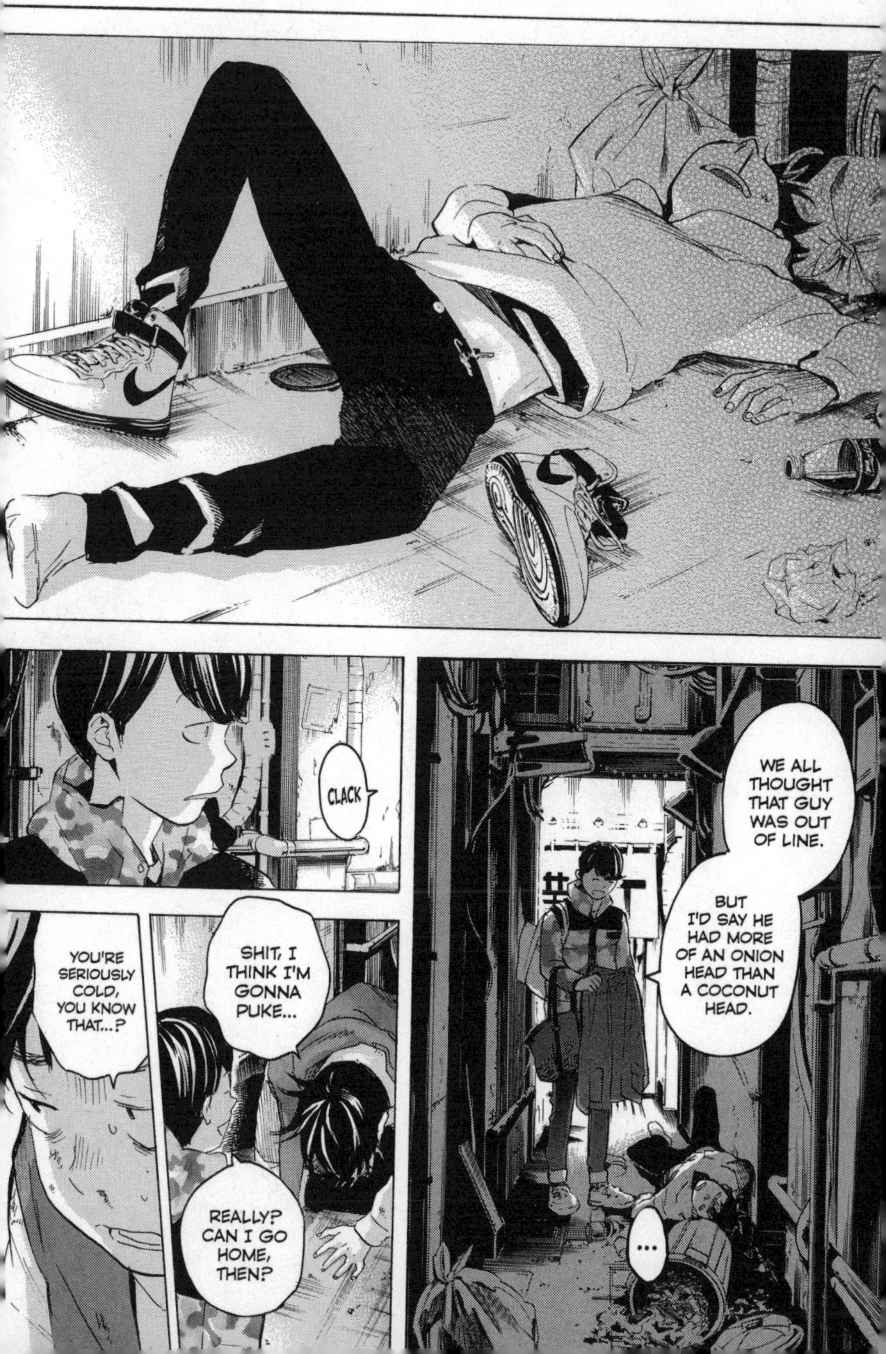
WE ALL THOUGHT THAT GUY WAS OUT OF LINE.
BUT I'D SAY HE HAD MORE OF AN ONION HEAD THAN A COCONUT HEAD.
...
CLACK
SHIT, I THINK I'M GONNA PUKE...
REALLY? CAN I GO HOME, THEN?
YOU'RE SERIOUSLY COLD, YOU KNOW THAT...?

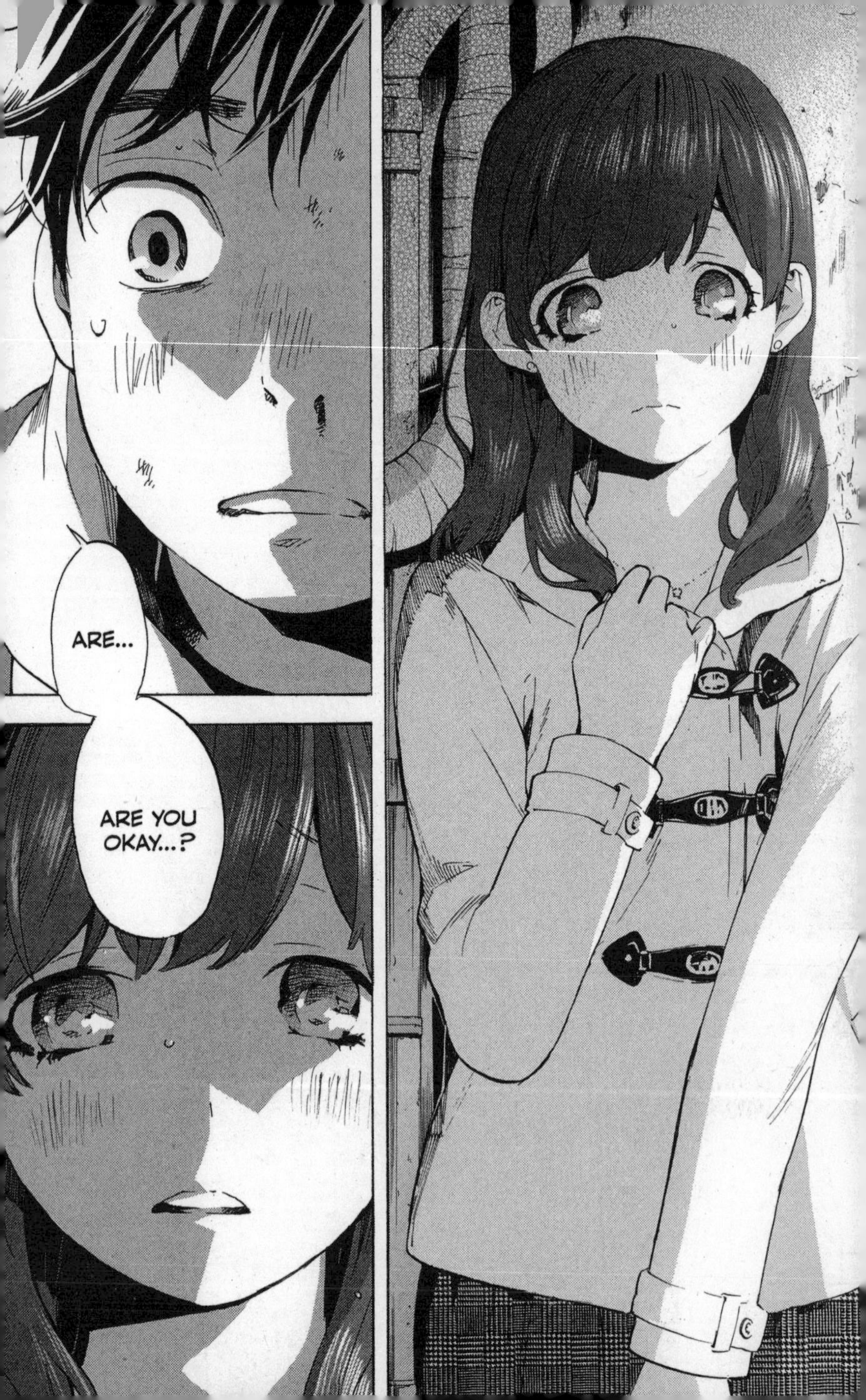
ARE...
ARE YOU OKAY...?

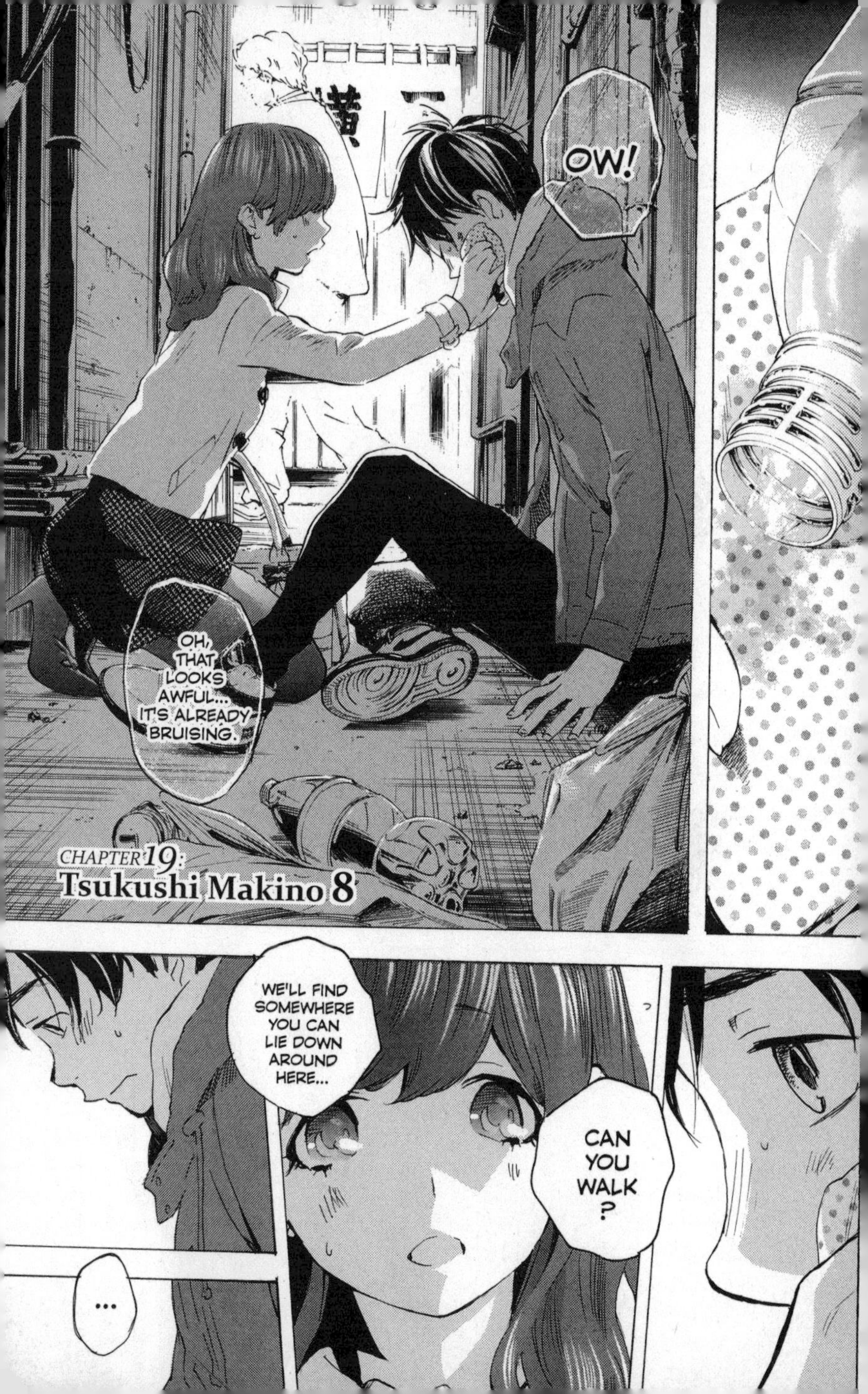
OW!
OH, THAT LOOKS AWFUL... IT'S ALREADY BRUISING.
CHAPTER 19:
Tsukushi Makino 8
WE'LL FIND SOMEWHERE YOU CAN LIE DOWN AROUND HERE...
CAN YOU WALK?
...

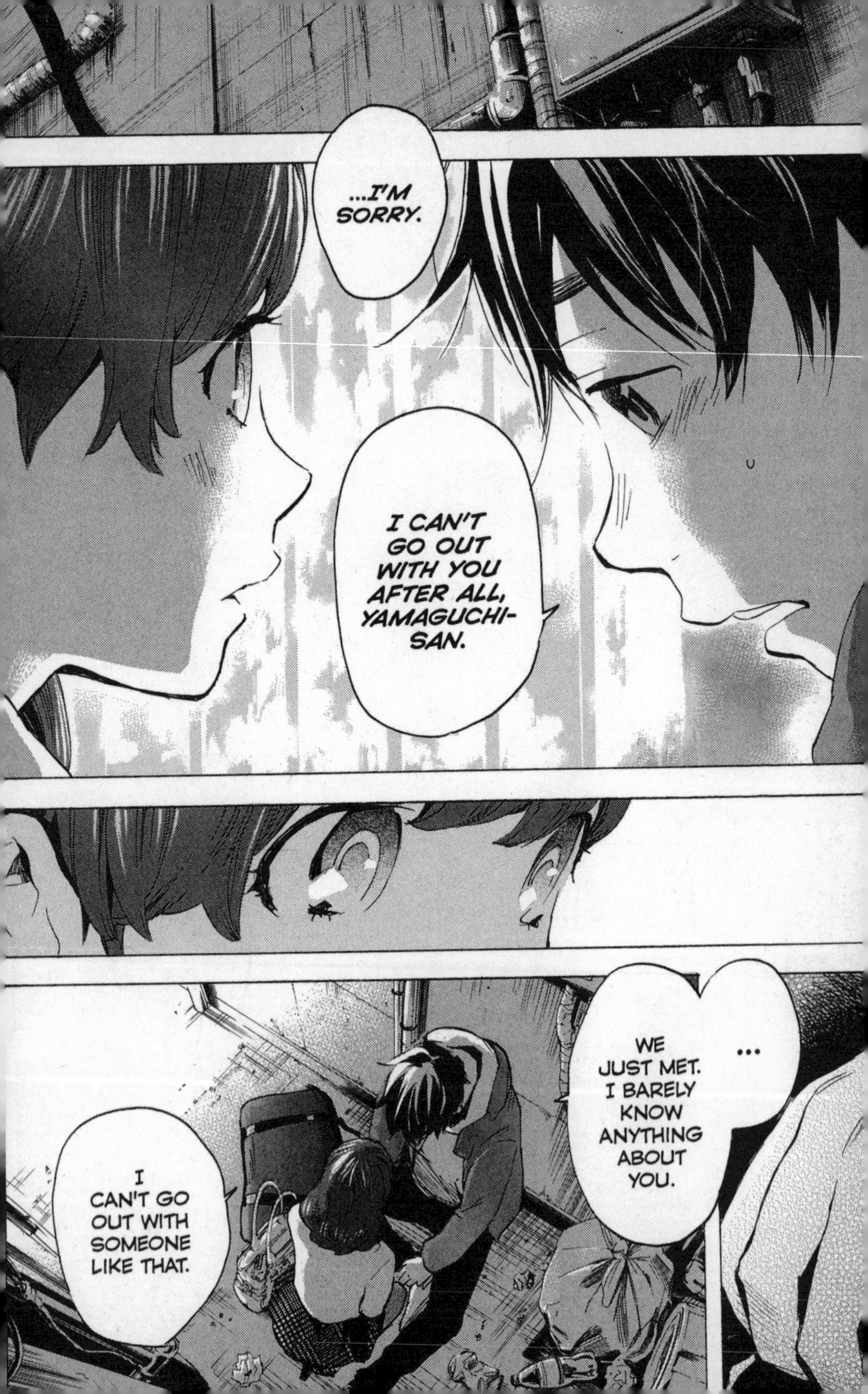
...I'M SORRY.
I CAN'T GO OUT WITH YOU AFTER ALL, YAMAGUCHI-SAN.
...
WE JUST MET. I BARELY KNOW ANYTHING ABOUT YOU.
I CAN'T GO OUT WITH SOMEONE LIKE THAT.

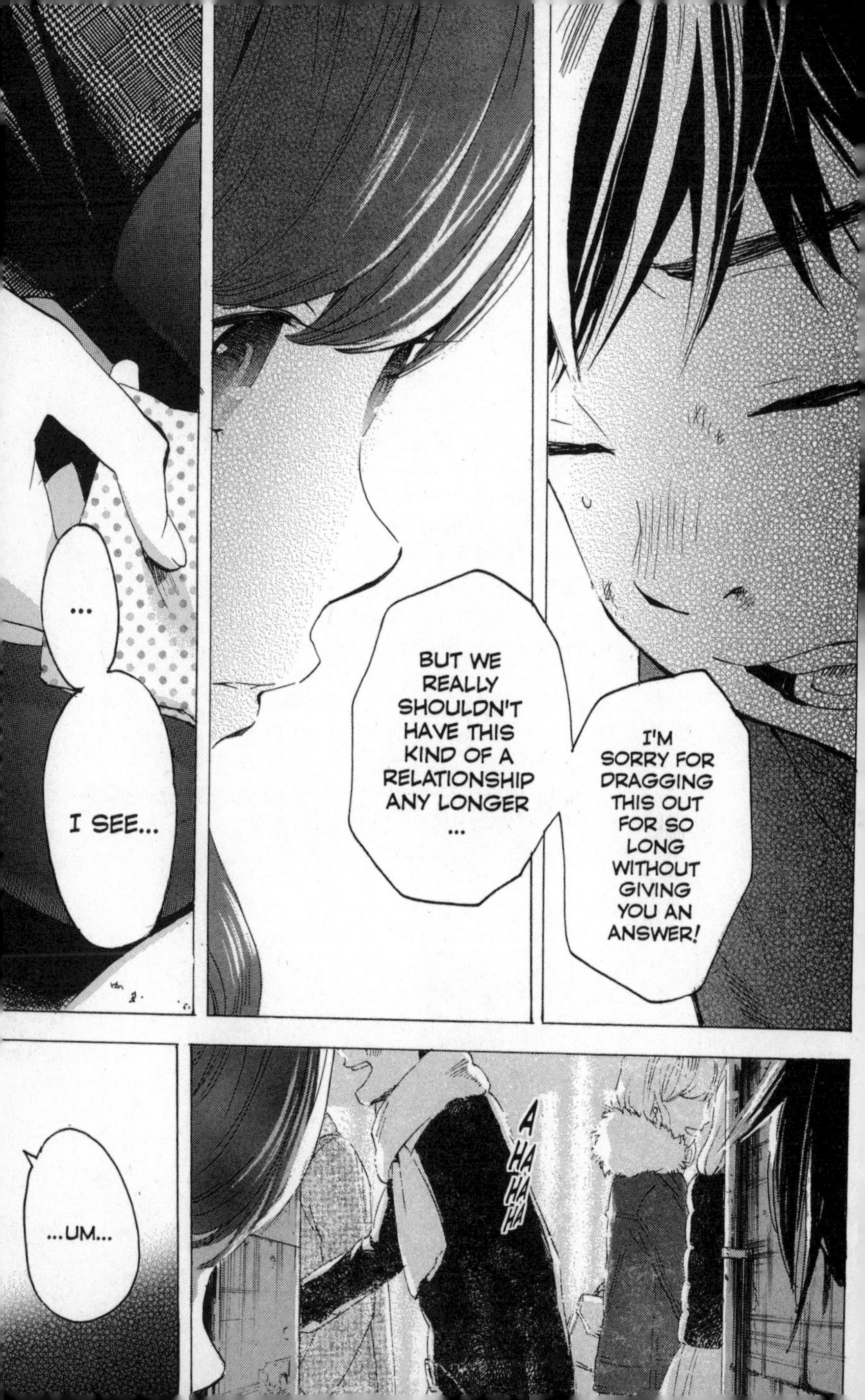
I'M SORRY FOR DRAGGING THIS OUT FOR SO LONG WITHOUT GIVING YOU AN ANSWER!
BUT WE REALLY SHOULDN'T HAVE THIS KIND OF A RELATIONSHIP ANY LONGER ...
...
I SEE...
AHAHAHA
...UM...

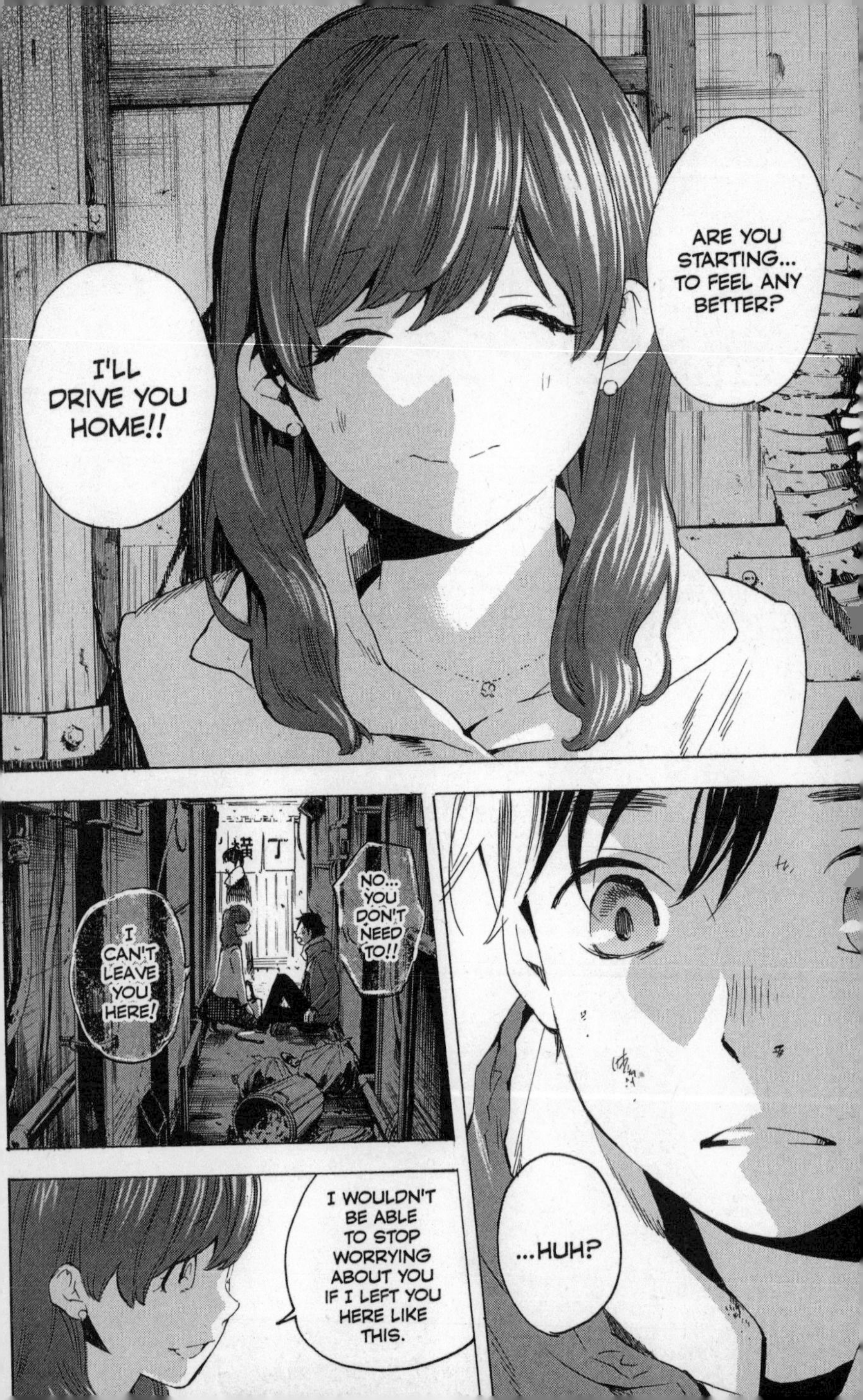
ARE YOU STARTING... TO FEEL ANY BETTER?
I'LL DRIVE YOU HOME!!
...HUH?
NO... YOU DON'T NEED TO!!
I CAN'T LEAVE YOU HERE!
I WOULDN'T BE ABLE TO STOP WORRYING ABOUT YOU IF I LEFT YOU HERE LIKE THIS.

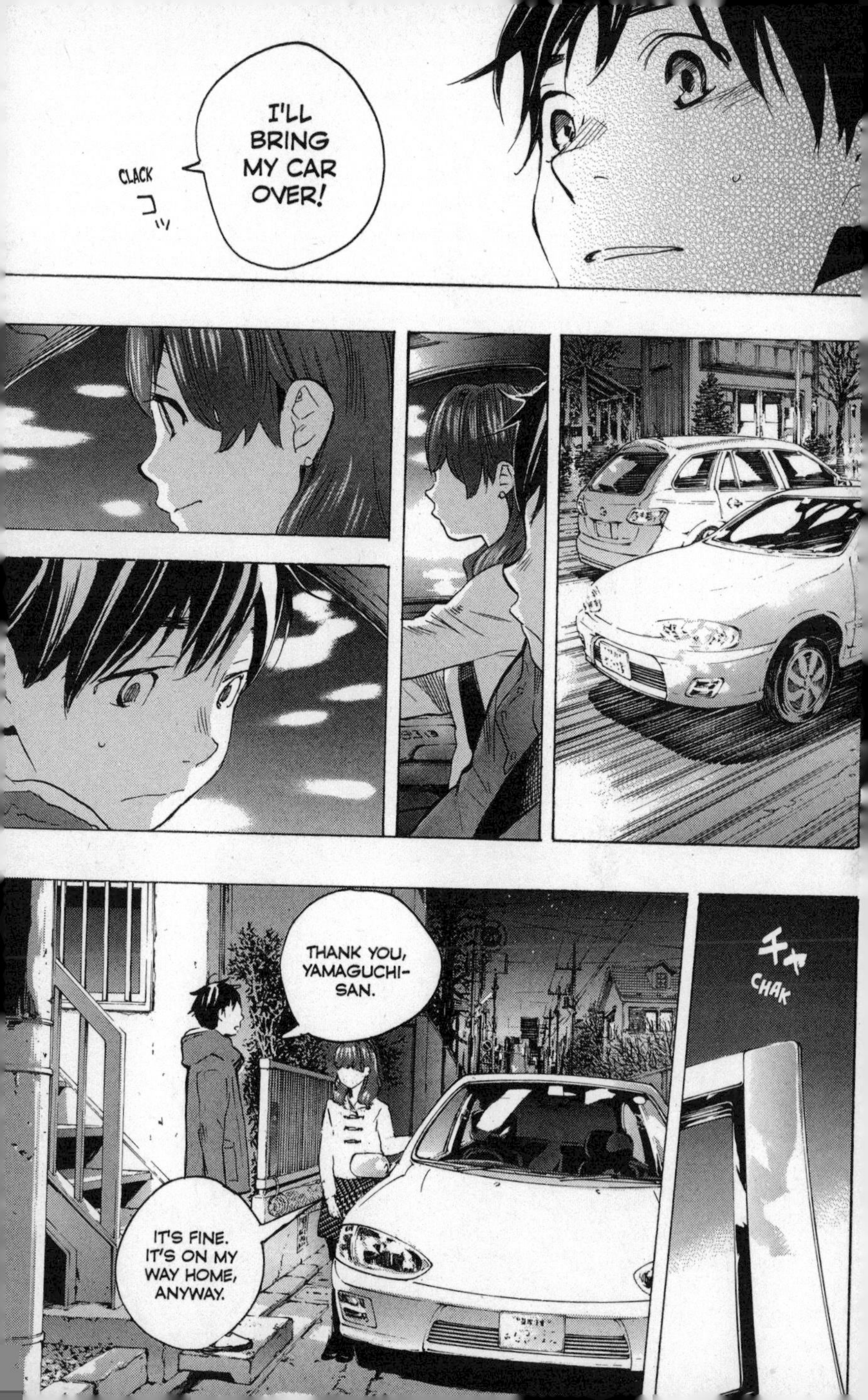
I'LL BRING MY CAR OVER!
CLACK
コッ
チャ
CHAK
THANK YOU, YAMAGUCHI-SAN.
IT'S FINE. IT'S ON MY WAY HOME, ANYWAY.

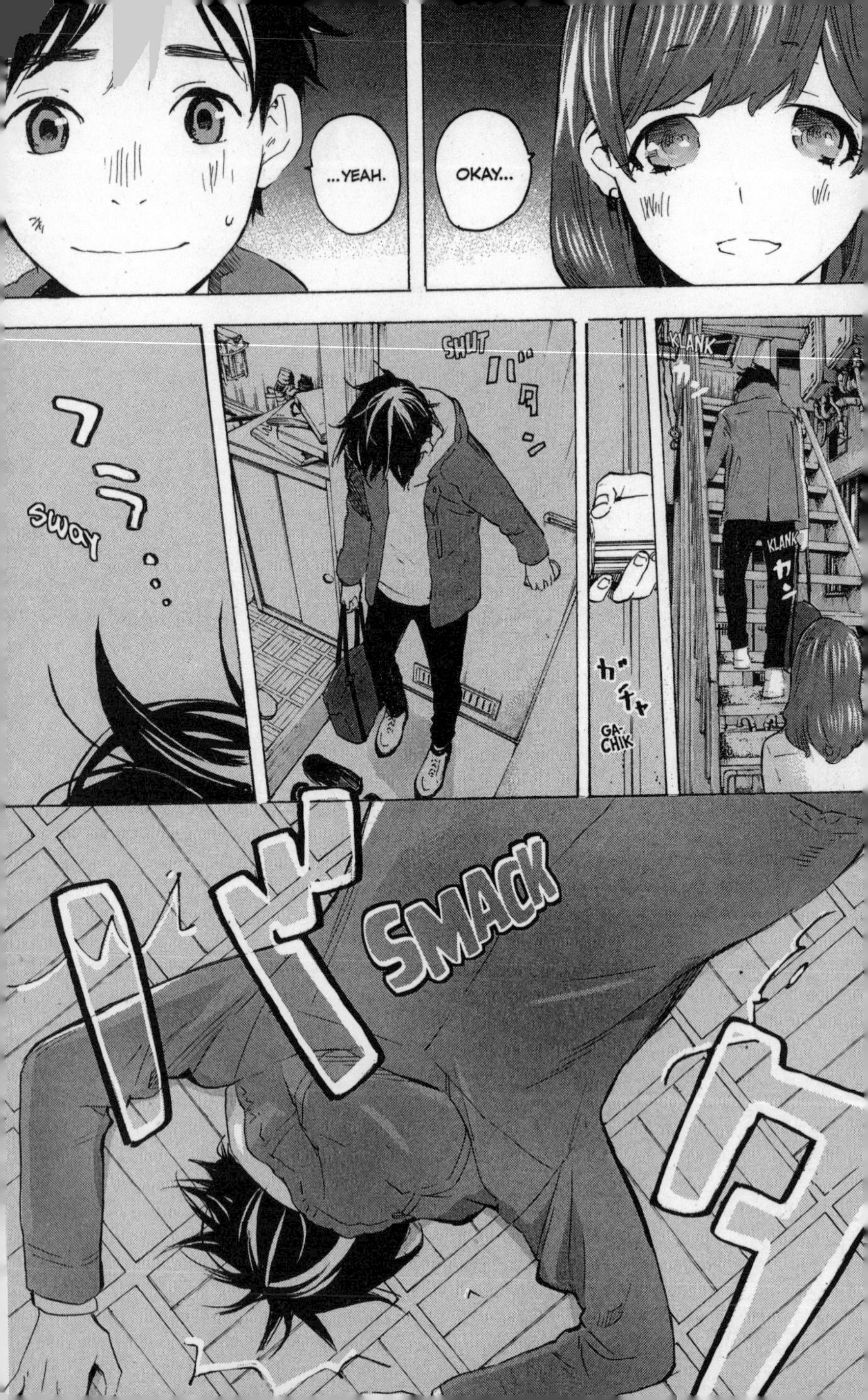
OKAY...
...YEAH.
KLANK
カン
KLANK
カン
ガチャ
GA-CHIK
SHUT
バタン
フラ
SWAY
SMACK

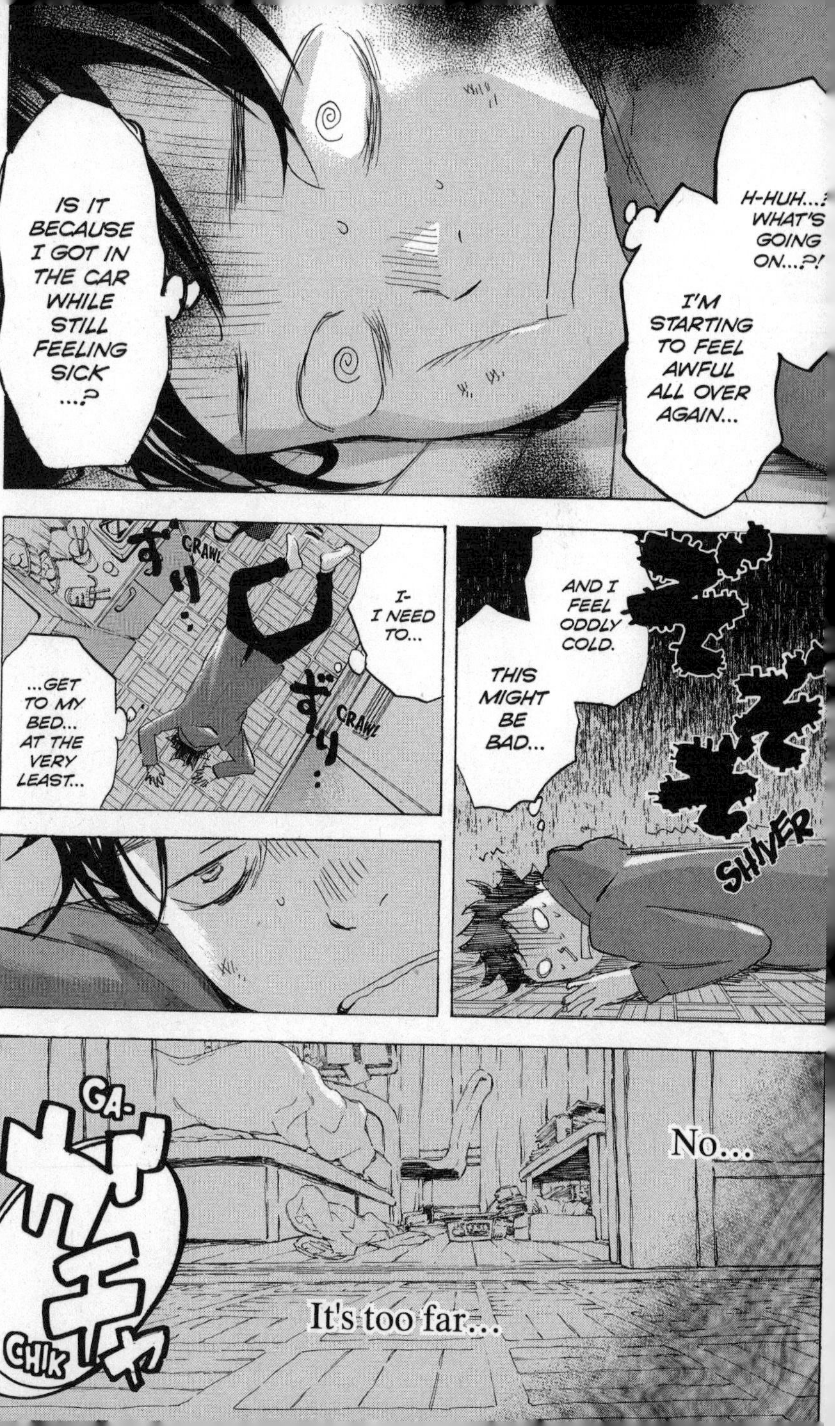
H-HUH...!? WHAT'S GOING ON...?!
I'M STARTING TO FEEL AWFUL ALL OVER AGAIN...
IS IT BECAUSE I GOT IN THE CAR WHILE STILL FEELING SICK ...?
AND I FEEL ODDLY COLD.
THIS MIGHT BE BAD...
SHIVER
I- I NEED TO...
CRAWL
...GET TO MY BED... AT THE VERY LEAST...
CRAWL
No...
GA-
It's too far...
CHIK

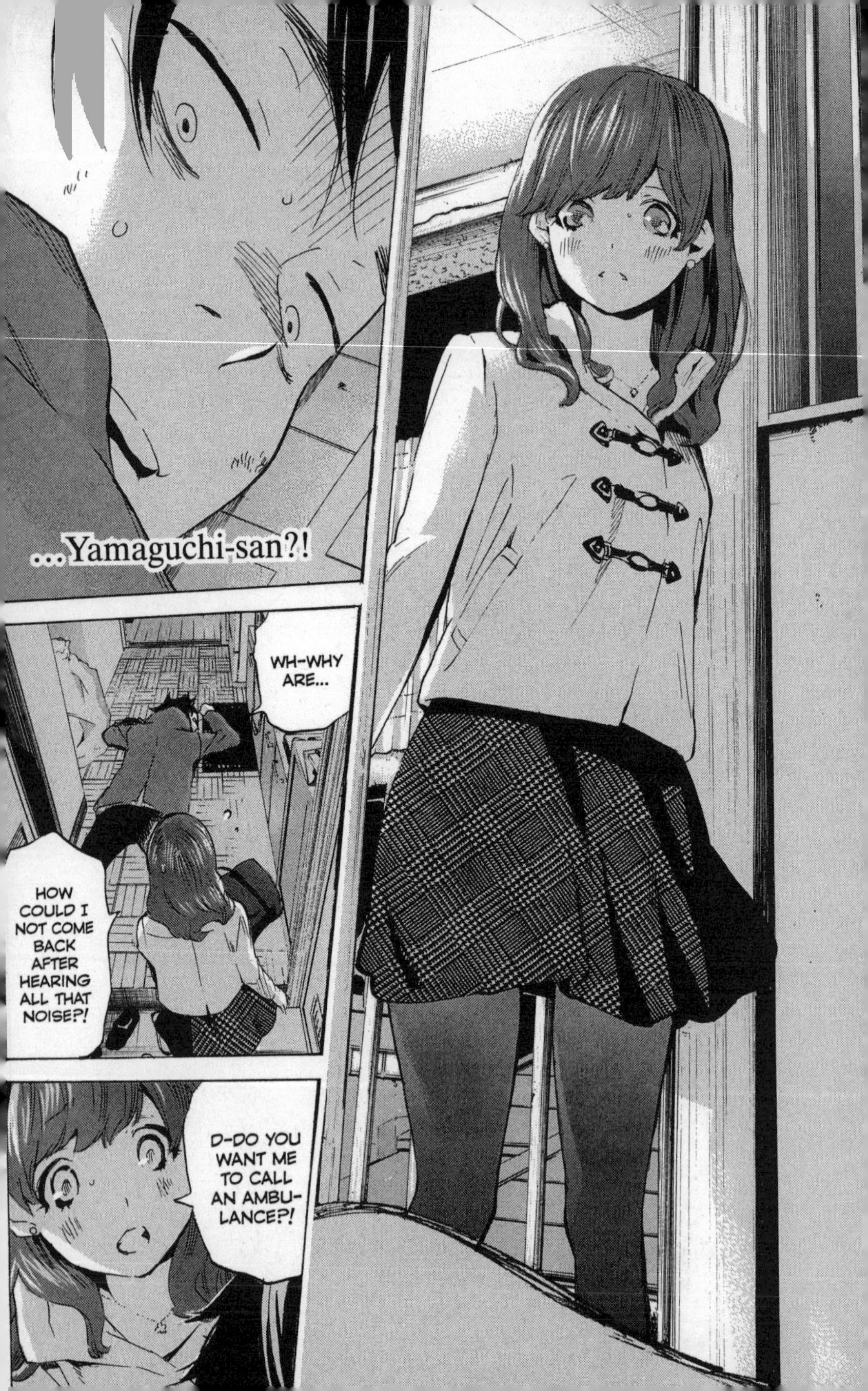
...Yamaguchi-san?!
WH-WHY ARE...
HOW COULD I NOT COME BACK AFTER HEARING ALL THAT NOISE?!
D-DO YOU WANT ME TO CALL AN AMBULANCE?!

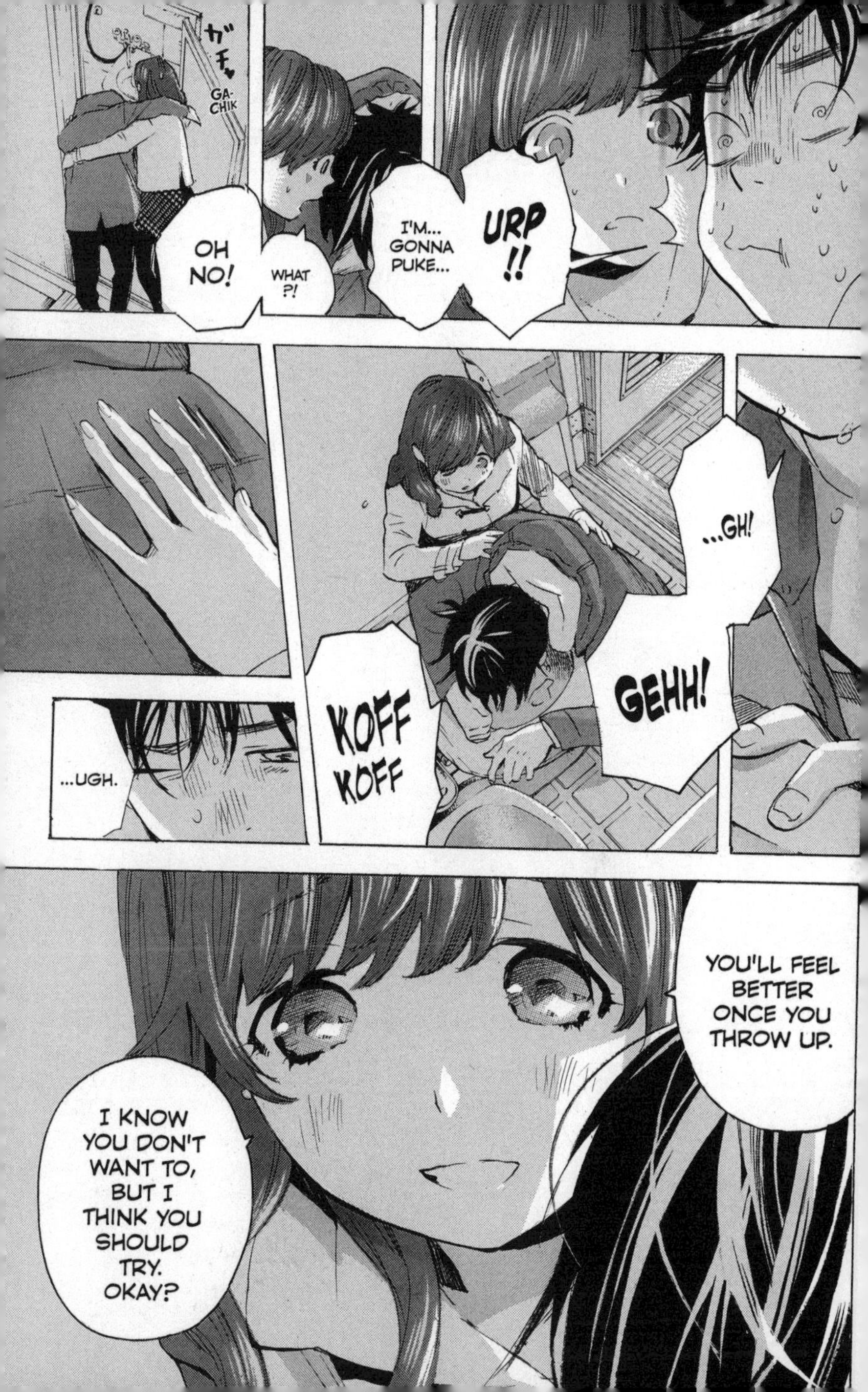
URP !!
I'M... GONNA PUKE...
WHAT ?!
ガチャ
GA-CHIK
OH NO!
...GH!
GEHH!
KOFF KOFF
...UGH.
YOU'LL FEEL BETTER ONCE YOU THROW UP.
I KNOW YOU DON'T WANT TO, BUT I THINK YOU SHOULD TRY. OKAY?

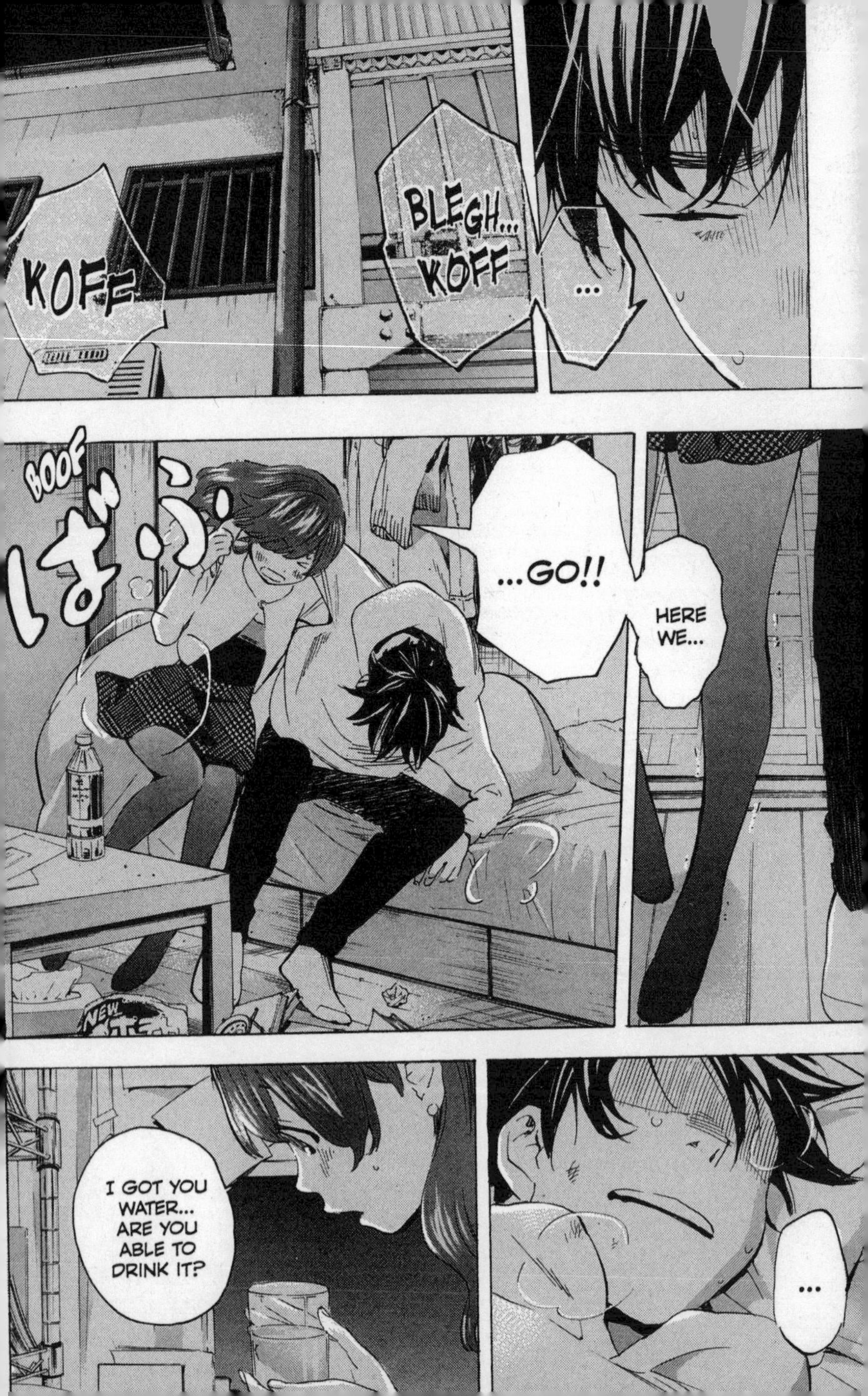
...
BLEGH... KOFF
KOFF
HERE WE...
...GO!!
BOOF
...
I GOT YOU WATER... ARE YOU ABLE TO DRINK IT?

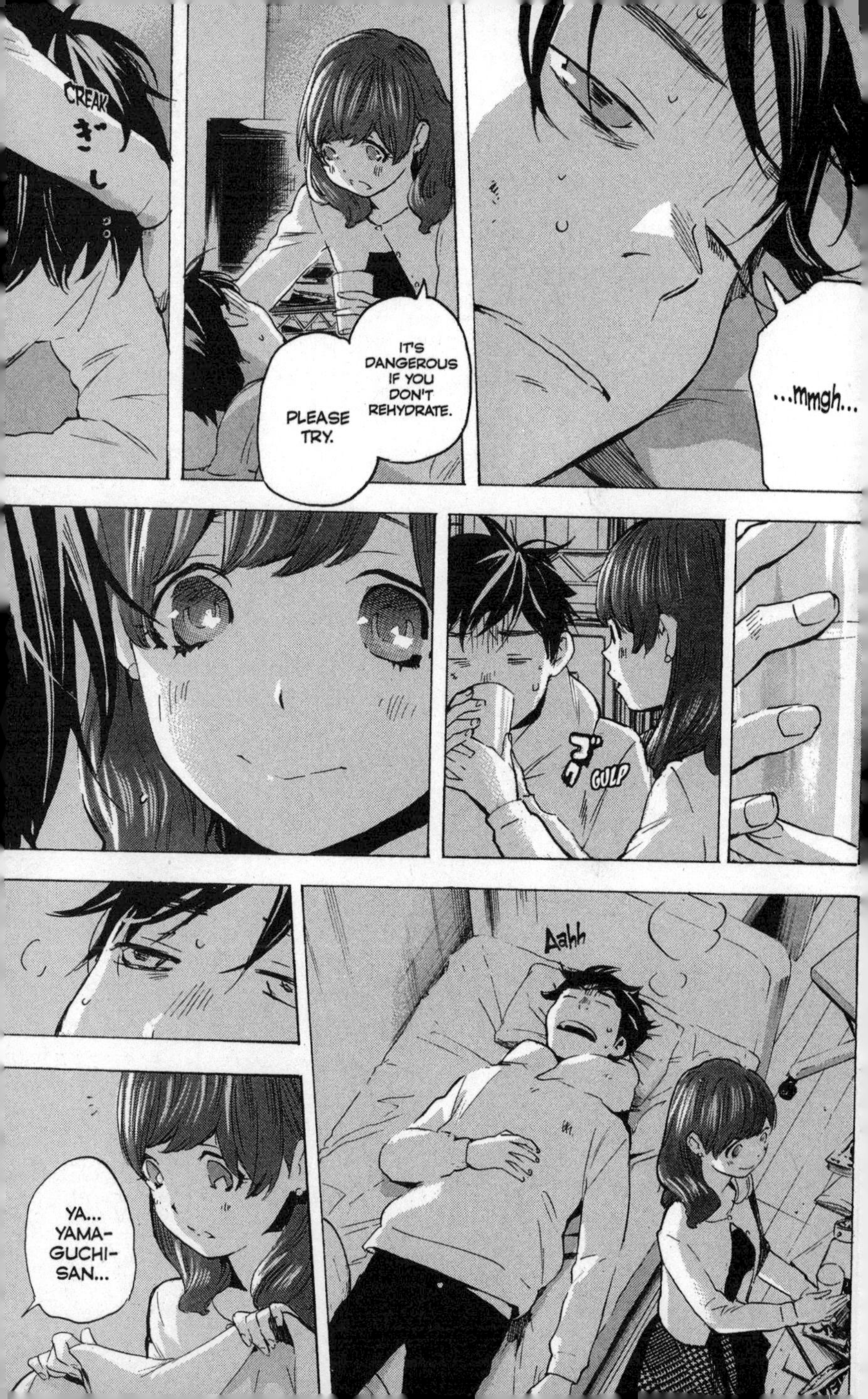
...mmgh...
IT'S DANGEROUS IF YOU DON'T REHYDRATE.
PLEASE TRY.
CREAK
きし
ゴク
GULP
Aahh
YA... YAMA-GUCHI-SAN...

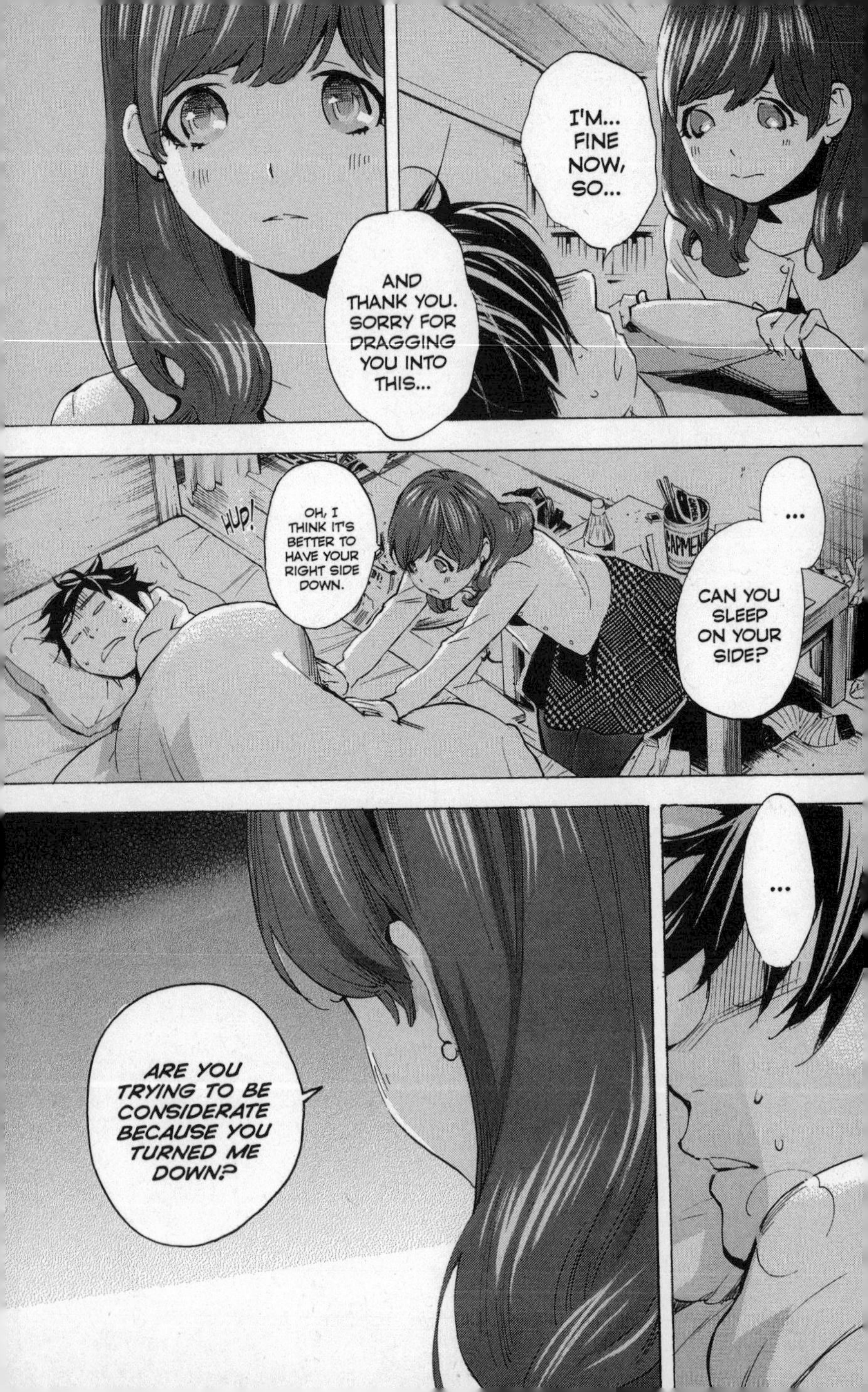
I'M... FINE NOW, SO...
AND THANK YOU. SORRY FOR DRAGGING YOU INTO THIS...
...
CAN YOU SLEEP ON YOUR SIDE?
OH, I THINK IT'S BETTER TO HAVE YOUR RIGHT SIDE DOWN.
HUP!
...
ARE YOU TRYING TO BE CONSIDERATE BECAUSE YOU TURNED ME DOWN?

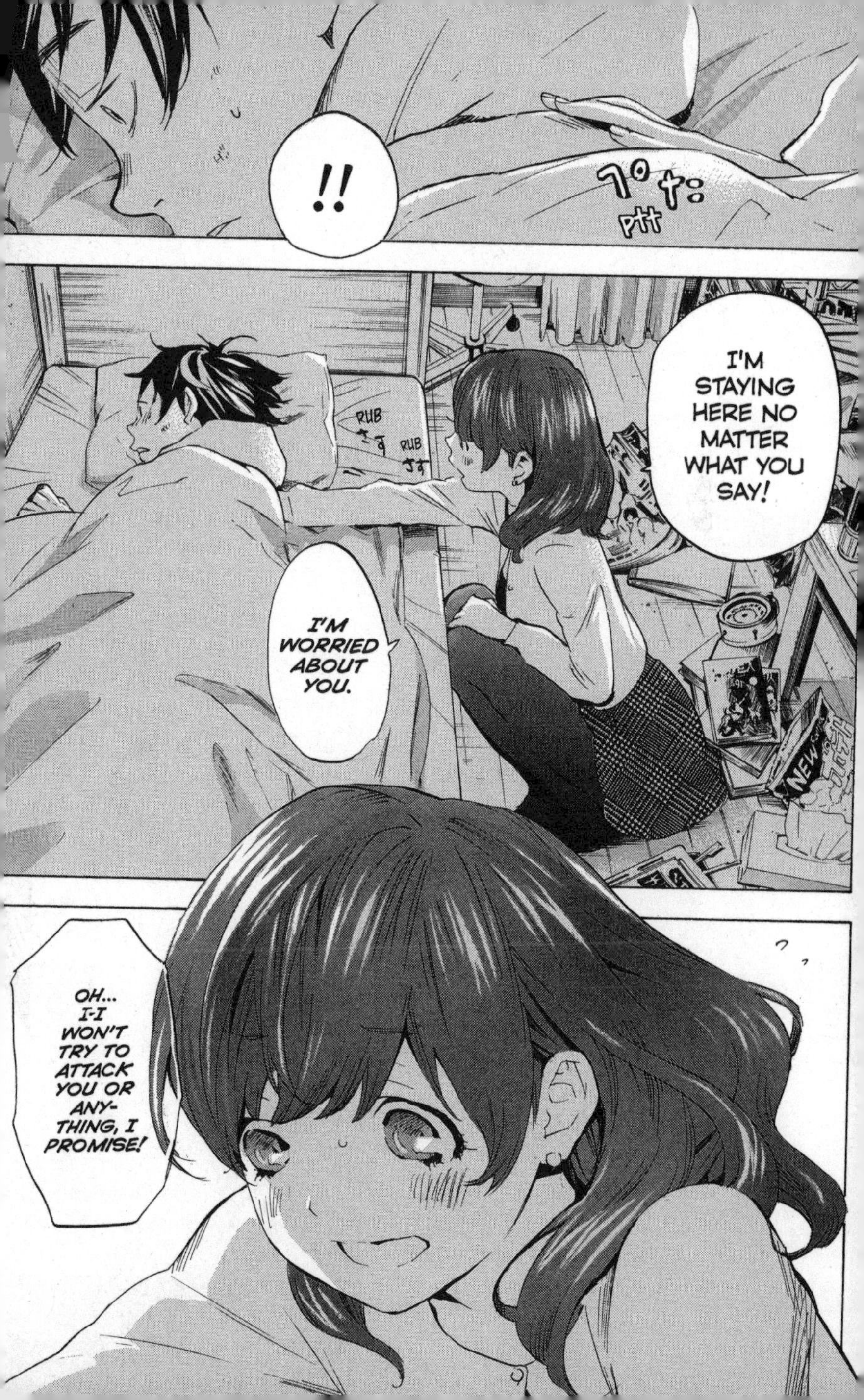
!!
ptt
I'M STAYING HERE NO MATTER WHAT YOU SAY!
RUB
RUB
I'M WORRIED ABOUT YOU.
OH... I-I WON'T TRY TO ATTACK YOU OR ANY-THING, I PROMISE!

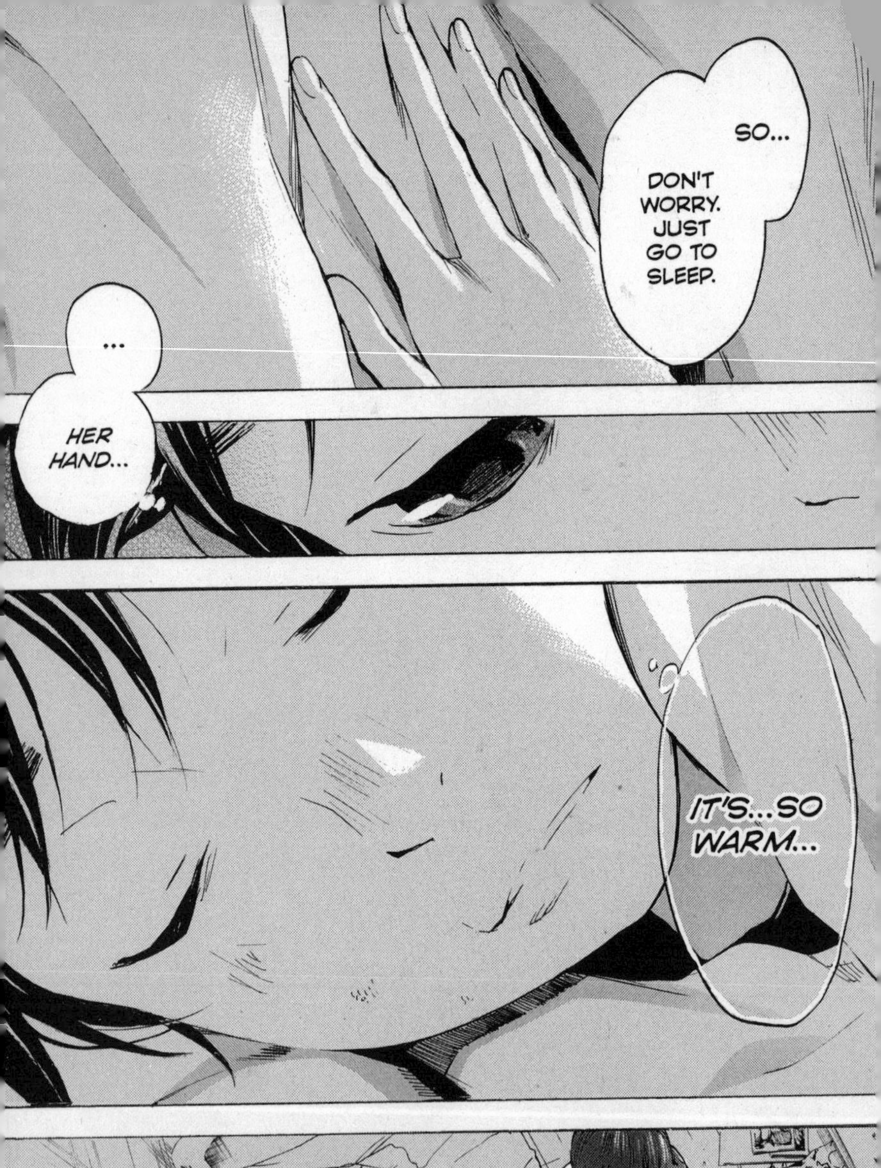
SO...
DON'T WORRY. JUST GO TO SLEEP.
...
HER HAND...
IT'S...SO WARM...

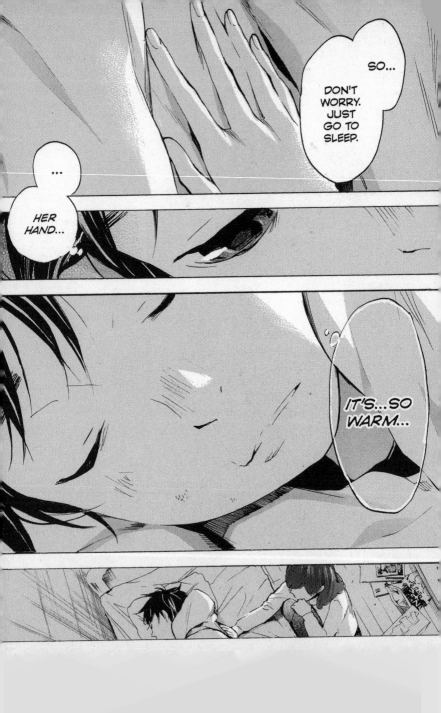

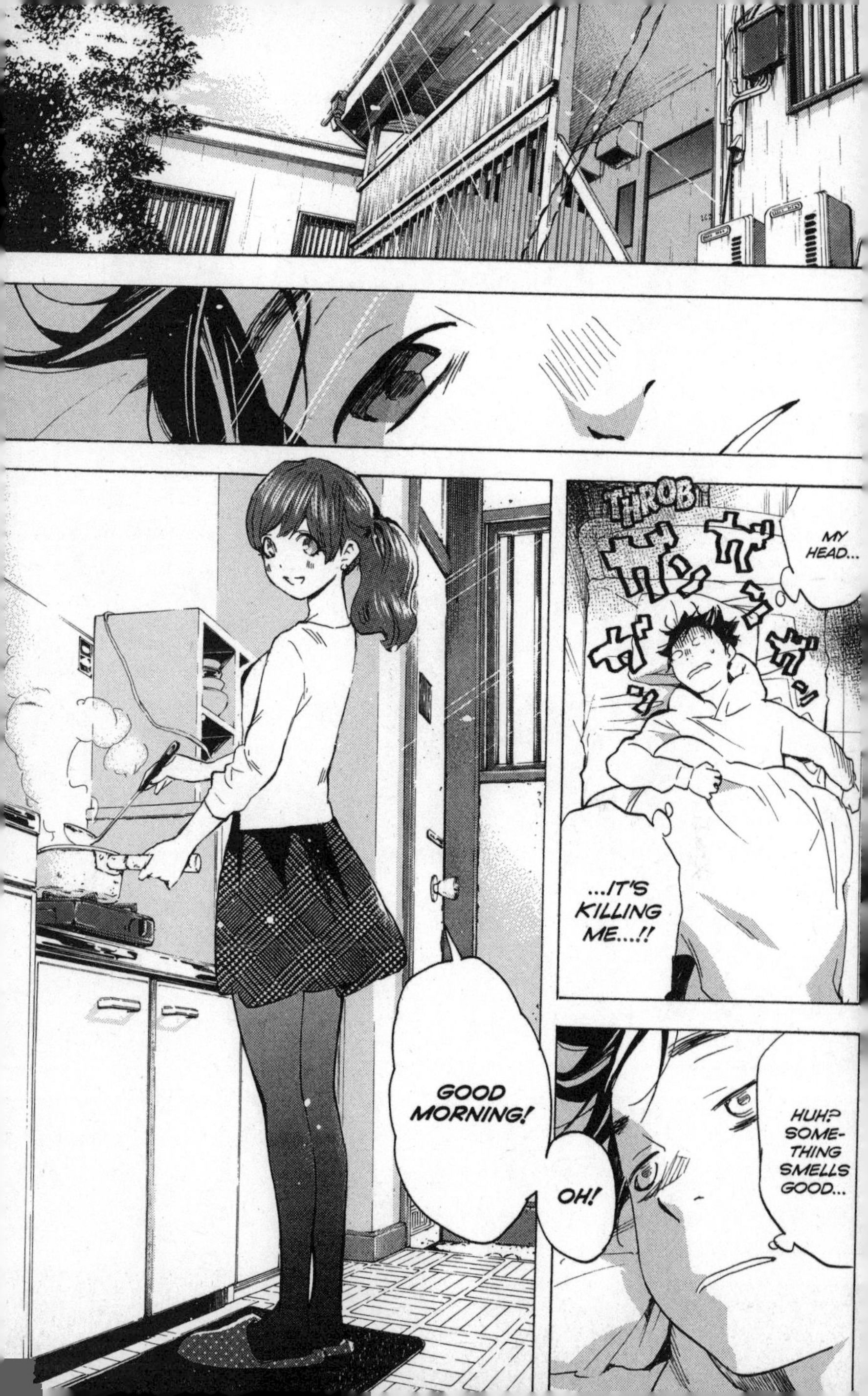
THROB
MY HEAD...
...IT'S KILLING ME...!!
HUH? SOME-THING SMELLS GOOD...
OH!
GOOD MORNING!

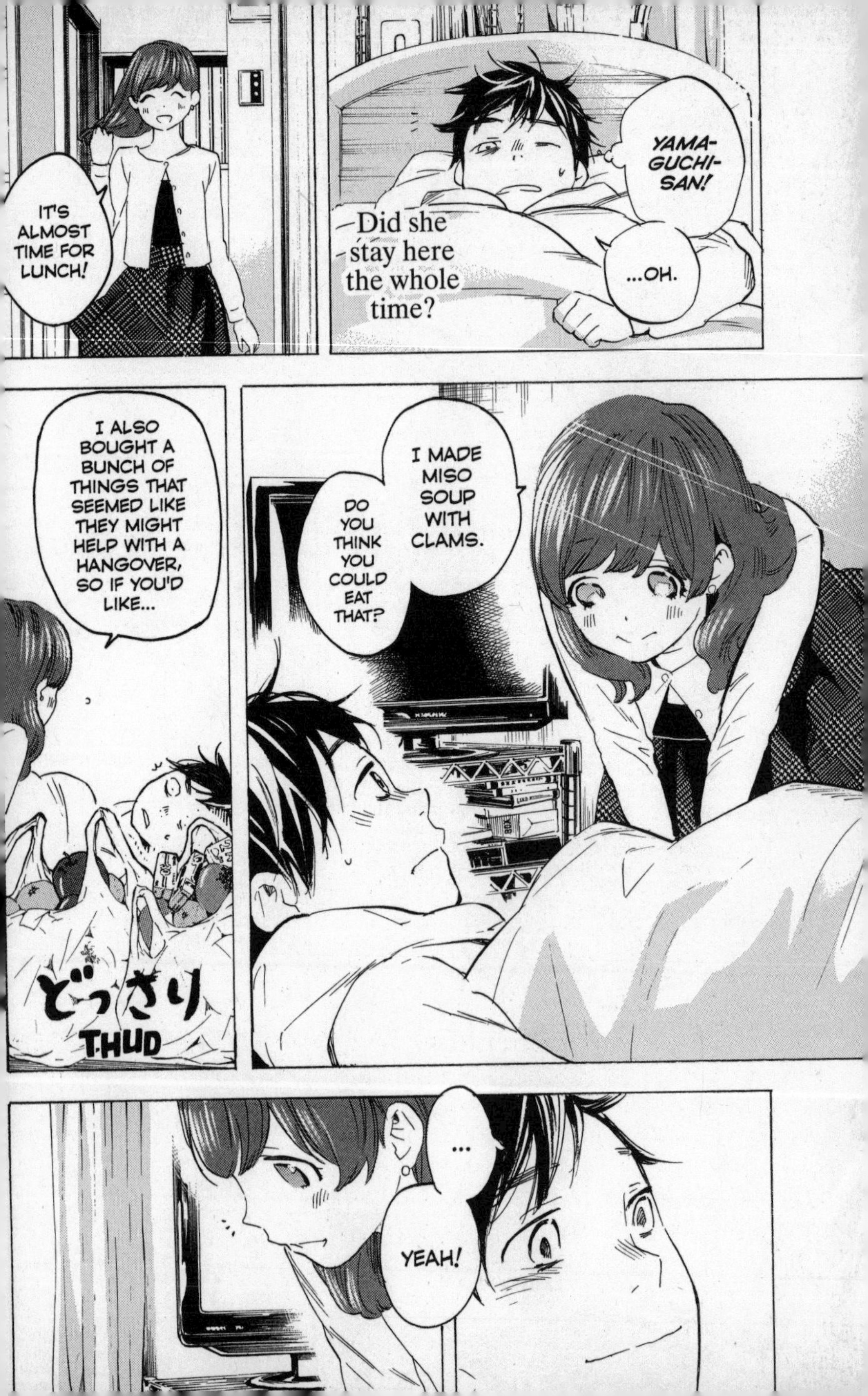
YAMA-GUCHI-SAN!
...OH.
Did she stay here the whole time?
IT'S ALMOST TIME FOR LUNCH!
I MADE MISO SOUP WITH CLAMS.
DO YOU THINK YOU COULD EAT THAT?
I ALSO BOUGHT A BUNCH OF THINGS THAT SEEMED LIKE THEY MIGHT HELP WITH A HANGOVER, SO IF YOU'D LIKE...
どっさり
THUD
...
YEAH!

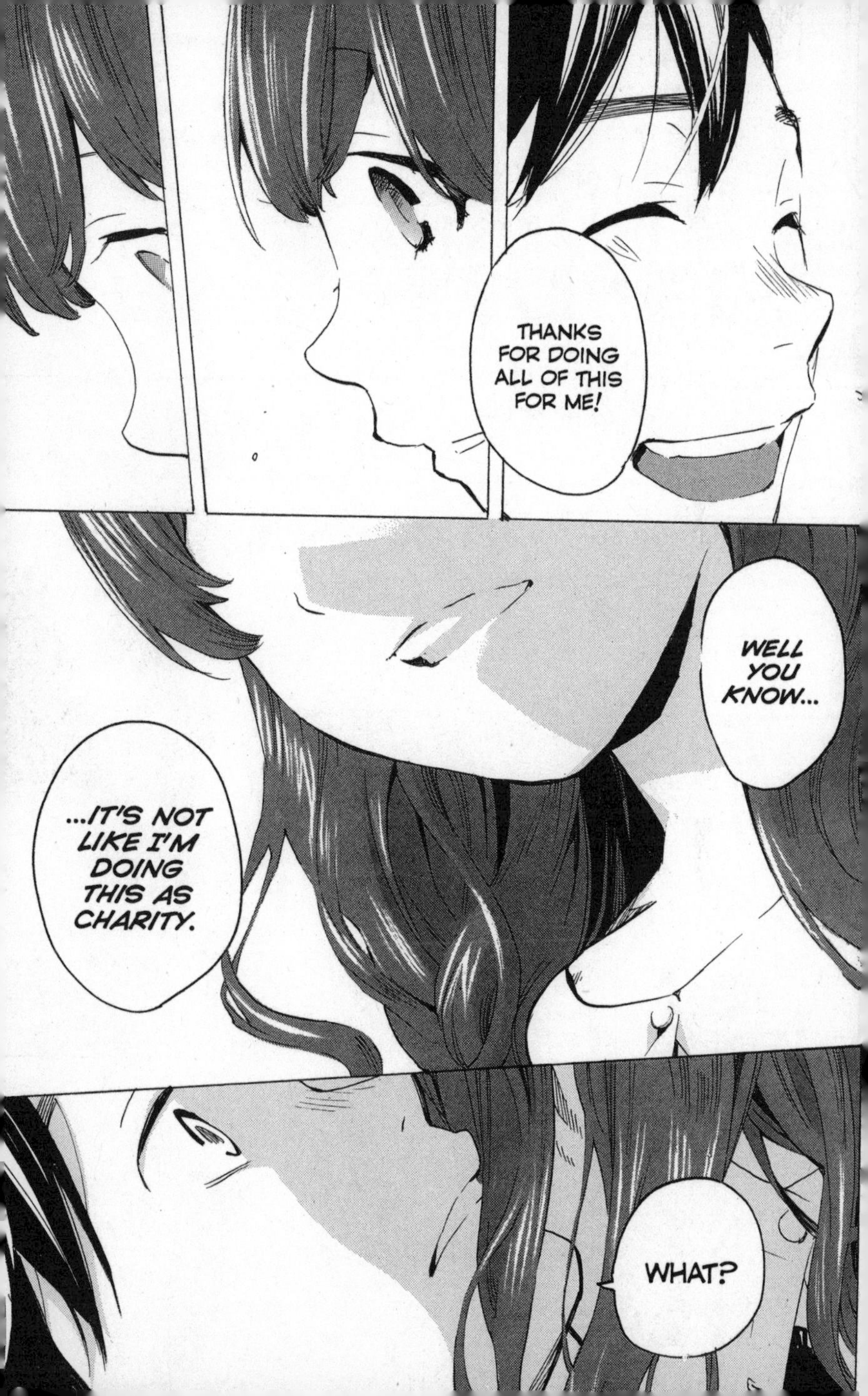
THANKS FOR DOING ALL OF THIS FOR ME!
WELL YOU KNOW...
...IT'S NOT LIKE I'M DOING THIS AS CHARITY.
WHAT?

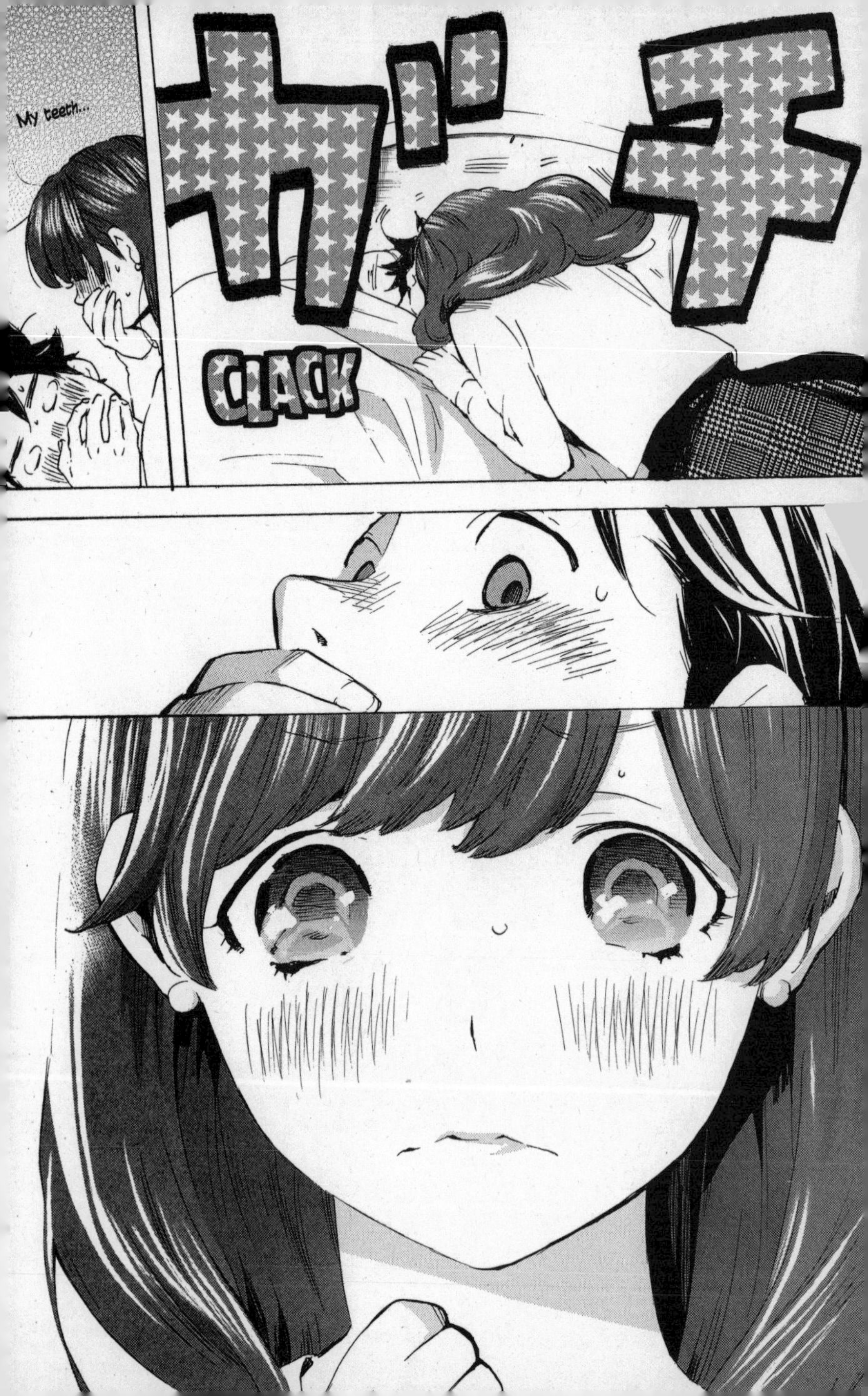
ガブ
CLACK
My teeth...

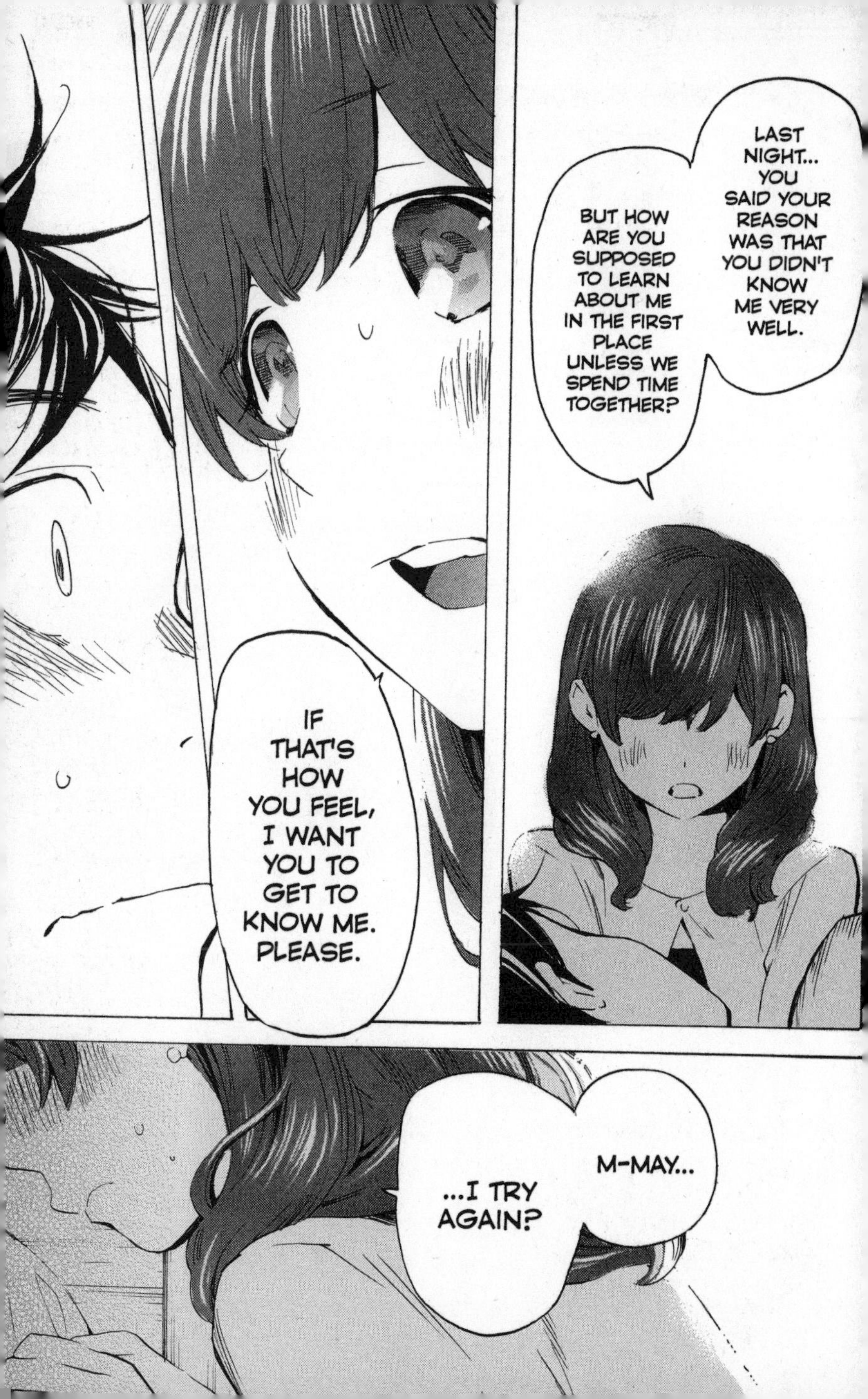
LAST NIGHT... YOU SAID YOUR REASON WAS THAT YOU DIDN'T KNOW ME VERY WELL.
BUT HOW ARE YOU SUPPOSED TO LEARN ABOUT ME IN THE FIRST PLACE UNLESS WE SPEND TIME TOGETHER?
IF THAT'S HOW YOU FEEL, I WANT YOU TO GET TO KNOW ME. PLEASE.
M-MAY...
...I TRY AGAIN?

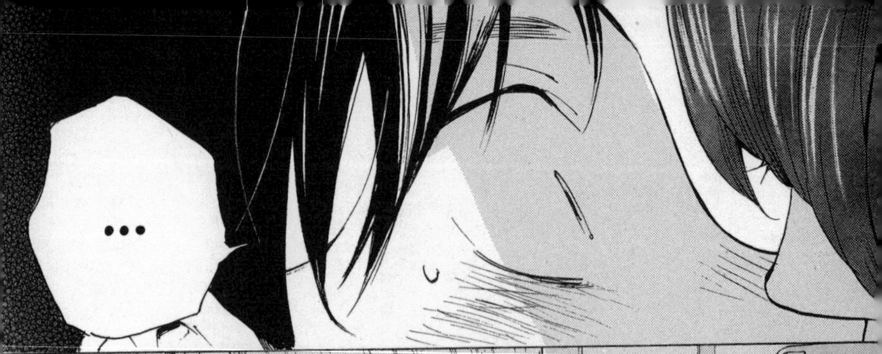
...
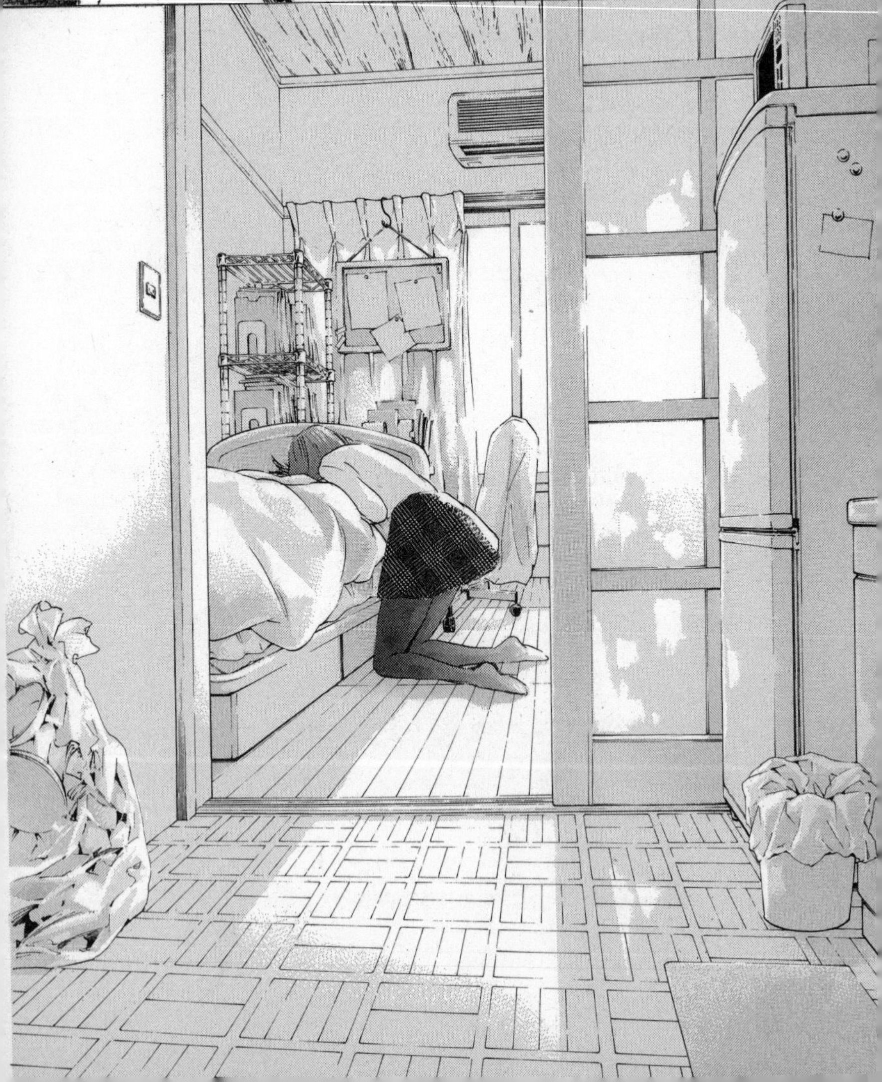

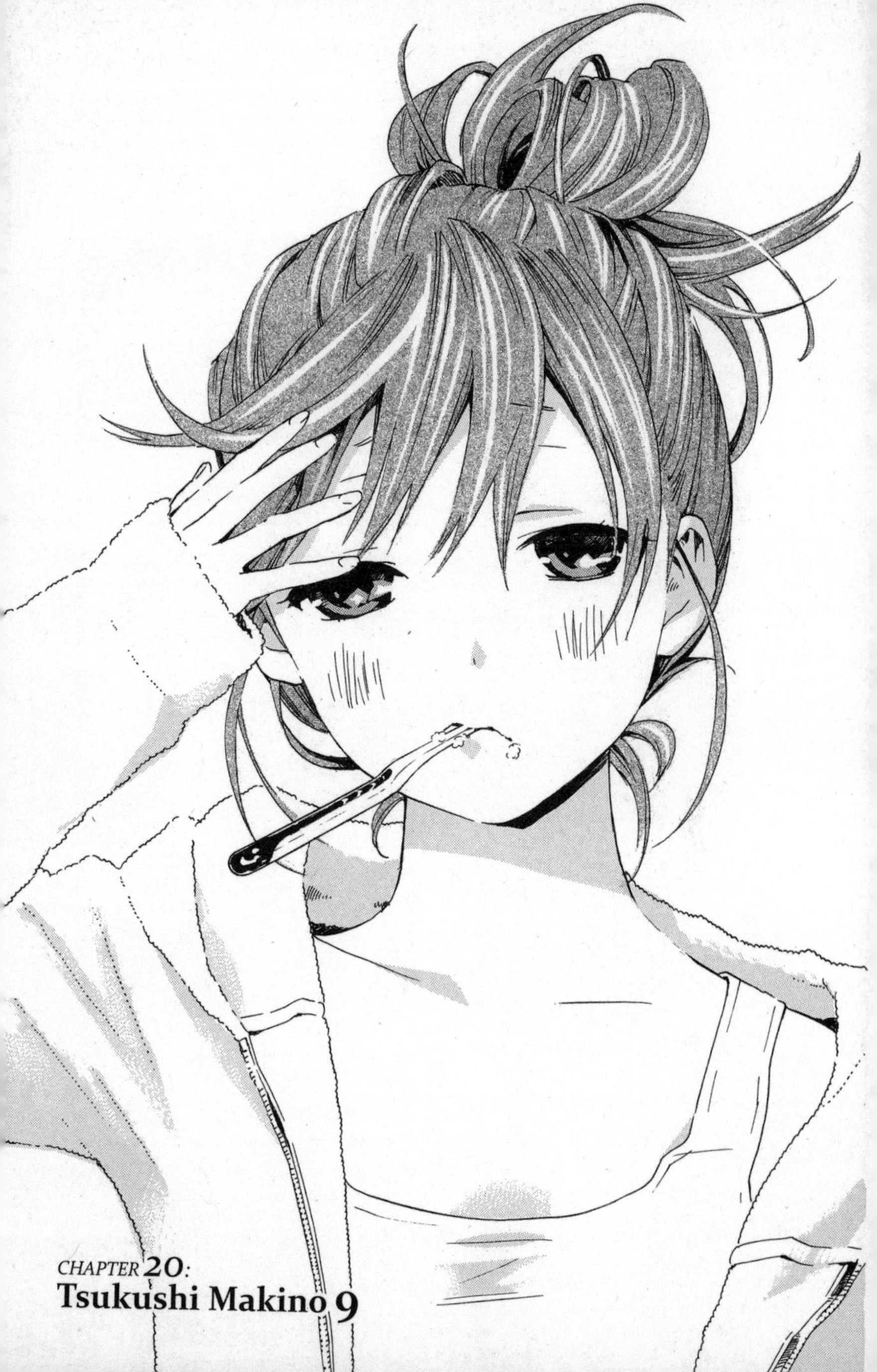

CHAPTER 20: Tsukushi Makino 9

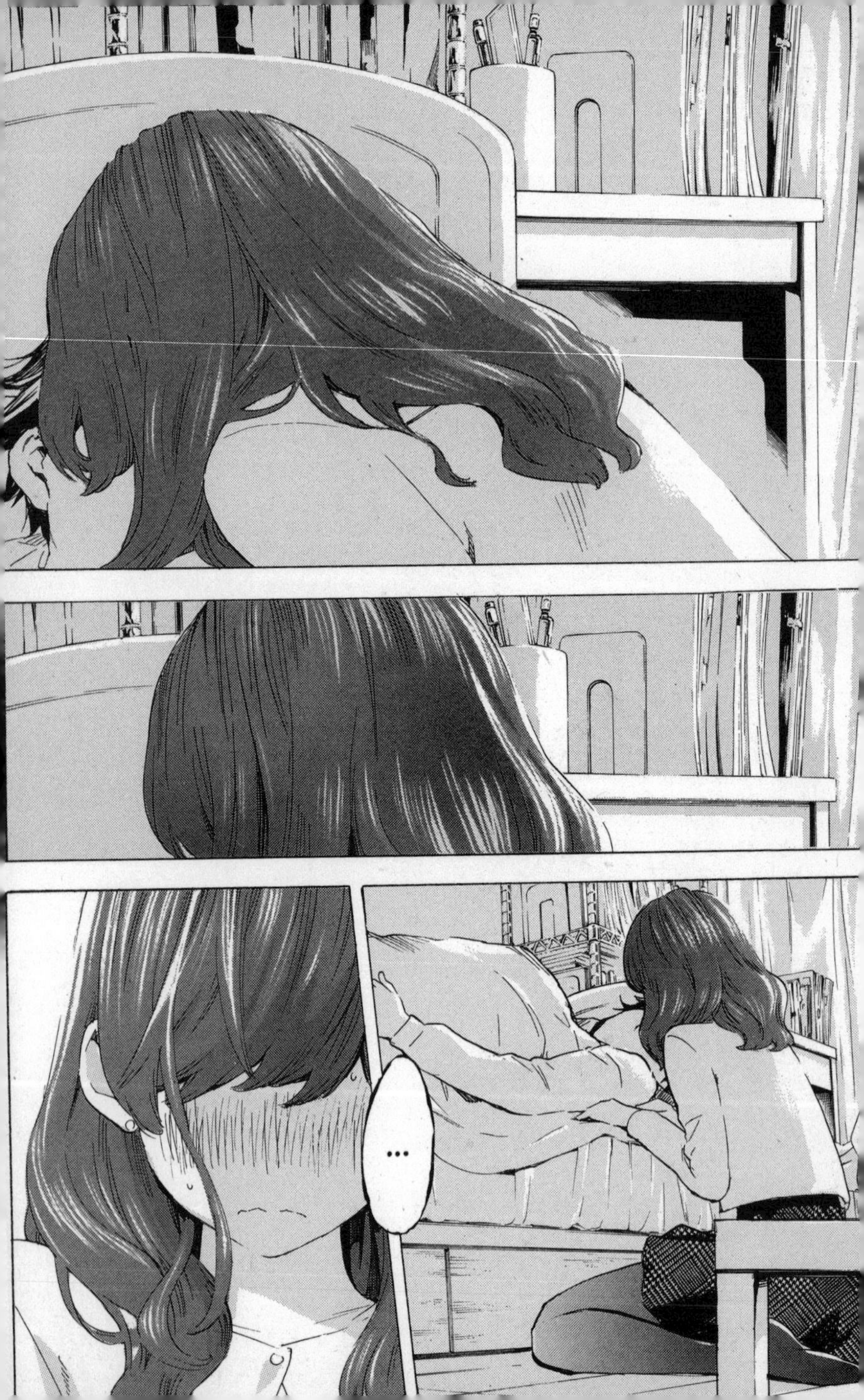
...

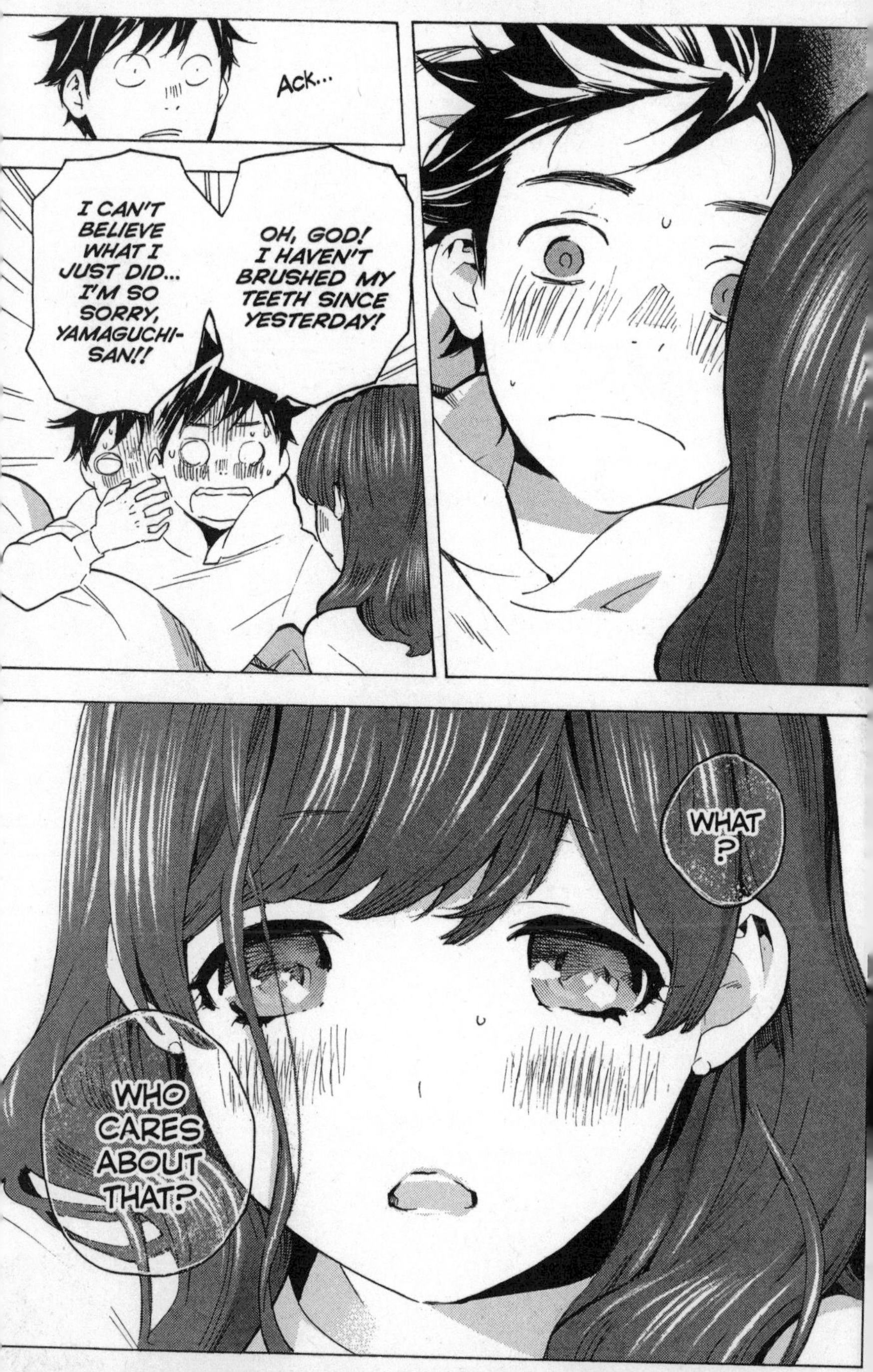
Ack...
OH, GOD! I HAVEN'T BRUSHED MY TEETH SINCE YESTERDAY!
I CAN'T BELIEVE WHAT I JUST DID... I'M SO SORRY, YAMAGUCHI-SAN!!
WHAT?
WHO CARES ABOUT THAT?

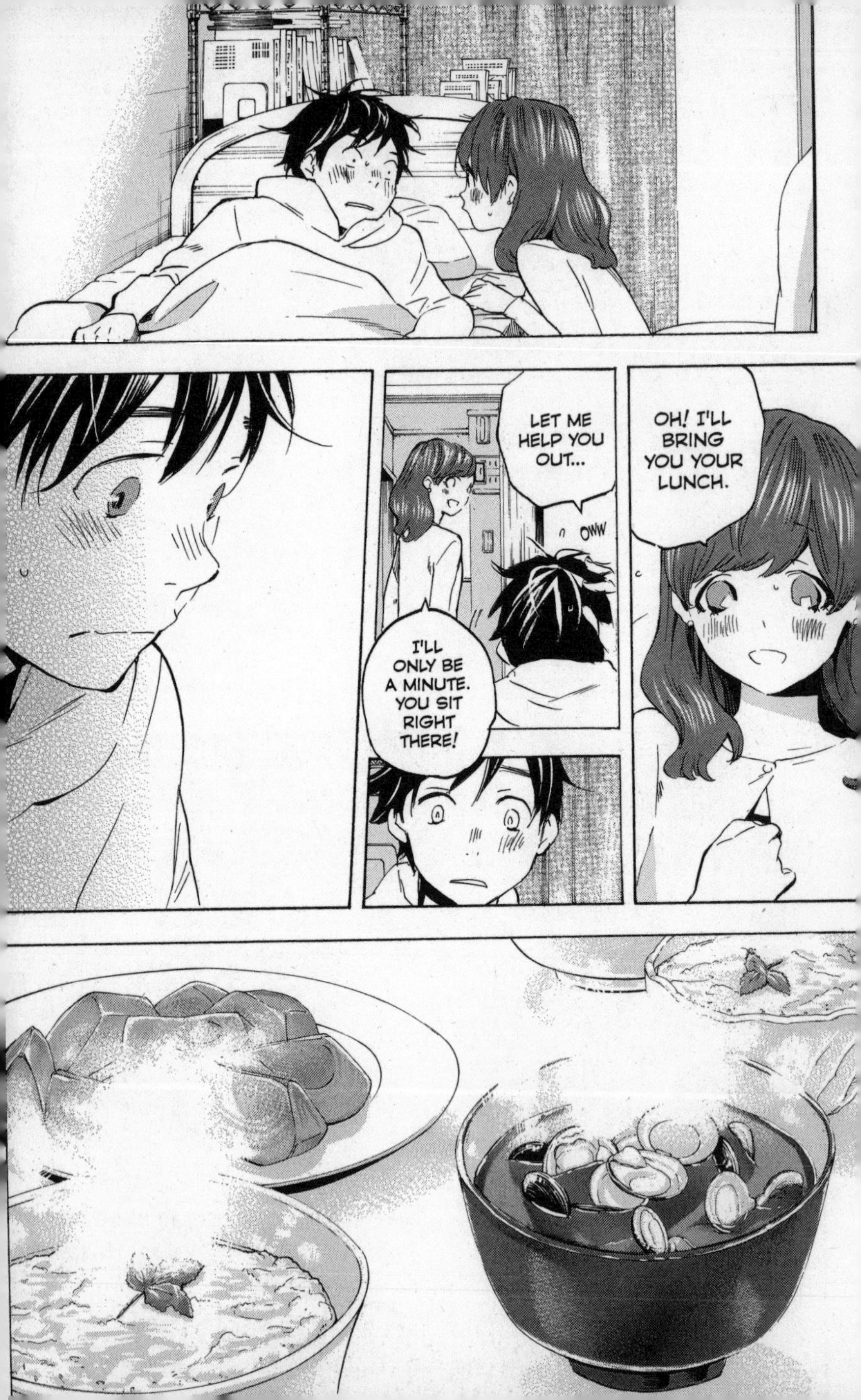
OH! I'LL BRING YOU YOUR LUNCH.
LET ME HELP YOU OUT...
OWW
I'LL ONLY BE A MINUTE. YOU SIT RIGHT THERE!

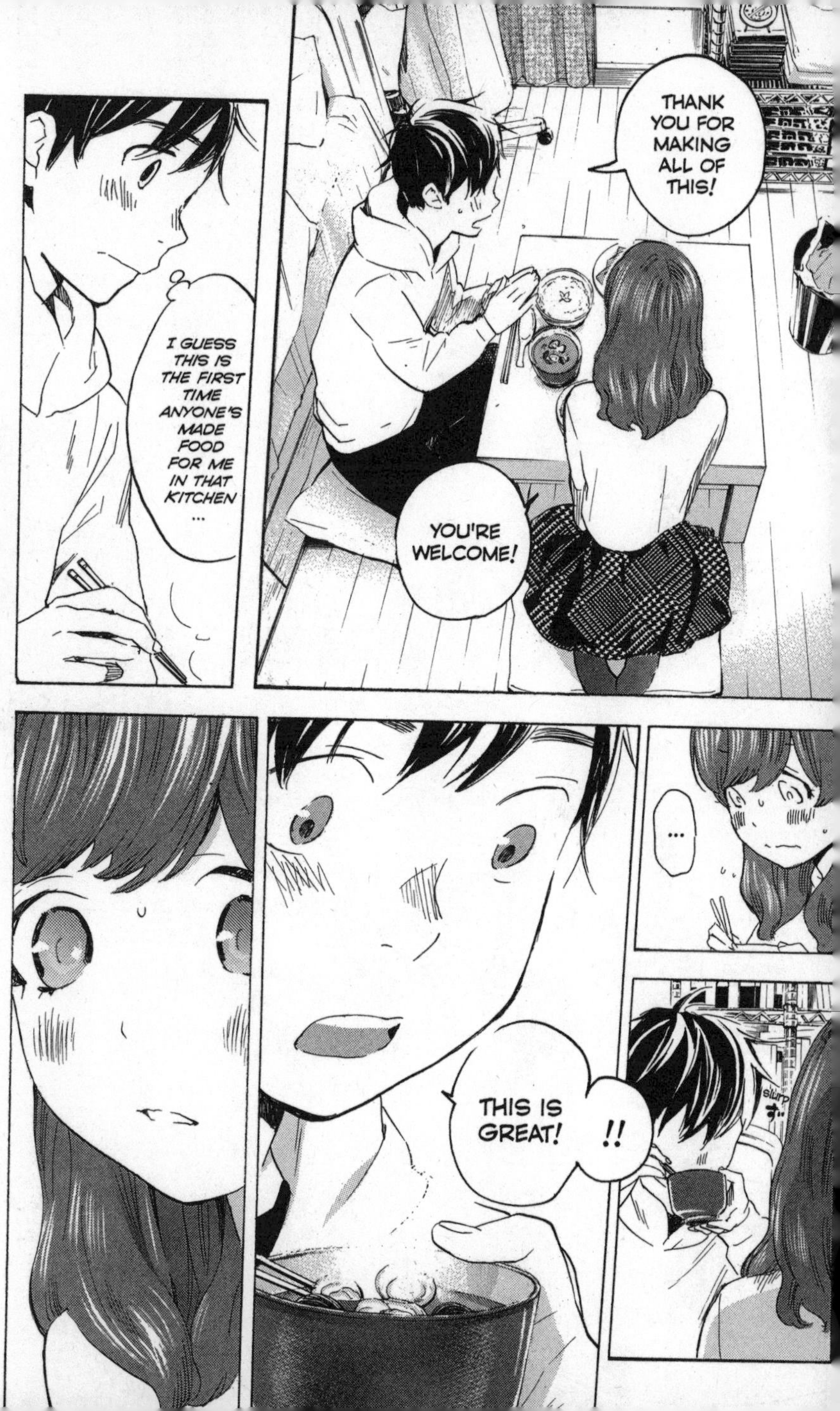
THANK YOU FOR MAKING ALL OF THIS!
YOU'RE WELCOME!
I GUESS THIS IS THE FIRST TIME ANYONE'S MADE FOOD FOR ME IN THAT KITCHEN ...
...
slurp
THIS IS GREAT!
!!

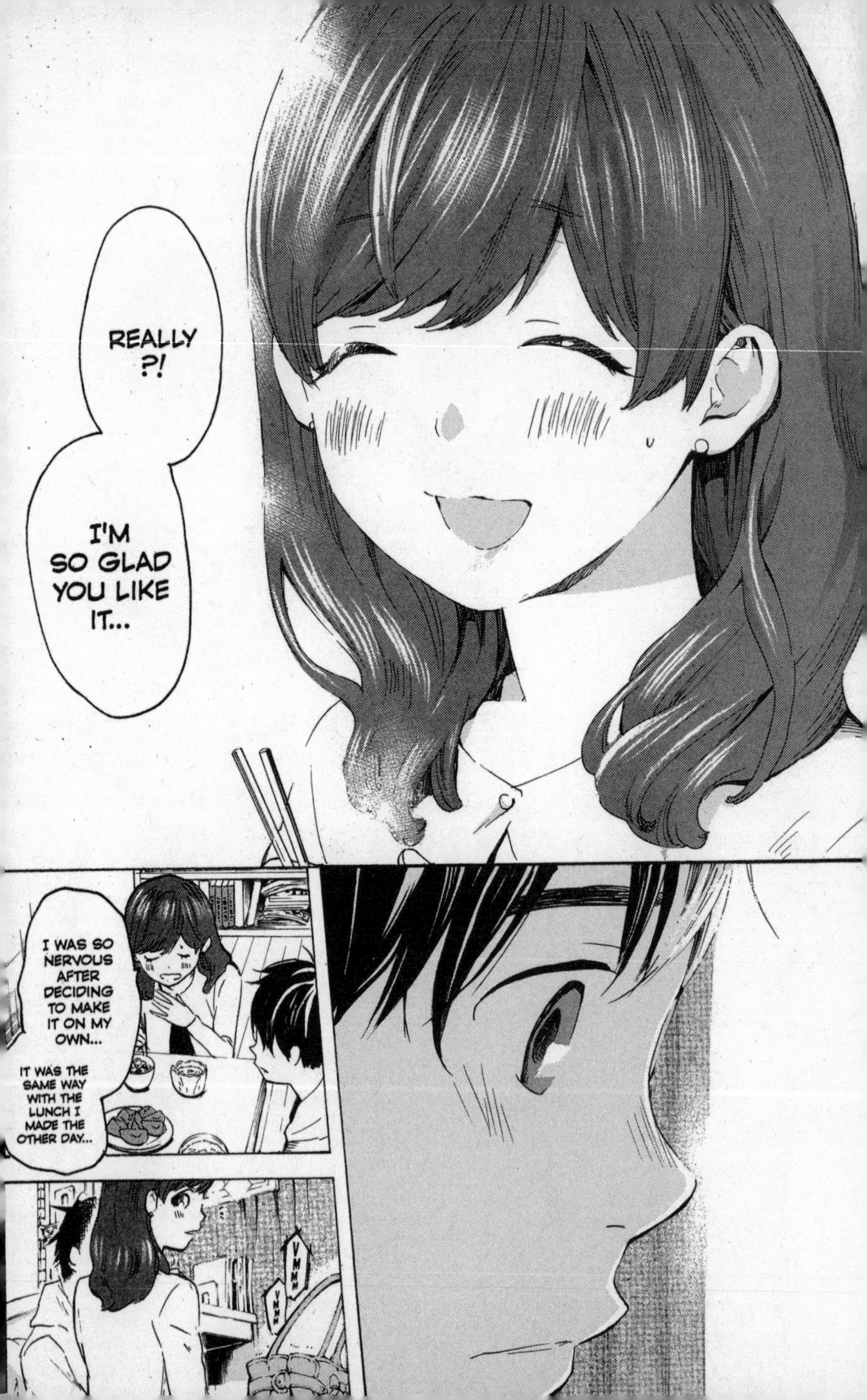
REALLY ?!
I'M SO GLAD YOU LIKE IT...
I WAS SO NERVOUS AFTER DECIDING TO MAKE IT ON MY OWN...
IT WAS THE SAME WAY WITH THE LUNCH I MADE THE OTHER DAY...
VMM
VMM

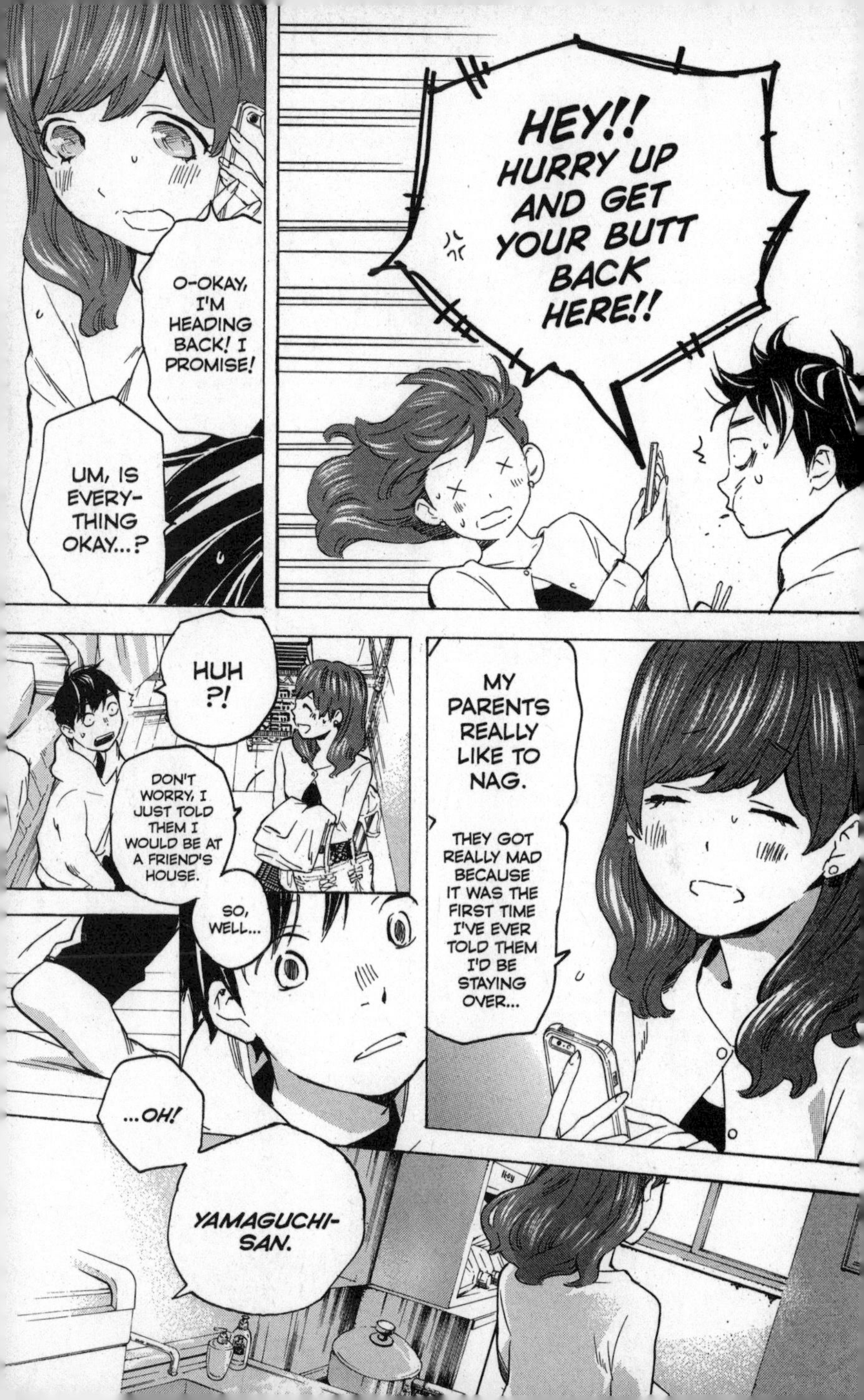
HEY!! HURRY UP AND GET YOUR BUTT BACK HERE!!
O-OKAY, I'M HEADING BACK! I PROMISE!
UM, IS EVERYTHING OKAY...?
MY PARENTS REALLY LIKE TO NAG.
THEY GOT REALLY MAD BECAUSE IT WAS THE FIRST TIME I'VE EVER TOLD THEM I'D BE STAYING OVER...
HUH ?!
DON'T WORRY, I JUST TOLD THEM I WOULD BE AT A FRIEND'S HOUSE.
SO, WELL...
...OH!
YAMAGUCHI-SAN.

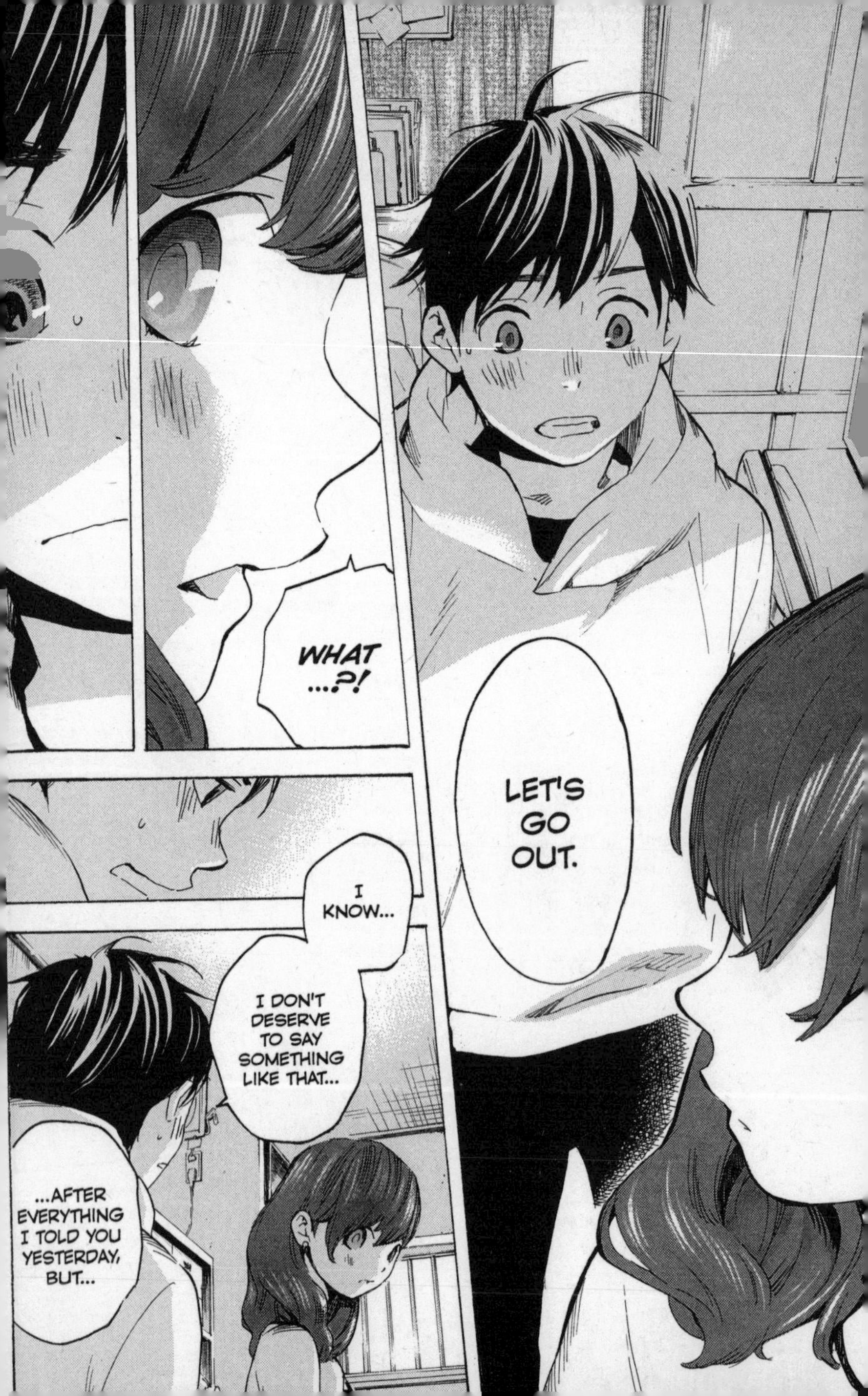
LET'S GO OUT.
WHAT ...?!
I KNOW...
I DON'T DESERVE TO SAY SOMETHING LIKE THAT...
...AFTER EVERYTHING I TOLD YOU YESTERDAY, BUT...

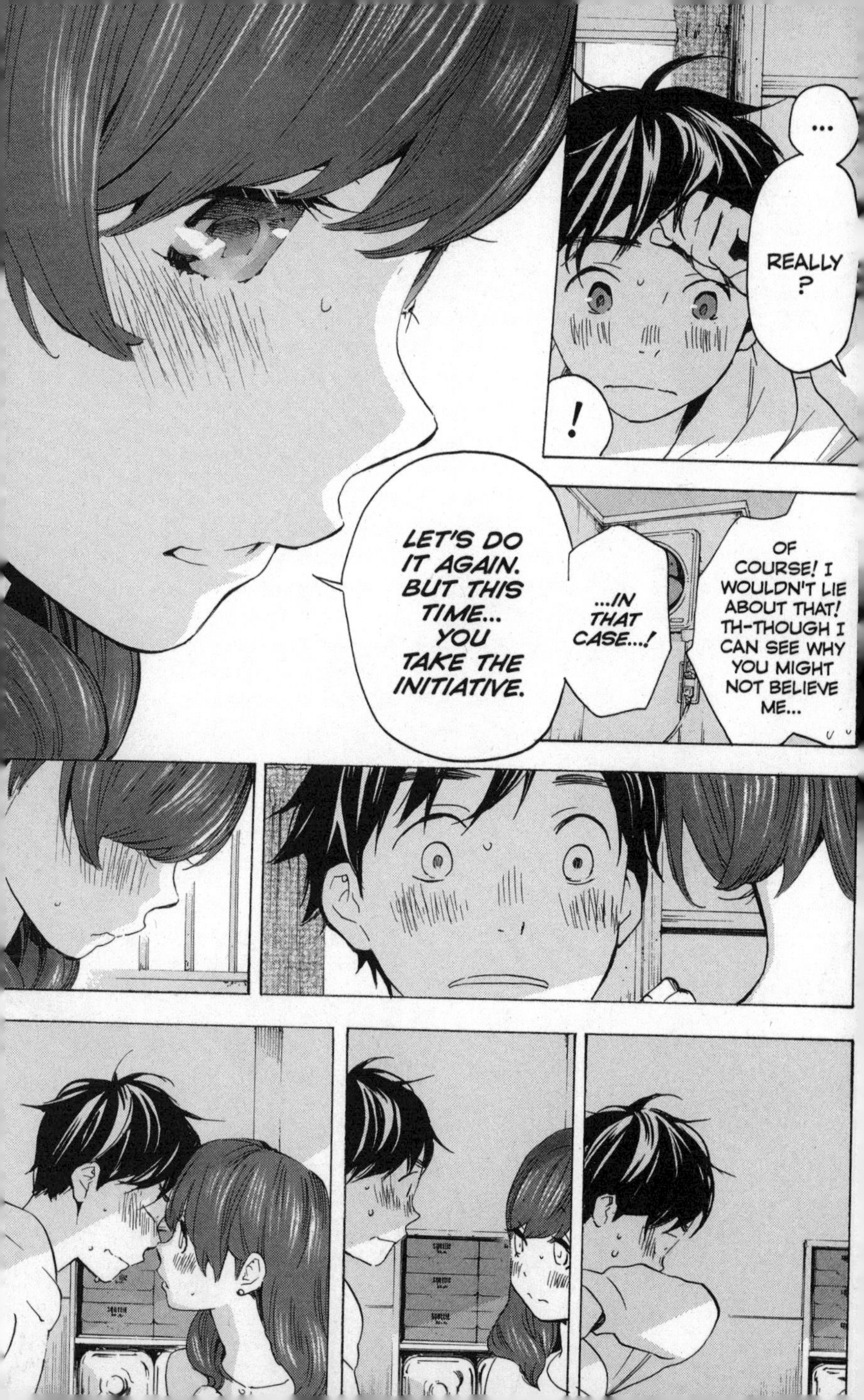
...
REALLY?
!
OF COURSE! I WOULDN'T LIE ABOUT THAT! TH-THOUGH I CAN SEE WHY YOU MIGHT NOT BELIEVE ME...
...IN THAT CASE...!
LET'S DO IT AGAIN. BUT THIS TIME... YOU TAKE THE INITIATIVE.

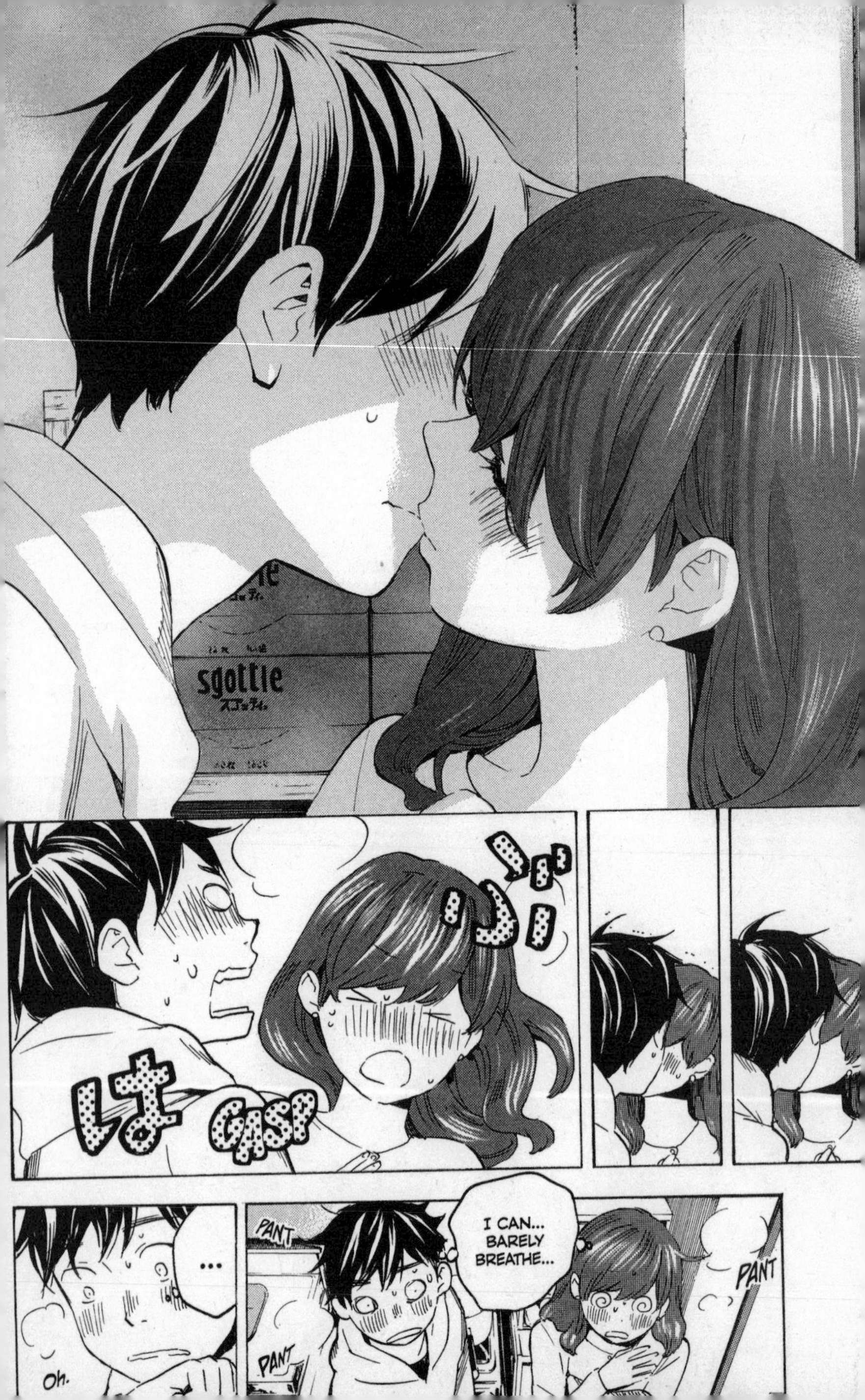
sgottle
GASP!
PANT
I CAN... BARELY BREATHE...
PANT
PANT
...
Oh.

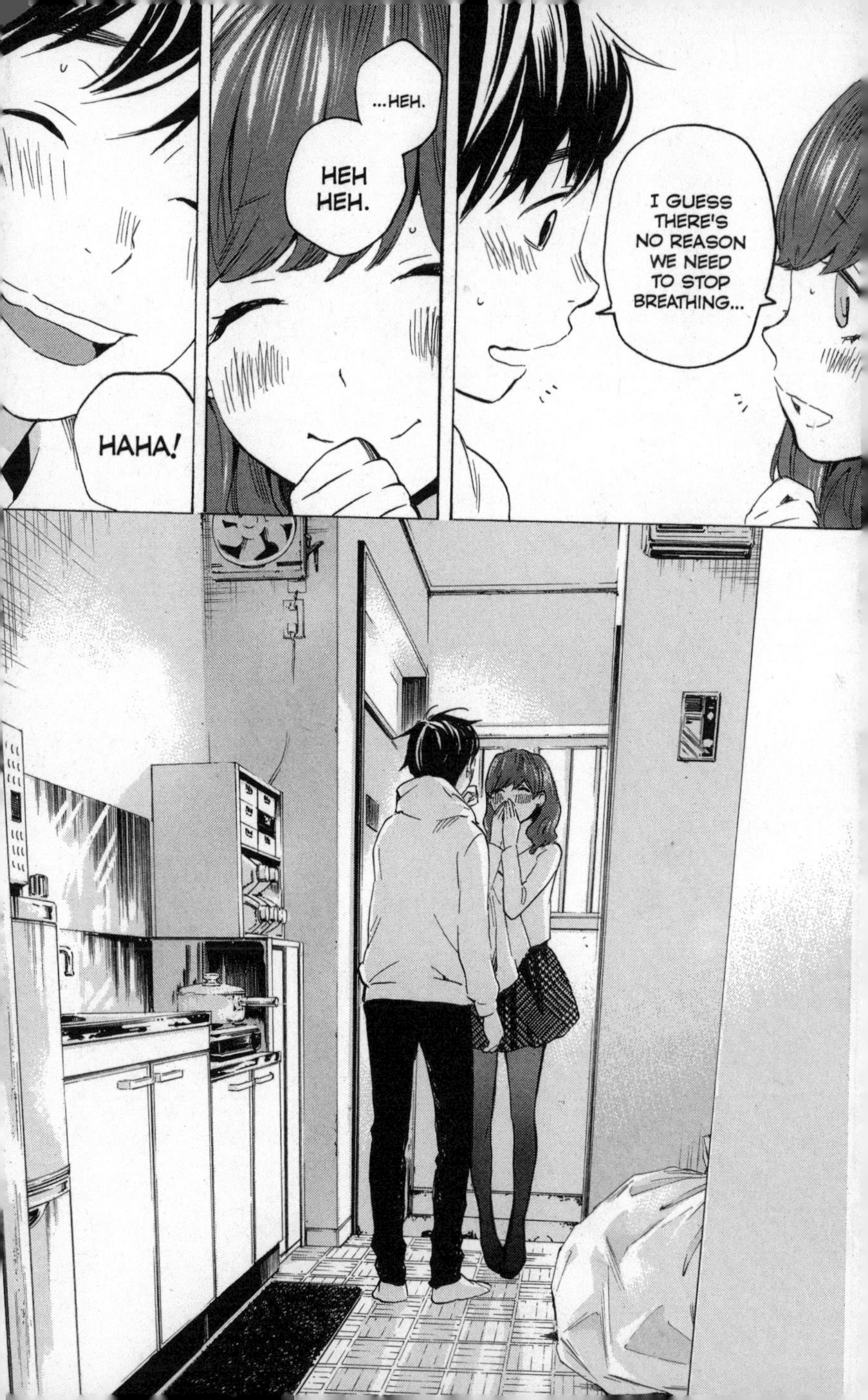
I GUESS THERE'S NO REASON WE NEED TO STOP BREATHING...
...HEH.
HEH HEH.
HAHA!

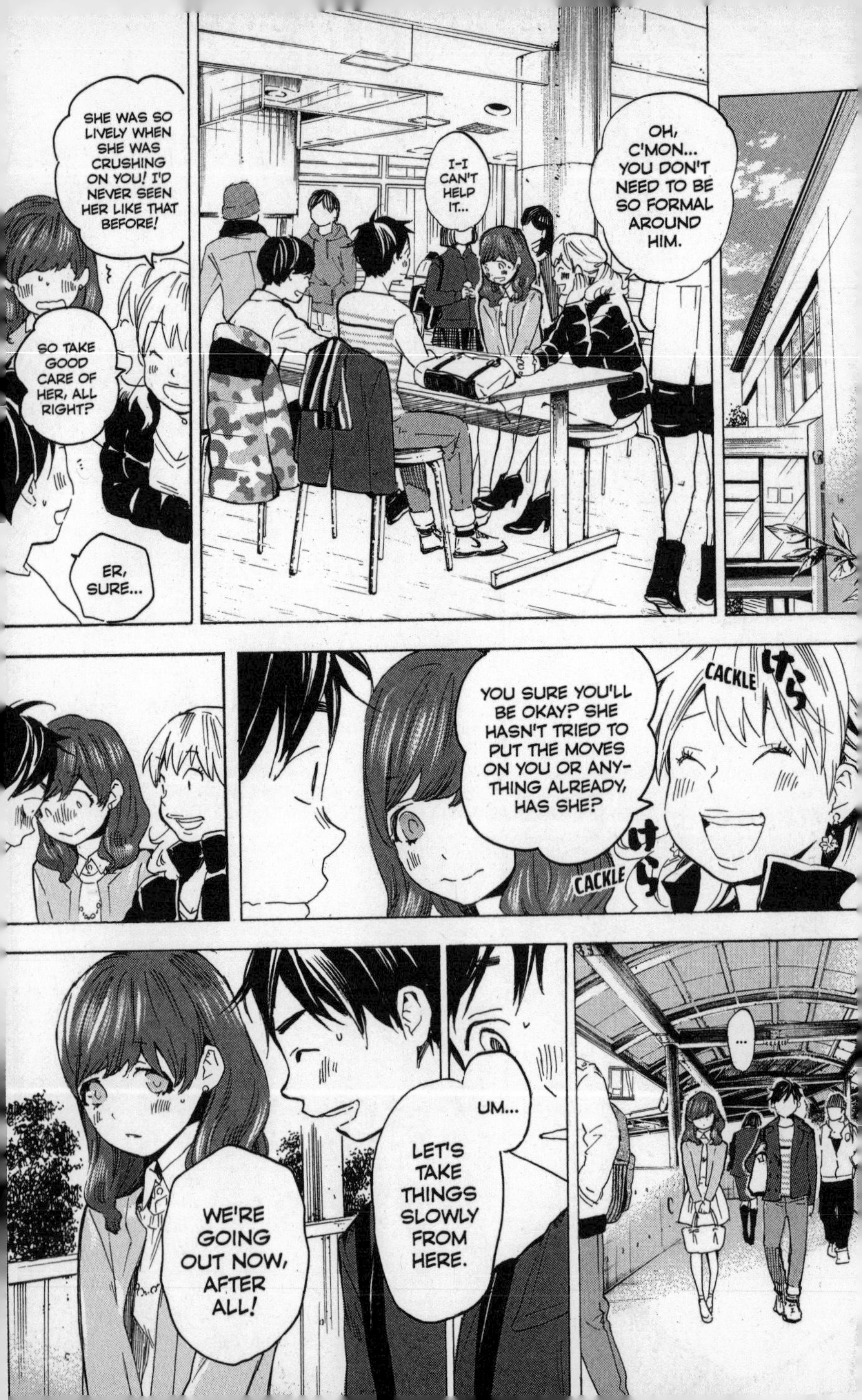
OH, C'MON... YOU DON'T NEED TO BE SO FORMAL AROUND HIM.
I-I CAN'T HELP IT...
SHE WAS SO LIVELY WHEN SHE WAS CRUSHING ON YOU! I'D NEVER SEEN HER LIKE THAT BEFORE!
SO TAKE GOOD CARE OF HER, ALL RIGHT?
ER, SURE...
CACKLE けら
YOU SURE YOU'LL BE OKAY? SHE HASN'T TRIED TO PUT THE MOVES ON YOU OR ANY-THING ALREADY, HAS SHE?
CACKLE けら
...
UM...
LET'S TAKE THINGS SLOWLY FROM HERE.
WE'RE GOING OUT NOW, AFTER ALL!

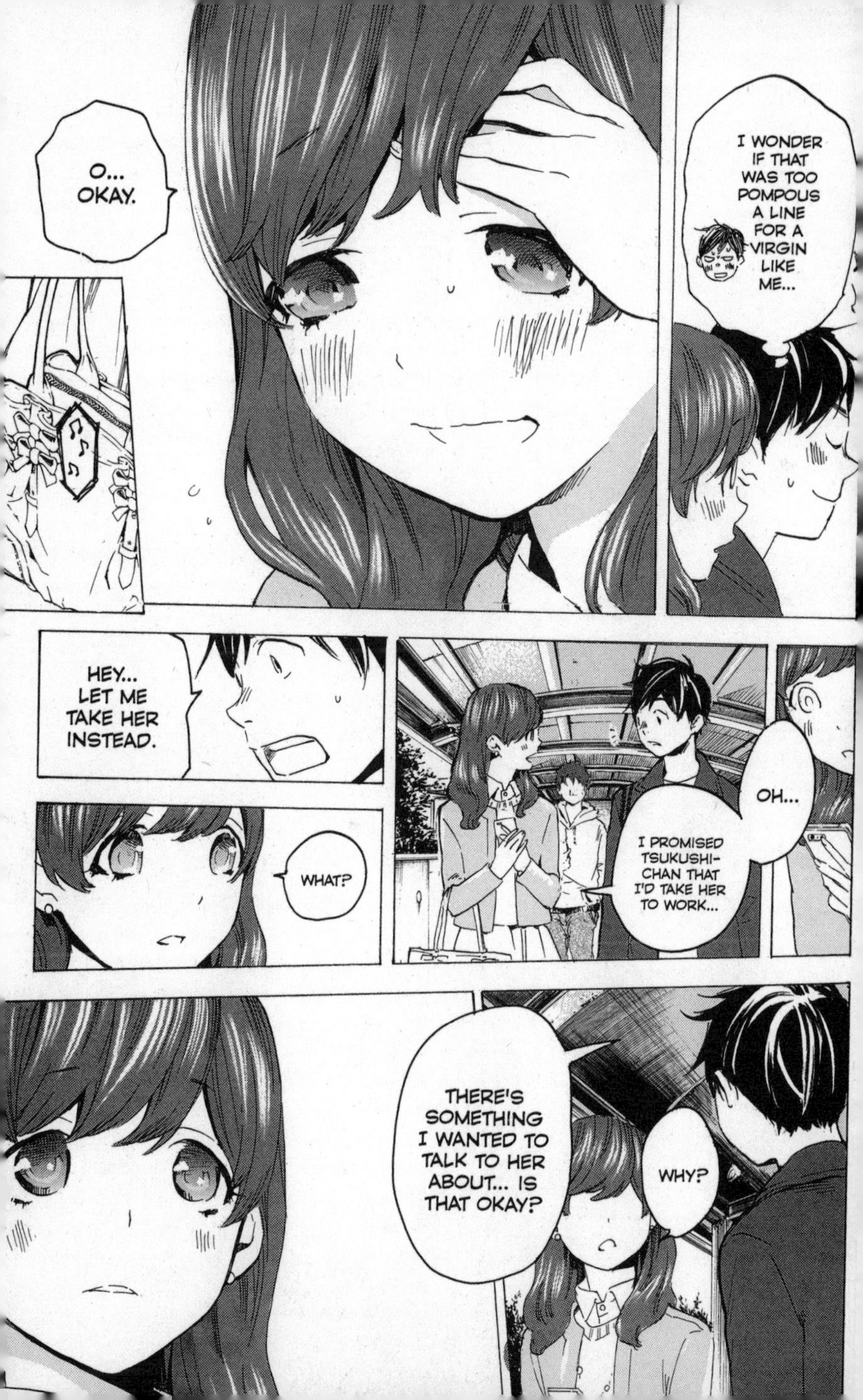
I WONDER IF THAT WAS TOO POMPOUS A LINE FOR A VIRGIN LIKE ME...
O... OKAY.
OH...
I PROMISED TSUKUSHI-CHAN THAT I'D TAKE HER TO WORK...
HEY... LET ME TAKE HER INSTEAD.
WHAT?
THERE'S SOMETHING I WANTED TO TALK TO HER ABOUT... IS THAT OKAY?
WHY?

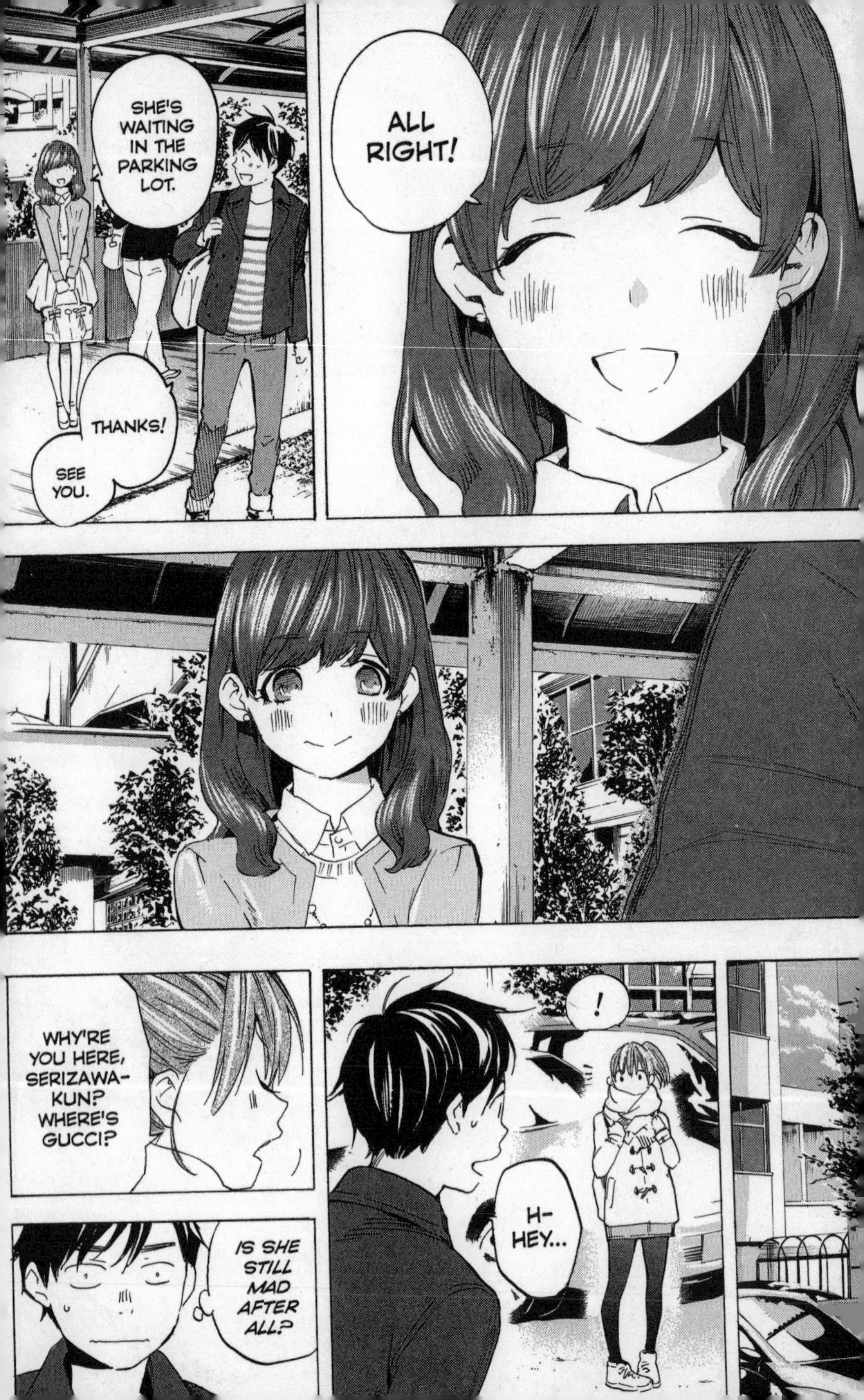
ALL RIGHT!
SHE'S WAITING IN THE PARKING LOT.
THANKS!
SEE YOU.
!
H-HEY...
WHY'RE YOU HERE, SERIZAWA-KUN? WHERE'S GUCCI?
IS SHE STILL MAD AFTER ALL?

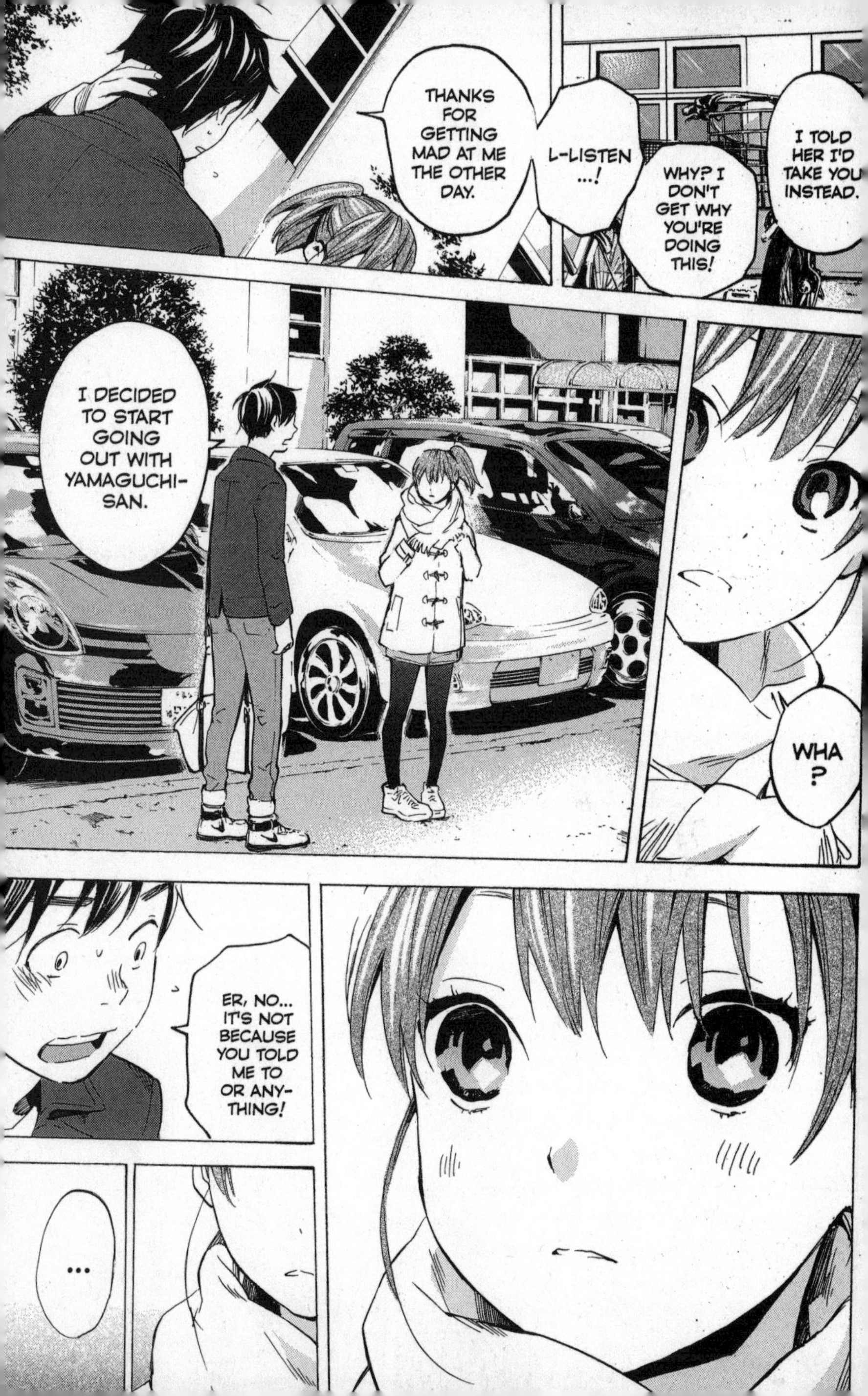
I TOLD HER I'D TAKE YOU INSTEAD.
WHY? I DON'T GET WHY YOU'RE DOING THIS!
L-LISTEN ...!
THANKS FOR GETTING MAD AT ME THE OTHER DAY.
WHA ?
I DECIDED TO START GOING OUT WITH YAMAGUCHI-SAN.
ER, NO... IT'S NOT BECAUSE YOU TOLD ME TO OR ANY-THING!
...

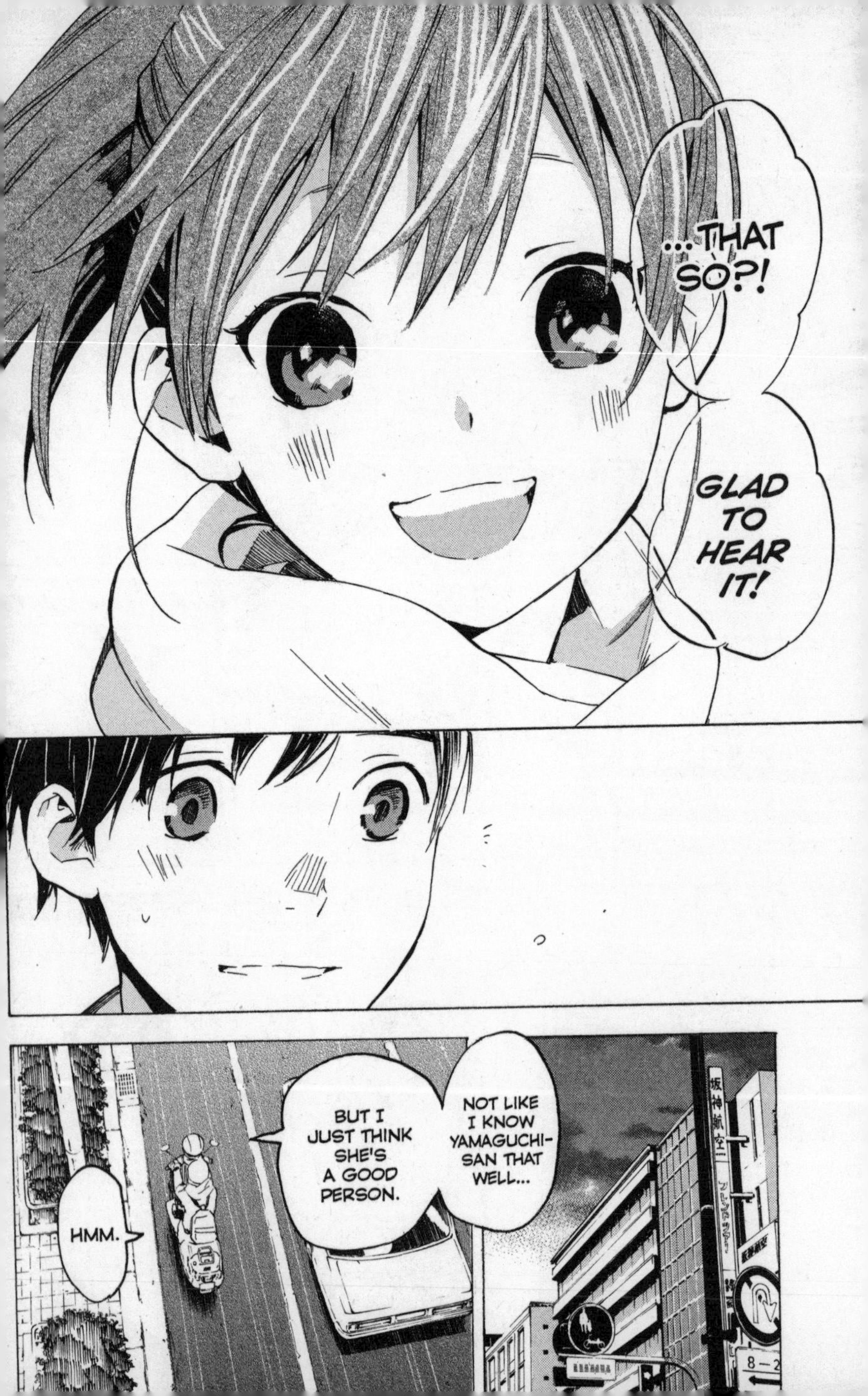
...THAT SO?!
GLAD TO HEAR IT!
NOT LIKE I KNOW YAMAGUCHI-SAN THAT WELL...
BUT I JUST THINK SHE'S A GOOD PERSON.
HMM.

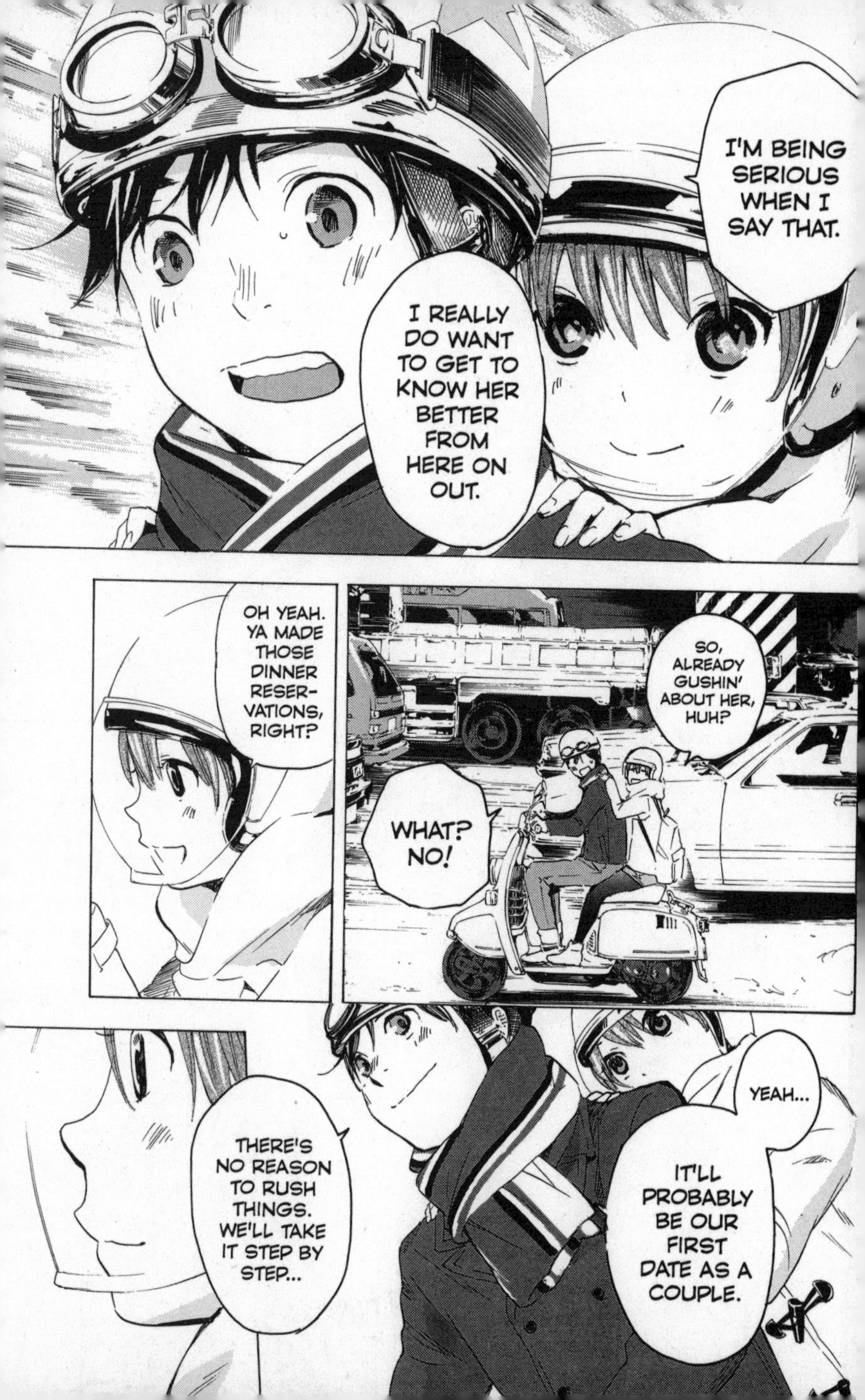
I'M BEING SERIOUS WHEN I SAY THAT.
I REALLY DO WANT TO GET TO KNOW HER BETTER FROM HERE ON OUT.
SO, ALREADY GUSHIN' ABOUT HER, HUH?
WHAT? NO!
OH YEAH. YA MADE THOSE DINNER RESER-VATIONS, RIGHT?
YEAH...
IT'LL PROBABLY BE OUR FIRST DATE AS A COUPLE.
THERE'S NO REASON TO RUSH THINGS. WE'LL TAKE IT STEP BY STEP...

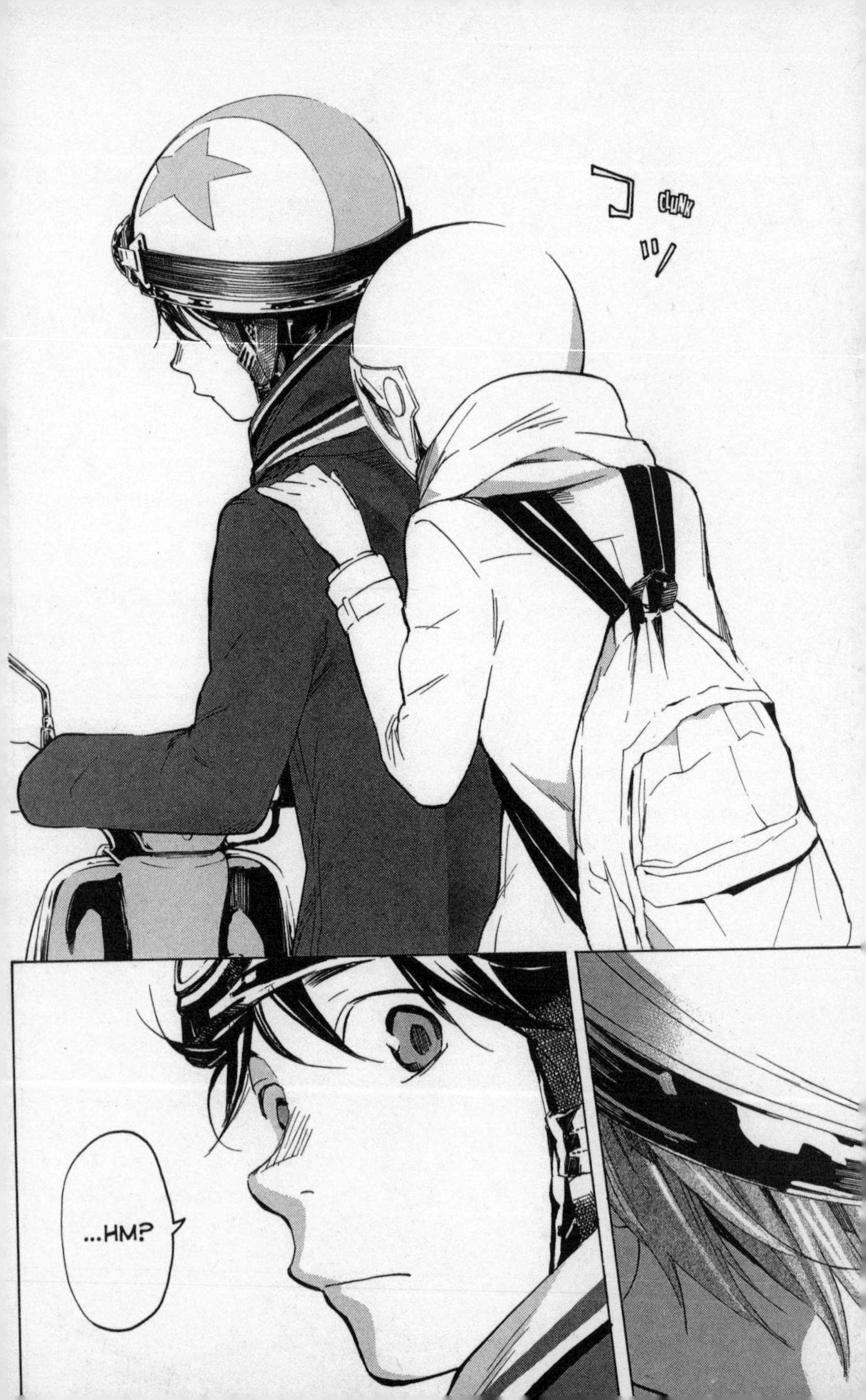
CLUNK
...HM?

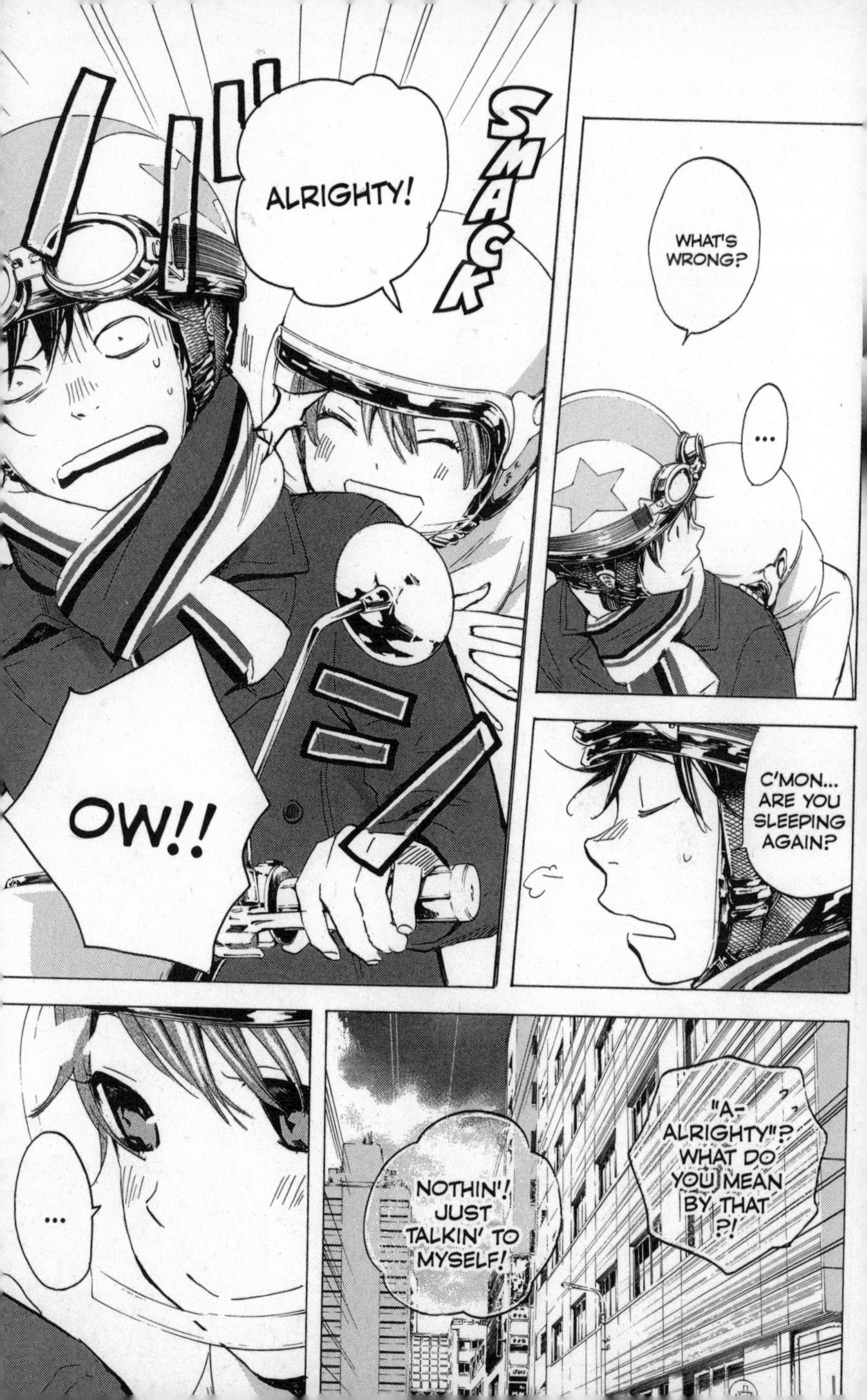
WHAT'S WRONG?
...
C'MON... ARE YOU SLEEPING AGAIN?
ALRIGHTY!
SMACK
OW!!
"A-ALRIGHTY"?! WHAT DO YOU MEAN BY THAT?!
NOTHIN'! JUST TALKIN' TO MYSELF!
...

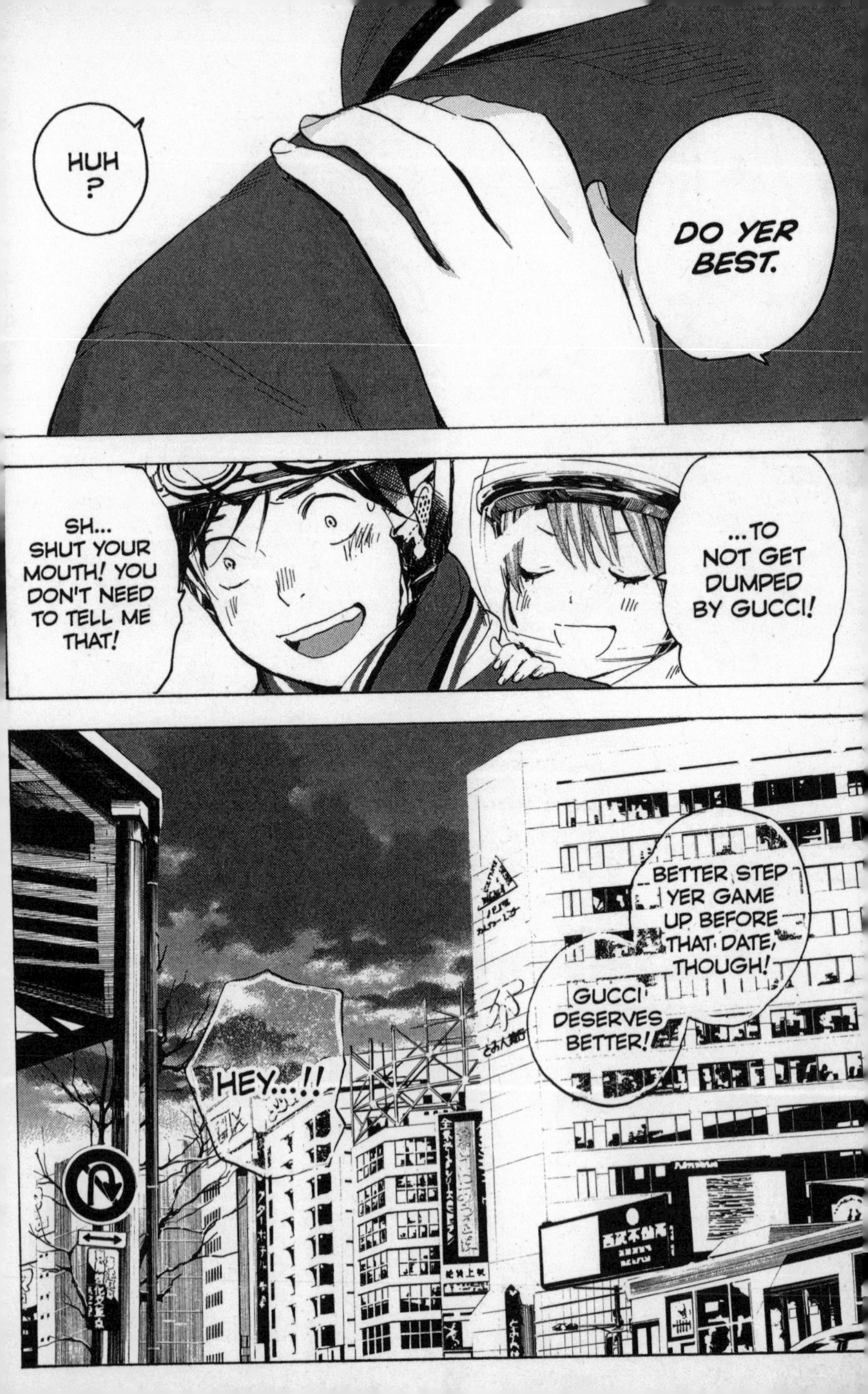
DO YER BEST.
HUH?
...TO NOT GET DUMPED BY GUCCI!
SH... SHUT YOUR MOUTH! YOU DON'T NEED TO TELL ME THAT!
BETTER STEP YER GAME UP BEFORE THAT DATE, THOUGH!
GUCCI DESERVES BETTER!
HEY...!!

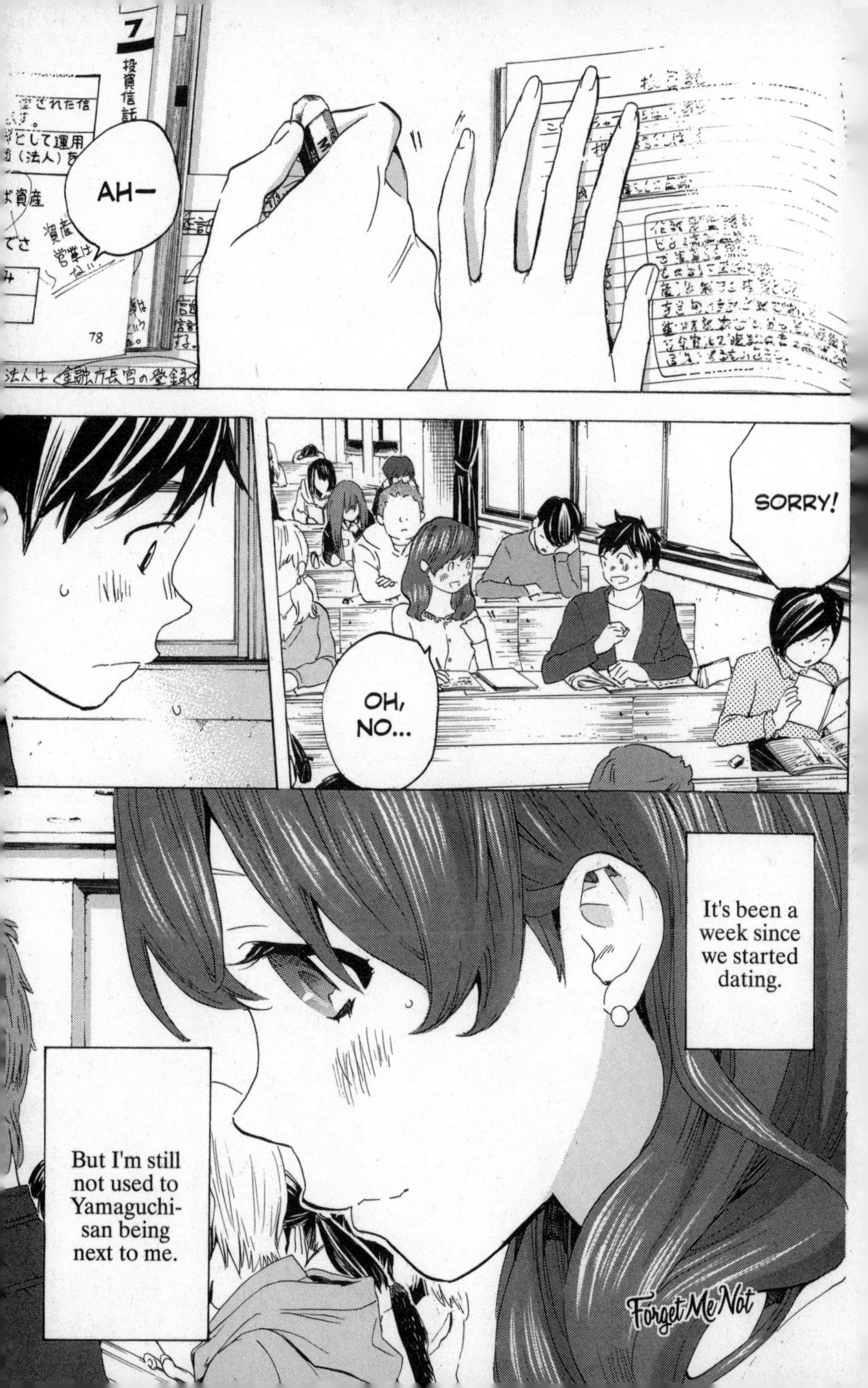
AH—
SORRY!
OH, NO...
It's been a week since we started dating.
But I'm still not used to Yamaguchi-san being next to me.
Forget Me Not

CHAPTER 21: Tsukushi Makino 10

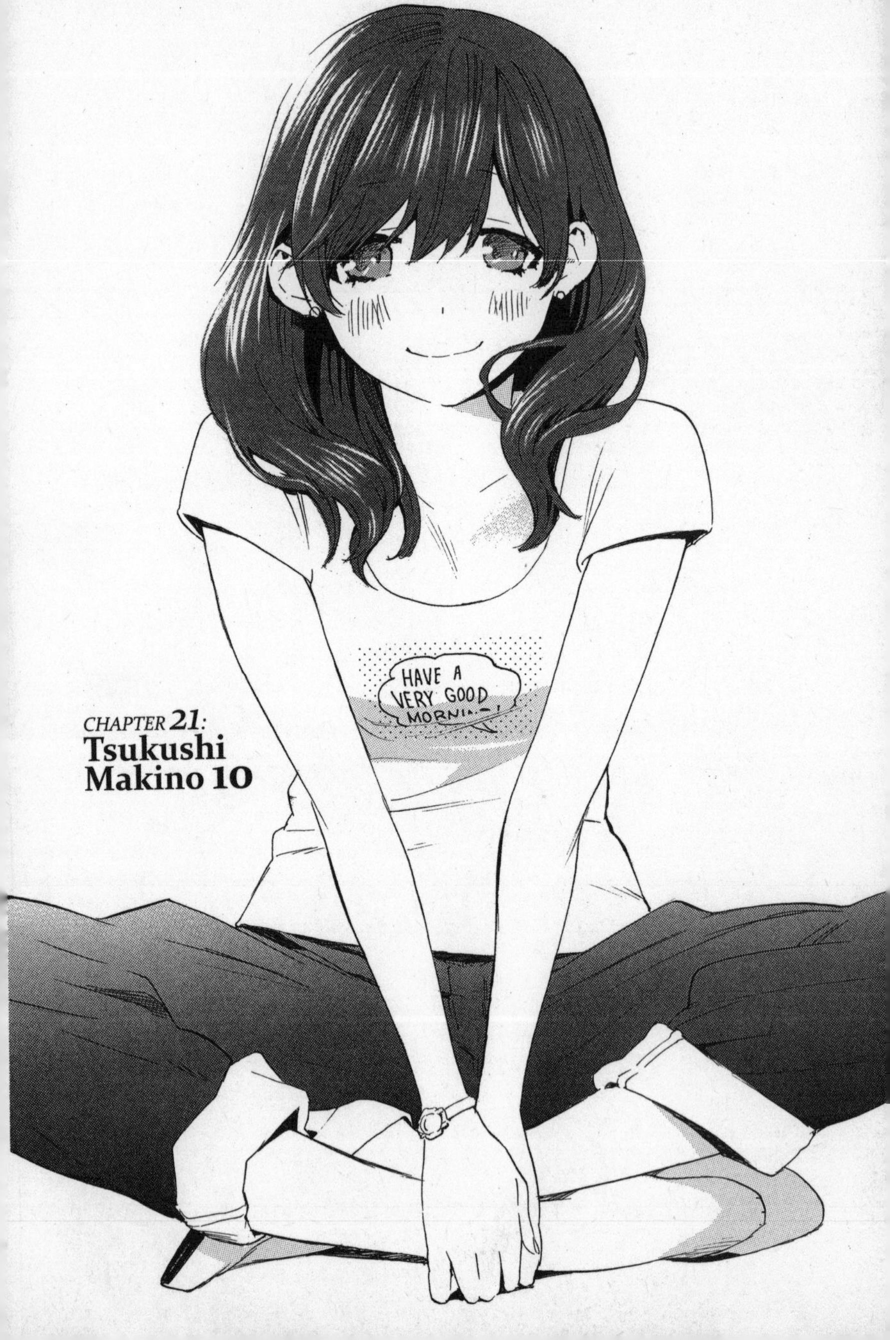
HAVE A VERY GOOD

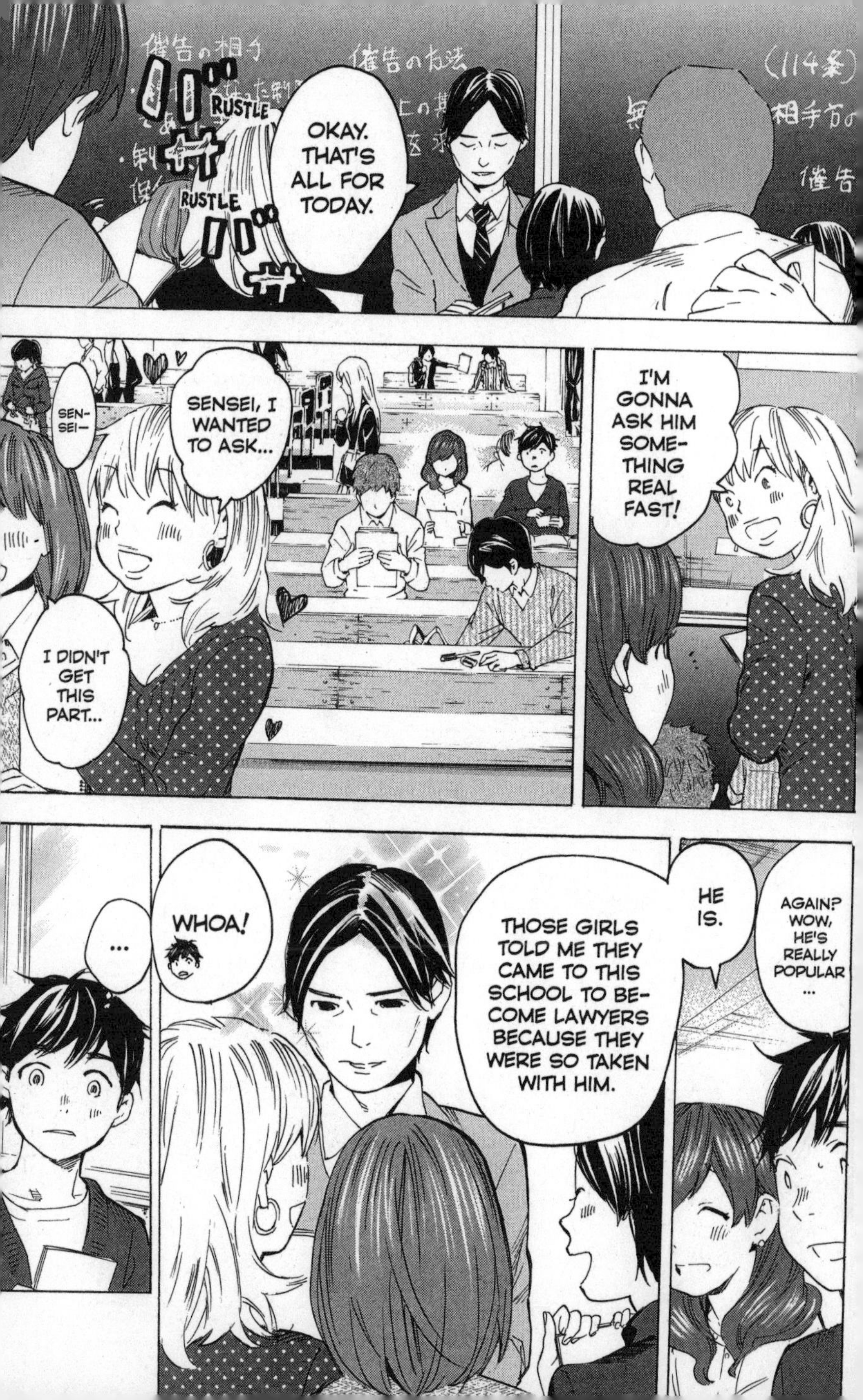
(114条)
催告の方法
OKAY. THAT'S ALL FOR TODAY.
RUSTLE
RUSTLE
I'M GONNA ASK HIM SOME-THING REAL FAST!
SENSEI, I WANTED TO ASK...
SEN-SEI—
I DIDN'T GET THIS PART...
AGAIN? WOW, HE'S REALLY POPULAR...
HE IS.
THOSE GIRLS TOLD ME THEY CAME TO THIS SCHOOL TO BE-COME LAWYERS BECAUSE THEY WERE SO TAKEN WITH HIM.
WHOA!
...

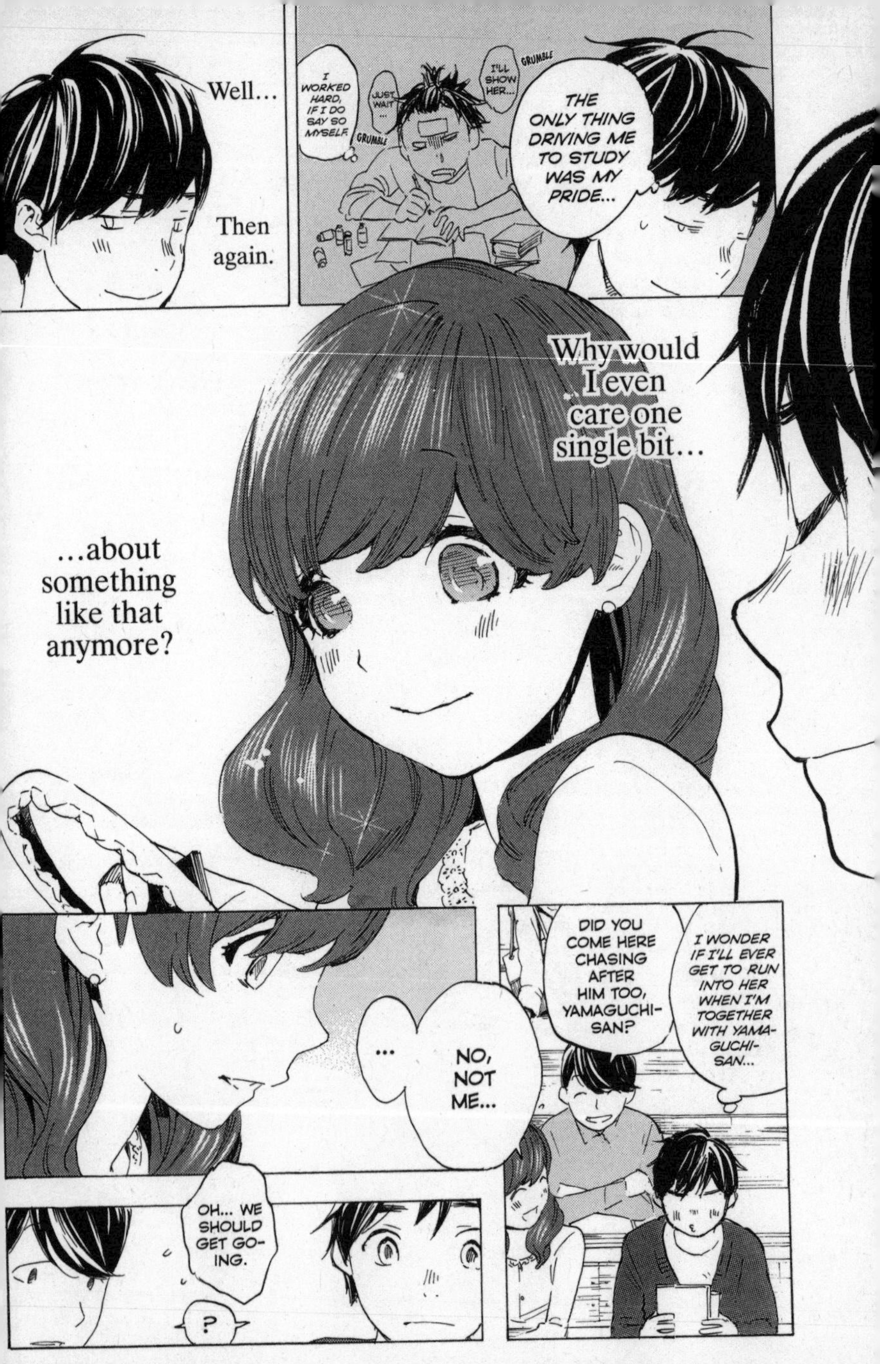
THE ONLY THING DRIVING ME TO STUDY WAS MY PRIDE...
GRUMBLE
I'LL SHOW HER...
JUST WAIT...
I WORKED HARD, IF I DO SAY SO MYSELF.
GRUMBLE
Well...
Then again.
Why would I even care one single bit...
...about something like that anymore?
I WONDER IF I'LL EVER GET TO RUN INTO HER WHEN I'M TOGETHER WITH YAMA-GUCHI-SAN...
DID YOU COME HERE CHASING AFTER HIM TOO, YAMAGUCHI-SAN?
NO, NOT ME...
...
OH... WE SHOULD GET GO-ING.
?

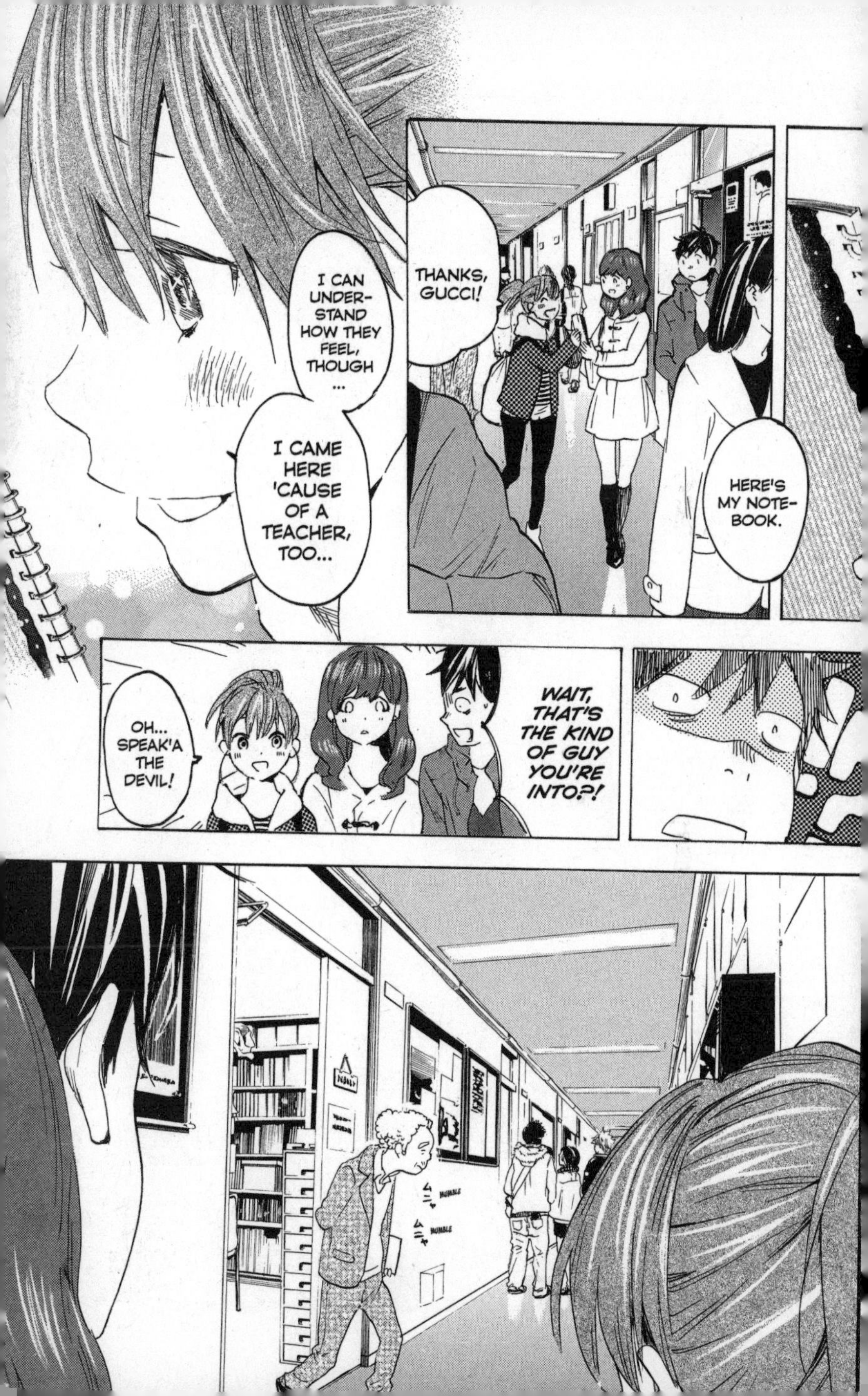
HERE'S MY NOTEBOOK.
THANKS, GUCCI!
I CAN UNDERSTAND HOW THEY FEEL, THOUGH...
I CAME HERE 'CAUSE OF A TEACHER, TOO...
WAIT, THAT'S THE KIND OF GUY YOU'RE INTO?!
OH... SPEAK'A THE DEVIL!
ムニャ MUMBLE
ムニャ MUMBLE

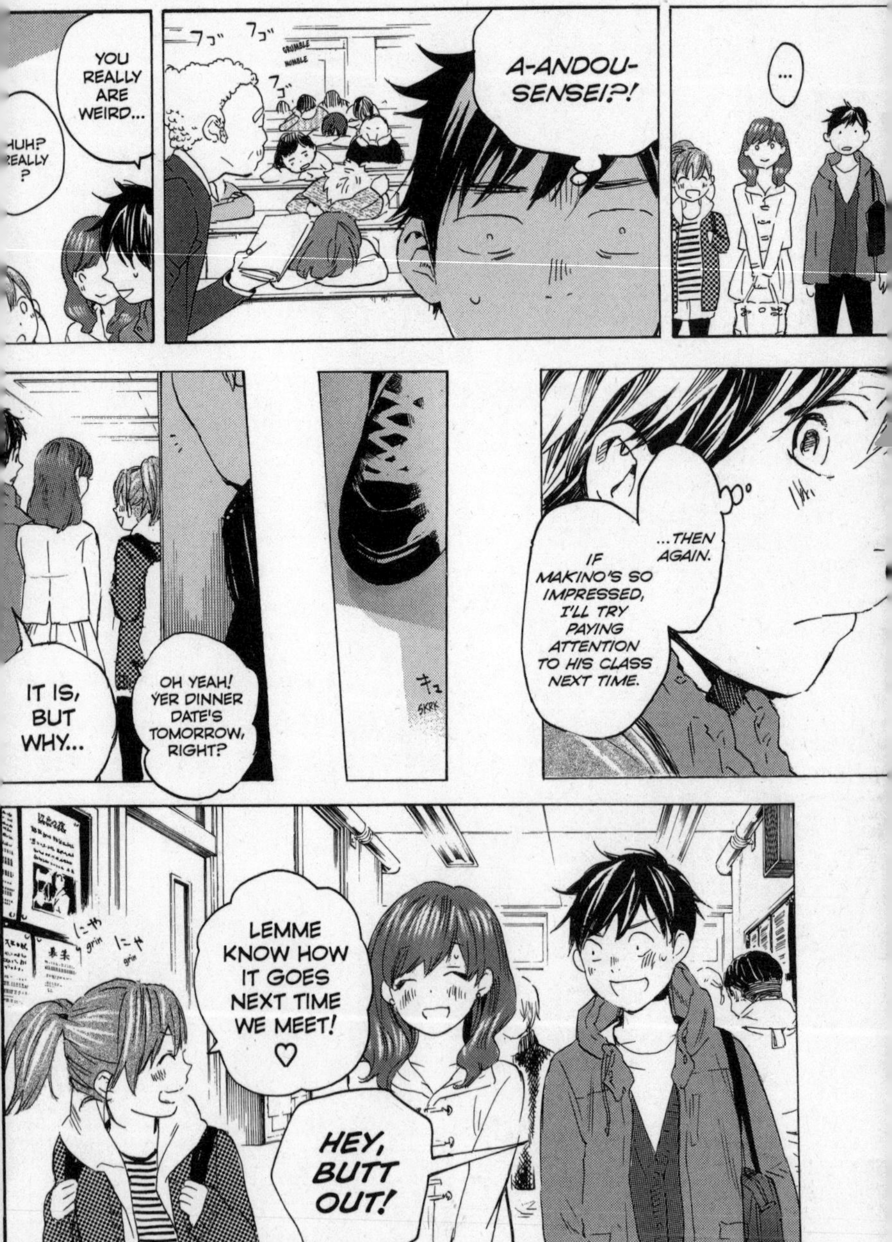
...
A-ANDOU-SENSEI?!
フゴ フゴ
GRUMBLE MUMBLE
フゴ
YOU REALLY ARE WEIRD...
HUH? EALLY ?
...THEN AGAIN.
IF MAKINO'S SO IMPRESSED, I'LL TRY PAYING ATTENTION TO HIS CLASS NEXT TIME.
キュ SKRK
OH YEAH! YER DINNER DATE'S TOMORROW, RIGHT?
IT IS, BUT WHY...
LEMME KNOW HOW IT GOES NEXT TIME WE MEET! ♡
にや grin
にや grin
HEY, BUTT OUT!

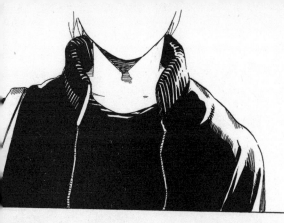

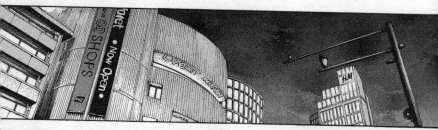

SHOPS
Now Open
DON'T WORRY, I JUST GOT HERE!
EH... MAYBE THE SUNGLASSES AREN'T A GOOD FIT AFTER ALL?
I MIGHT BE OVER-DOING IT A LITTLE WITH THESE...
I NEED TO START ACTING MORE LIKE THE KIND OF MAN YAMAGUCHI-SAN WANTS ME TO BE.
SORRY TO KEEP YOU WAITING.
OH...

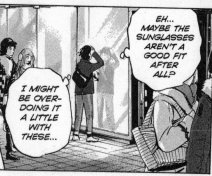

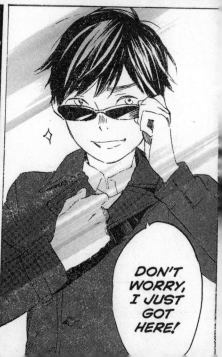

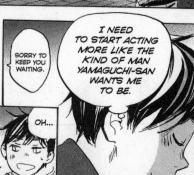

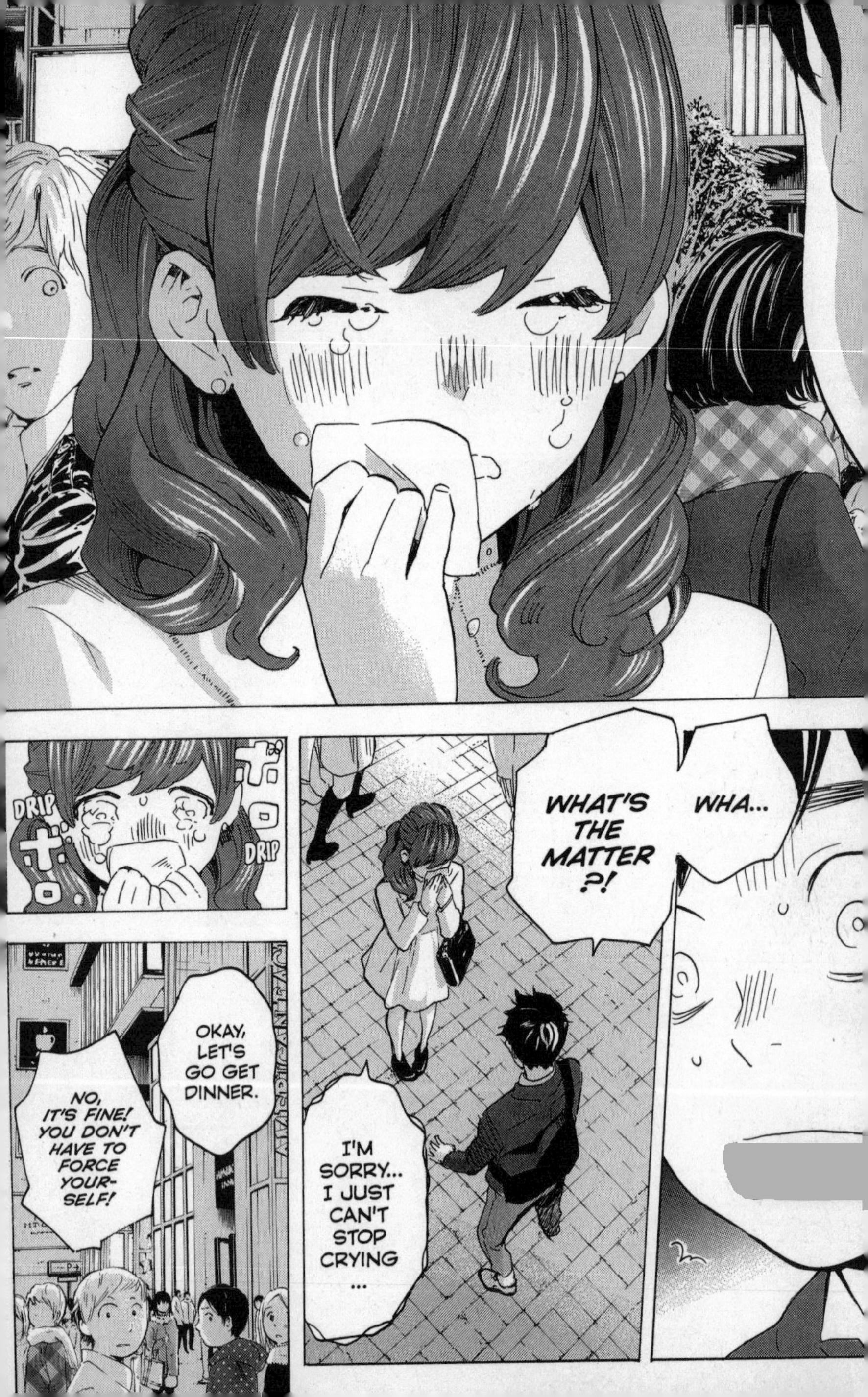
WHA...
WHAT'S THE MATTER ?!
I'M SORRY... I JUST CAN'T STOP CRYING ...
ポロ
DRIP
ポロ
DRIP
OKAY, LET'S GO GET DINNER.
NO, IT'S FINE! YOU DON'T HAVE TO FORCE YOUR-SELF!

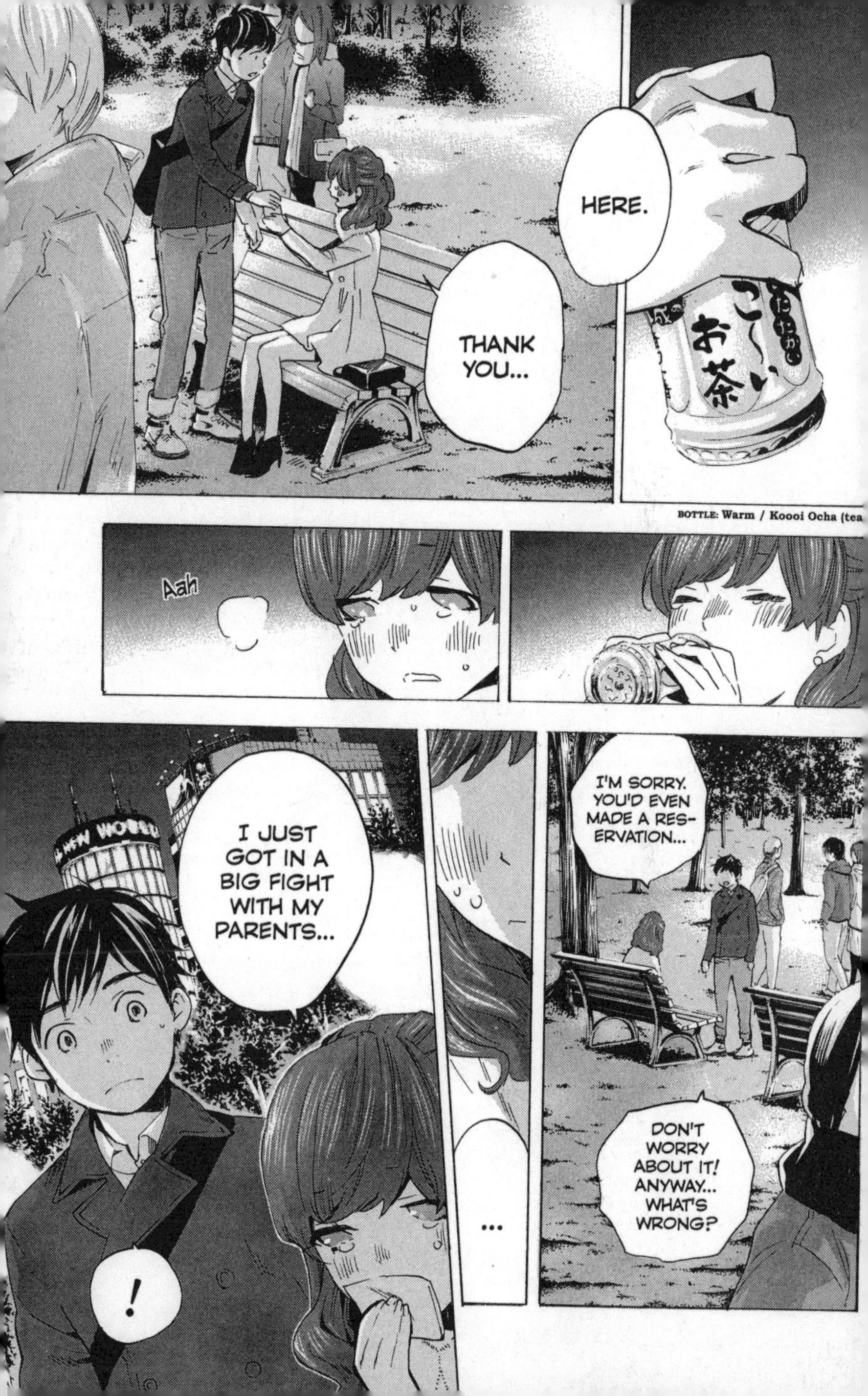
HERE.
THANK YOU...
BOTTLE: Warm / Koooi Ocha (tea
Aah
I'M SORRY. YOU'D EVEN MADE A RES-ERVATION...
DON'T WORRY ABOUT IT! ANYWAY... WHAT'S WRONG?
...
I JUST GOT IN A BIG FIGHT WITH MY PARENTS...
!

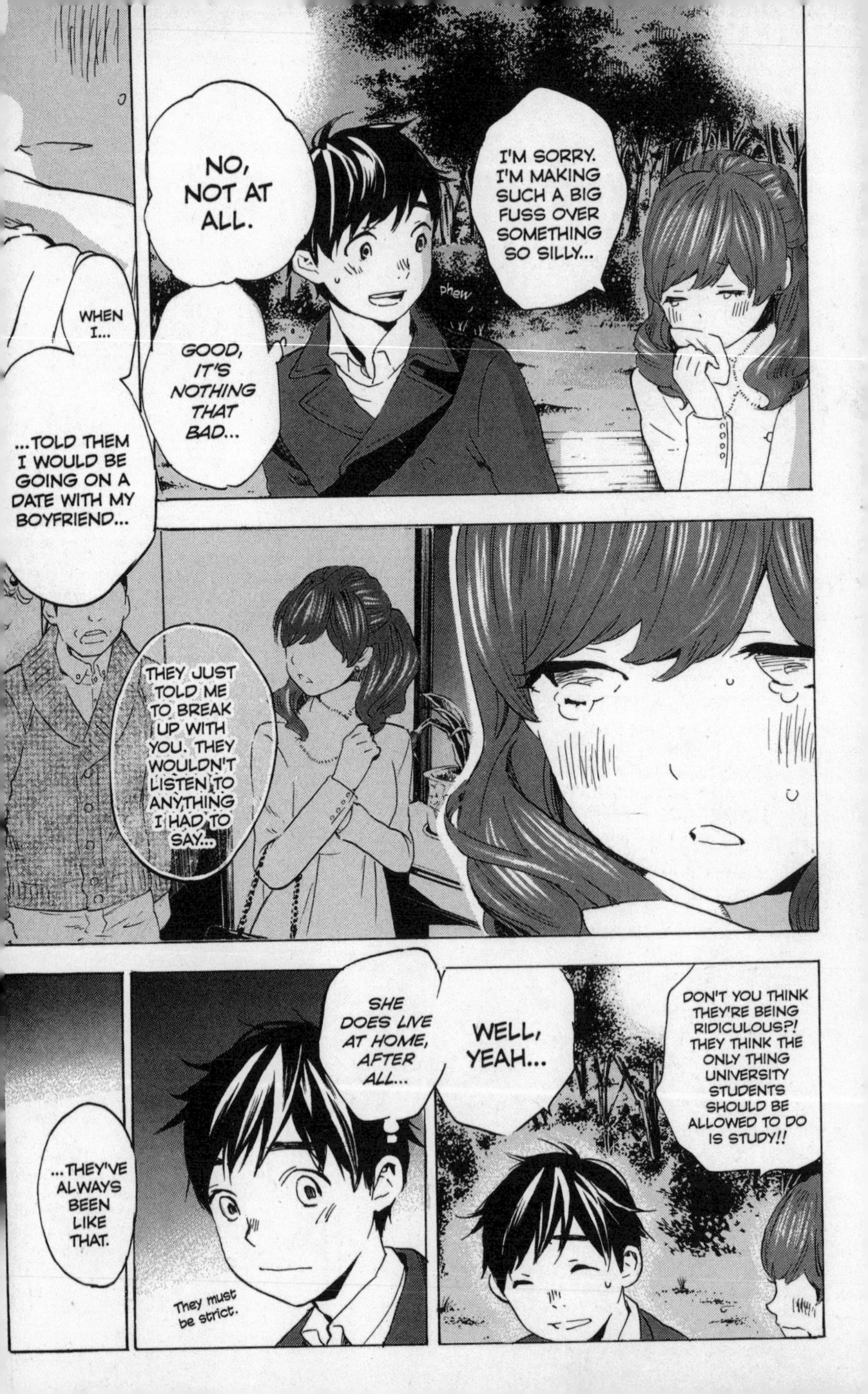
I'M SORRY. I'M MAKING SUCH A BIG FUSS OVER SOMETHING SO SILLY...
NO, NOT AT ALL.
phew
GOOD, IT'S NOTHING THAT BAD...
WHEN I...
...TOLD THEM I WOULD BE GOING ON A DATE WITH MY BOYFRIEND...
THEY JUST TOLD ME TO BREAK UP WITH YOU. THEY WOULDN'T LISTEN TO ANYTHING I HAD TO SAY...
DON'T YOU THINK THEY'RE BEING RIDICULOUS?! THEY THINK THE ONLY THING UNIVERSITY STUDENTS SHOULD BE ALLOWED TO DO IS STUDY!!
WELL, YEAH...
SHE DOES LIVE AT HOME, AFTER ALL...
They must be strict.
...THEY'VE ALWAYS BEEN LIKE THAT.

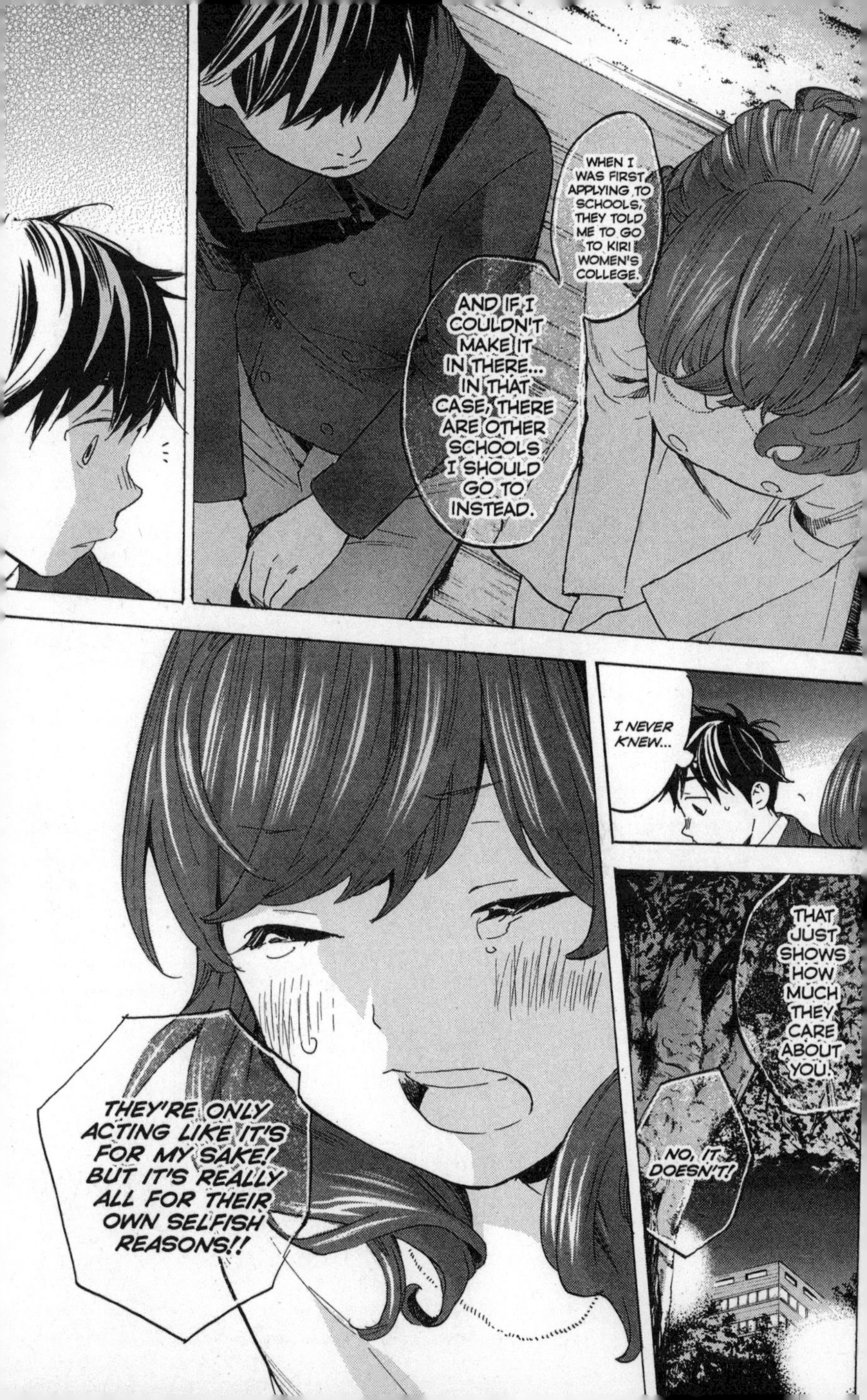
WHEN I WAS FIRST APPLYING TO SCHOOLS, THEY TOLD ME TO GO TO KIRI WOMEN'S COLLEGE.
AND IF I COULDN'T MAKE IT IN THERE... IN THAT CASE, THERE ARE OTHER SCHOOLS I SHOULD GO TO INSTEAD.
I NEVER KNEW...
THAT JUST SHOWS HOW MUCH THEY CARE ABOUT YOU.
NO, IT DOESN'T!
THEY'RE ONLY ACTING LIKE IT'S FOR MY SAKE! BUT IT'S REALLY ALL FOR THEIR OWN SELFISH REASONS!!

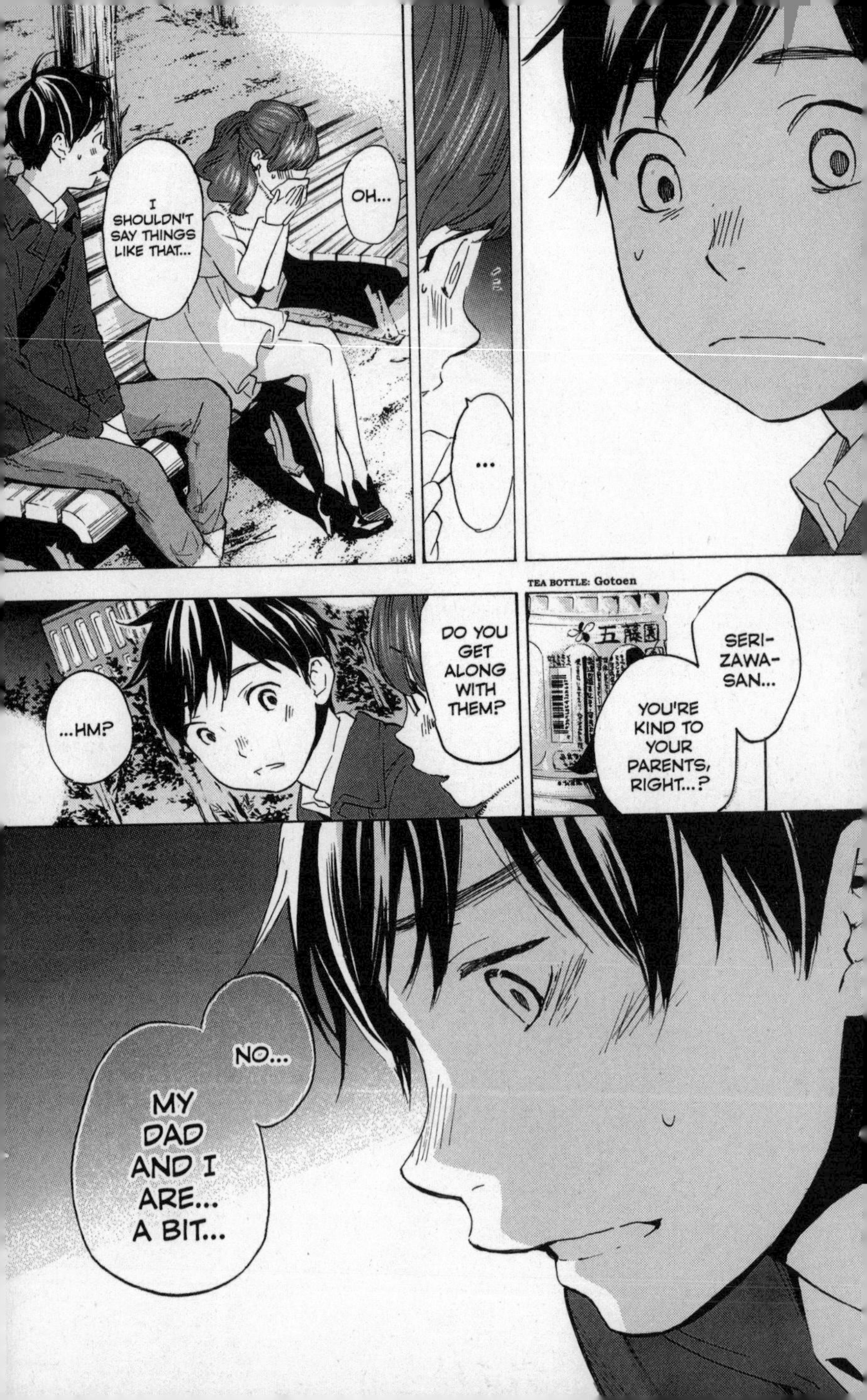
OH...
...
I SHOULDN'T SAY THINGS LIKE THAT...
TEA BOTTLE: Gotoen
SERI-ZAWA-SAN...
YOU'RE KIND TO YOUR PARENTS, RIGHT...?
DO YOU GET ALONG WITH THEM?
...HM?
NO...
MY DAD AND I ARE... A BIT...

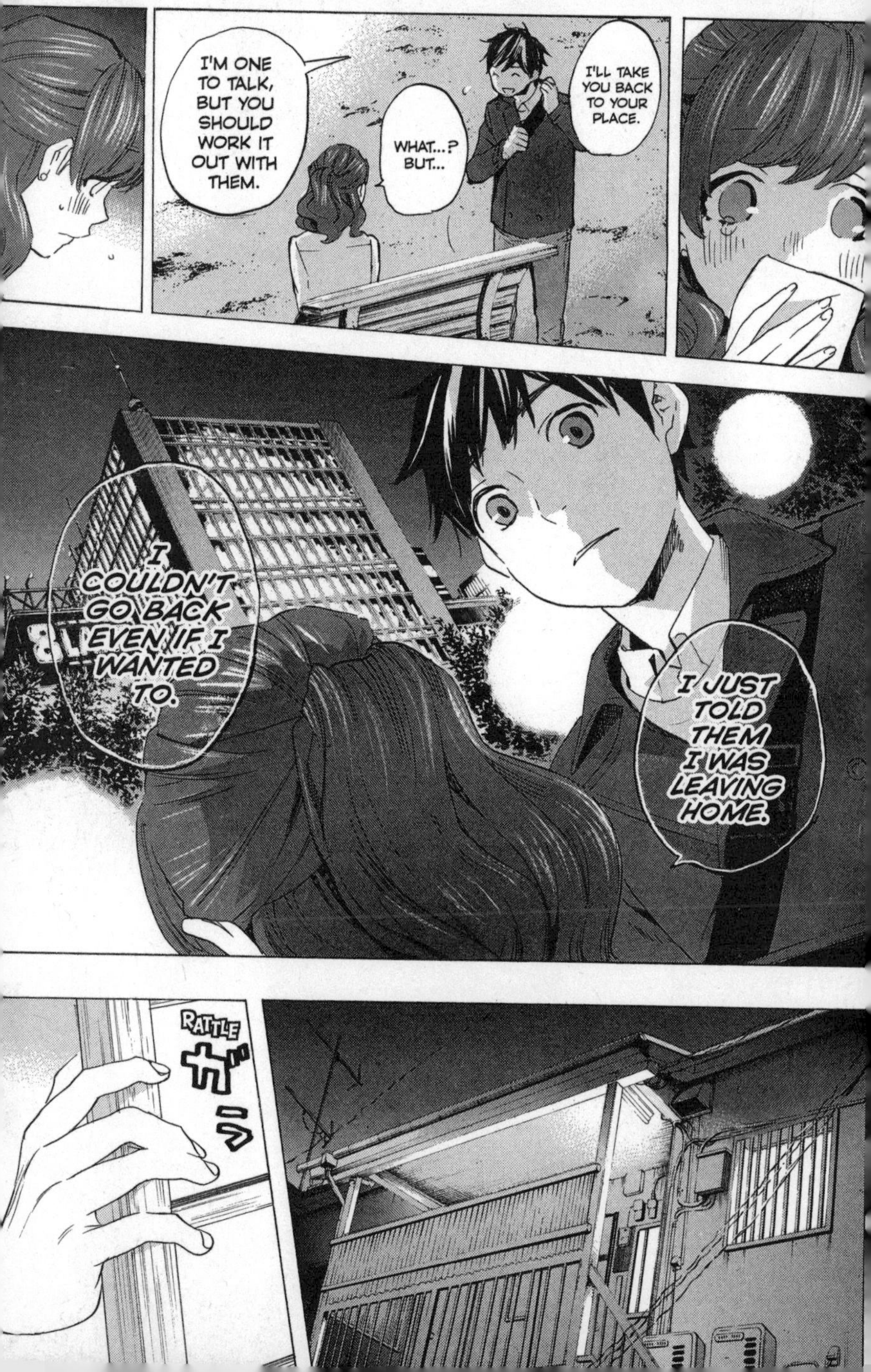
I'LL TAKE YOU BACK TO YOUR PLACE.
WHAT...? BUT...
I'M ONE TO TALK, BUT YOU SHOULD WORK IT OUT WITH THEM.
I JUST TOLD THEM I WAS LEAVING HOME.
I COULDN'T GO BACK EVEN IF I WANTED TO.
RATTLE
ガラ

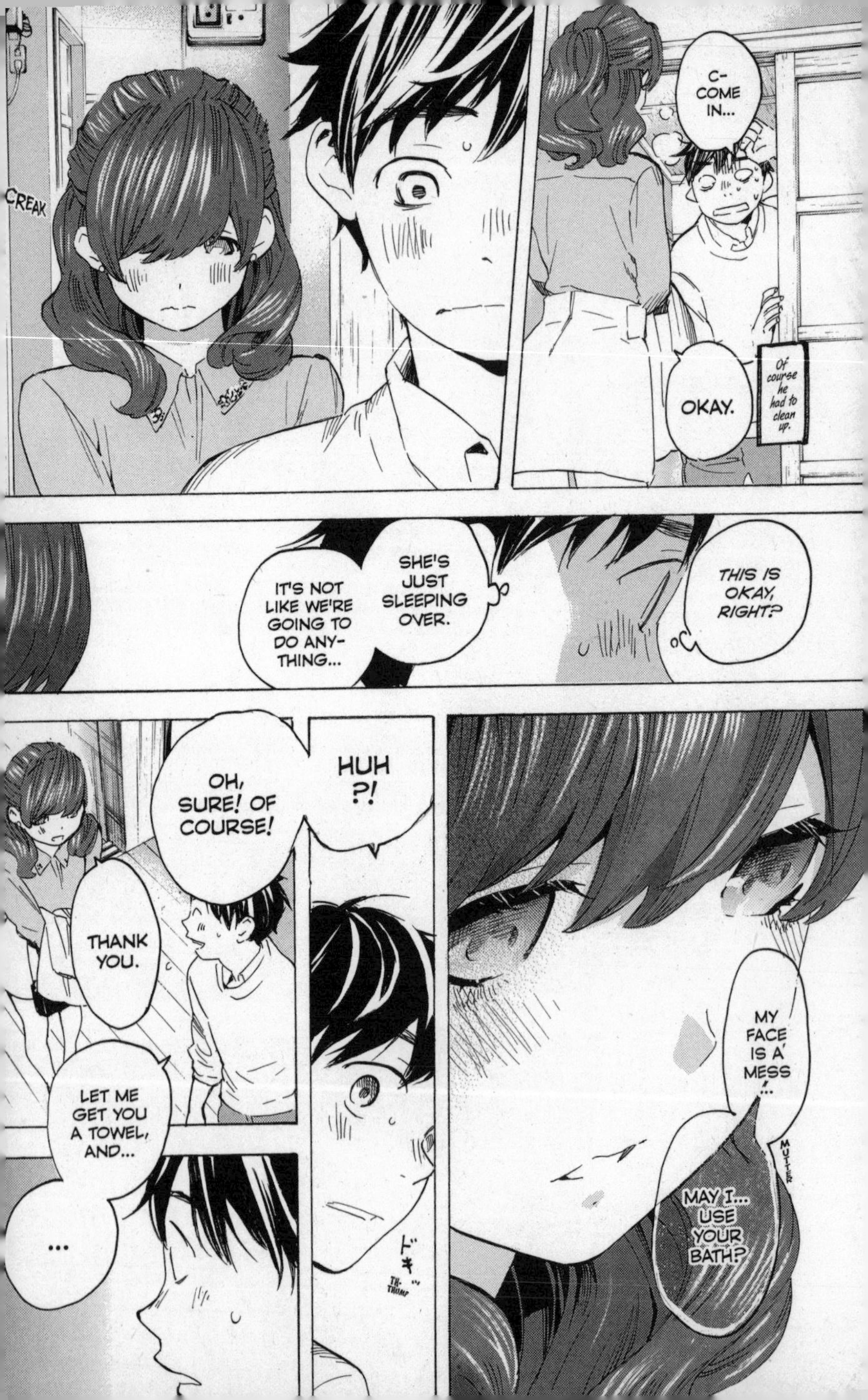
C-COME IN...
OKAY.
Of course he had to clean up.
CREAK
THIS IS OKAY, RIGHT?
SHE'S JUST SLEEPING OVER.
IT'S NOT LIKE WE'RE GOING TO DO ANYTHING...
MY FACE IS A MESS...
MUTTER
MAY I... USE YOUR BATH?
HUH?!
ドキッ
TH-THUMP
OH, SURE! OF COURSE!
THANK YOU.
LET ME GET YOU A TOWEL, AND...
...

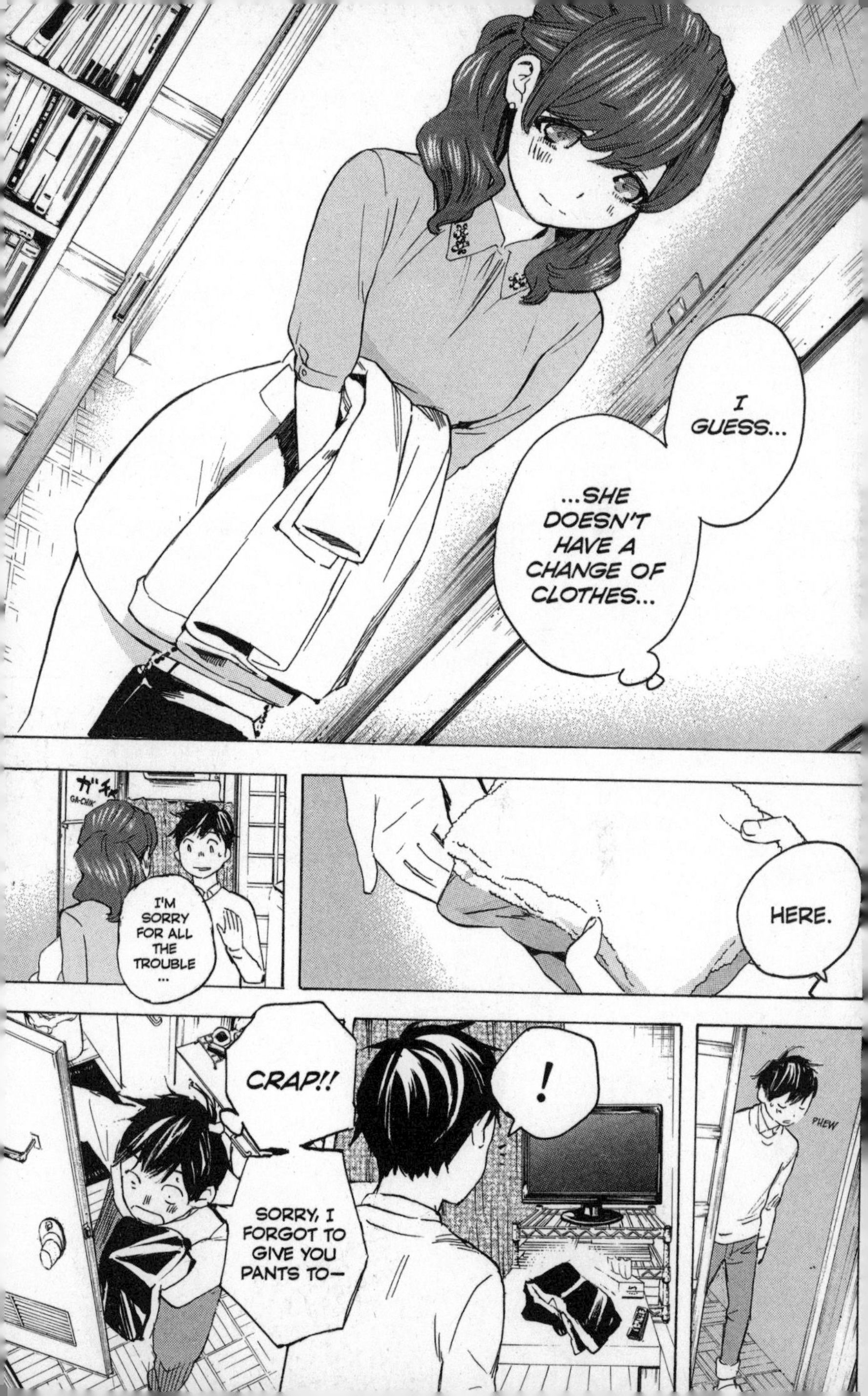
I GUESS...
...SHE DOESN'T HAVE A CHANGE OF CLOTHES...
HERE.
GA-CHIK
I'M SORRY FOR ALL THE TROUBLE ...
PHEW
!
CRAP!!
SORRY, I FORGOT TO GIVE YOU PANTS TO—

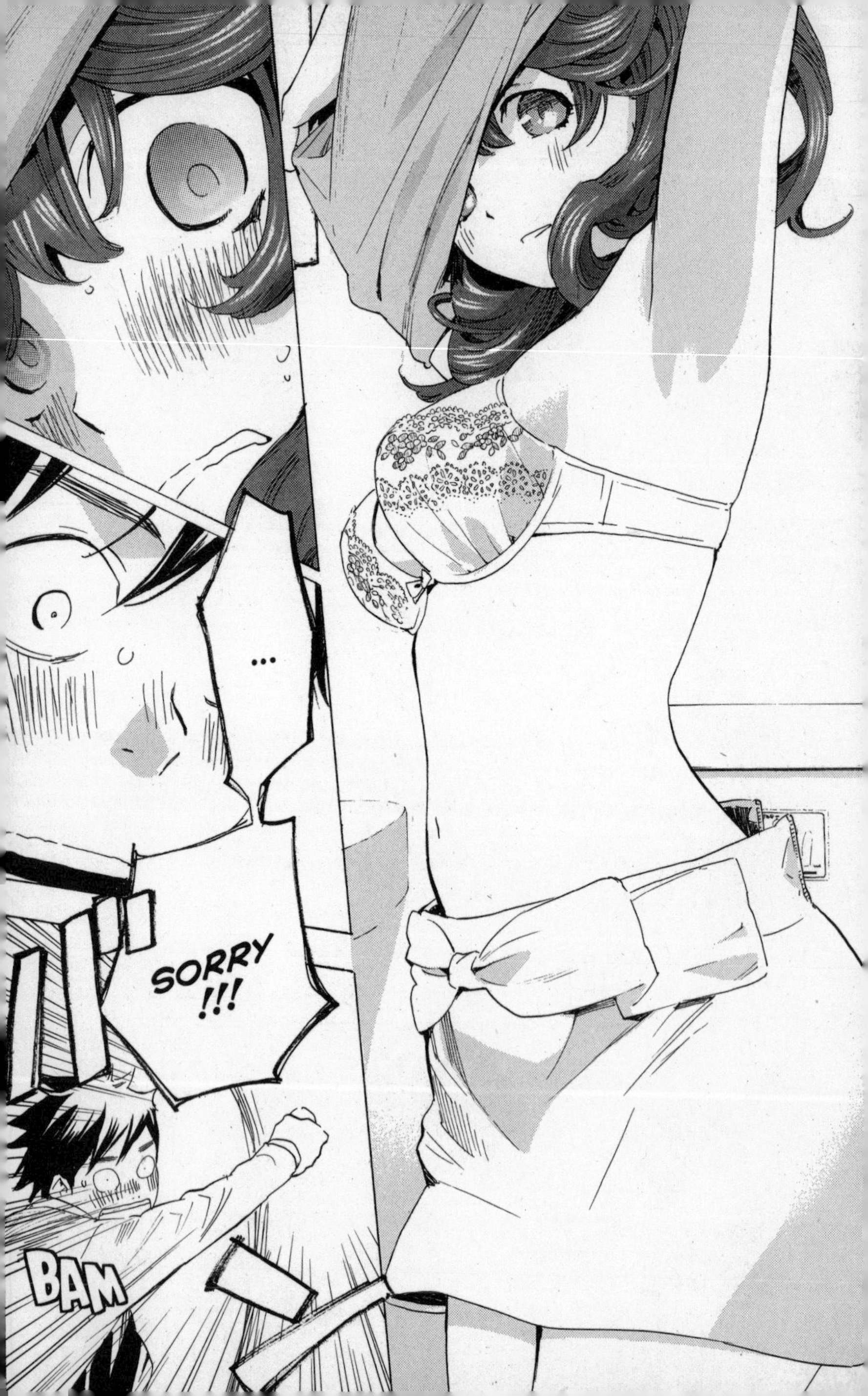
...
SORRY !!!
BAM

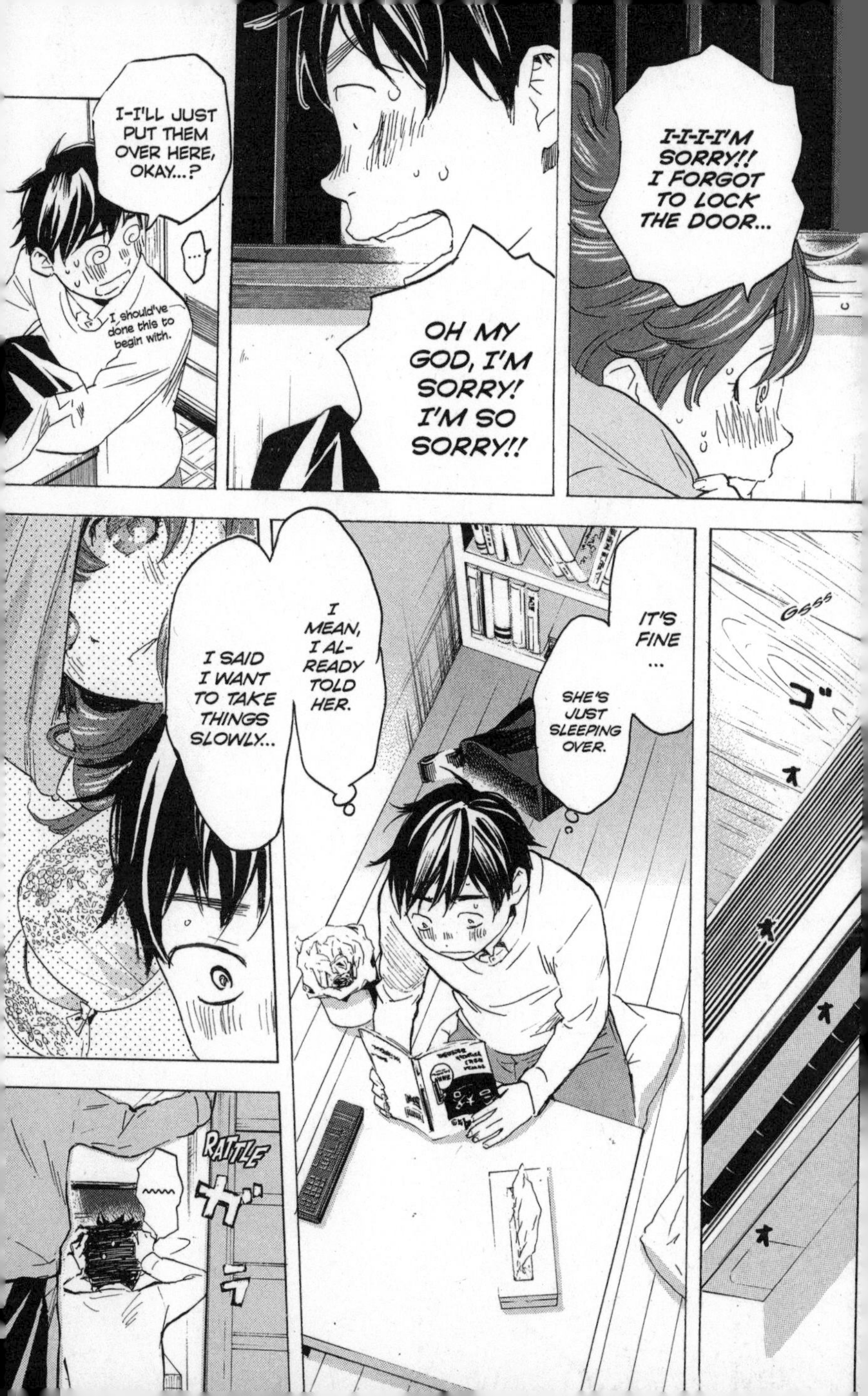
I-I-I-I'M SORRY!! I FORGOT TO LOCK THE DOOR...
OH MY GOD, I'M SORRY! I'M SO SORRY!!
I-I'LL JUST PUT THEM OVER HERE, OKAY...?
...
I should've done this to begin with.
Gsss
ゴ
IT'S FINE ...
SHE'S JUST SLEEPING OVER.
I MEAN, I ALREADY TOLD HER.
I SAID I WANT TO TAKE THINGS SLOWLY...
RATTLE
ガ
ラ

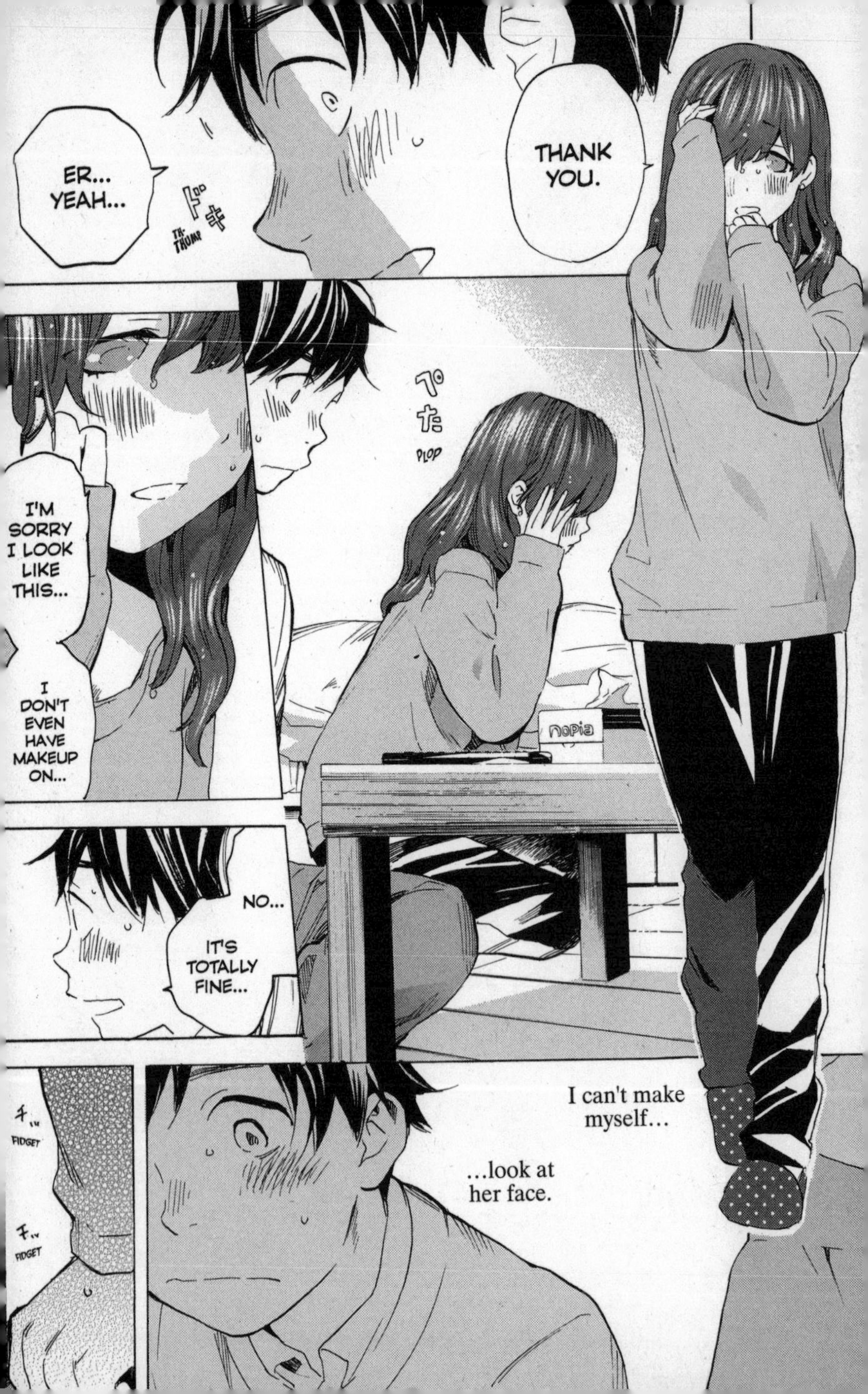
THANK YOU.
ER... YEAH...
ドキ
TH-THUMP
ペた
PLOP
I'M SORRY I LOOK LIKE THIS...
I DON'T EVEN HAVE MAKEUP ON...
NO...
IT'S TOTALLY FINE...
I can't make myself…
…look at her face.
FIDGET
FIDGET

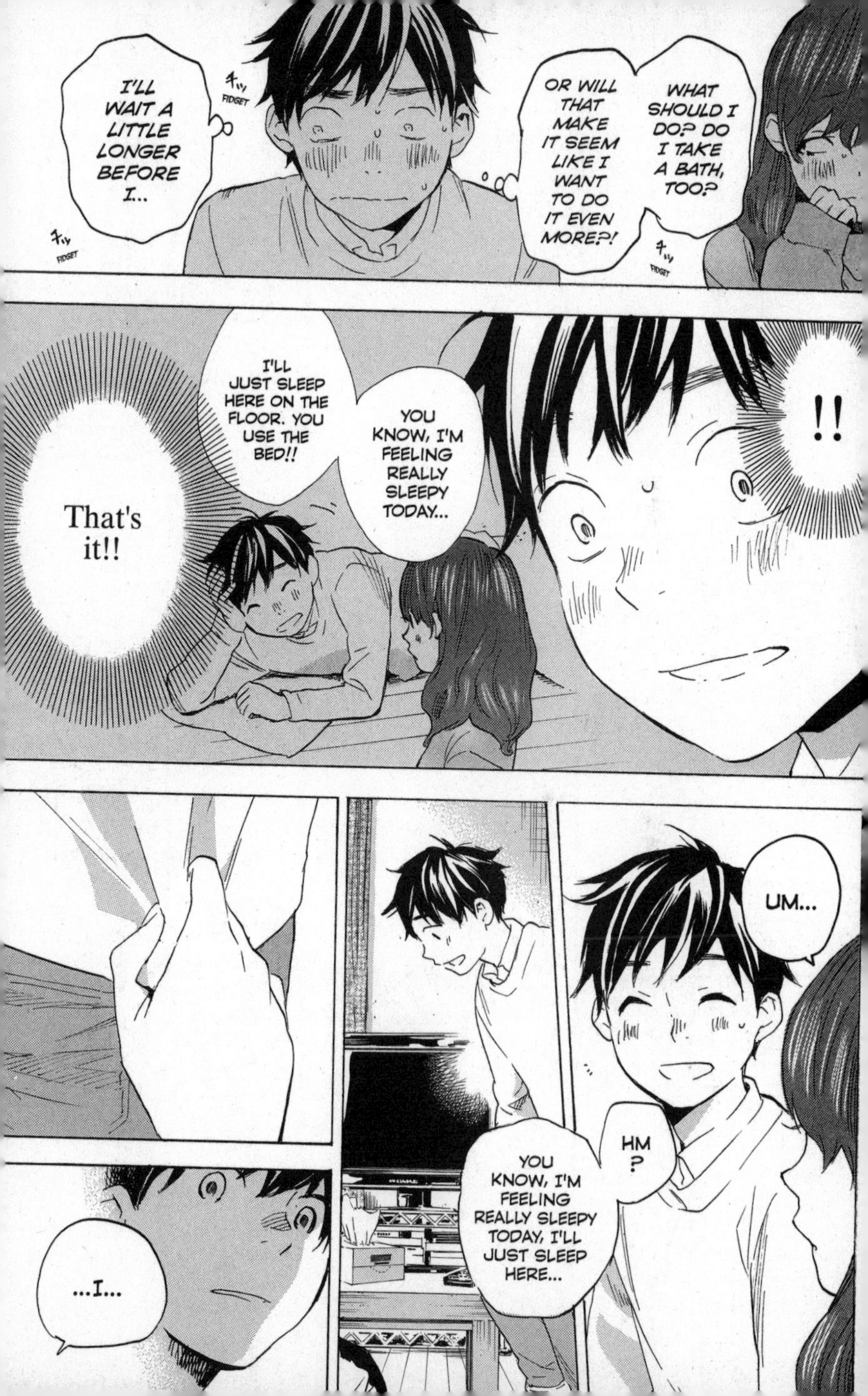
WHAT SHOULD I DO? DO I TAKE A BATH, TOO?
OR WILL THAT MAKE IT SEEM LIKE I WANT TO DO IT EVEN MORE?!
FIDGET
I'LL WAIT A LITTLE LONGER BEFORE I...
FIDGET
FIDGET
!!
YOU KNOW, I'M FEELING REALLY SLEEPY TODAY...
I'LL JUST SLEEP HERE ON THE FLOOR. YOU USE THE BED!!
That's it!!
UM...
HM?
YOU KNOW, I'M FEELING REALLY SLEEPY TODAY, I'LL JUST SLEEP HERE...
...I...

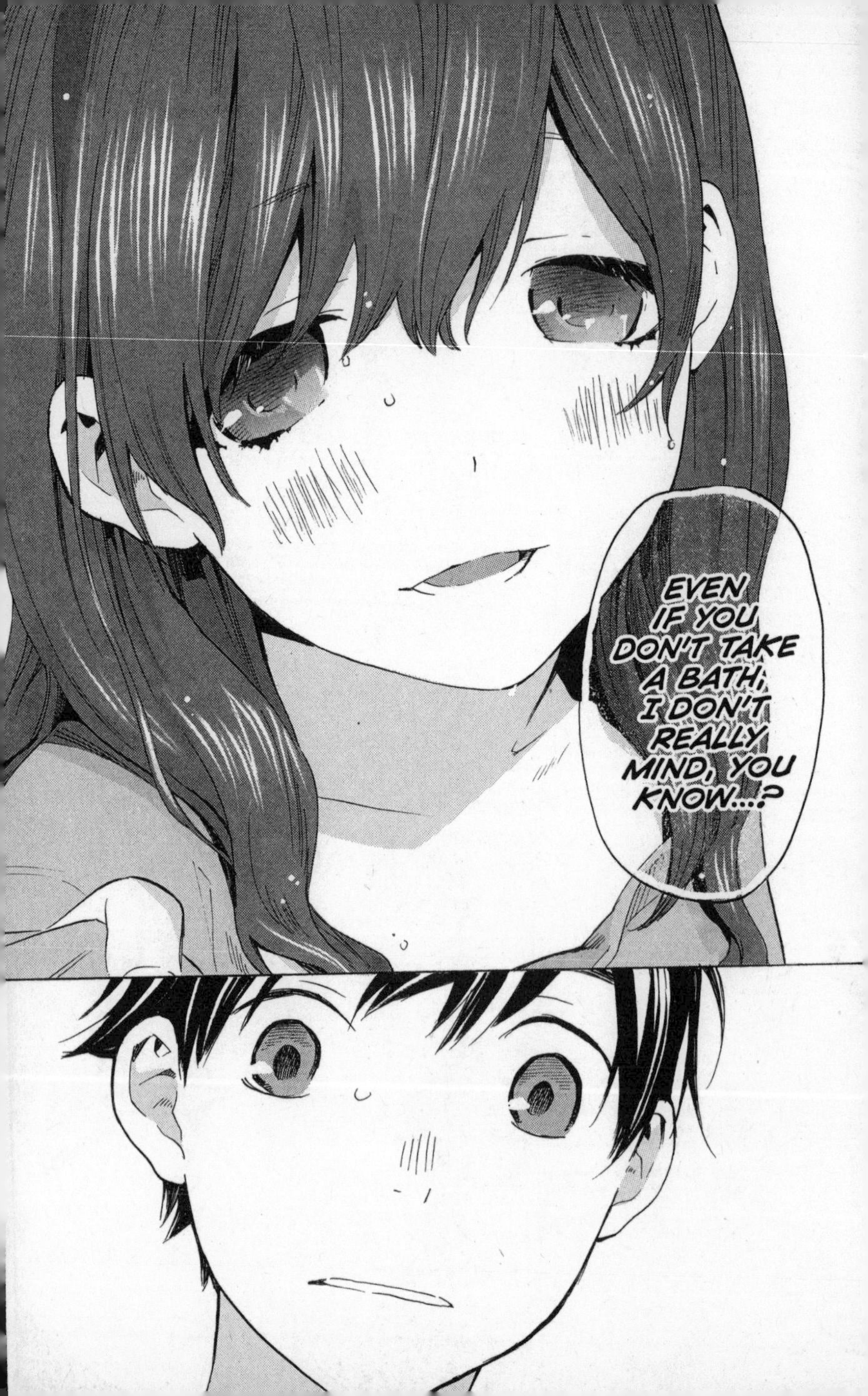
EVEN IF YOU DON'T TAKE A BATH, I DON'T REALLY MIND, YOU KNOW...?

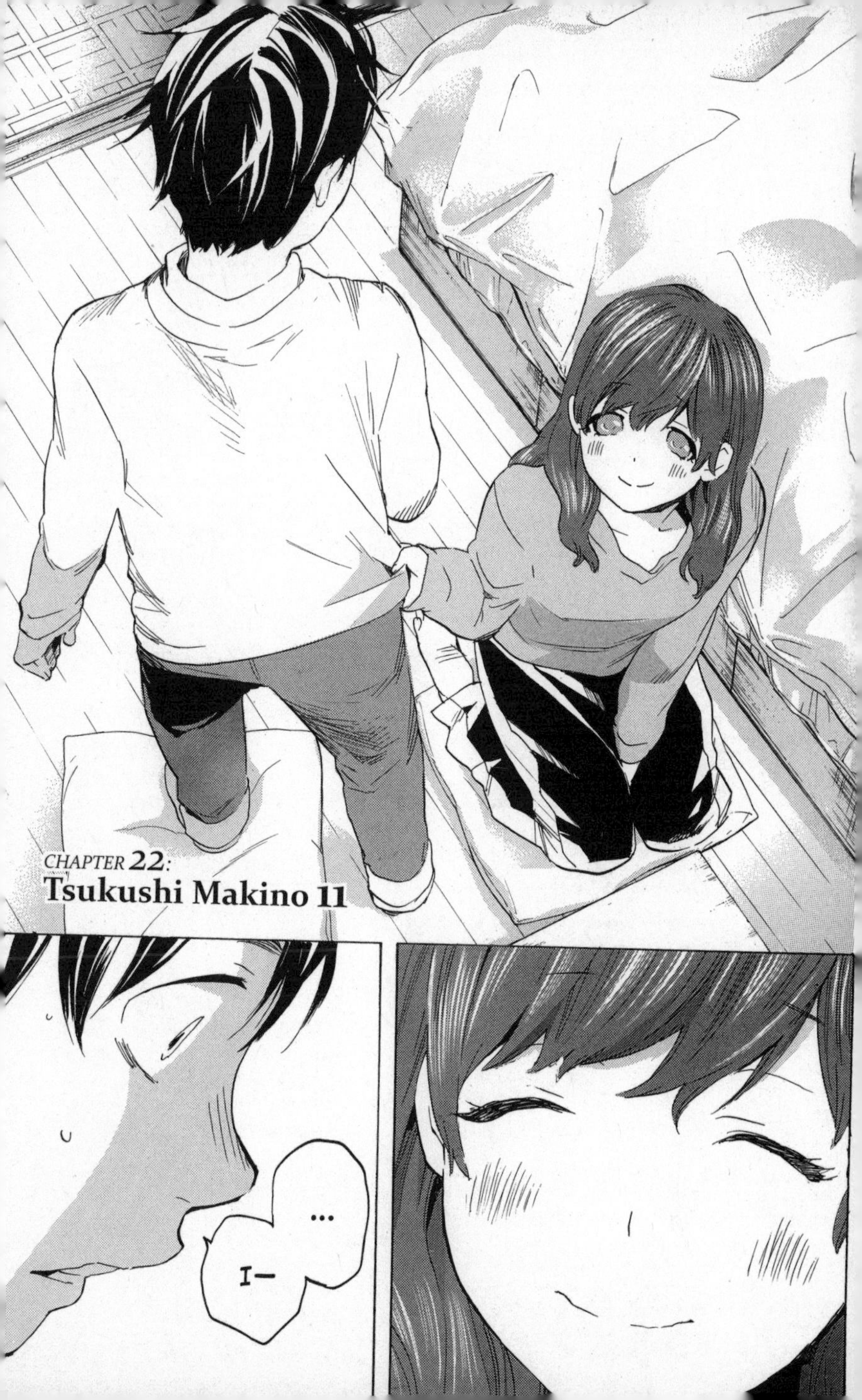
CHAPTER 22:
Tsukushi Makino 11
...
I—

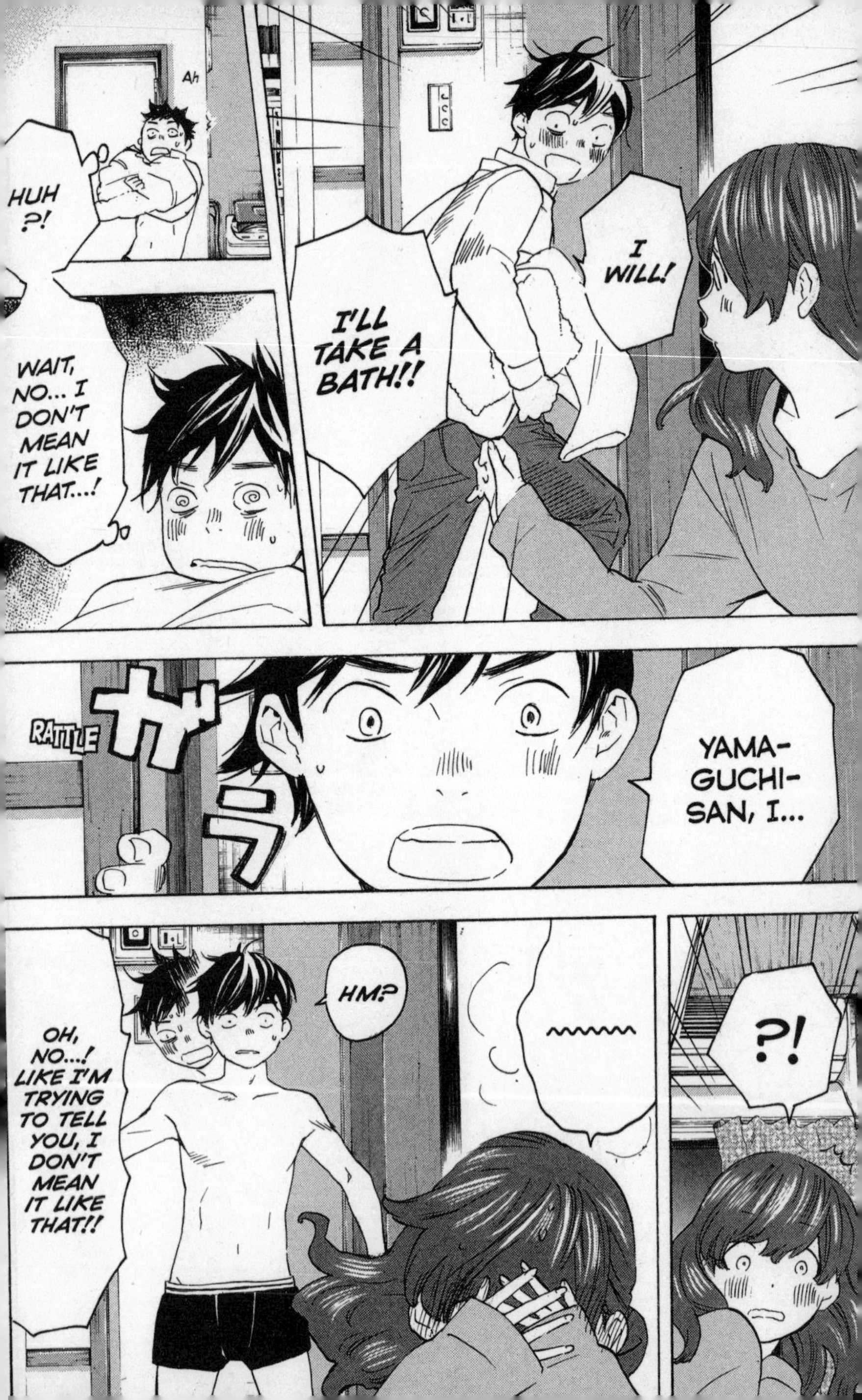
I WILL!
I'LL TAKE A BATH!!
Ah
HUH ?!
WAIT, NO... I DON'T MEAN IT LIKE THAT...!
YAMA-GUCHI-SAN, I...
RATTLE
?!
~~~~~
HM?
OH, NO...! LIKE I'M TRYING TO TELL YOU, I DON'T MEAN IT LIKE THAT!!
~~~~~

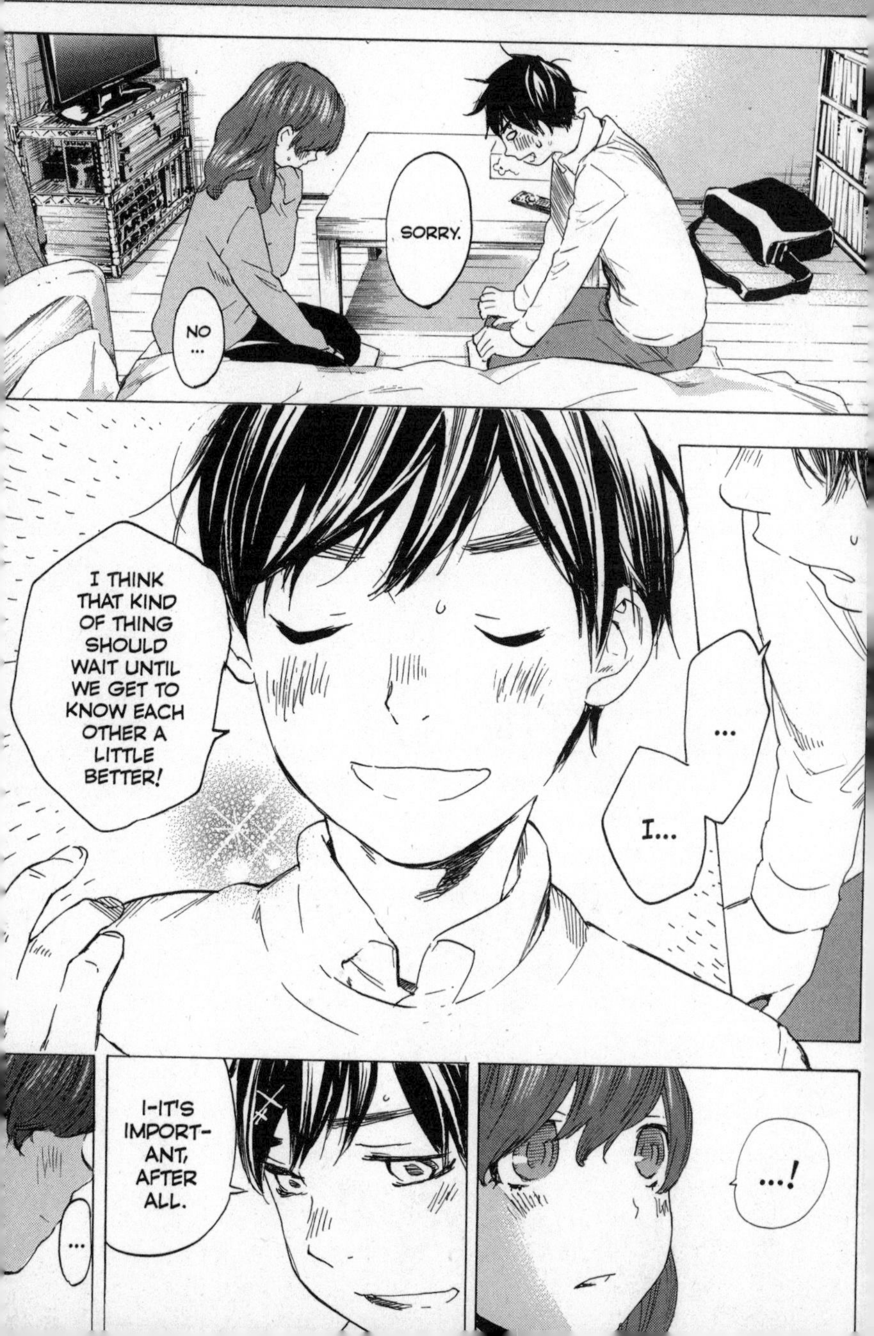
SORRY.
NO ...
...
I...
I THINK THAT KIND OF THING SHOULD WAIT UNTIL WE GET TO KNOW EACH OTHER A LITTLE BETTER!
...!
I-IT'S IMPORT-ANT, AFTER ALL.
...

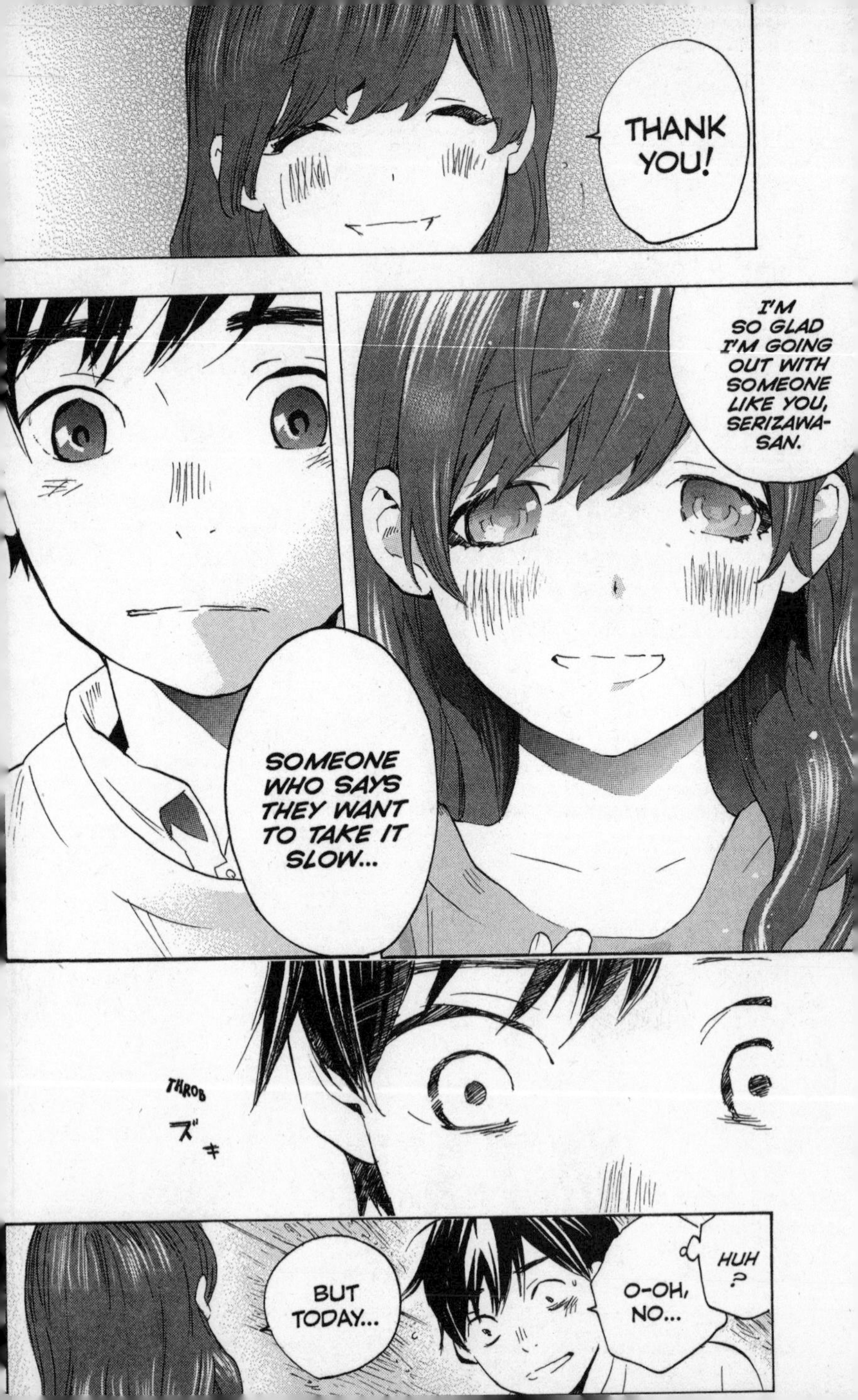
THANK YOU!
I'M SO GLAD I'M GOING OUT WITH SOMEONE LIKE YOU, SERIZAWA-SAN.
SOMEONE WHO SAYS THEY WANT TO TAKE IT SLOW...
THROB
ズキ
HUH?
O-OH, NO...
BUT TODAY...

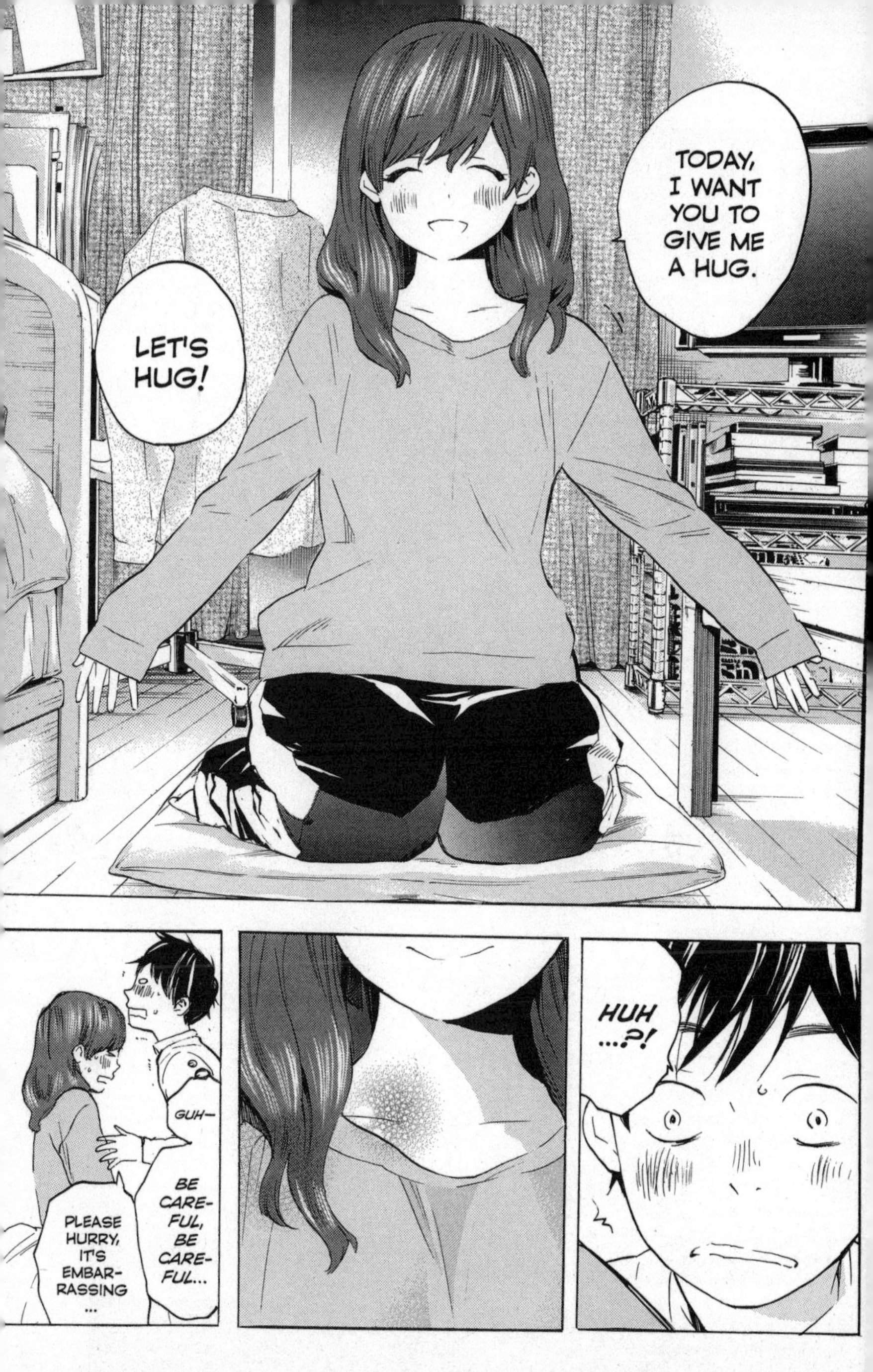
TODAY, I WANT YOU TO GIVE ME A HUG.
LET'S HUG!
HUH ...?!
GUH—
BE CARE-FUL, BE CARE-FUL...
PLEASE HURRY, IT'S EMBAR-RASSING ...

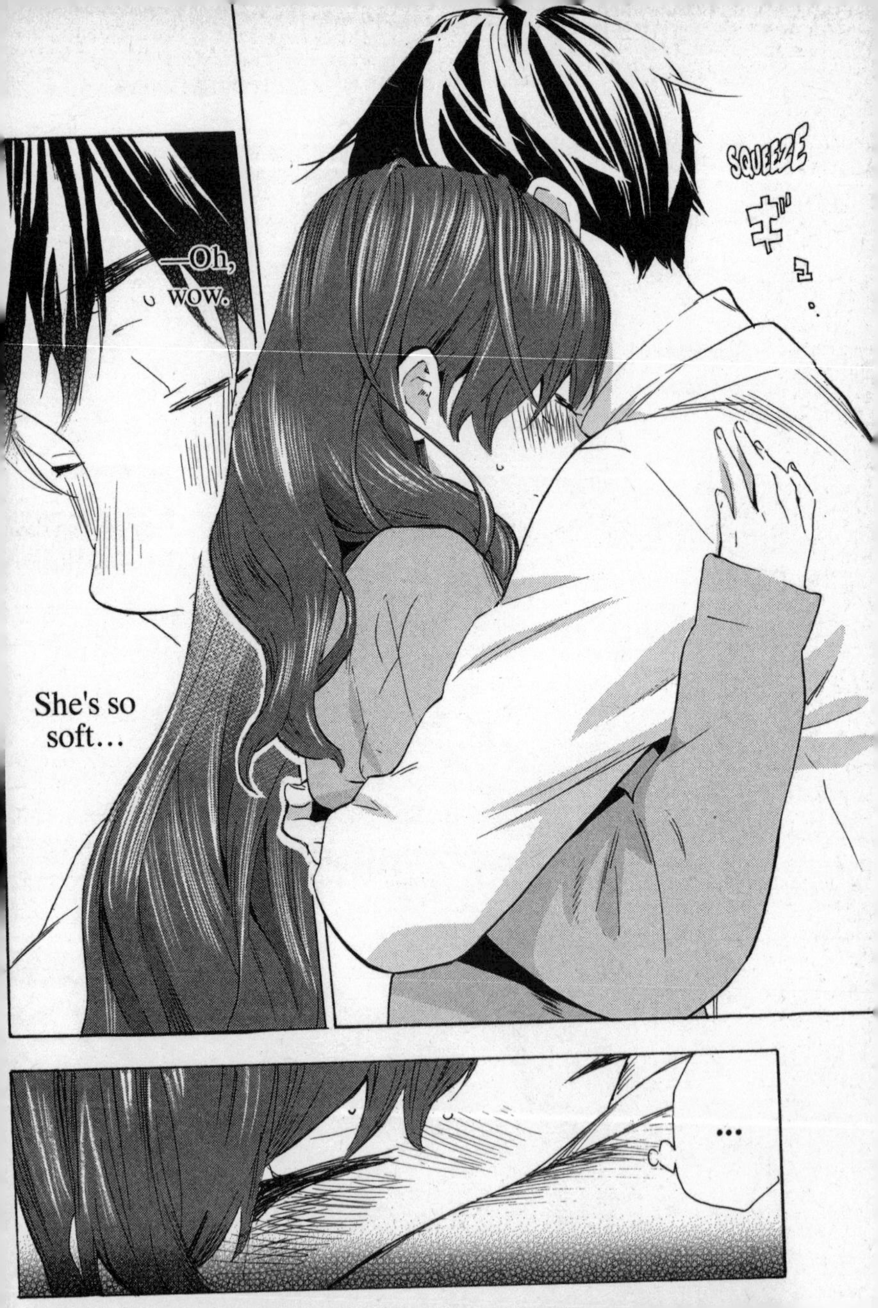
SQUEEZE
ギュ
—Oh, wow.
She's so soft…
…

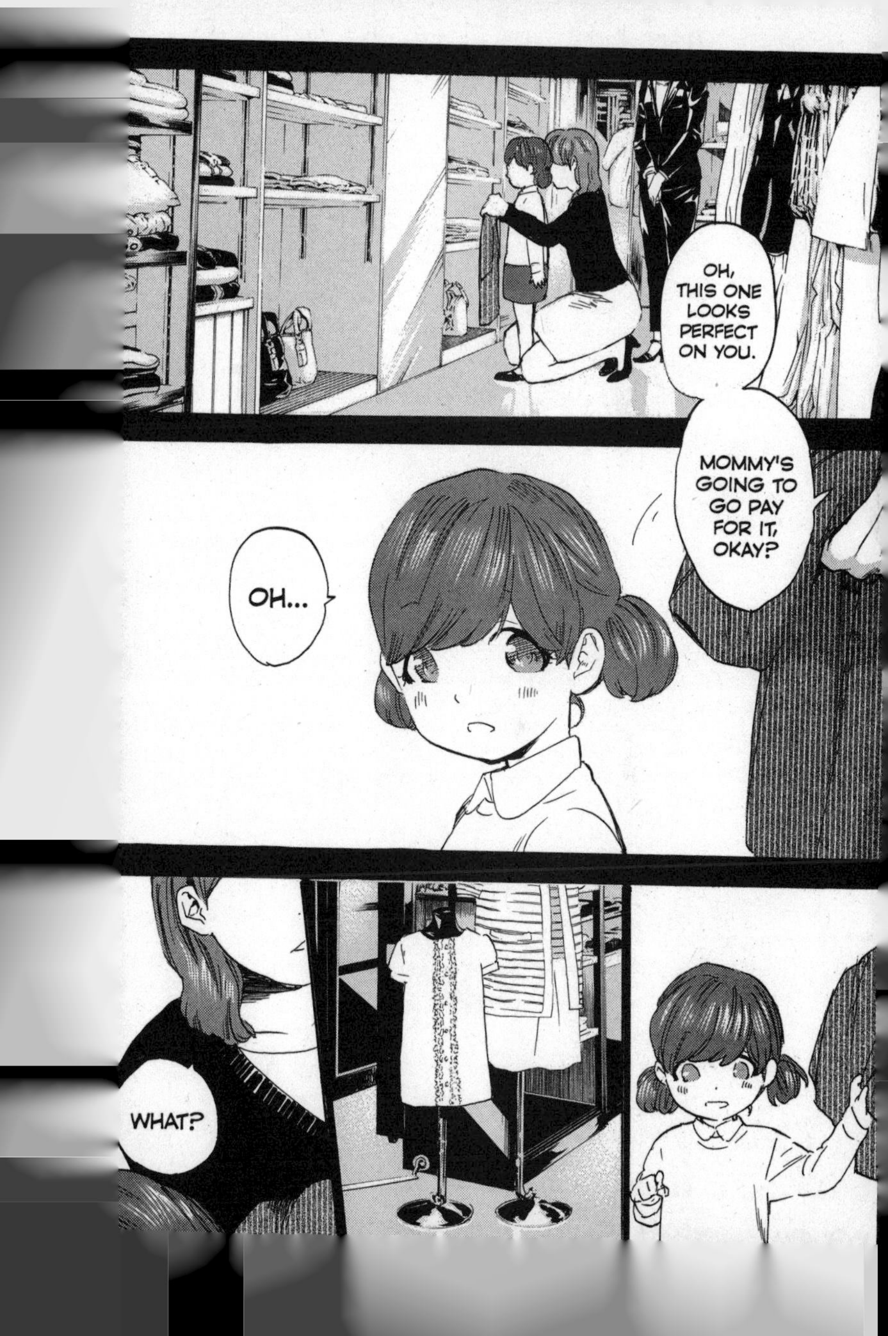
OH, THIS ONE LOOKS PERFECT ON YOU.
MOMMY'S GOING TO GO PAY FOR IT, OKAY?
OH...
WHAT?

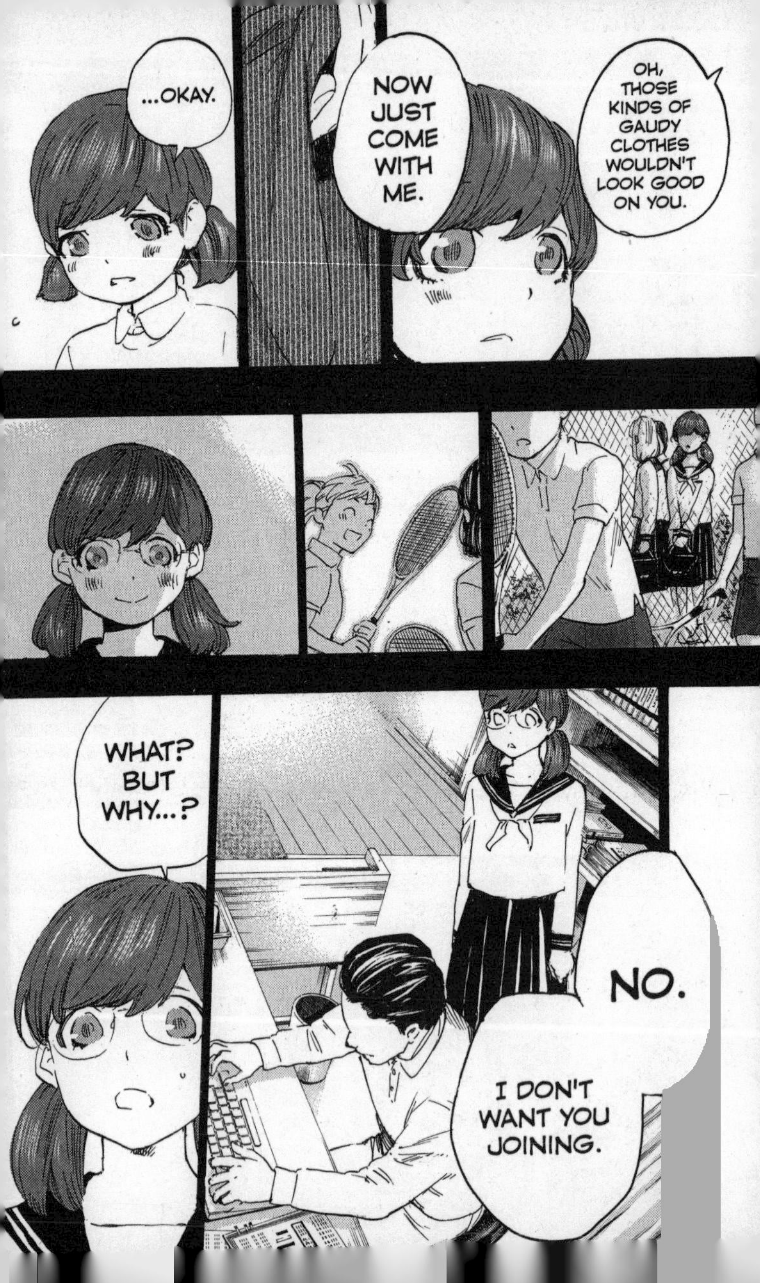
OH, THOSE KINDS OF GAUDY CLOTHES WOULDN'T LOOK GOOD ON YOU.
NOW JUST COME WITH ME.
...OKAY.
NO.
I DON'T WANT YOU JOINING.
WHAT? BUT WHY...?

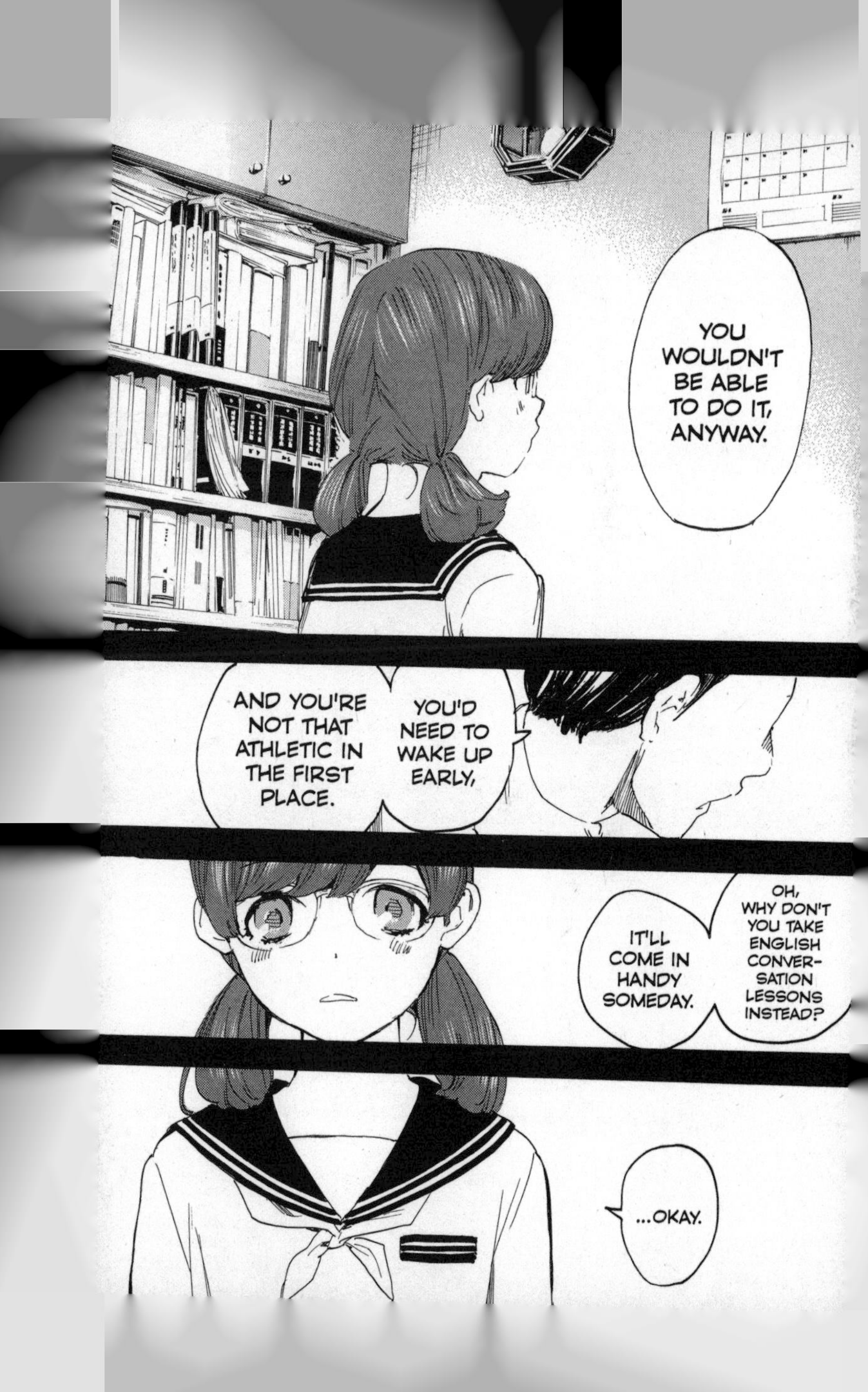
YOU WOULDN'T BE ABLE TO DO IT, ANYWAY.
YOU'D NEED TO WAKE UP EARLY,
AND YOU'RE NOT THAT ATHLETIC IN THE FIRST PLACE.
OH, WHY DON'T YOU TAKE ENGLISH CONVERSATION LESSONS INSTEAD?
IT'LL COME IN HANDY SOMEDAY.
...OKAY.

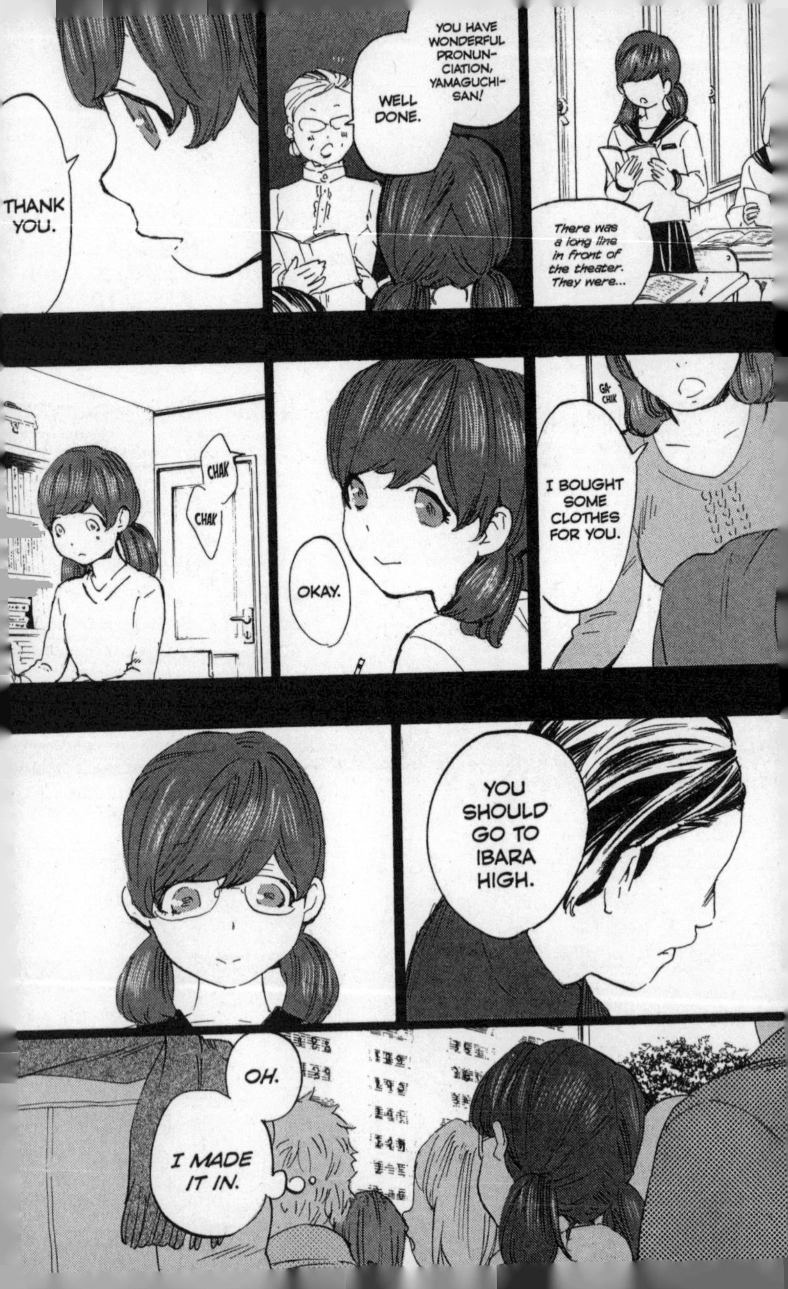
There was a long line in front of the theater. They were...
YOU HAVE WONDERFUL PRONUN-CIATION, YAMAGUCHI-SAN!
WELL DONE.
THANK YOU.
GA-CHIK
I BOUGHT SOME CLOTHES FOR YOU.
OKAY.
CHAK
CHAK
YOU SHOULD GO TO IBARA HIGH.
OH.
I MADE IT IN.

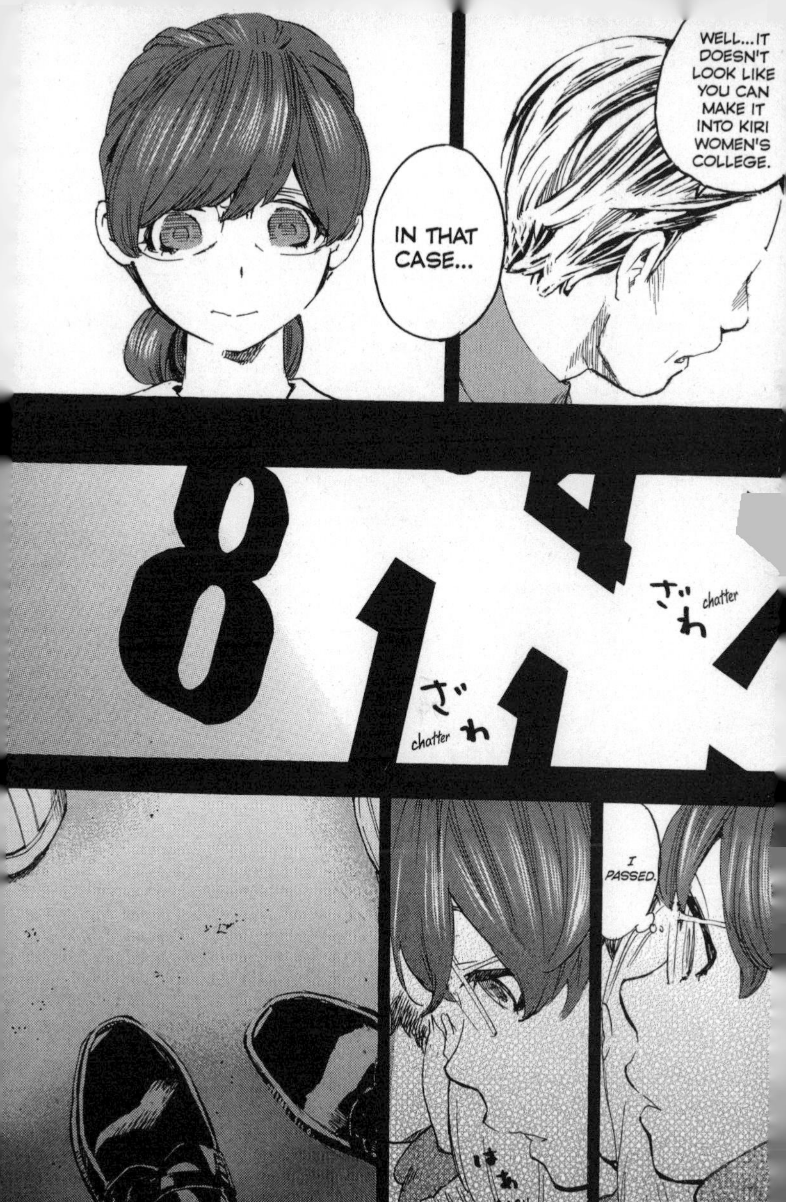
WELL...IT DOESN'T LOOK LIKE YOU CAN MAKE IT INTO KIRI WOMEN'S COLLEGE.
IN THAT CASE...
ざわ chatter
ざわ chatter
I PASSED.
はぁ SIGH

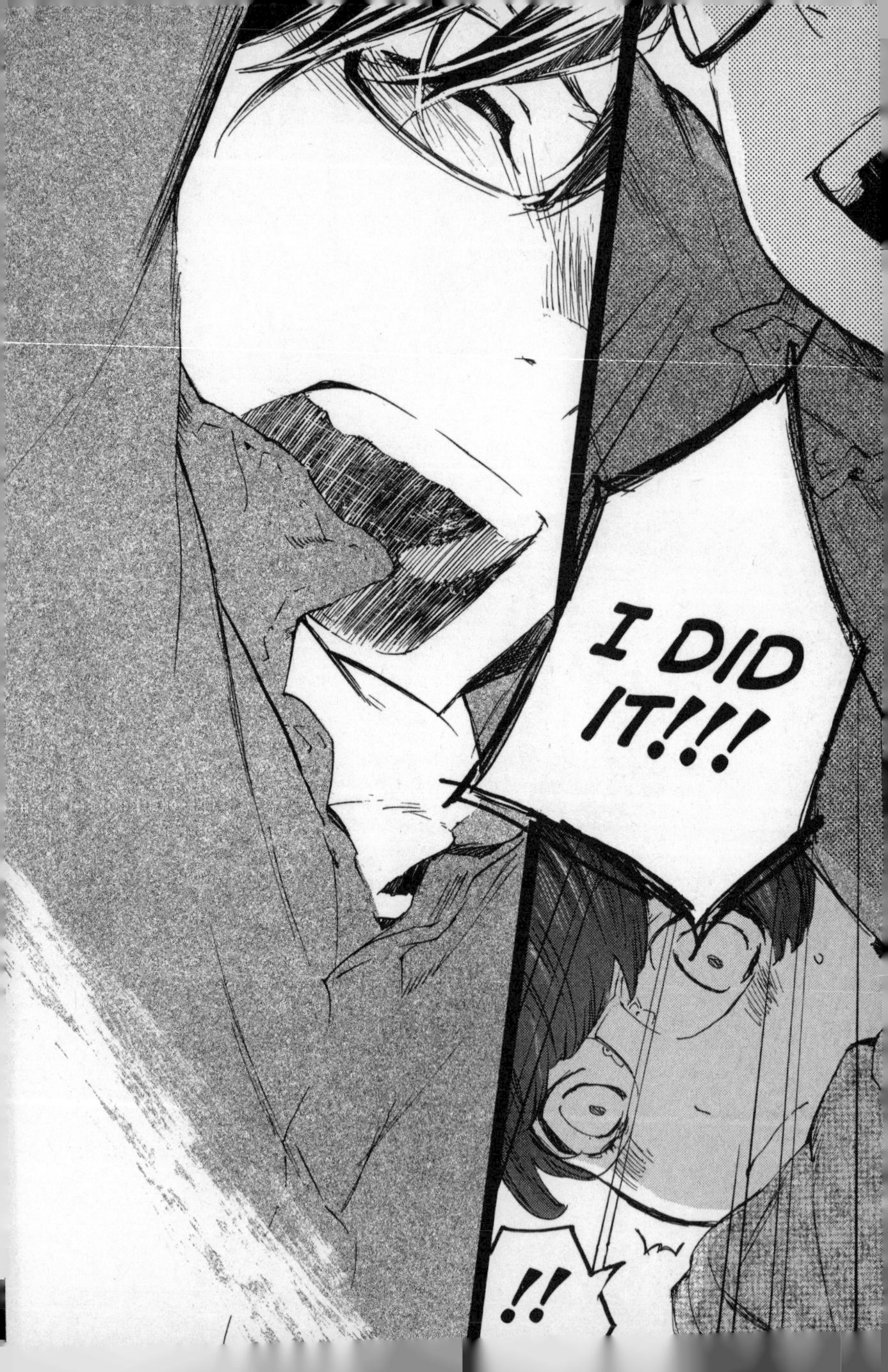
I DID IT!!!
!!

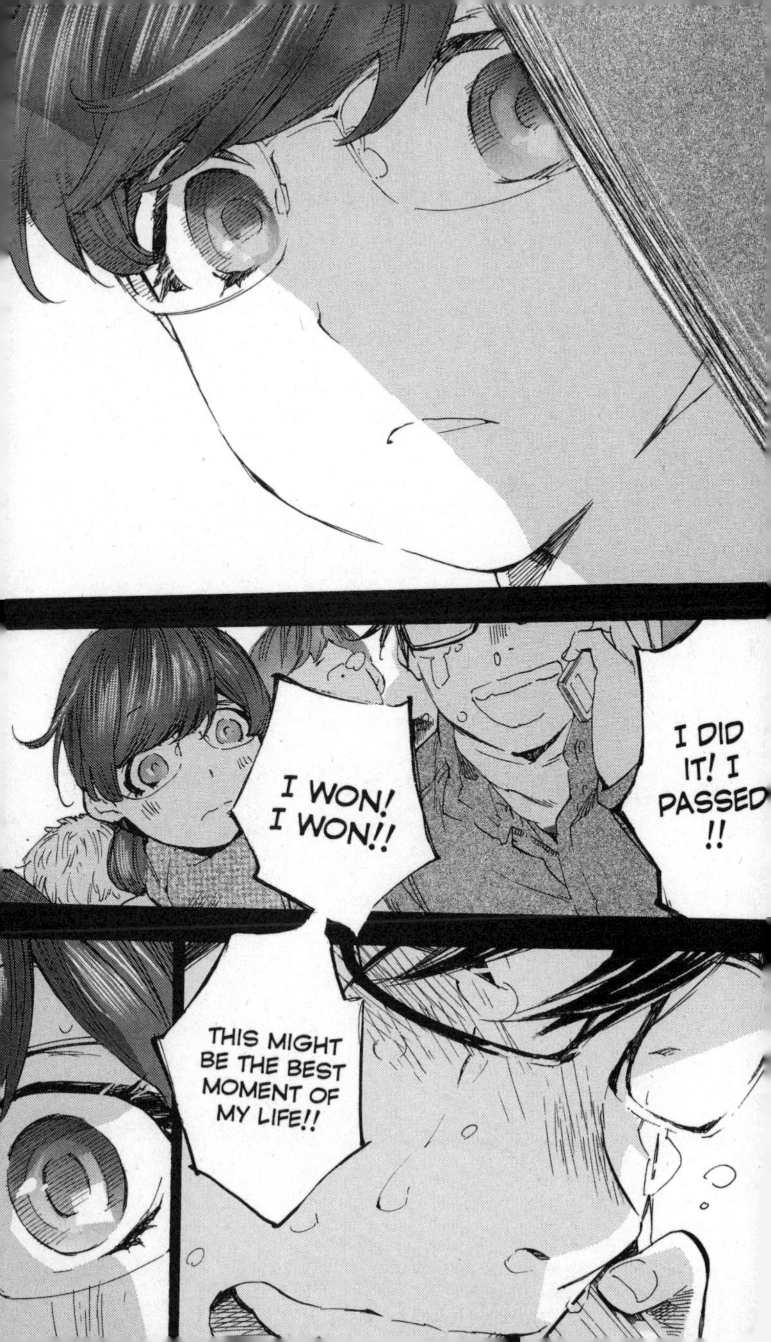
I DID IT! I PASSED!!
I WON! I WON!!
THIS MIGHT BE THE BEST MOMENT OF MY LIFE!!

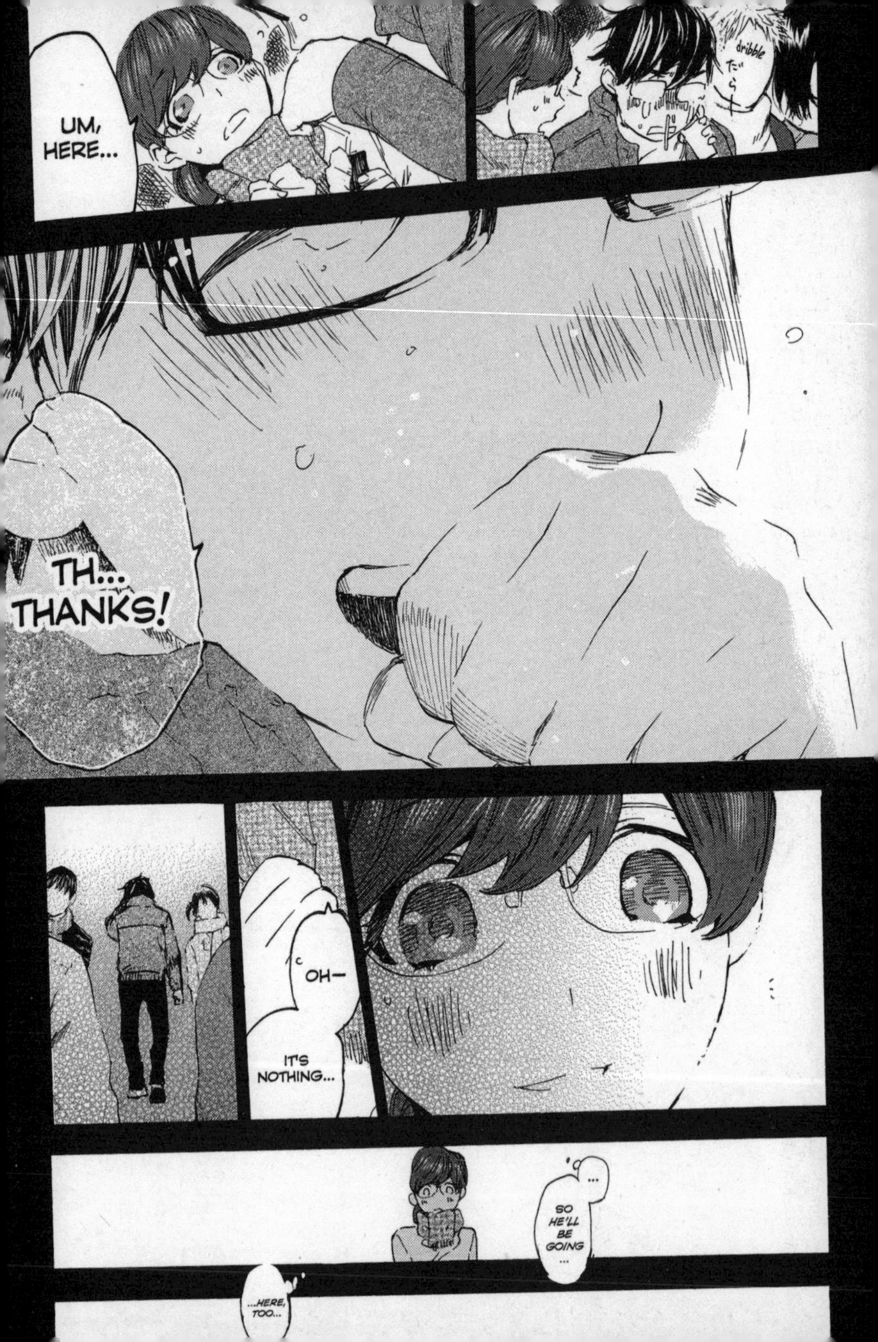
dribble
だら
UM, HERE...
TH... THANKS!
OH—
IT'S NOTHING...
...
SO HE'LL BE GOING ...
...HERE, TOO...

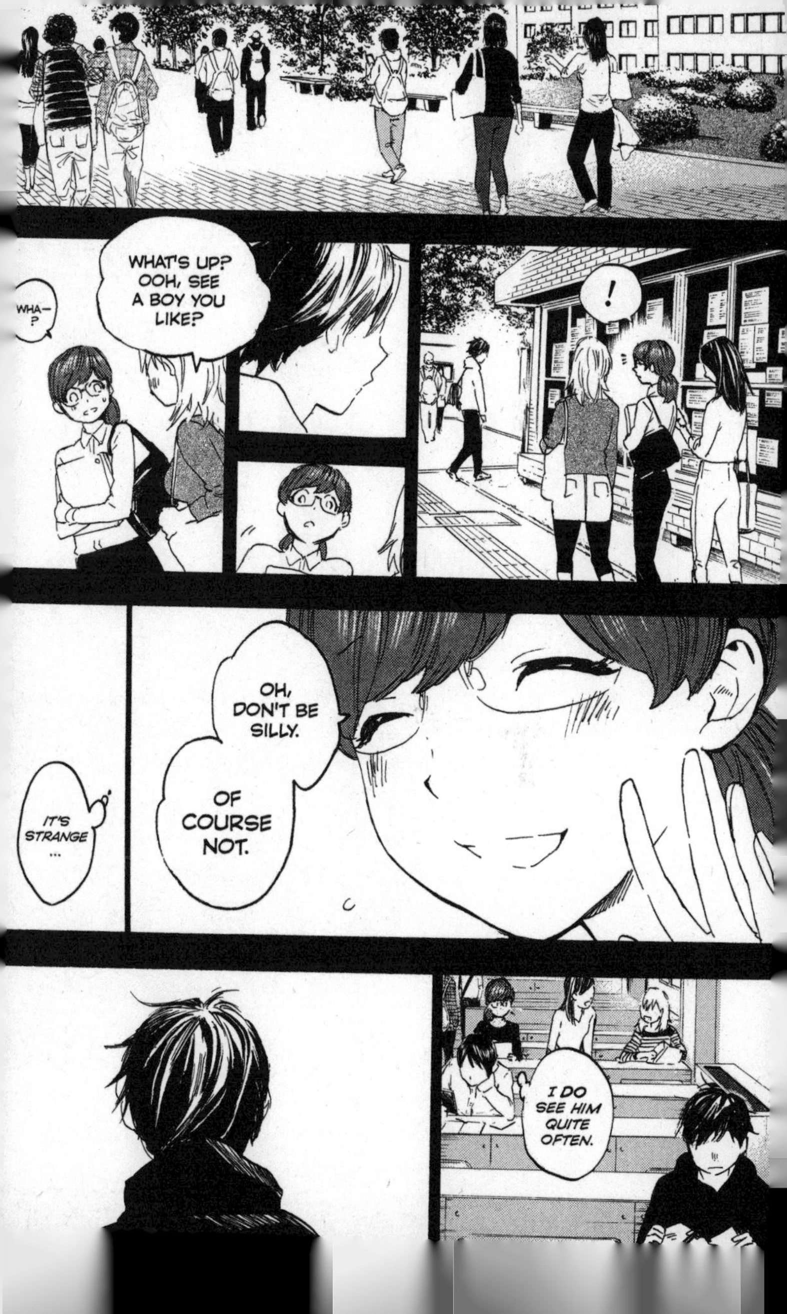
!
WHAT'S UP? OOH, SEE A BOY YOU LIKE?
WHA-?
OH, DON'T BE SILLY.
OF COURSE NOT.
IT'S STRANGE ...
I DO SEE HIM QUITE OFTEN.

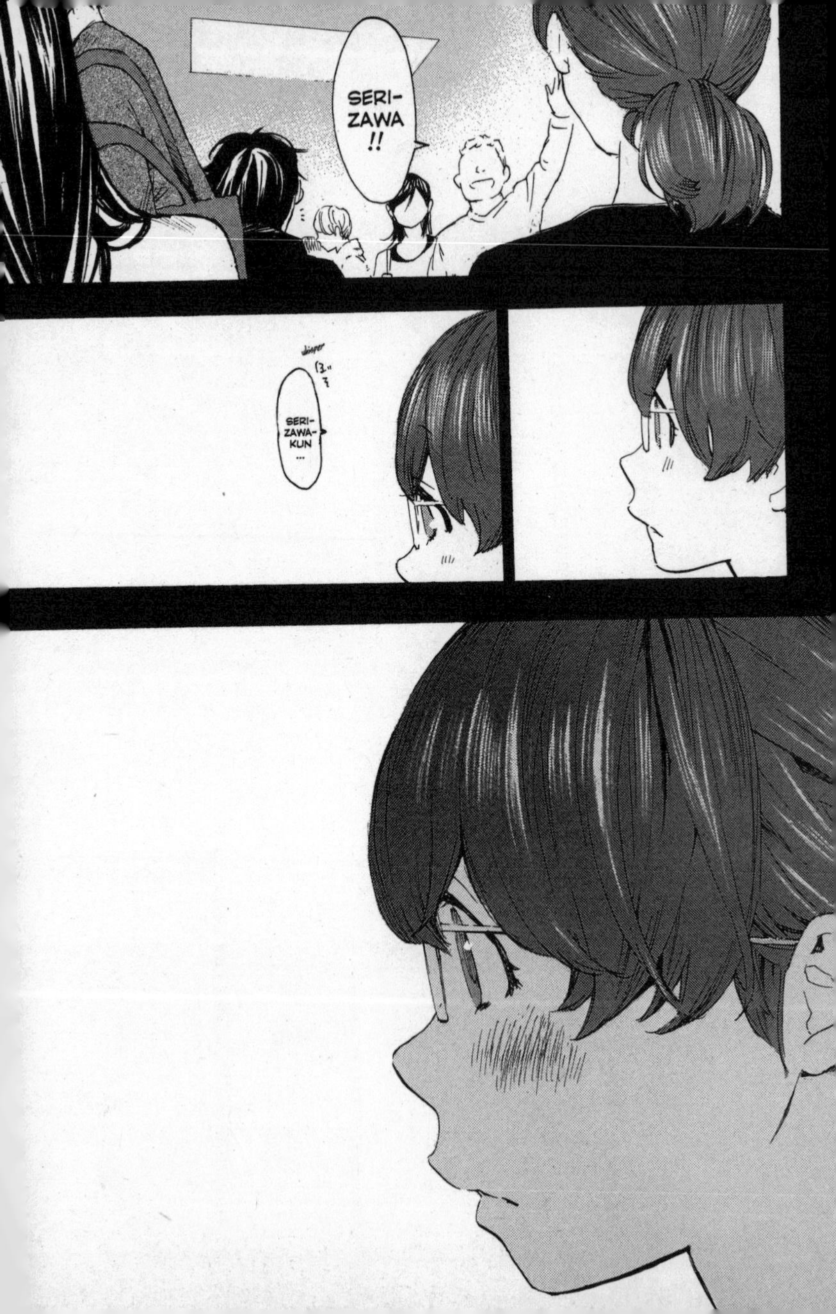
SERI-ZAWA !!
SERI-ZAWA-KUN ...

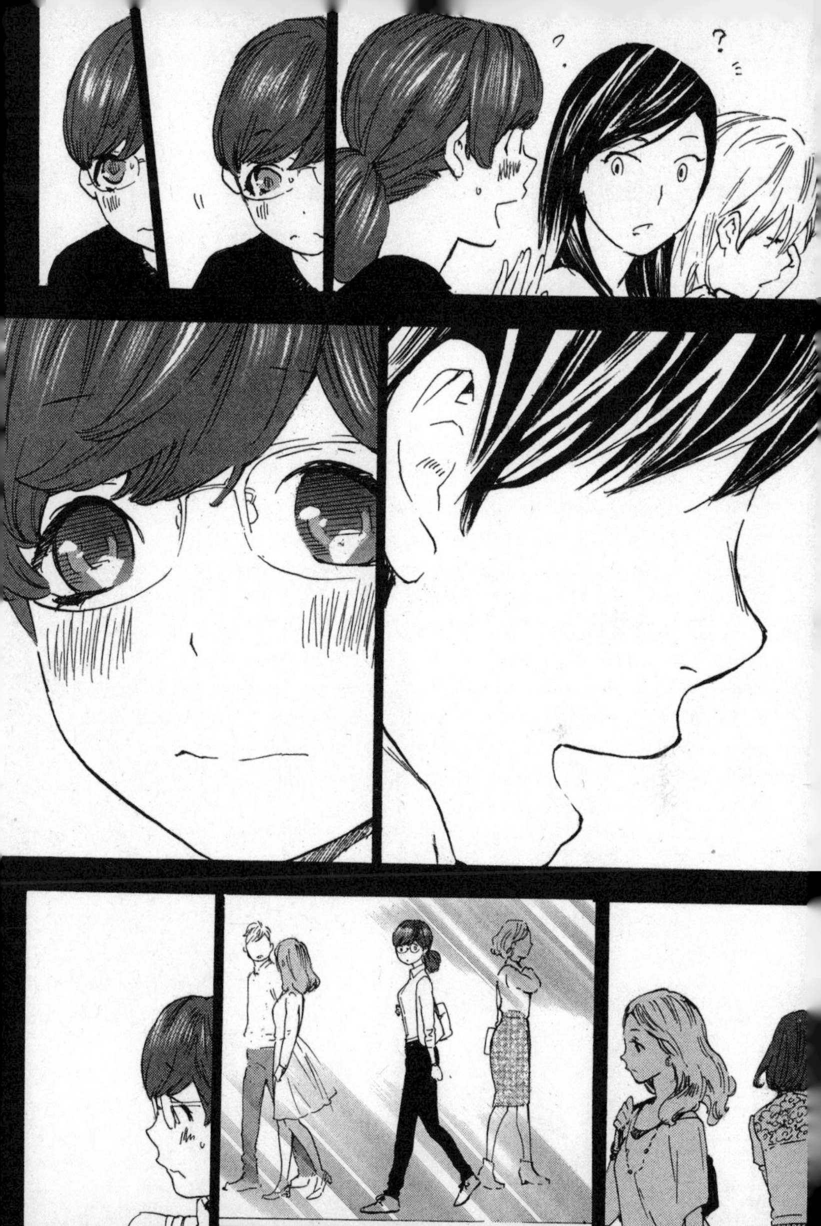
?
?

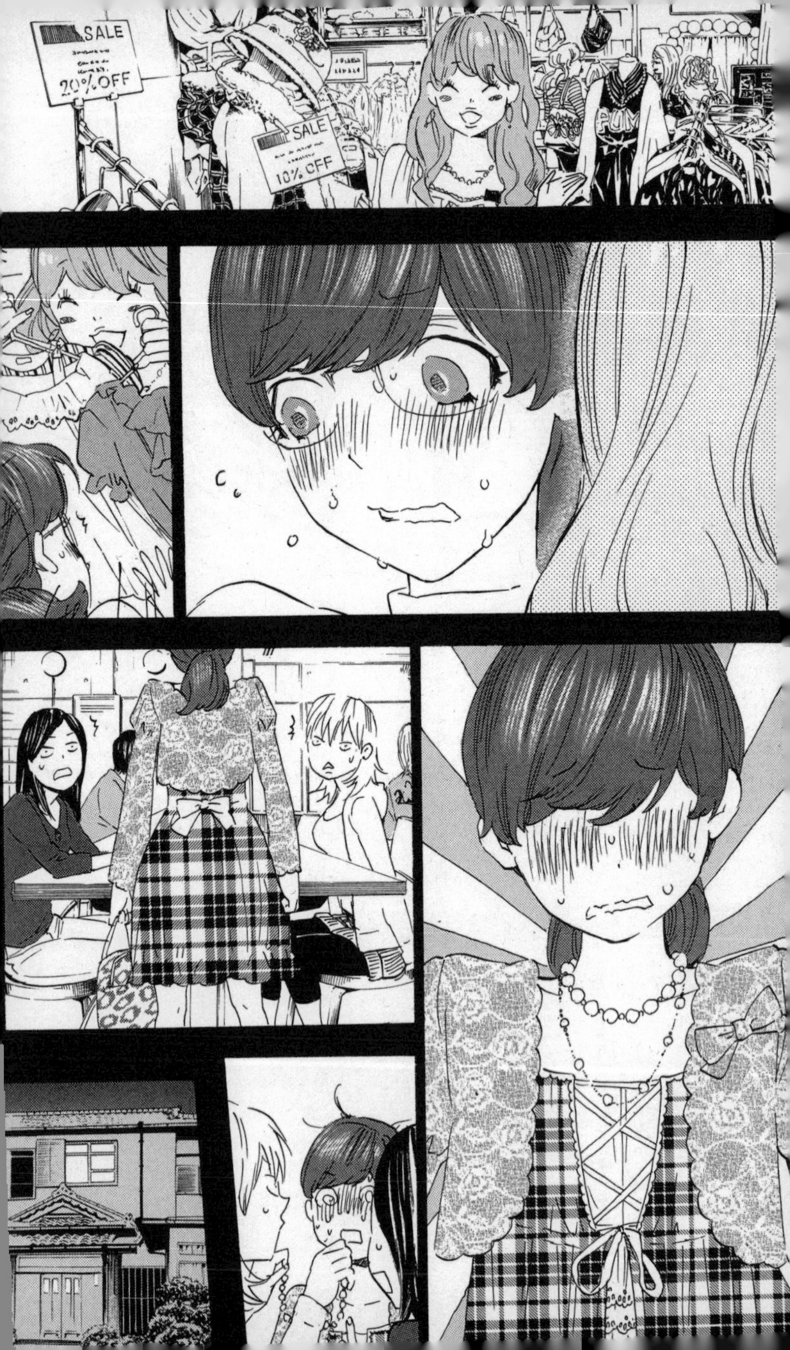
SALE
10% OFF
SALE
20% OFF

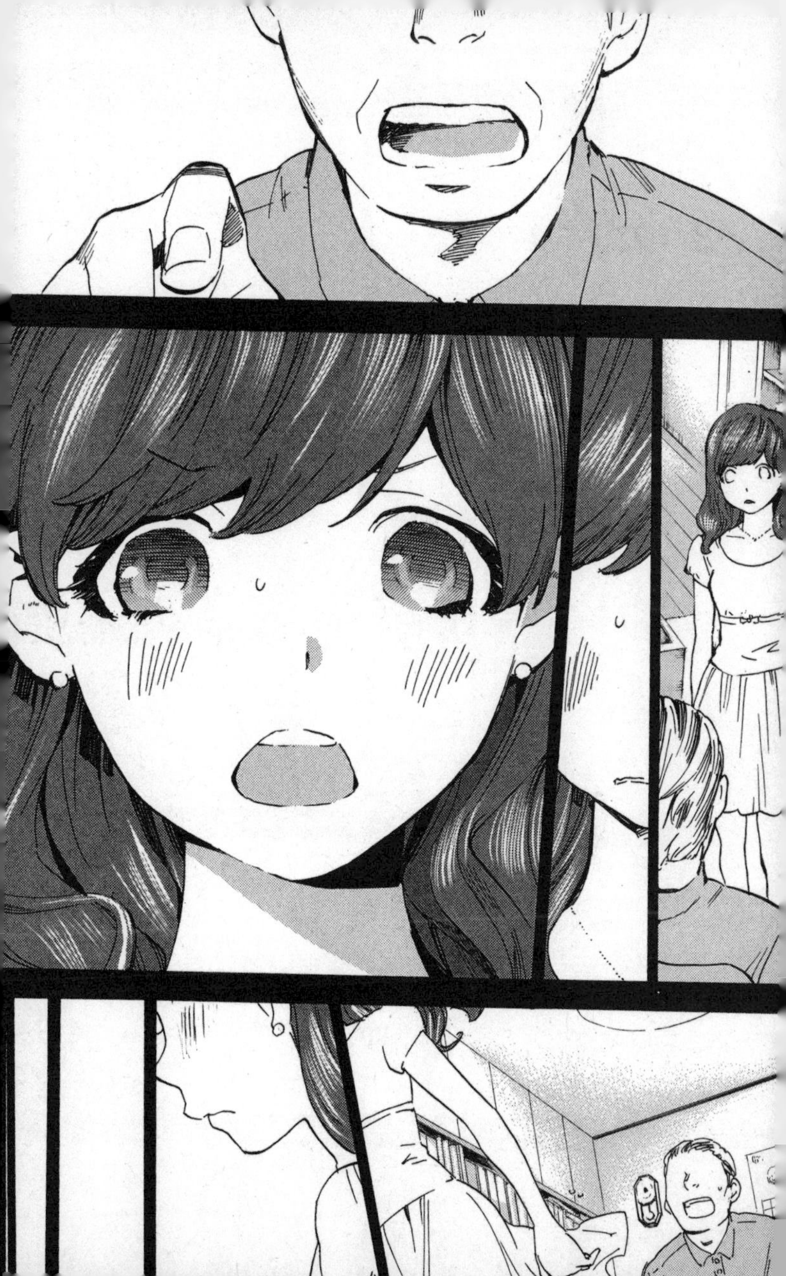

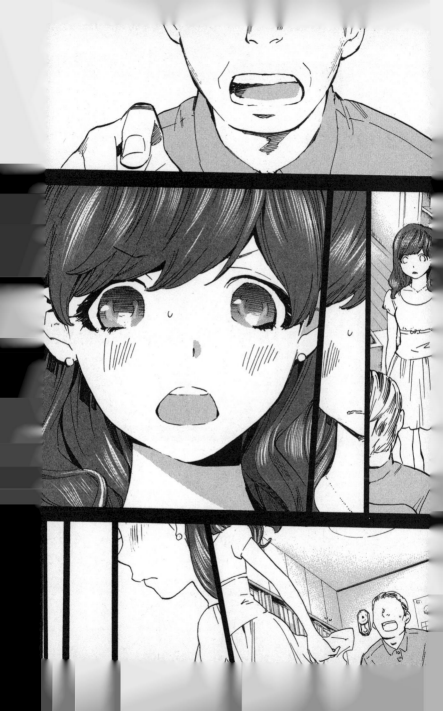

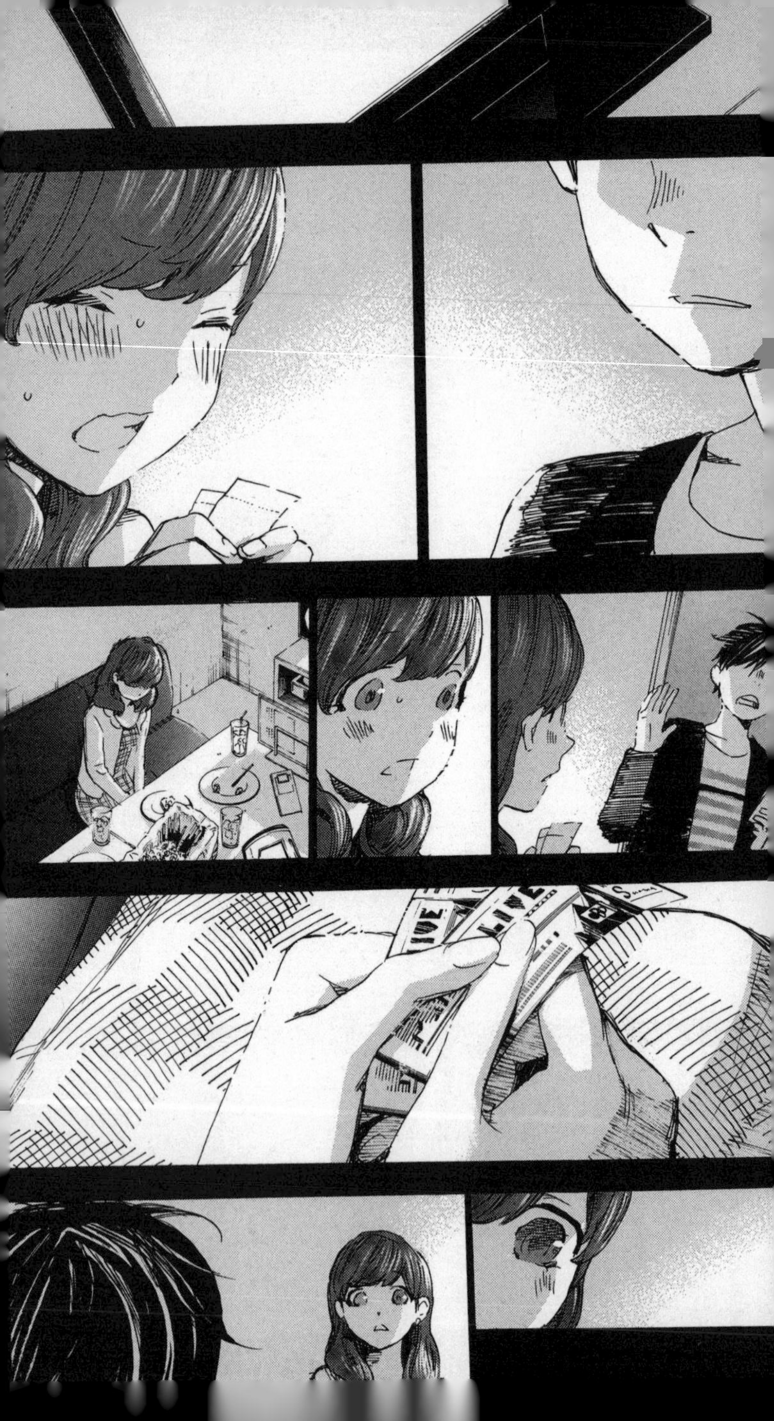
LIVE

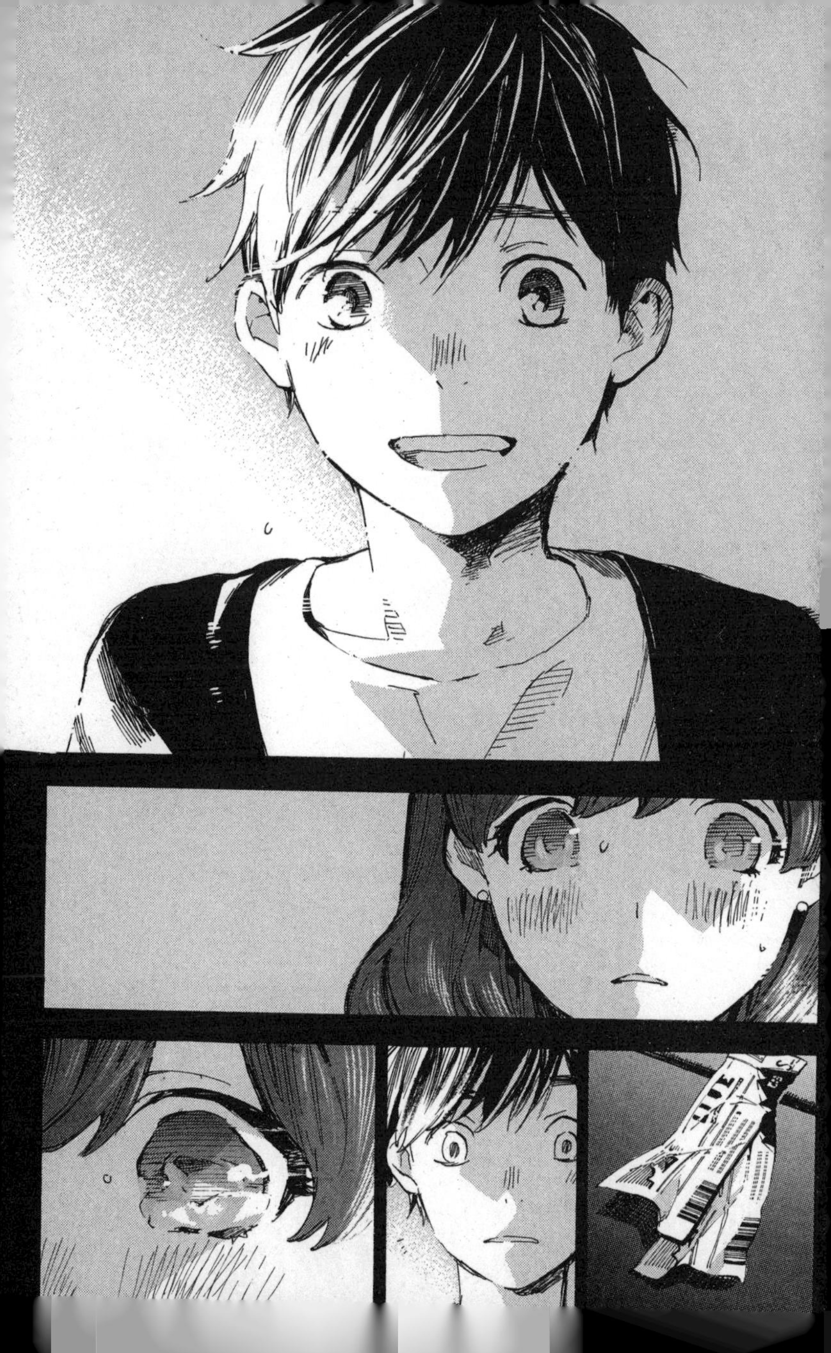

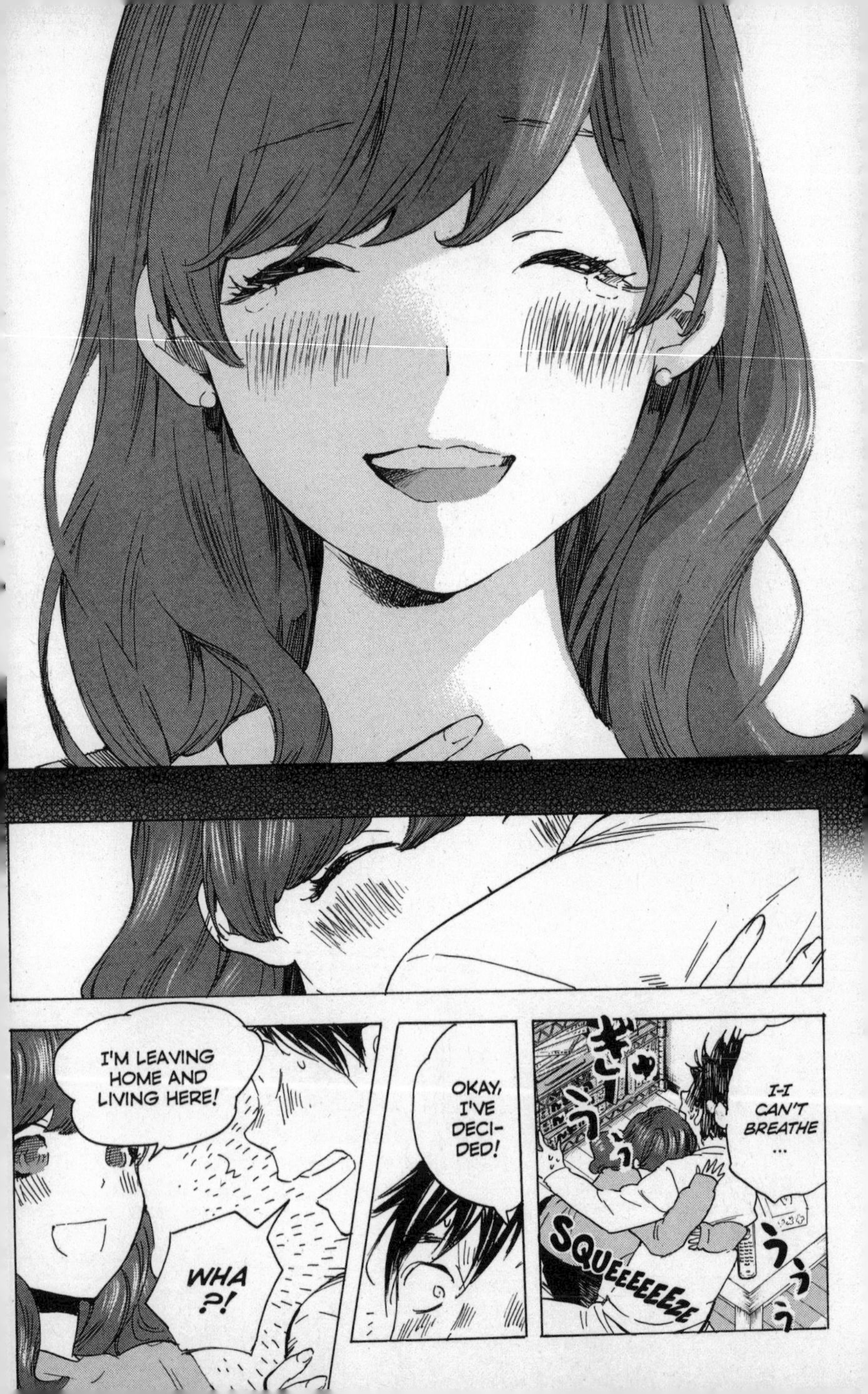
I-I CAN'T BREATHE ...
SQUEEEEEEEZE
OKAY, I'VE DECI-DED!
I'M LEAVING HOME AND LIVING HERE!
WHA ?!

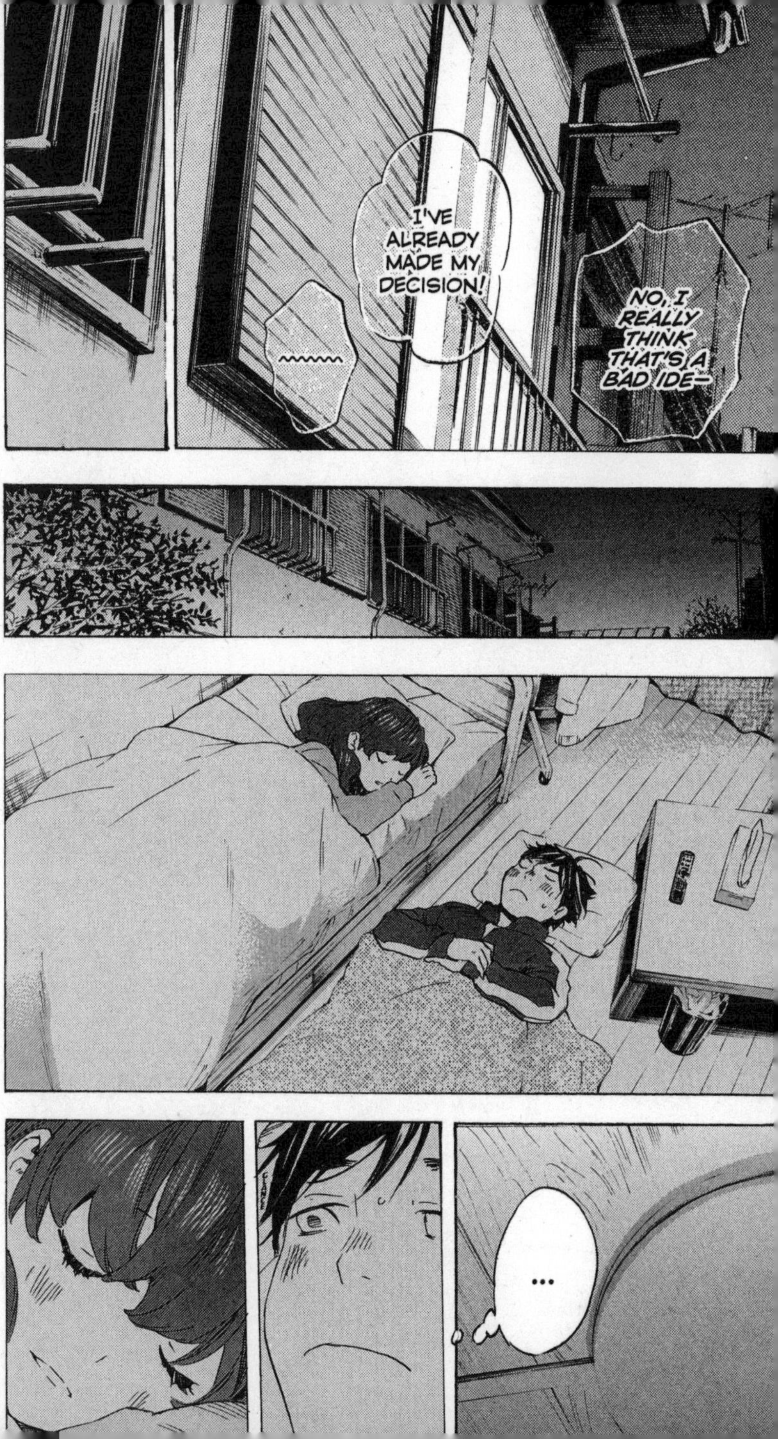
NO, I REALLY THINK THAT'S A BAD IDE—
I'VE ALREADY MADE MY DECISION!
...

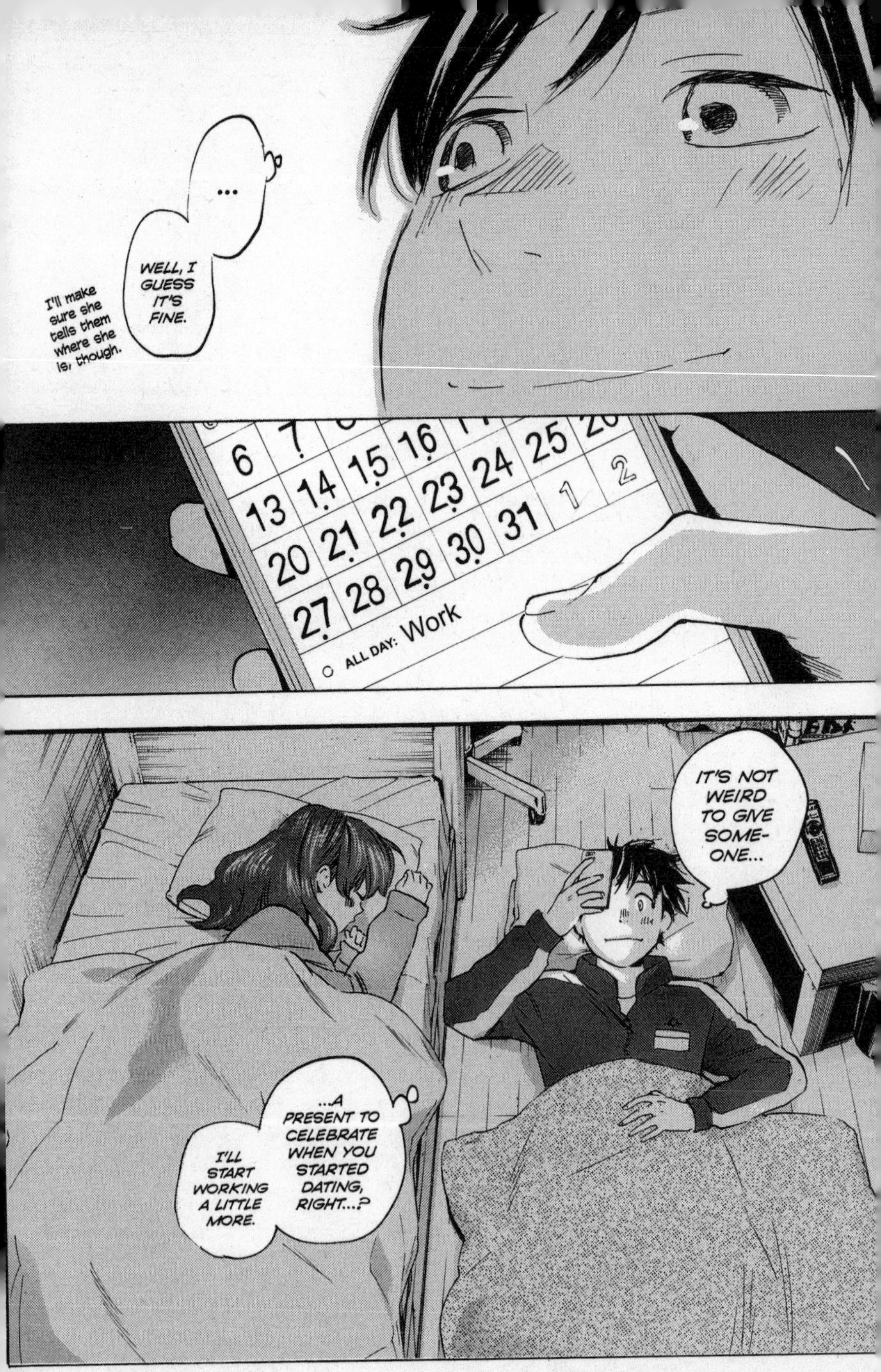
...
WELL, I GUESS IT'S FINE.
I'll make sure she tells them where she is, though.
ALL DAY: Work
IT'S NOT WEIRD TO GIVE SOME-ONE...
...A PRESENT TO CELEBRATE WHEN YOU STARTED DATING, RIGHT...?
I'LL START WORKING A LITTLE MORE.

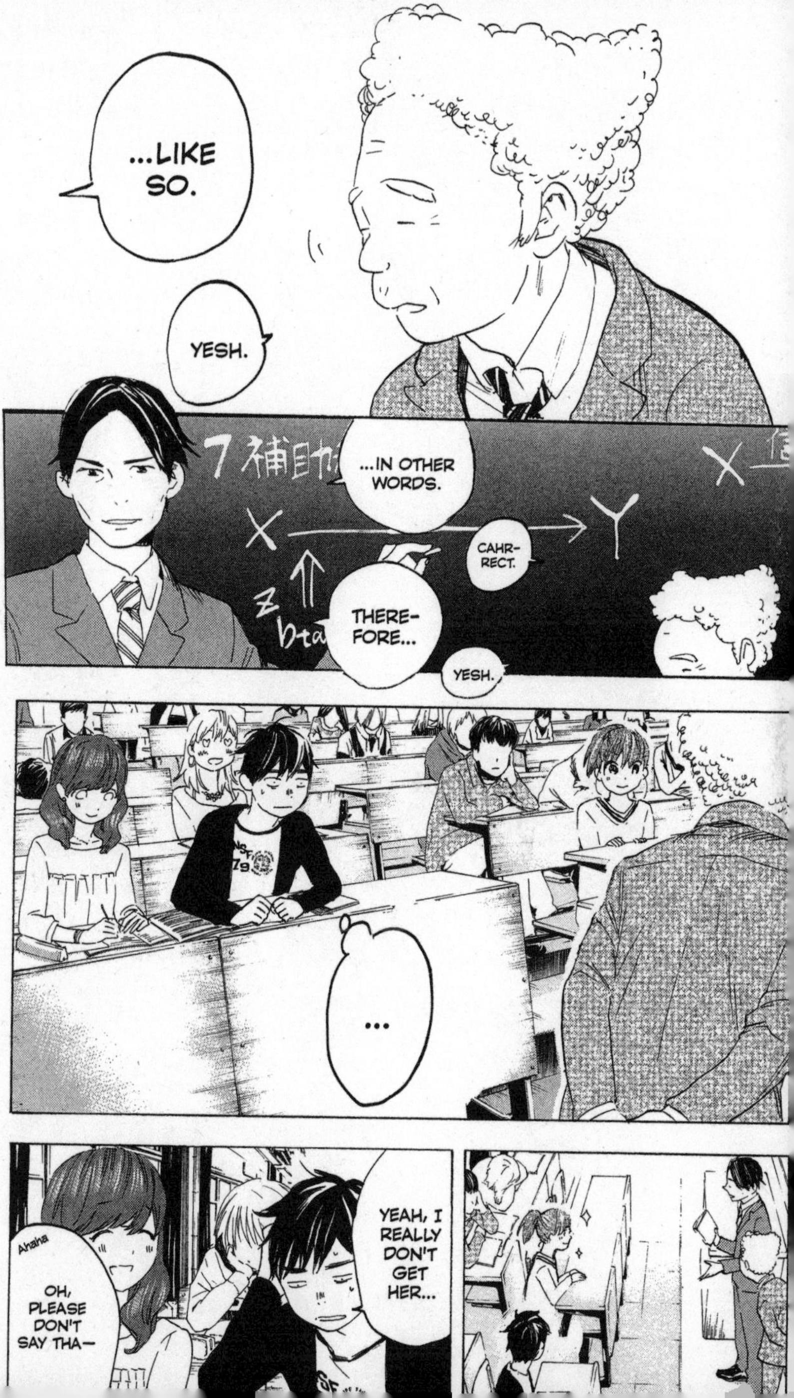
...LIKE SO.
YESH.
...IN OTHER WORDS.
CAHR-RECT.
THERE-FORE...
YESH.
...
YEAH, I REALLY DON'T GET HER...
Ahaha
OH, PLEASE DON'T SAY THA—

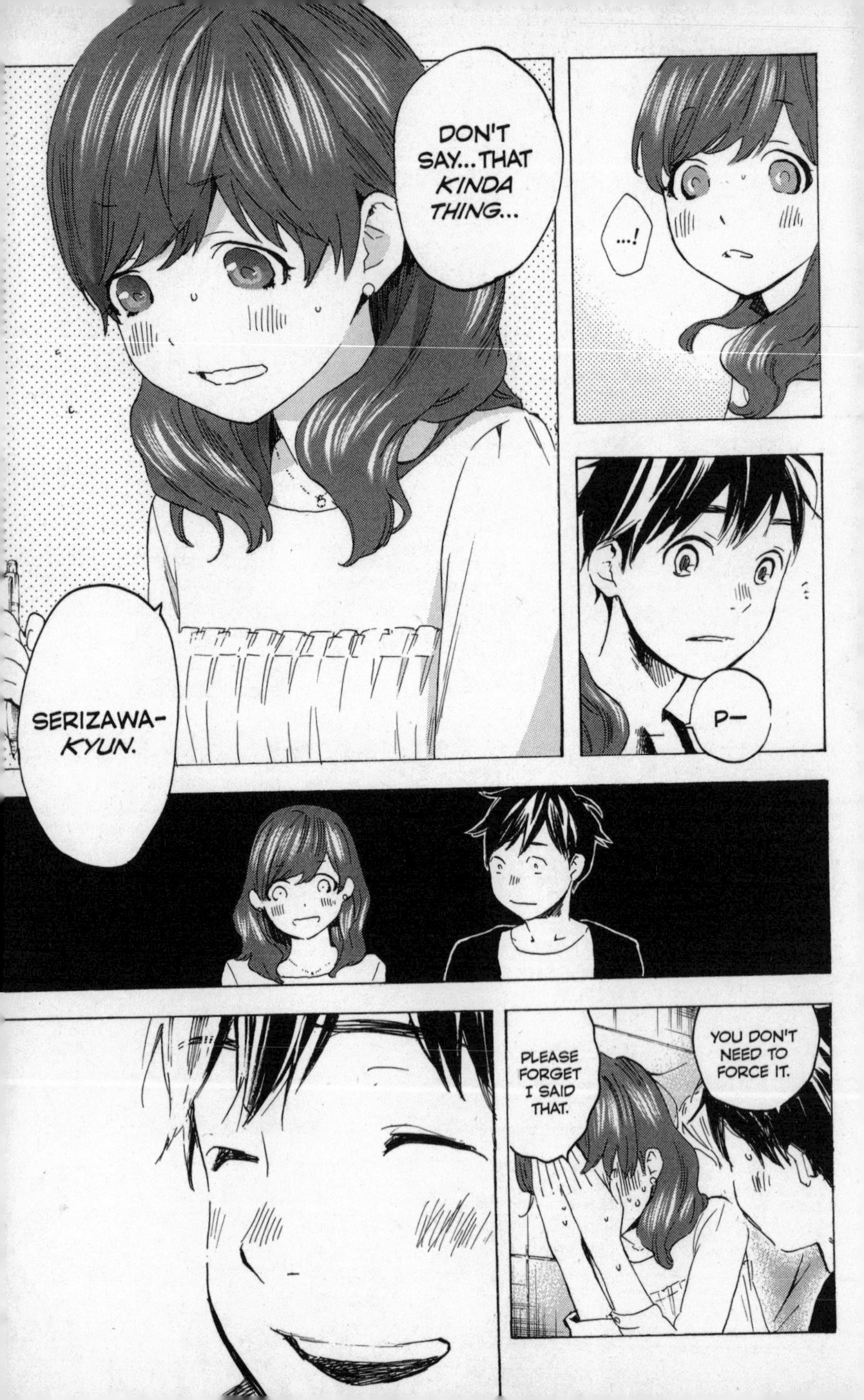
...!
P—
DON'T SAY...THAT KINDA THING...
SERIZAWA-KYUN.
YOU DON'T NEED TO FORCE IT.
PLEASE FORGET I SAID THAT.

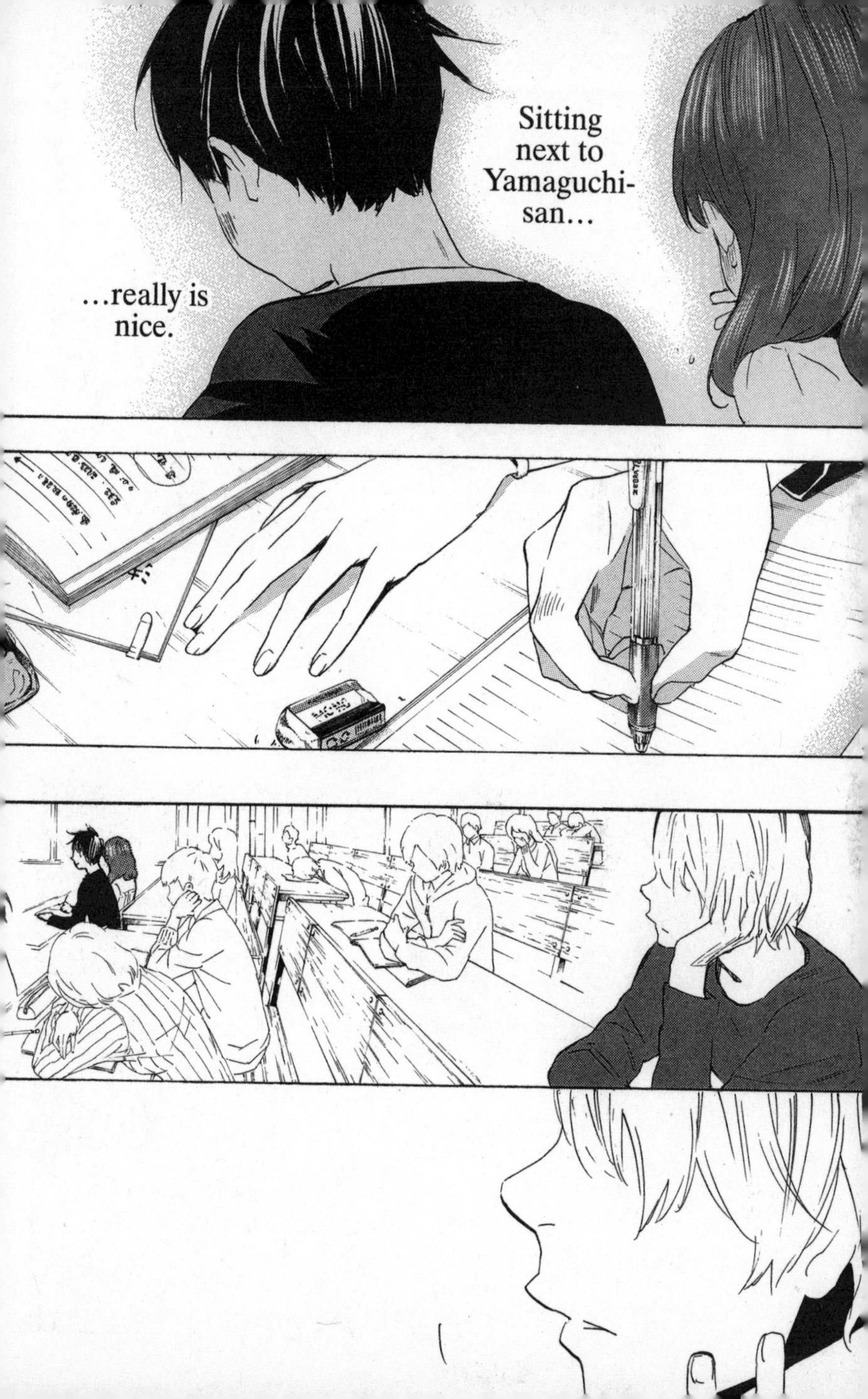
Sitting next to Yamaguchi-san…
…really is nice.

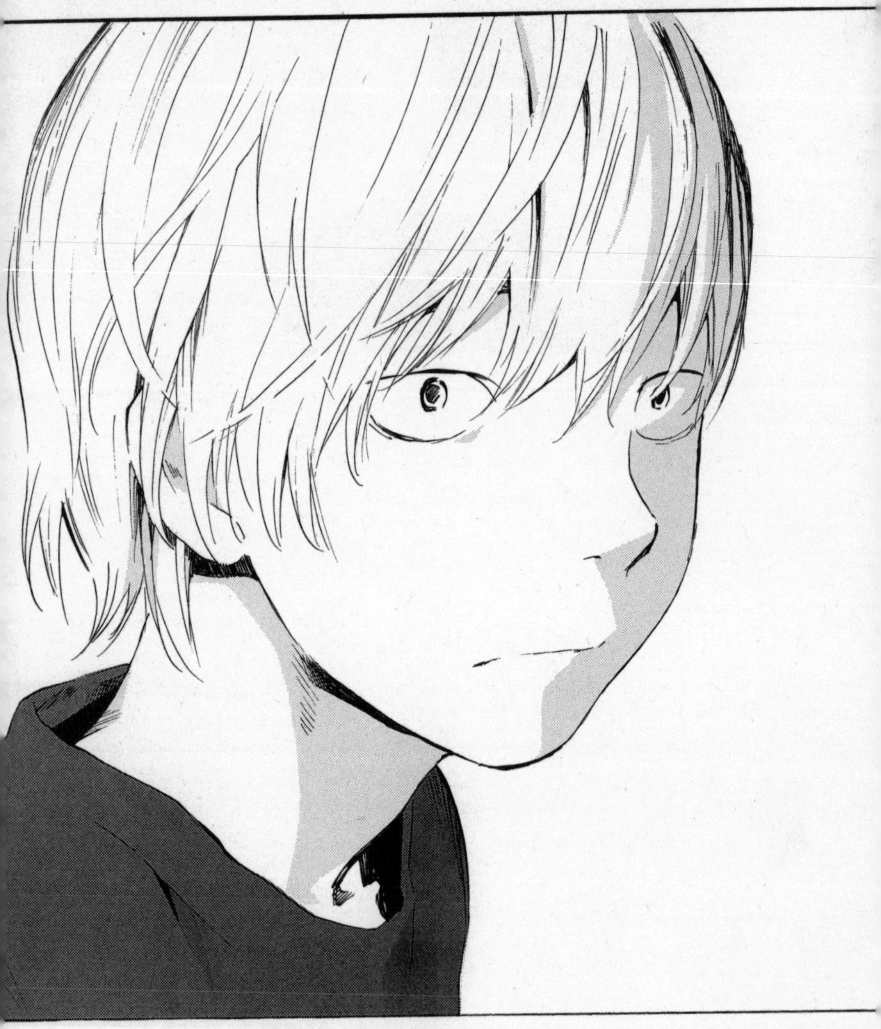

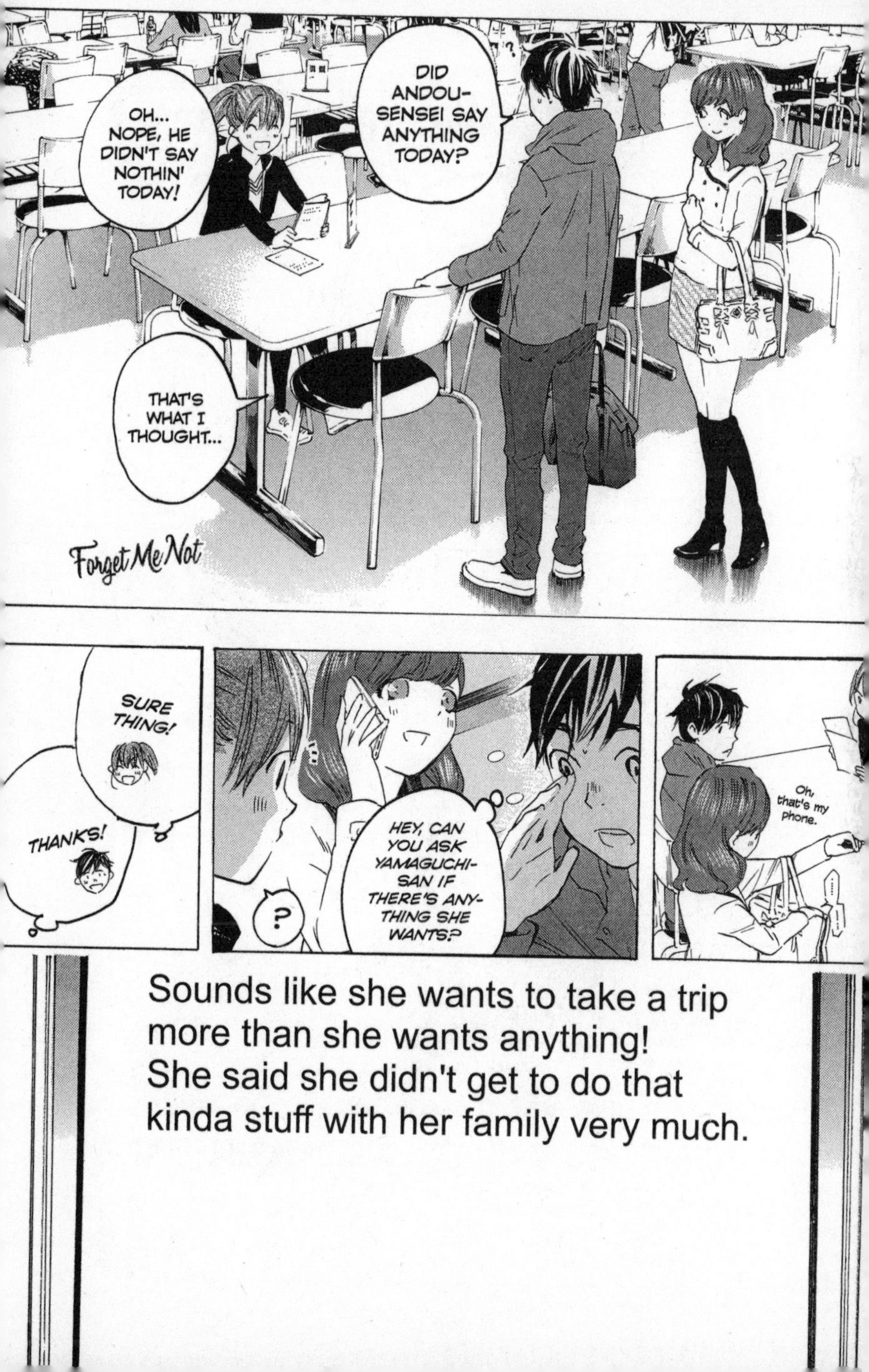
DID ANDOU-SENSEI SAY ANYTHING TODAY?
OH... NOPE, HE DIDN'T SAY NOTHIN' TODAY!
THAT'S WHAT I THOUGHT...
Forget Me Not
Oh, that's my phone.
HEY, CAN YOU ASK YAMAGUCHI-SAN IF THERE'S ANYTHING SHE WANTS?
?
SURE THING!
THANKS!
Sounds like she wants to take a trip more than she wants anything! She said she didn't get to do that kinda stuff with her family very much.

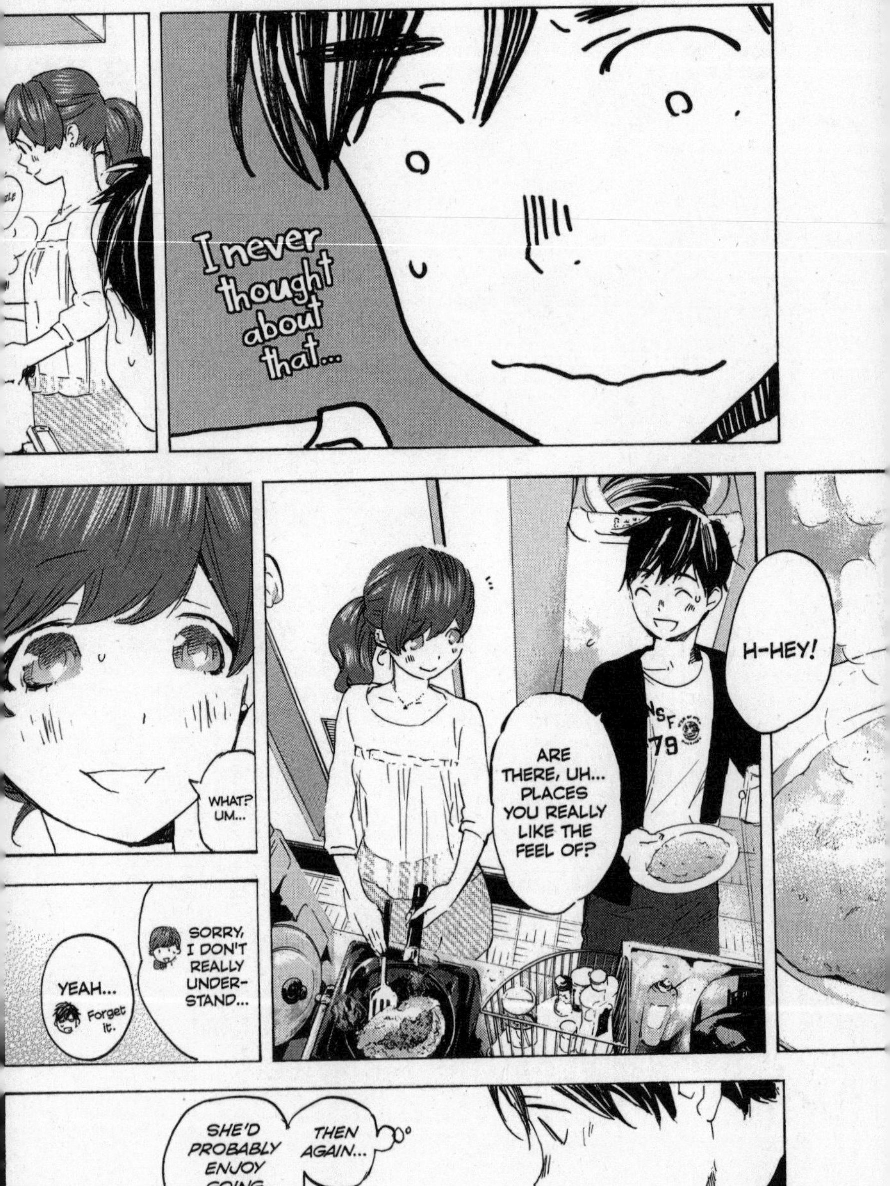
I never thought about that...
H-HEY!
ARE THERE, UH... PLACES YOU REALLY LIKE THE FEEL OF?
WHAT? UM...
SORRY, I DON'T REALLY UNDER-STAND...
YEAH... Forget it.
THEN AGAIN...
SHE'D PROBABLY ENJOY GOING ANYWHERE.

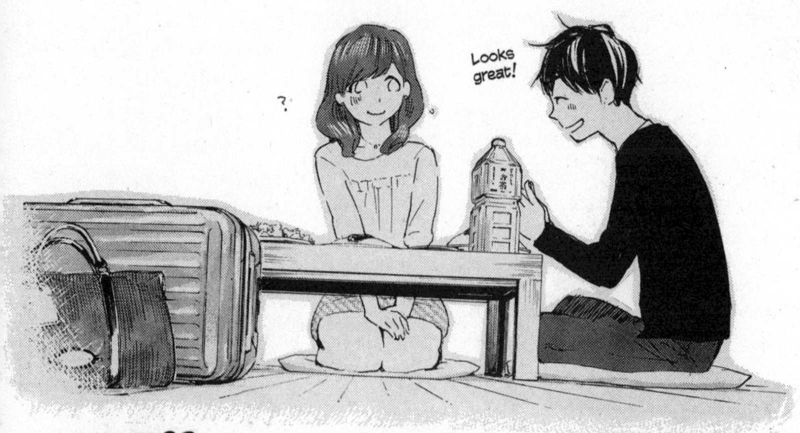
Looks great!
?

CHAPTER 23:
Tsukushi Makino 12

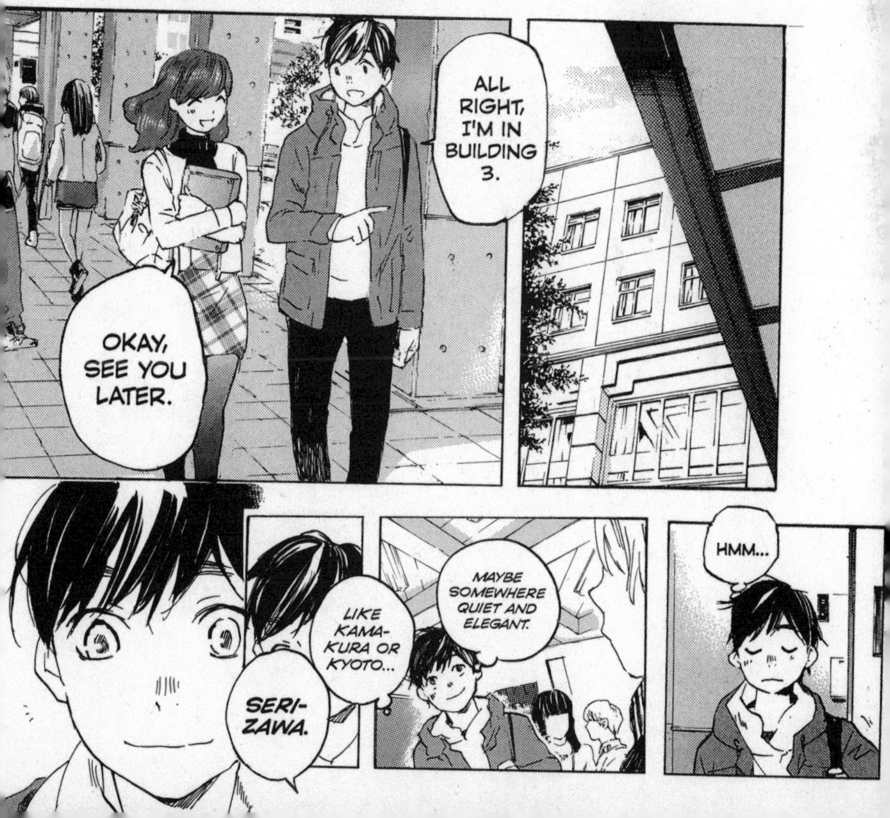
ALL RIGHT, I'M IN BUILDING 3.
OKAY, SEE YOU LATER.
HMM...
MAYBE SOMEWHERE QUIET AND ELEGANT.
LIKE KAMA-KURA OR KYOTO...
SERI-ZAWA.

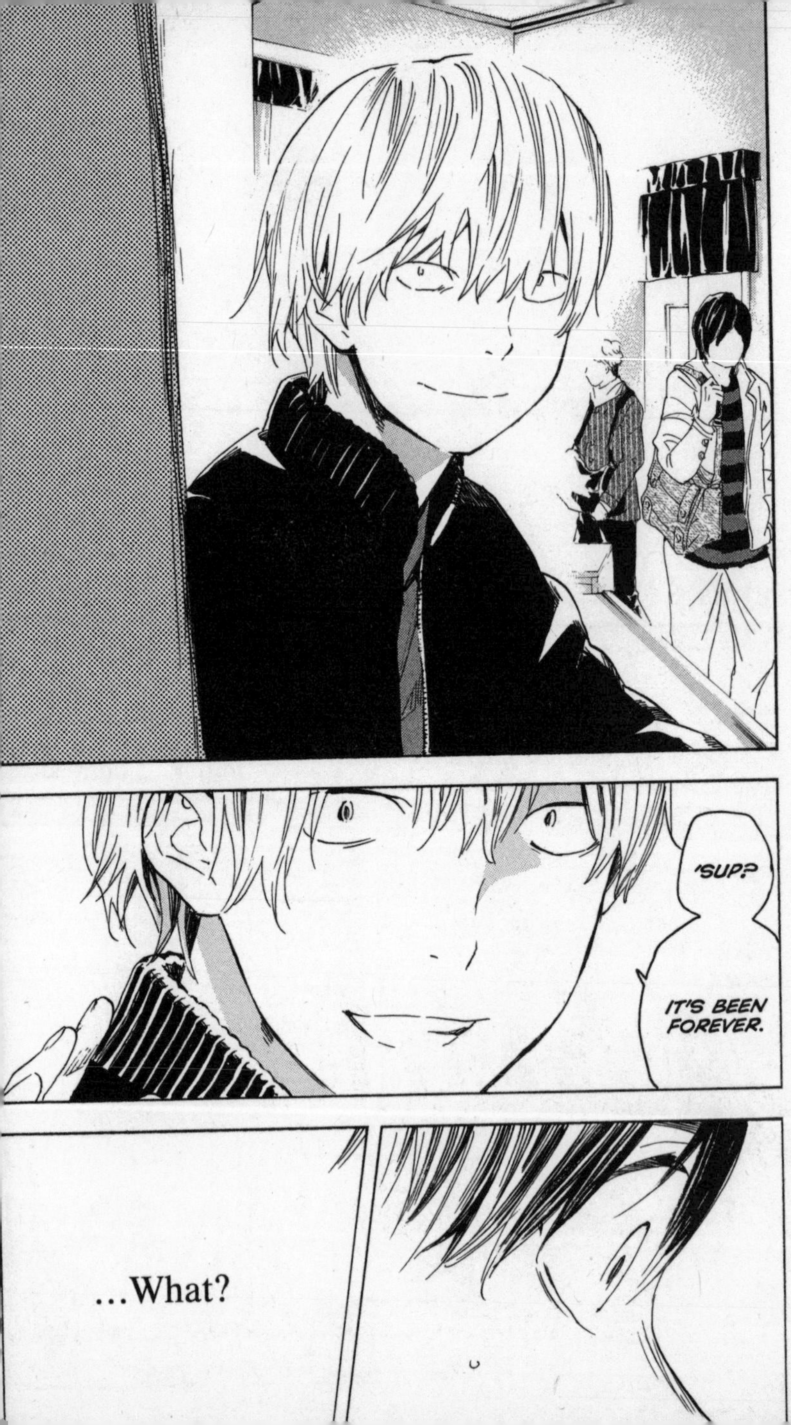
'SUP?
IT'S BEEN FOREVER.
...What?

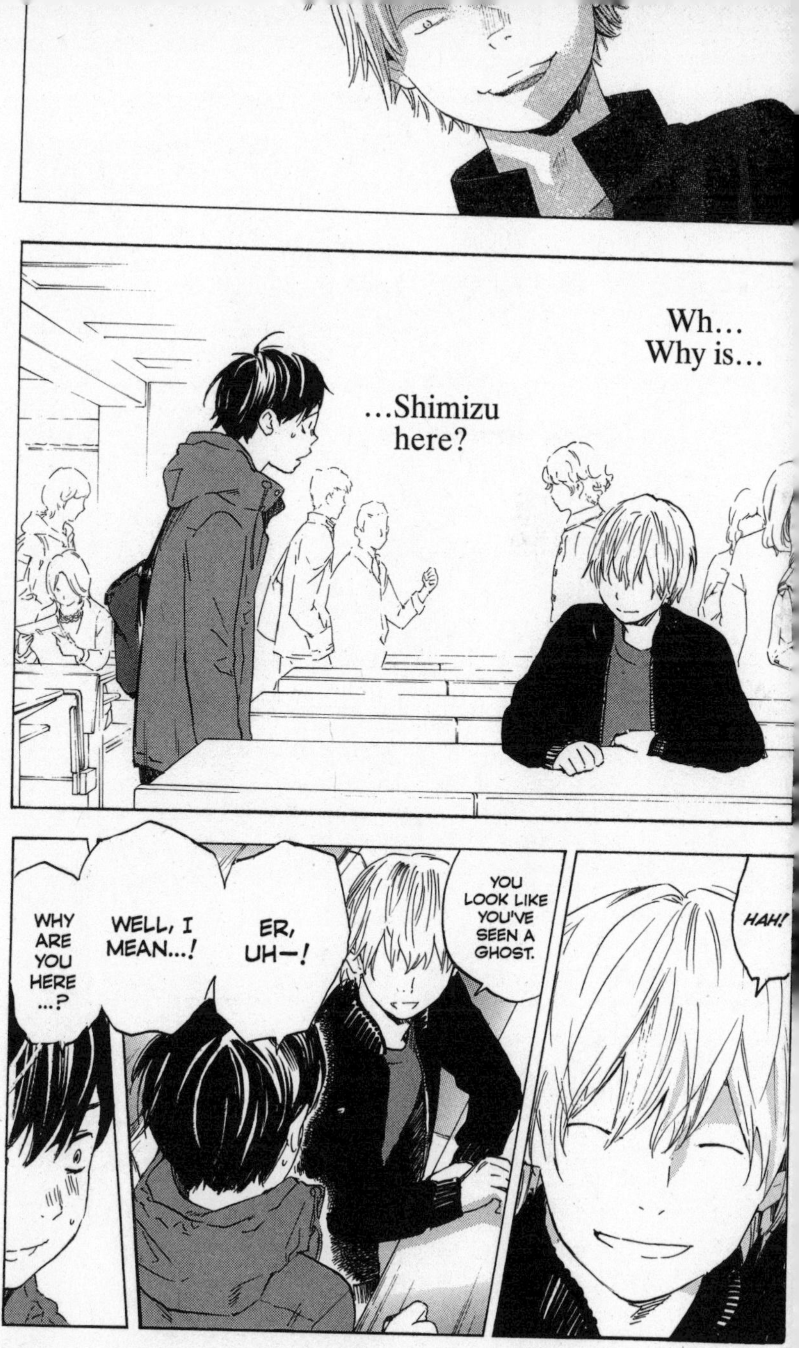

Wh…
Why is…
…Shimizu
here?
HAH!
YOU LOOK LIKE YOU'VE SEEN A GHOST.
ER, UH—!
WELL, I MEAN…!
WHY ARE YOU HERE …?

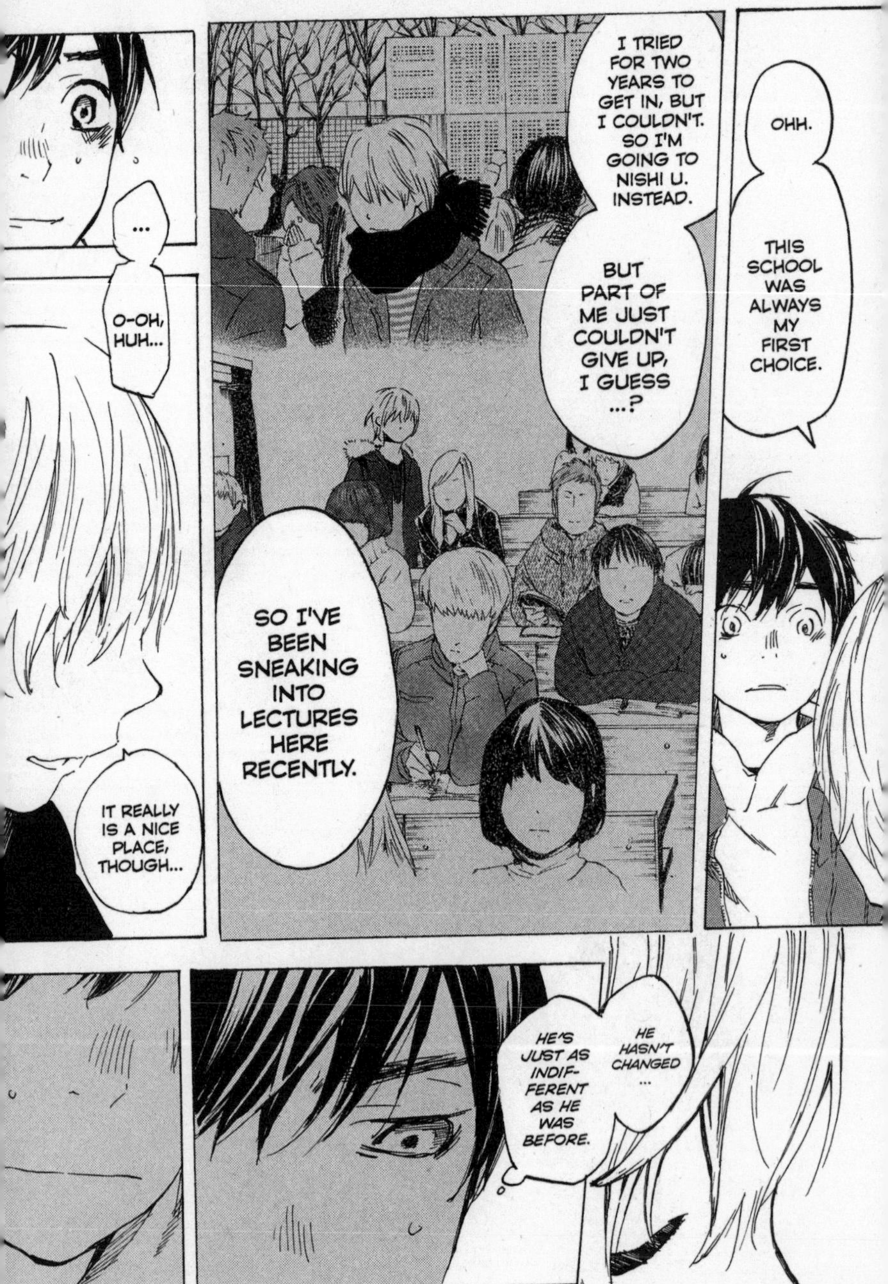
OHH.
THIS SCHOOL WAS ALWAYS MY FIRST CHOICE.
I TRIED FOR TWO YEARS TO GET IN, BUT I COULDN'T. SO I'M GOING TO NISHI U. INSTEAD.
BUT PART OF ME JUST COULDN'T GIVE UP, I GUESS ...?
SO I'VE BEEN SNEAKING INTO LECTURES HERE RECENTLY.
...
O-OH, HUH...
IT REALLY IS A NICE PLACE, THOUGH...
HE HASN'T CHANGED ...
HE'S JUST AS INDIF-FERENT AS HE WAS BEFORE.

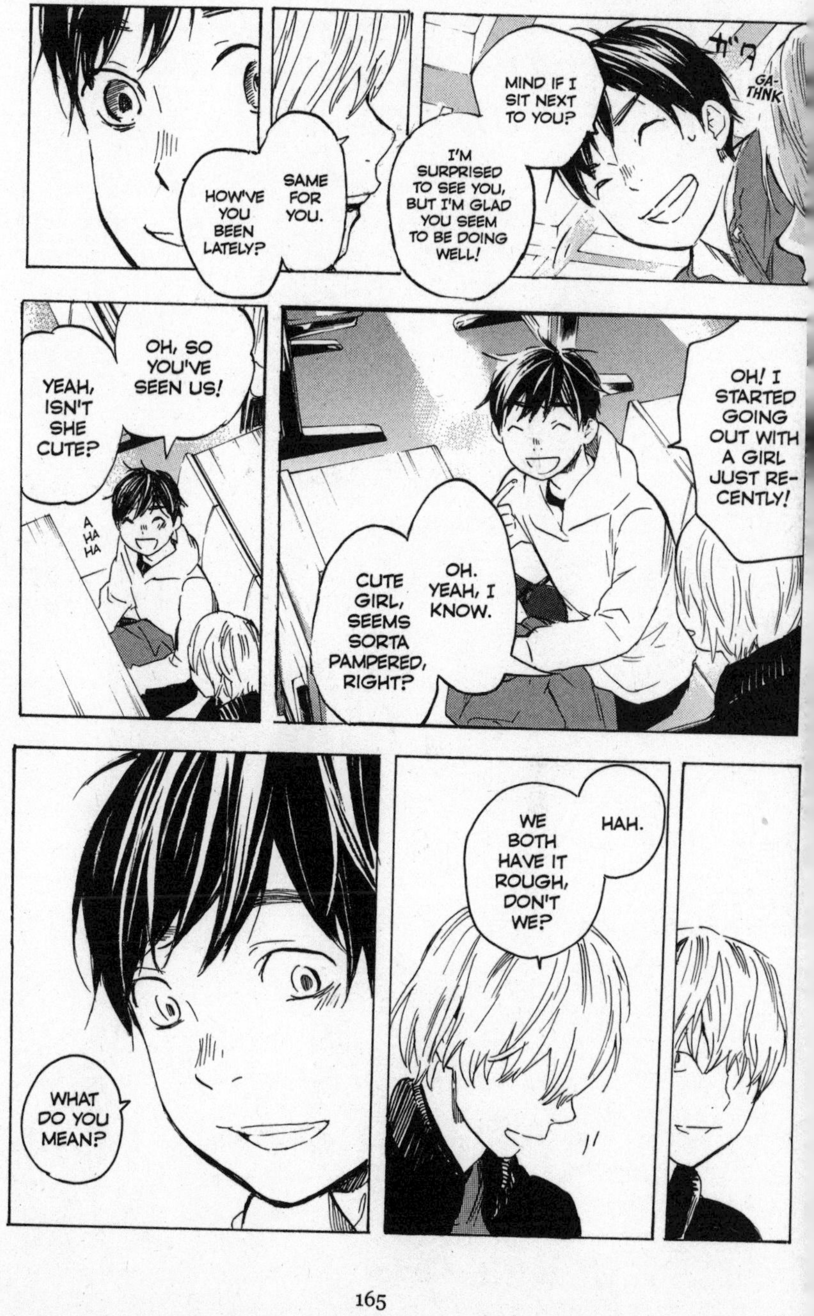
ガタ
GA-THNK
MIND IF I SIT NEXT TO YOU?
I'M SURPRISED TO SEE YOU, BUT I'M GLAD YOU SEEM TO BE DOING WELL!
SAME FOR YOU.
HOW'VE YOU BEEN LATELY?
OH! I STARTED GOING OUT WITH A GIRL JUST RE-CENTLY!
OH. YEAH, I KNOW.
CUTE GIRL, SEEMS SORTA PAMPERED, RIGHT?
OH, SO YOU'VE SEEN US!
YEAH, ISN'T SHE CUTE?
A HA HA
HAH.
WE BOTH HAVE IT ROUGH, DON'T WE?
WHAT DO YOU MEAN?

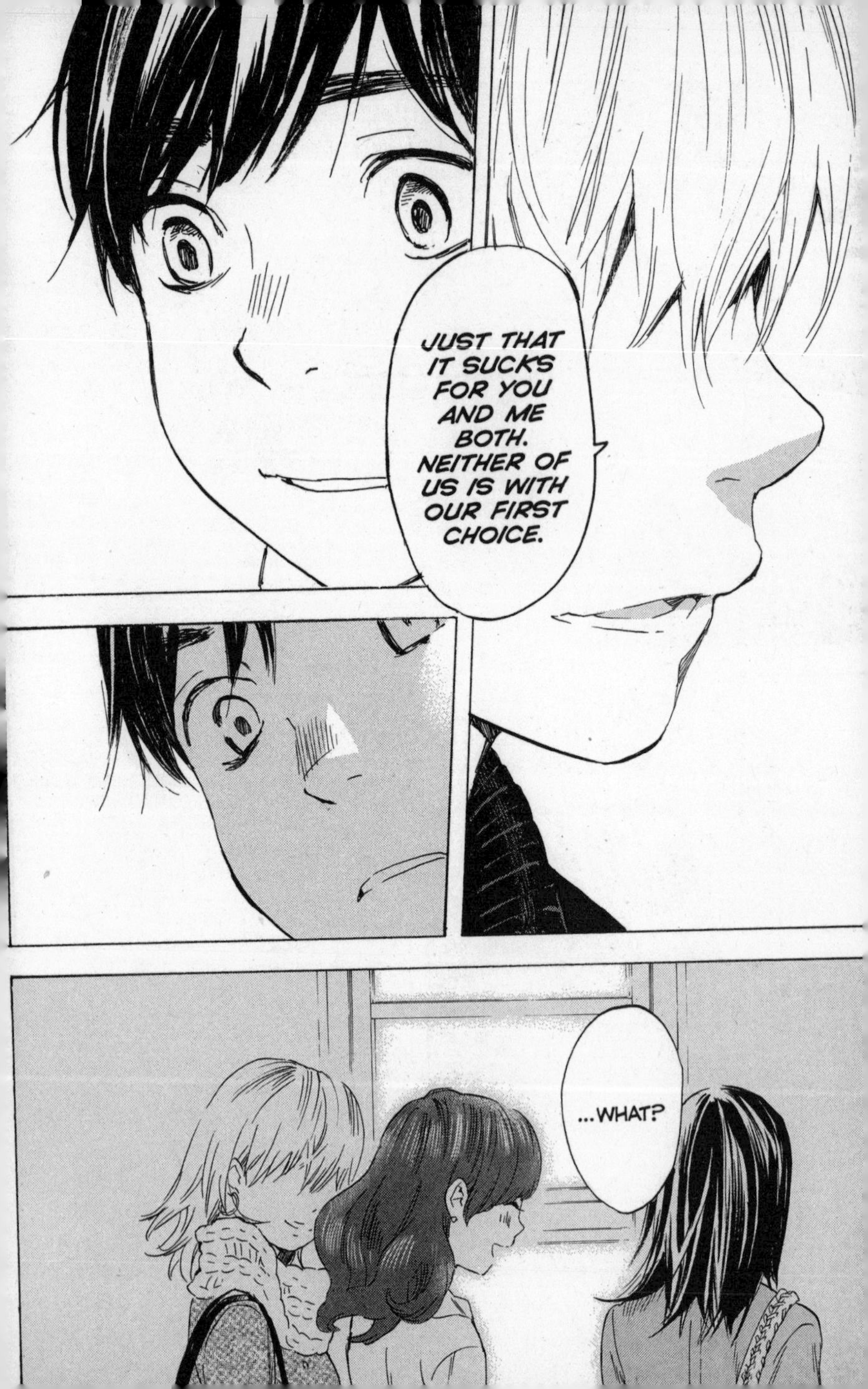
JUST THAT IT SUCKS FOR YOU AND ME BOTH. NEITHER OF US IS WITH OUR FIRST CHOICE.
...WHAT?

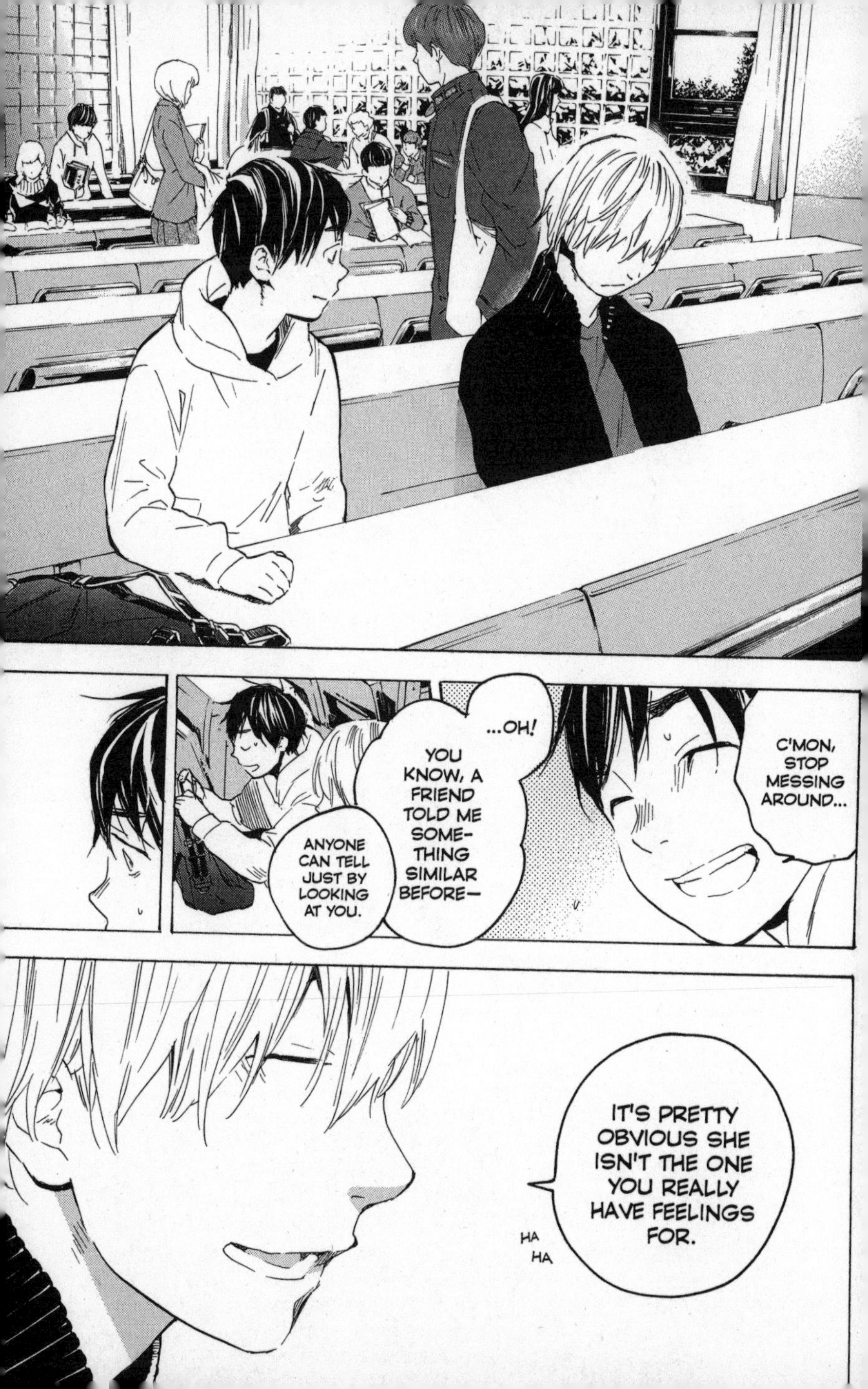
C'MON, STOP MESSING AROUND...
...OH!
YOU KNOW, A FRIEND TOLD ME SOME-THING SIMILAR BEFORE—
ANYONE CAN TELL JUST BY LOOKING AT YOU.
IT'S PRETTY OBVIOUS SHE ISN'T THE ONE YOU REALLY HAVE FEELINGS FOR.
HA HA

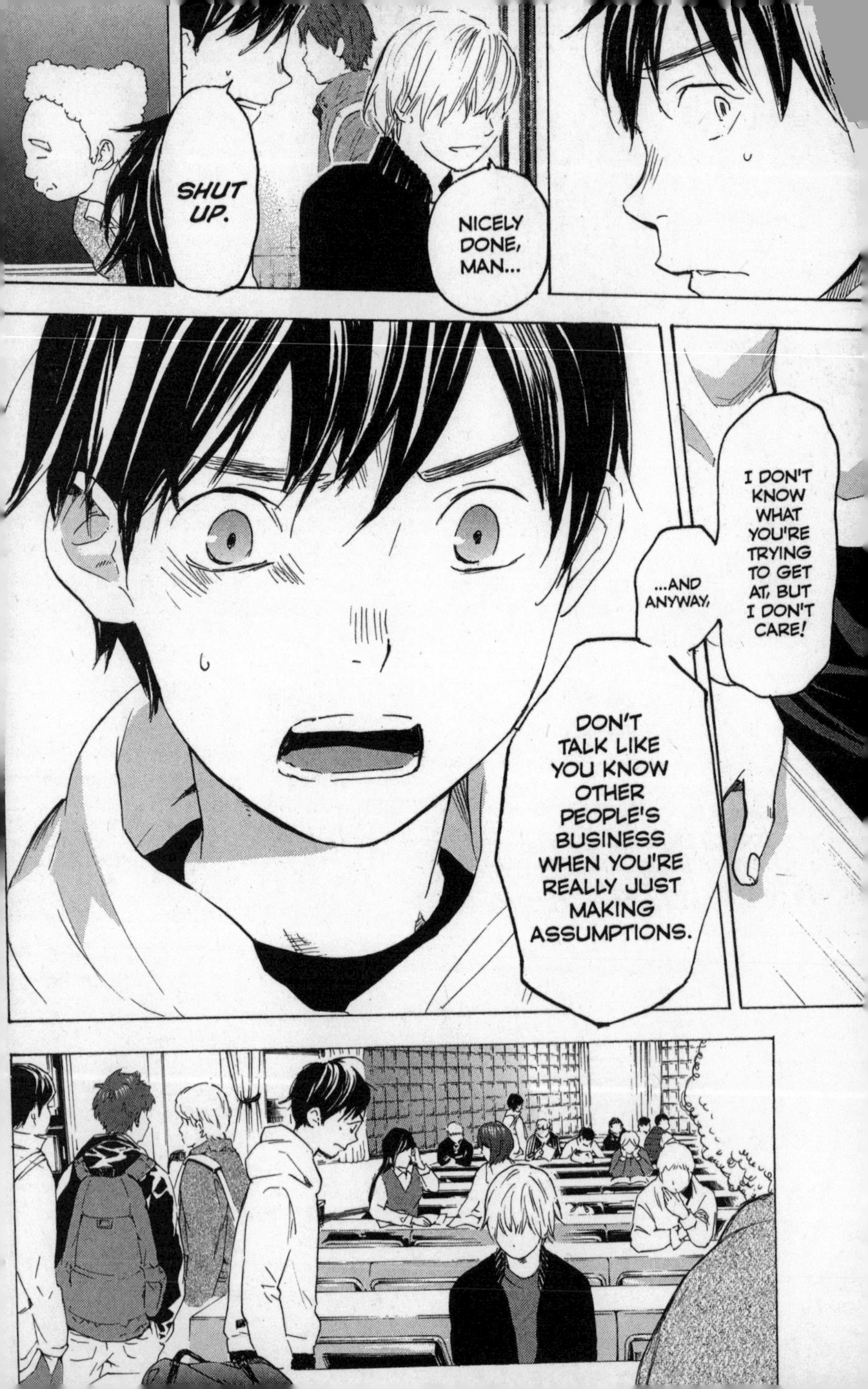
NICELY DONE, MAN...
SHUT UP.
I DON'T KNOW WHAT YOU'RE TRYING TO GET AT, BUT I DON'T CARE!
...AND ANYWAY,
DON'T TALK LIKE YOU KNOW OTHER PEOPLE'S BUSINESS WHEN YOU'RE REALLY JUST MAKING ASSUMPTIONS.

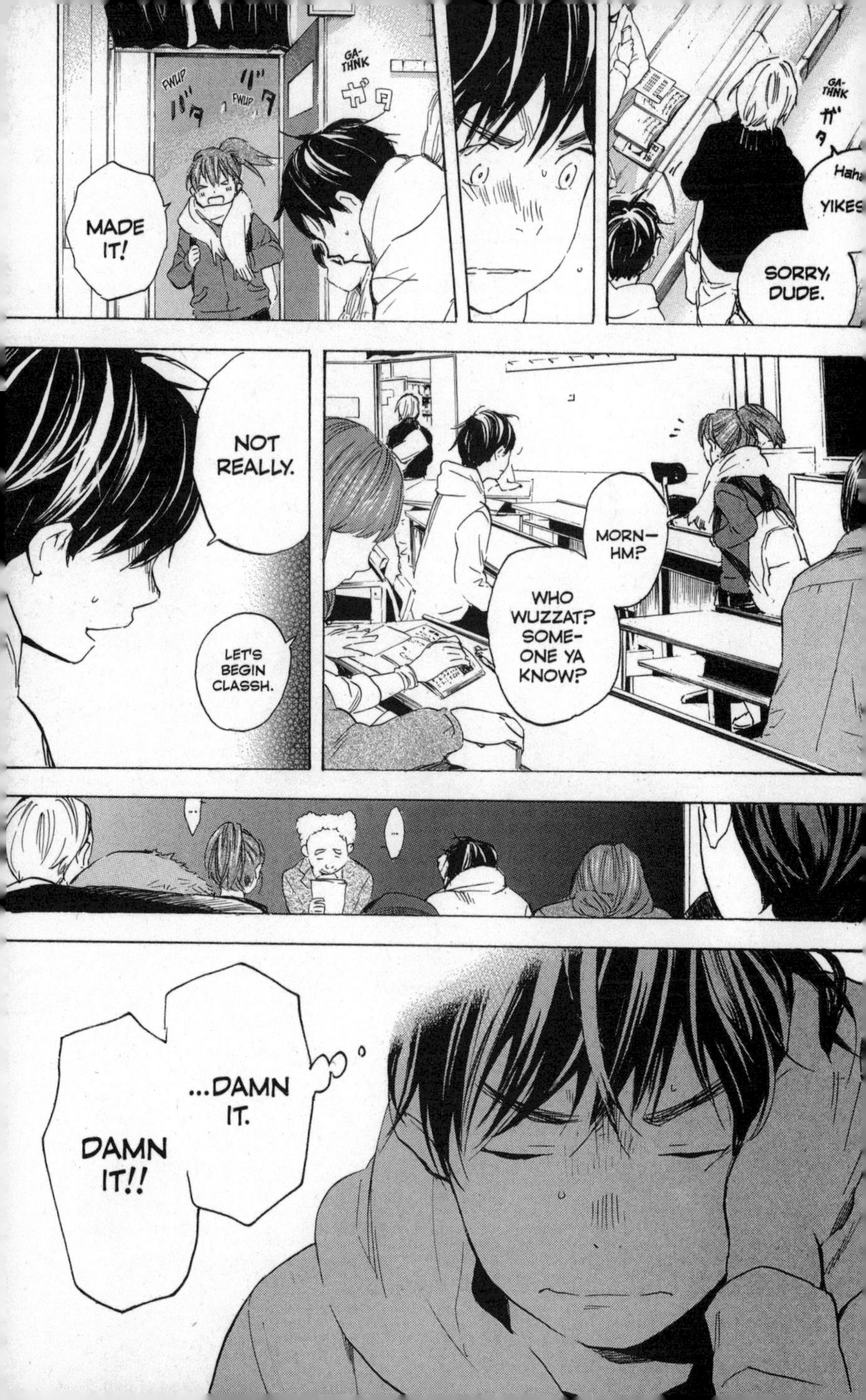
GA-THNK
ガタ
Haha
YIKES
SORRY, DUDE.
GA-THNK
ガタ
FWUP
FWUP
MADE IT!
MORN— HM?
WHO WUZZAT? SOME-ONE YA KNOW?
NOT REALLY.
LET'S BEGIN CLASSH.
...DAMN IT.
DAMN IT!!

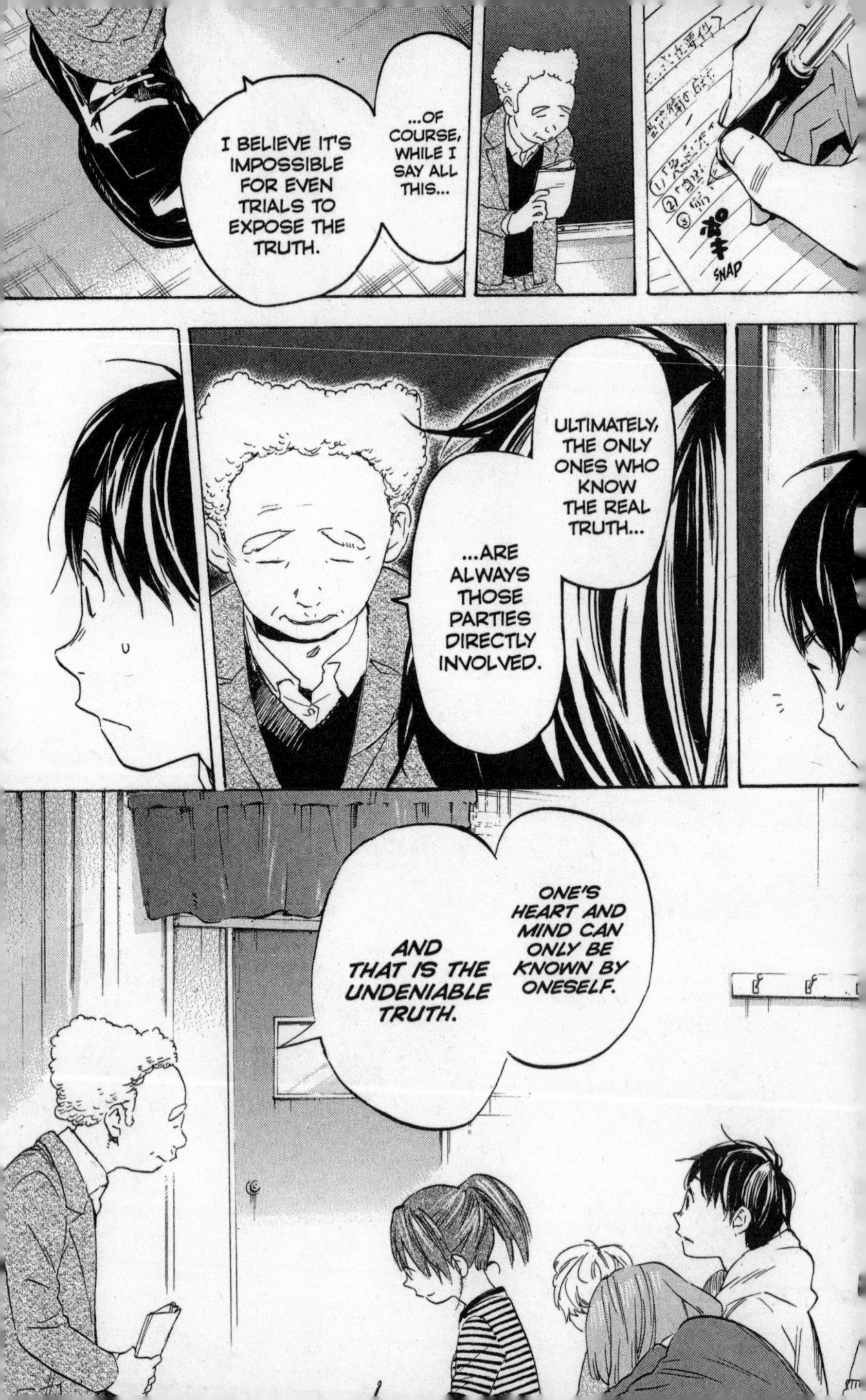
SNAP
...OF COURSE, WHILE I SAY ALL THIS...
I BELIEVE IT'S IMPOSSIBLE FOR EVEN TRIALS TO EXPOSE THE TRUTH.
ULTIMATELY, THE ONLY ONES WHO KNOW THE REAL TRUTH...
...ARE ALWAYS THOSE PARTIES DIRECTLY INVOLVED.
ONE'S HEART AND MIND CAN ONLY BE KNOWN BY ONESELF.
AND THAT IS THE UNDENIABLE TRUTH.

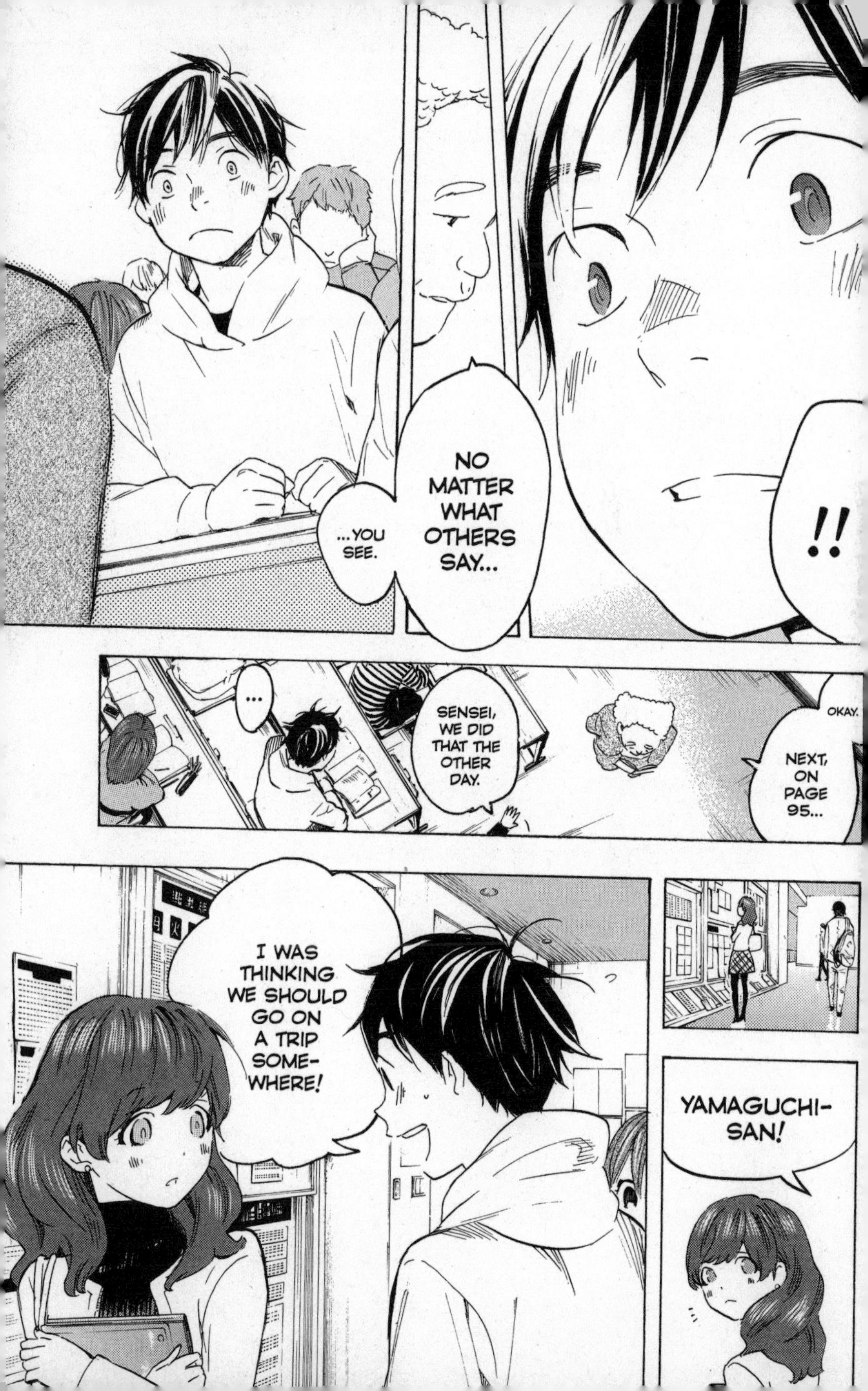
!!
NO MATTER WHAT OTHERS SAY...
...YOU SEE.
OKAY.
NEXT, ON PAGE 95...
SENSEI, WE DID THAT THE OTHER DAY.
...
YAMAGUCHI-SAN!
I WAS THINKING WE SHOULD GO ON A TRIP SOME-WHERE!

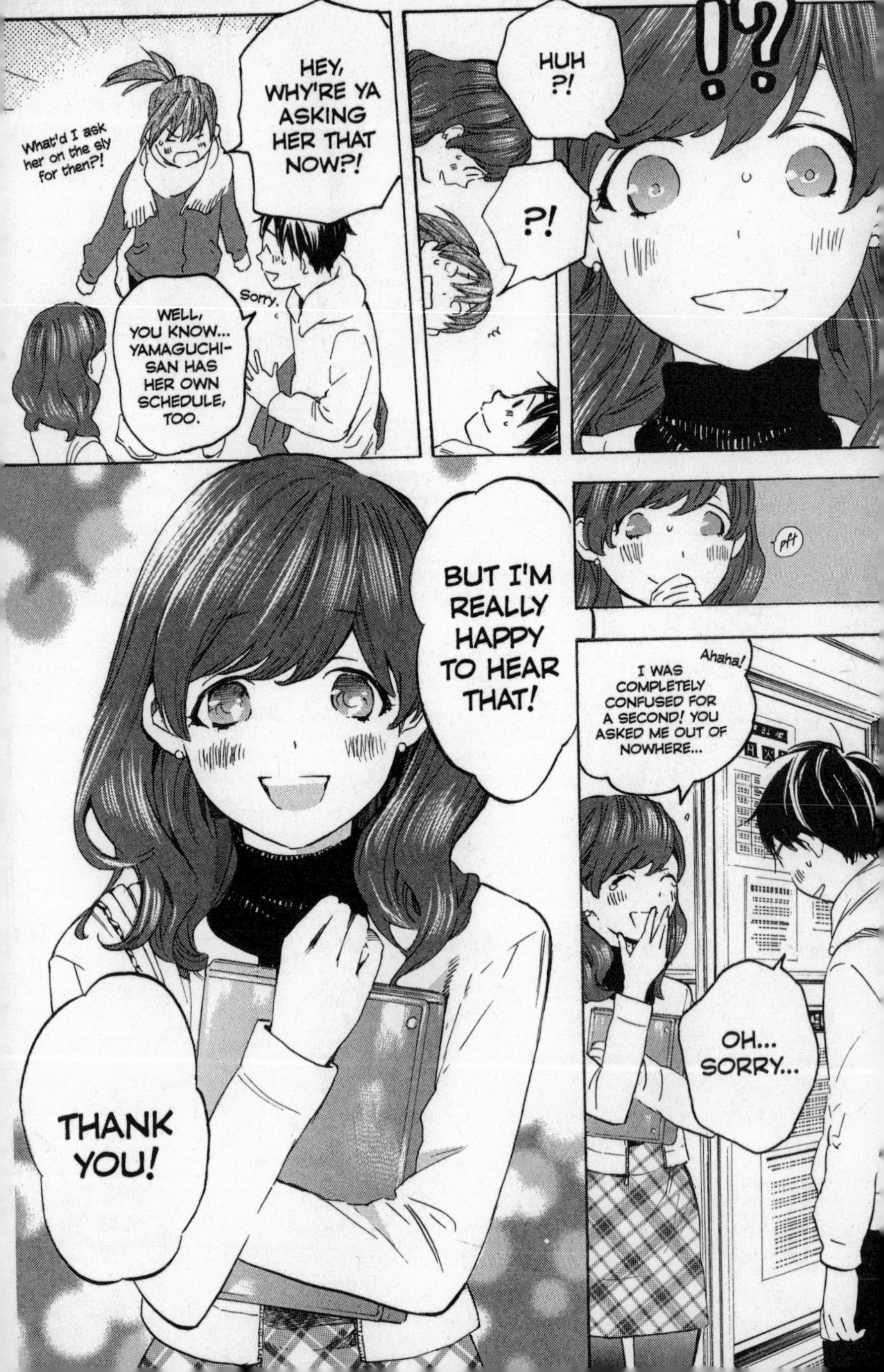
!?
HUH ?!
?!
HEY, WHY'RE YA ASKING HER THAT NOW?!
What'd I ask her on the sly for then?!
Sorry.
WELL, YOU KNOW... YAMAGUCHI-SAN HAS HER OWN SCHEDULE, TOO.
pft
Ahaha!
I WAS COMPLETELY CONFUSED FOR A SECOND! YOU ASKED ME OUT OF NOWHERE...
OH... SORRY...
BUT I'M REALLY HAPPY TO HEAR THAT!
THANK YOU!

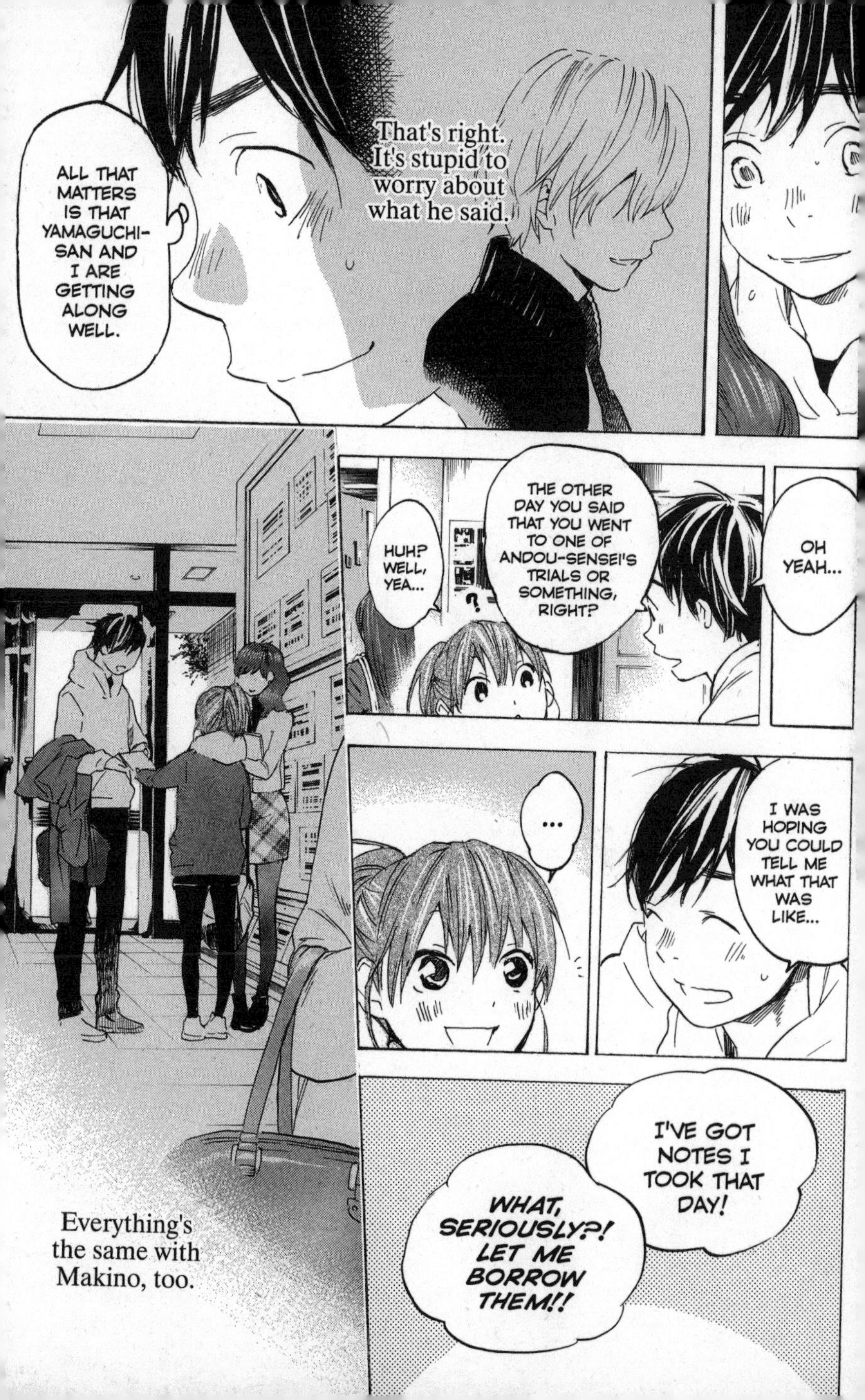

That's right. It's stupid to worry about what he said.
ALL THAT MATTERS IS THAT YAMAGUCHI-SAN AND I ARE GETTING ALONG WELL.
OH YEAH...
THE OTHER DAY YOU SAID THAT YOU WENT TO ONE OF ANDOU-SENSEI'S TRIALS OR SOMETHING, RIGHT?
HUH? WELL, YEA...
?
I WAS HOPING YOU COULD TELL ME WHAT THAT WAS LIKE...
...
I'VE GOT NOTES I TOOK THAT DAY!
WHAT, SERIOUSLY?! LET ME BORROW THEM!!
Everything's the same with Makino, too.

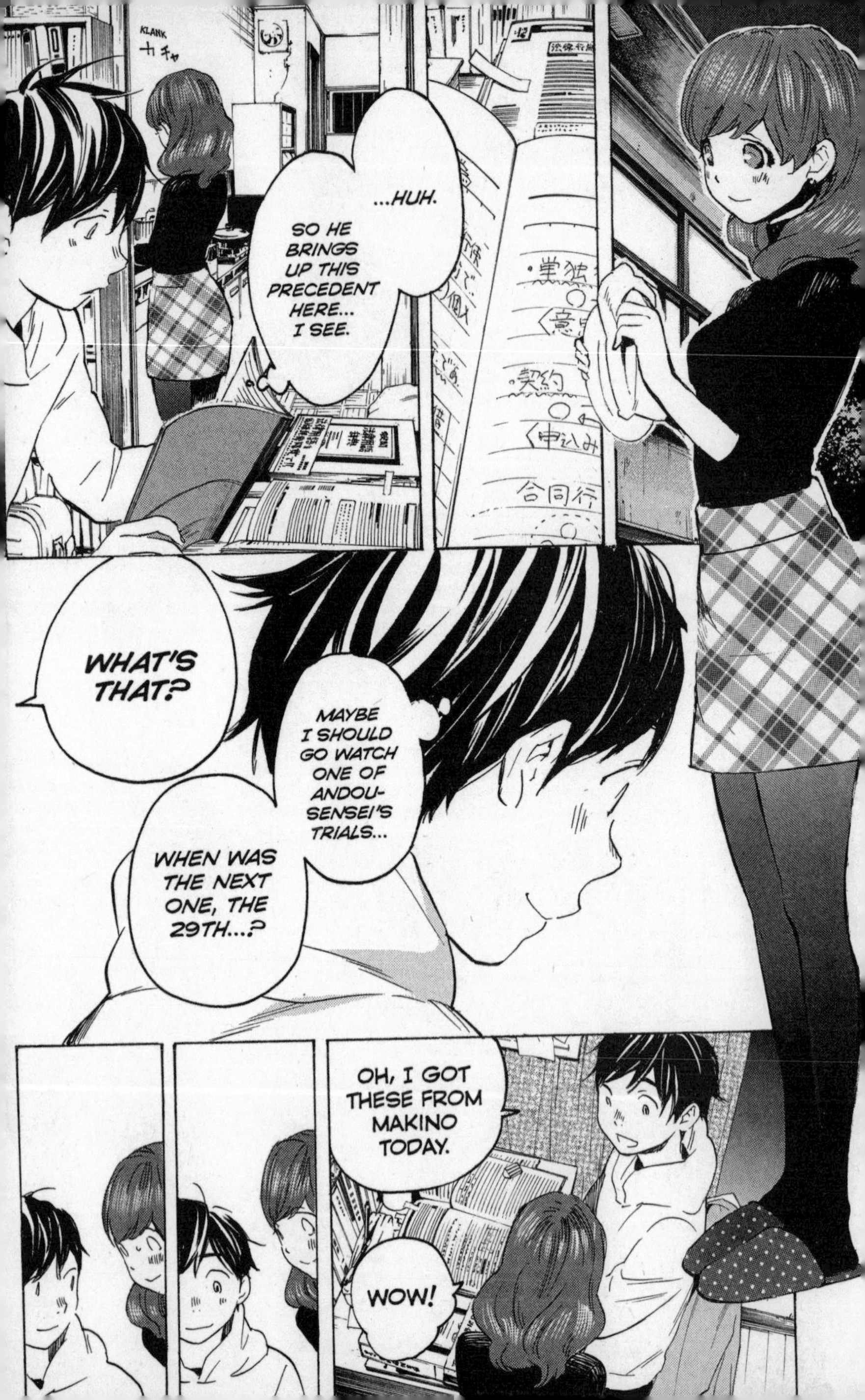
...HUH.
SO HE BRINGS UP THIS PRECEDENT HERE... I SEE.
KLANK
カチャ
MAYBE I SHOULD GO WATCH ONE OF ANDOU-SENSEI'S TRIALS...
WHEN WAS THE NEXT ONE, THE 29TH...?
WHAT'S THAT?
OH, I GOT THESE FROM MAKINO TODAY.
WOW!

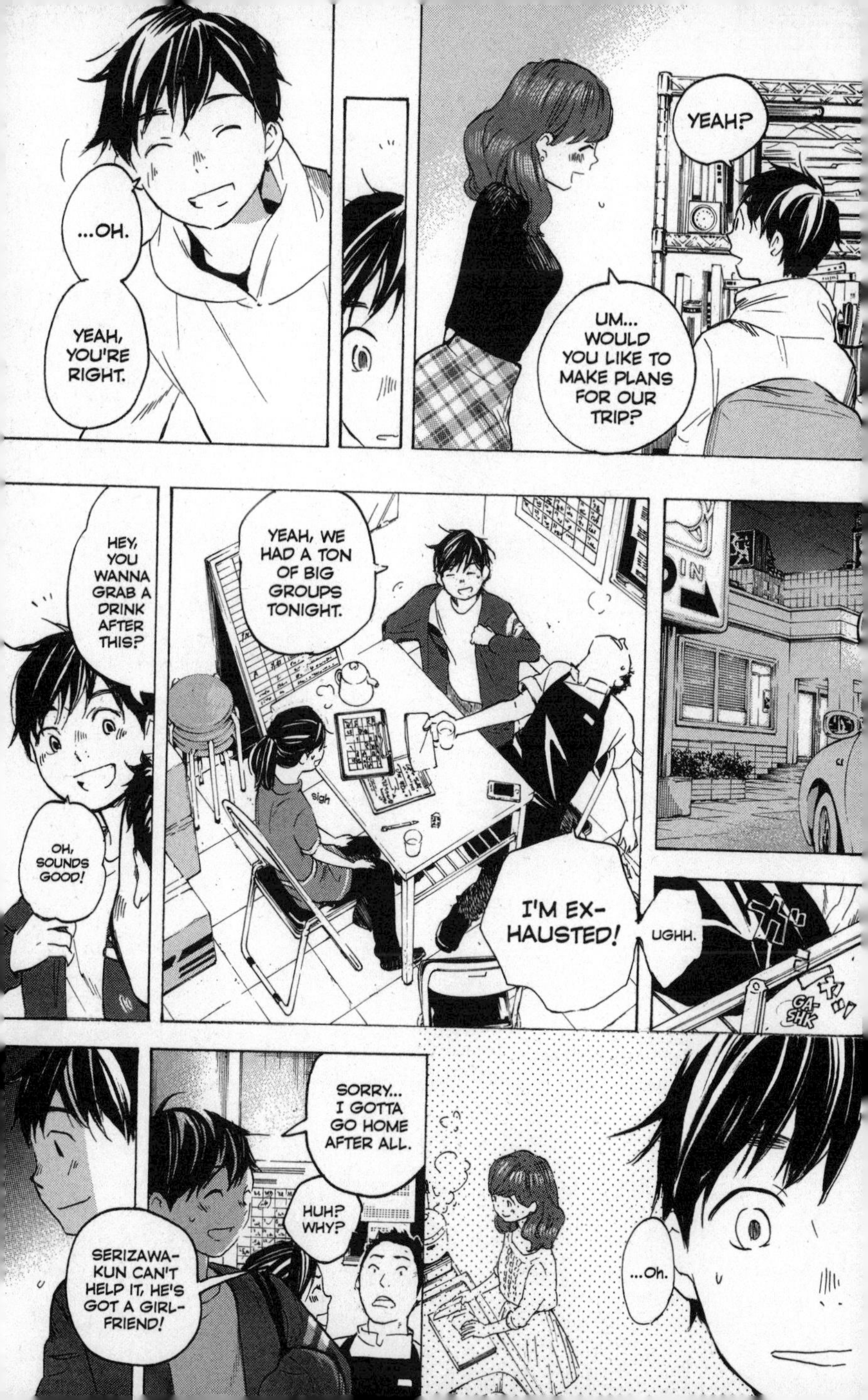
YEAH?
UM... WOULD YOU LIKE TO MAKE PLANS FOR OUR TRIP?
...OH.
YEAH, YOU'RE RIGHT.
IN
UGHH.
GA-SHK
I'M EX-HAUSTED!
YEAH, WE HAD A TON OF BIG GROUPS TONIGHT.
sigh
HEY, YOU WANNA GRAB A DRINK AFTER THIS?
OH, SOUNDS GOOD!
...Oh.
SORRY... I GOTTA GO HOME AFTER ALL.
HUH? WHY?
SERIZAWA-KUN CAN'T HELP IT, HE'S GOT A GIRL-FRIEND!

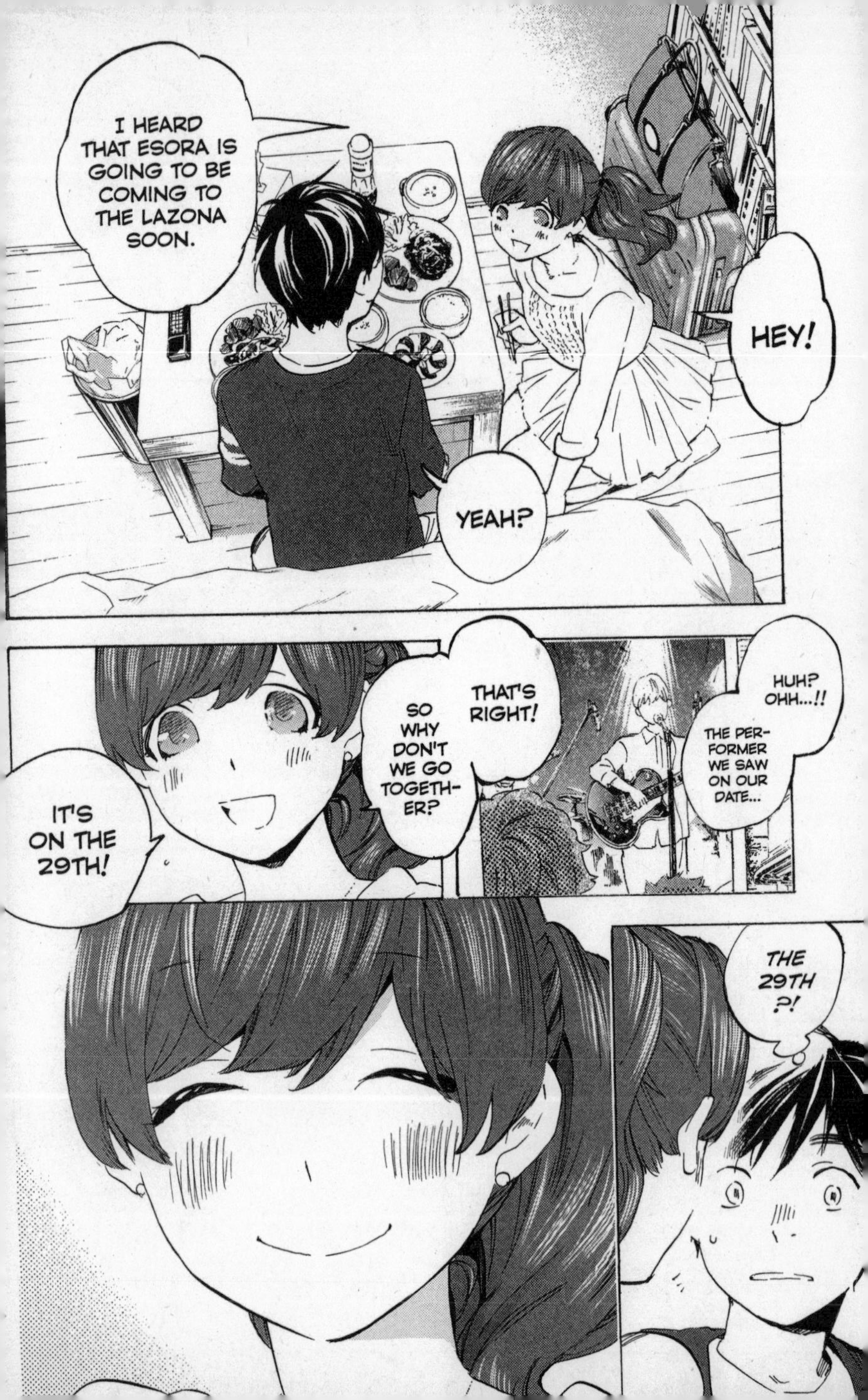
HEY!
YEAH?
I HEARD THAT ESORA IS GOING TO BE COMING TO THE LAZONA SOON.
HUH? OHH...!!
THE PER-FORMER WE SAW ON OUR DATE...
THAT'S RIGHT!
SO WHY DON'T WE GO TOGETH-ER?
IT'S ON THE 29TH!
THE 29TH?!

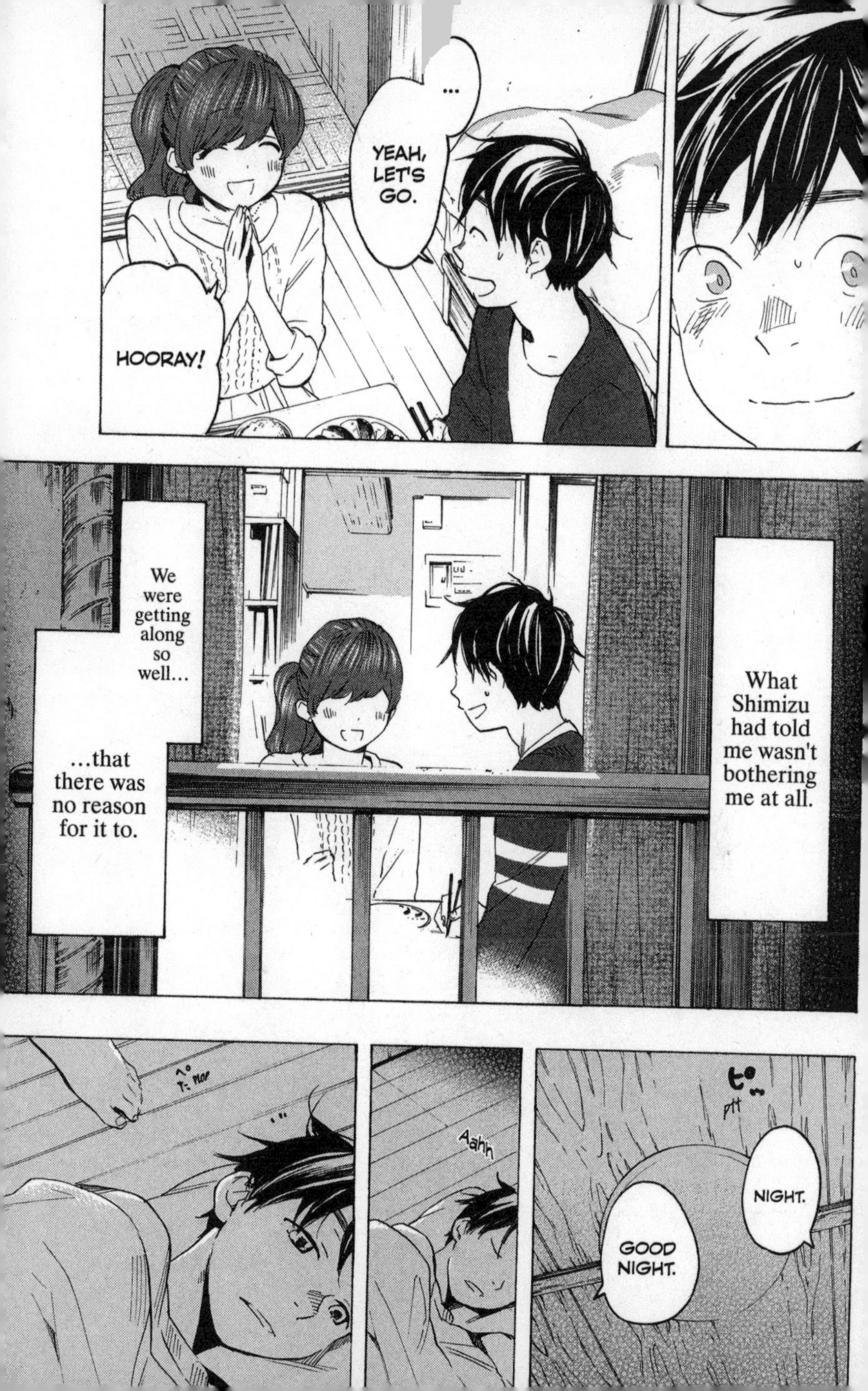
...
YEAH, LET'S GO.
HOORAY!
What Shimizu had told me wasn't bothering me at all.
We were getting along so well...
...that there was no reason for it to.
pit
NIGHT.
GOOD NIGHT.
Aahn
plop

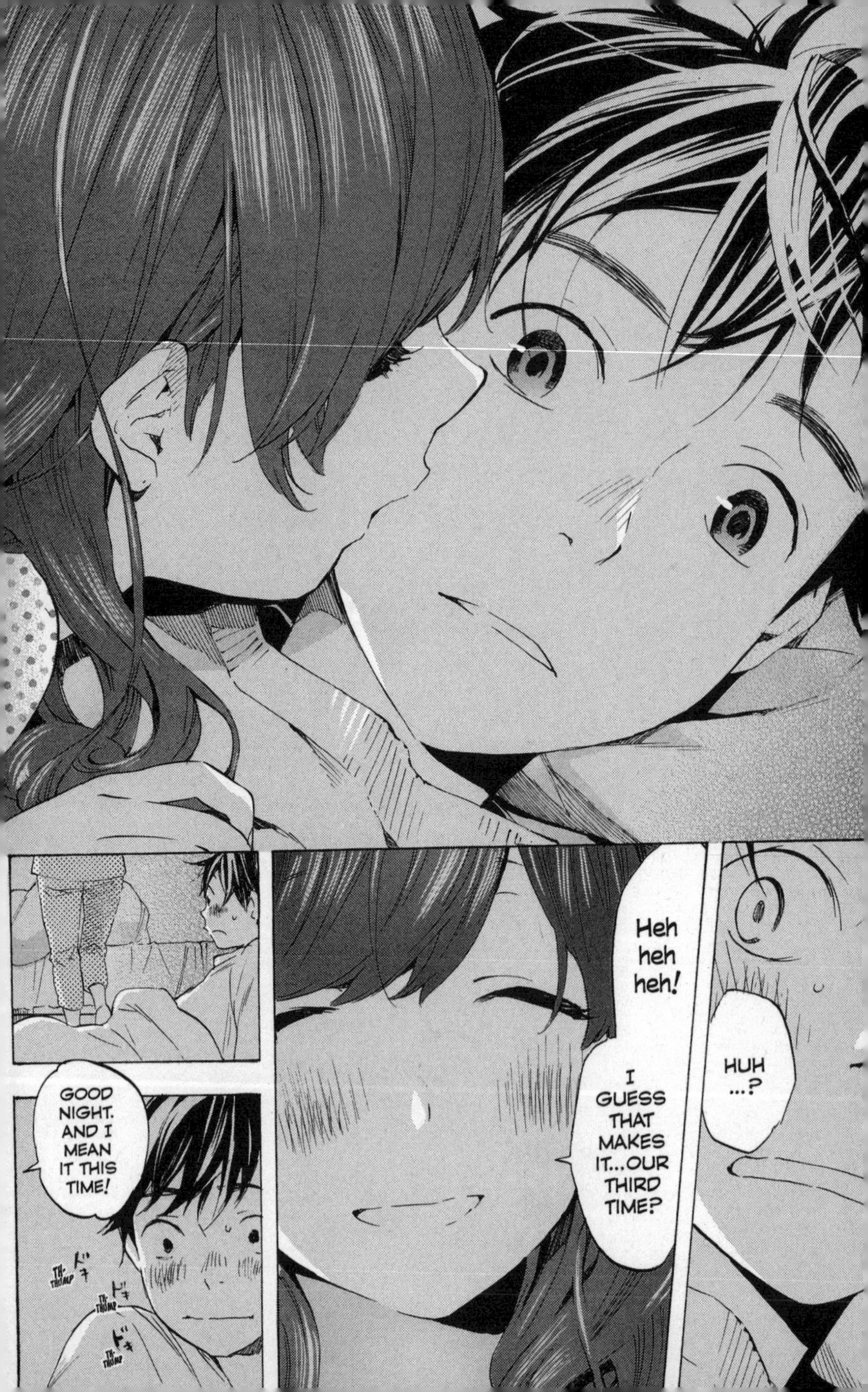
HUH ...?
Heh heh heh!
I GUESS THAT MAKES IT...OUR THIRD TIME?
GOOD NIGHT. AND I MEAN IT THIS TIME!
ドキ
TH-THUMP
ドキ
TH-THUMP
ドキ
TH-THUMP

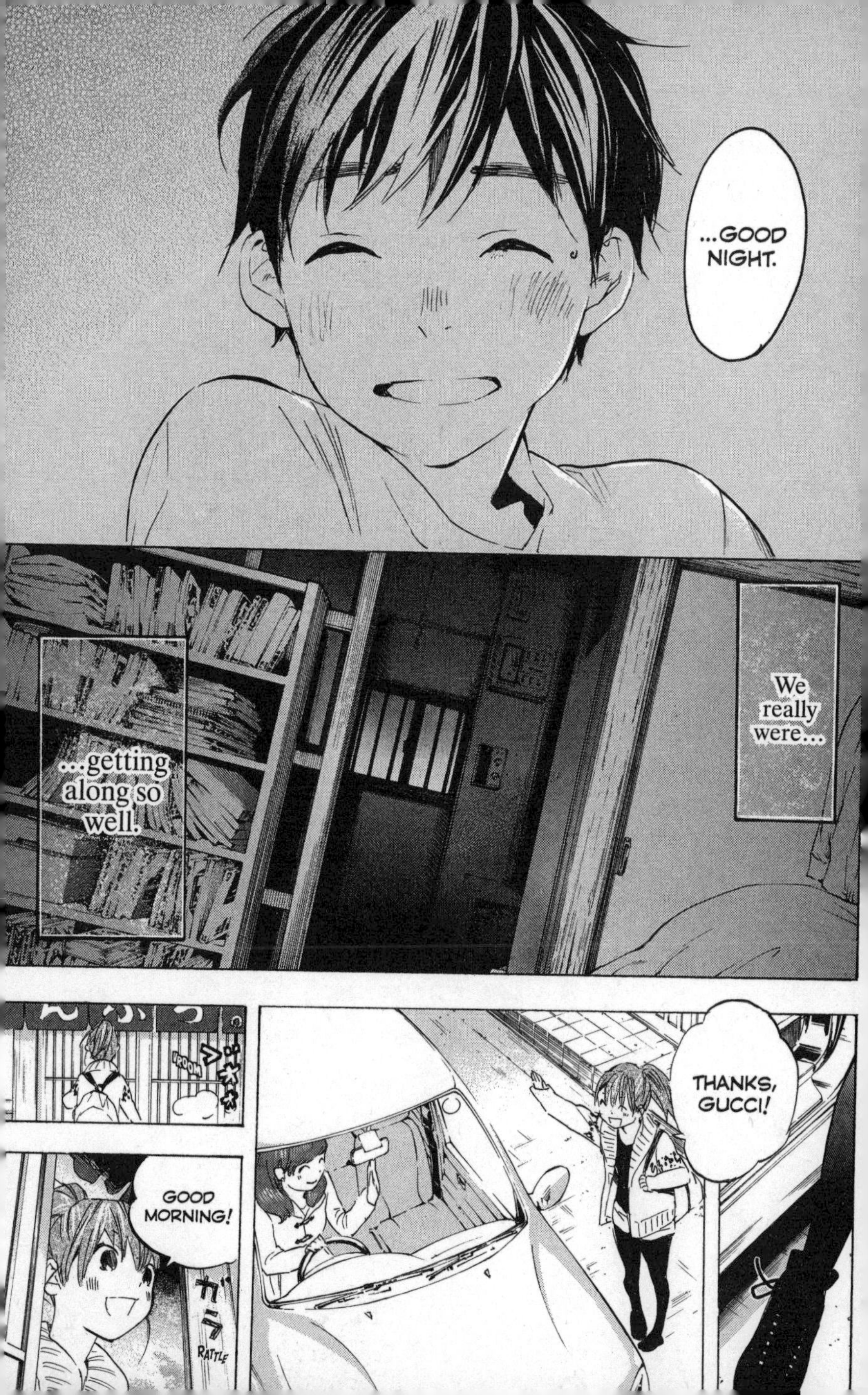
...GOOD NIGHT.
We really were...
...getting along so well.
THANKS, GUCCI!
VROOM
GOOD MORNING!
ガラ
RATTLE

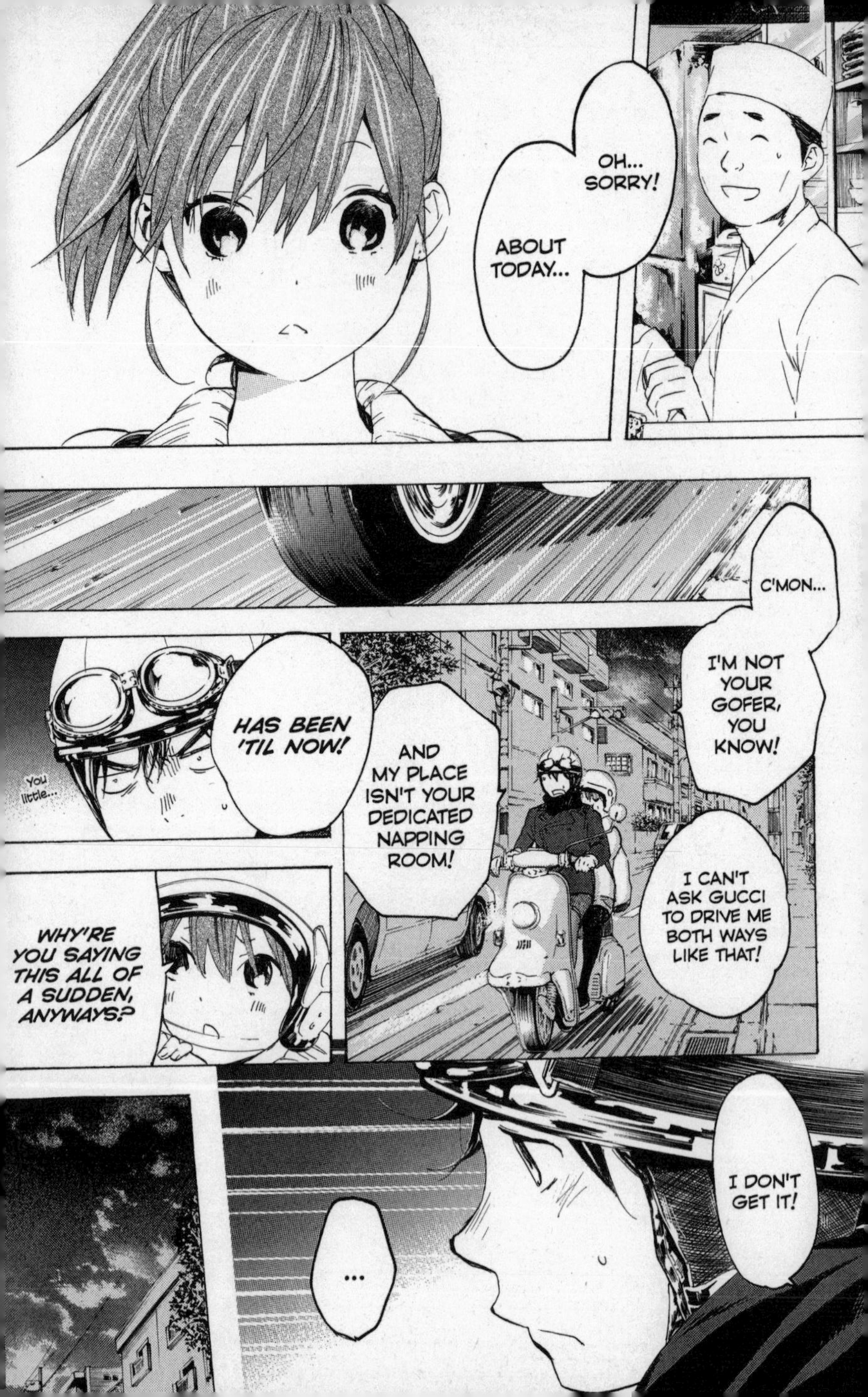
OH... SORRY!
ABOUT TODAY...
C'MON...
I'M NOT YOUR GOFER, YOU KNOW!
AND MY PLACE ISN'T YOUR DEDICATED NAPPING ROOM!
I CAN'T ASK GUCCI TO DRIVE ME BOTH WAYS LIKE THAT!
HAS BEEN 'TIL NOW!
You little...
WHY'RE YOU SAYING THIS ALL OF A SUDDEN, ANYWAYS?
I DON'T GET IT!
...

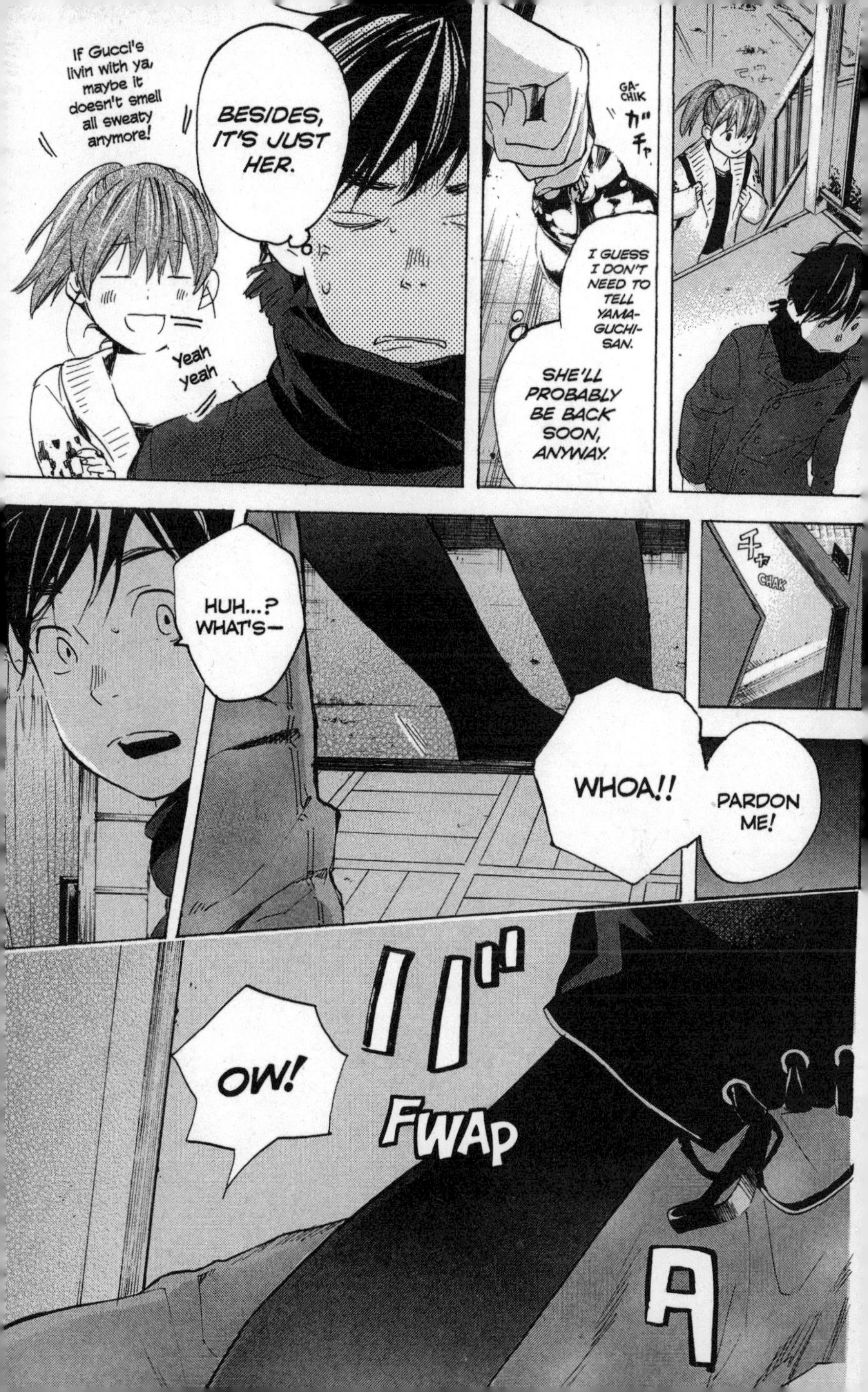
GA-CHIK
ガチャ
I GUESS I DON'T NEED TO TELL YAMAGUCHI-SAN.
SHE'LL PROBABLY BE BACK SOON, ANYWAY.
BESIDES, IT'S JUST HER.
If Gucci's livin with ya, maybe it doesn't smell all sweaty anymore!
Yeah yeah
チャ
CHAK
PARDON ME!
WHOA!!
HUH...? WHAT'S—
A
FWAP
OW!

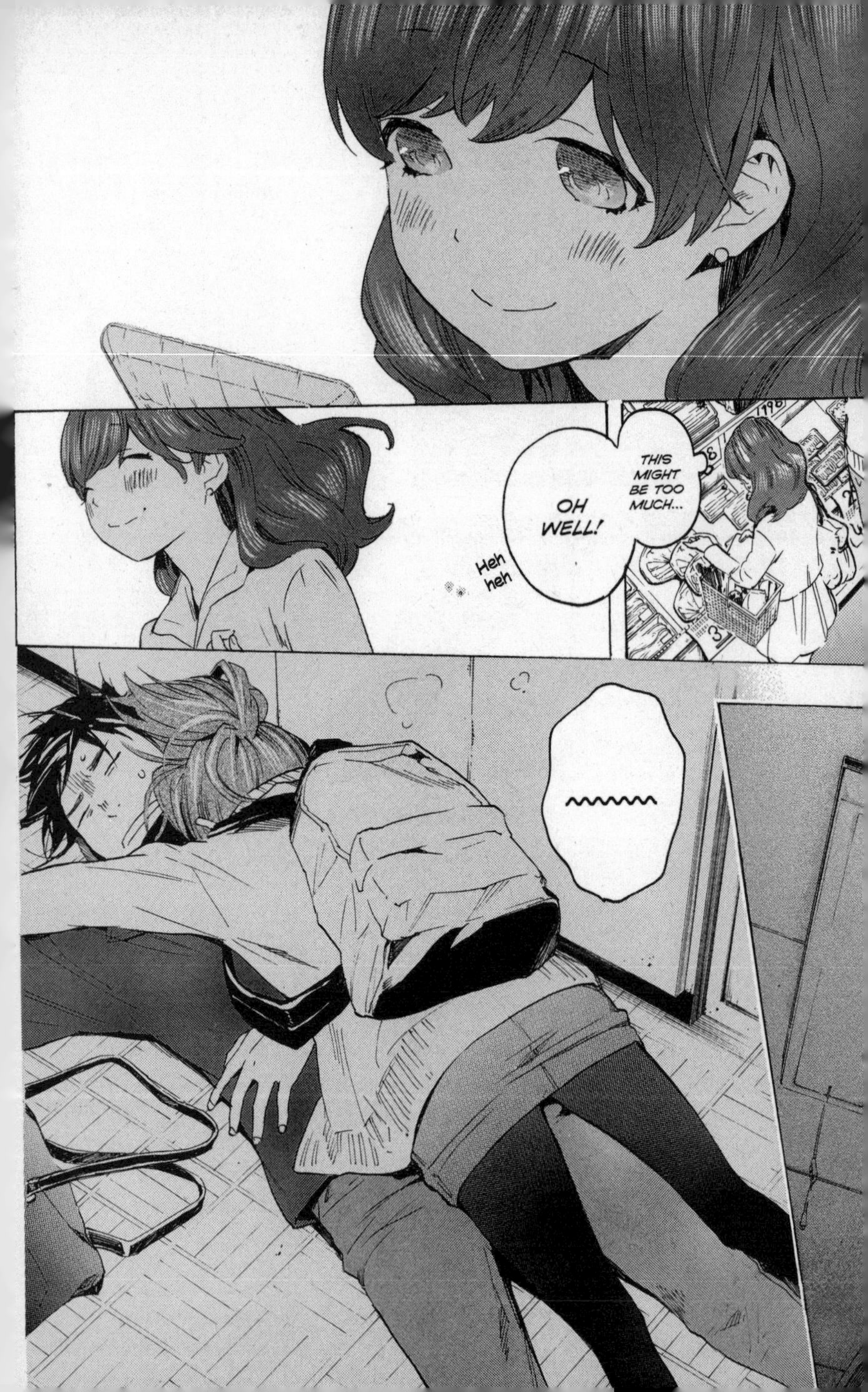
THIS MIGHT BE TOO MUCH...
OH WELL!
Heh heh
~~~~~~
~~~~~~

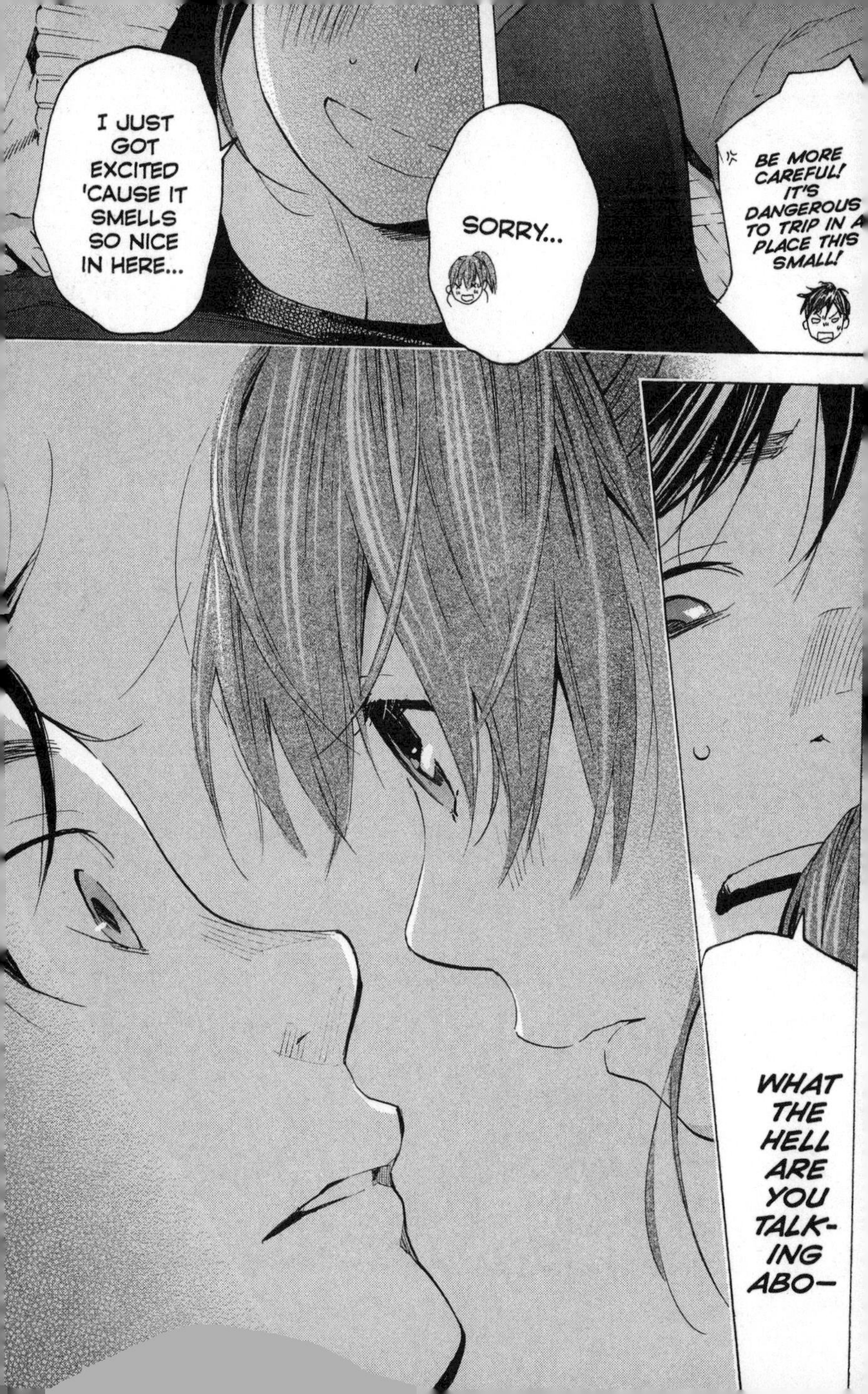

BE MORE CAREFUL! IT'S DANGEROUS TO TRIP IN A PLACE THIS SMALL!
SORRY...
I JUST GOT EXCITED 'CAUSE IT SMELLS SO NICE IN HERE...
WHAT THE HELL ARE YOU TALK-ING ABO—

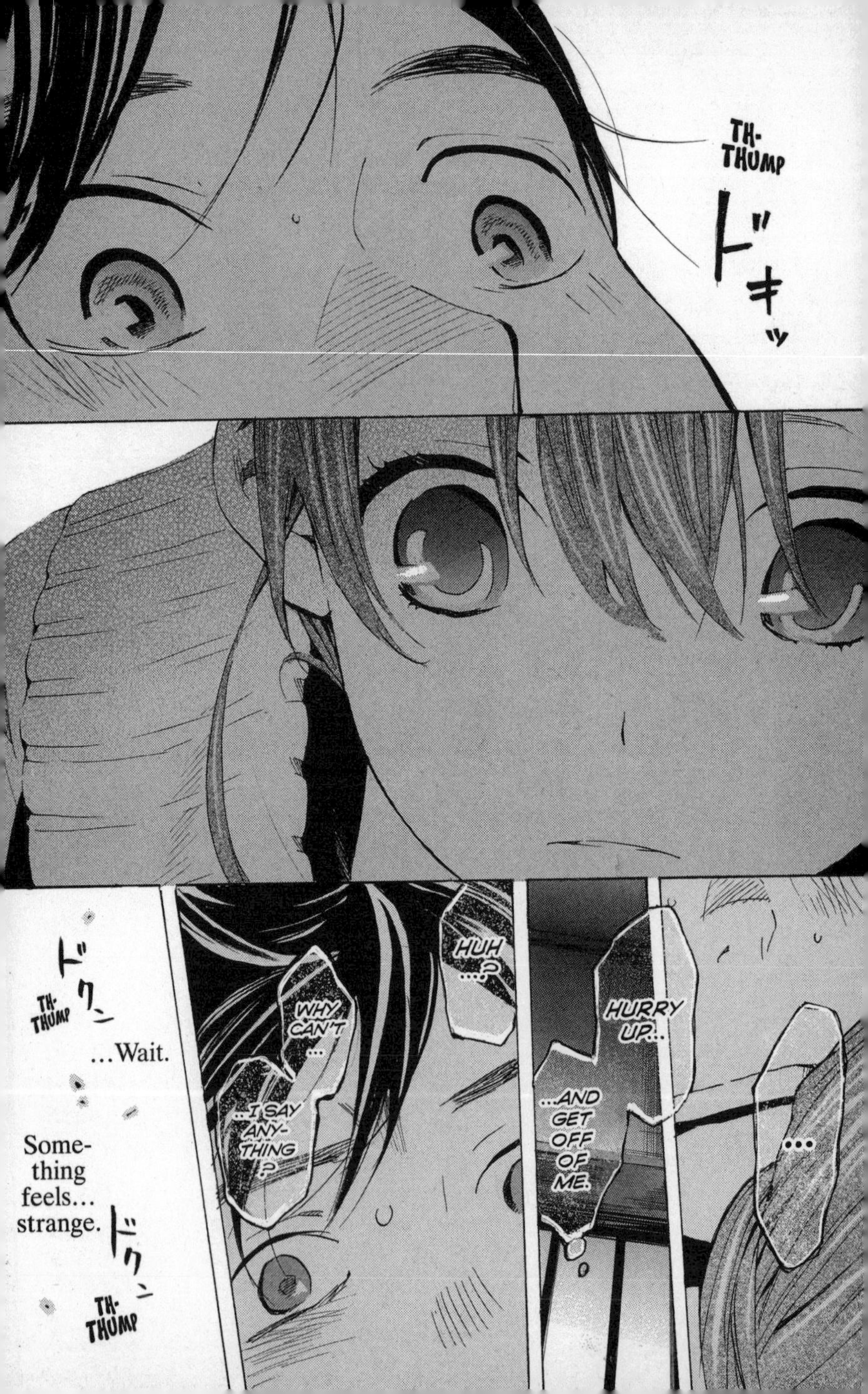
TH-THUMP
ドキッ
...
HURRY UP...
...AND GET OFF OF ME.
HUH...?
WHY CAN'T...
...I SAY ANYTHING?
ドクン
TH-THUMP
...Wait.
Something feels... strange.
ドクン
TH-THUMP

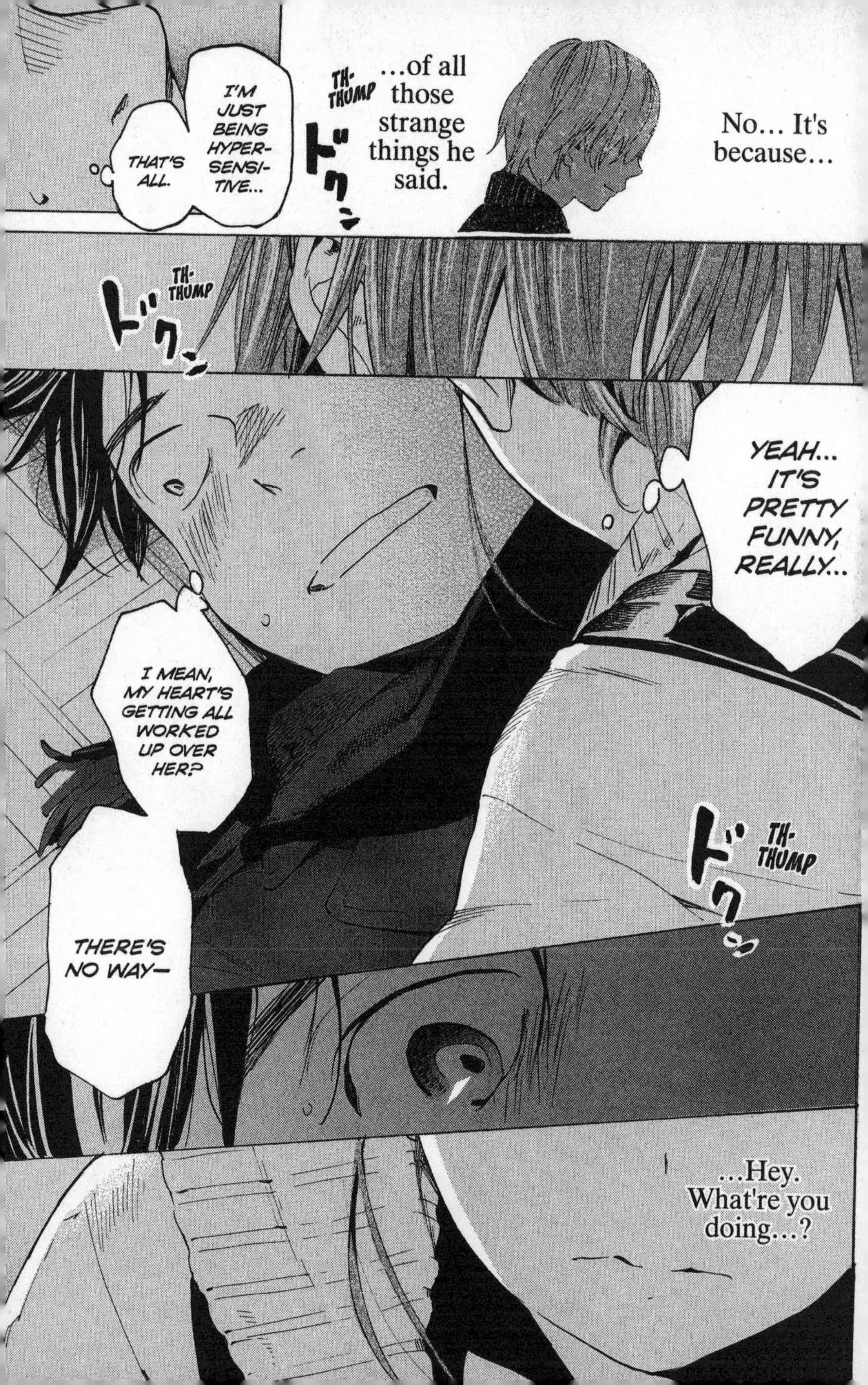
No… It's because…
TH-THUMP
ドクン
…of all those strange things he said.
I'M JUST BEING HYPER-SENSI-TIVE...
THAT'S ALL.
TH-THUMP
ドクン
YEAH... IT'S PRETTY FUNNY, REALLY...
I MEAN, MY HEART'S GETTING ALL WORKED UP OVER HER?
TH-THUMP
ドクン
THERE'S NO WAY—
…Hey. What're you doing…?

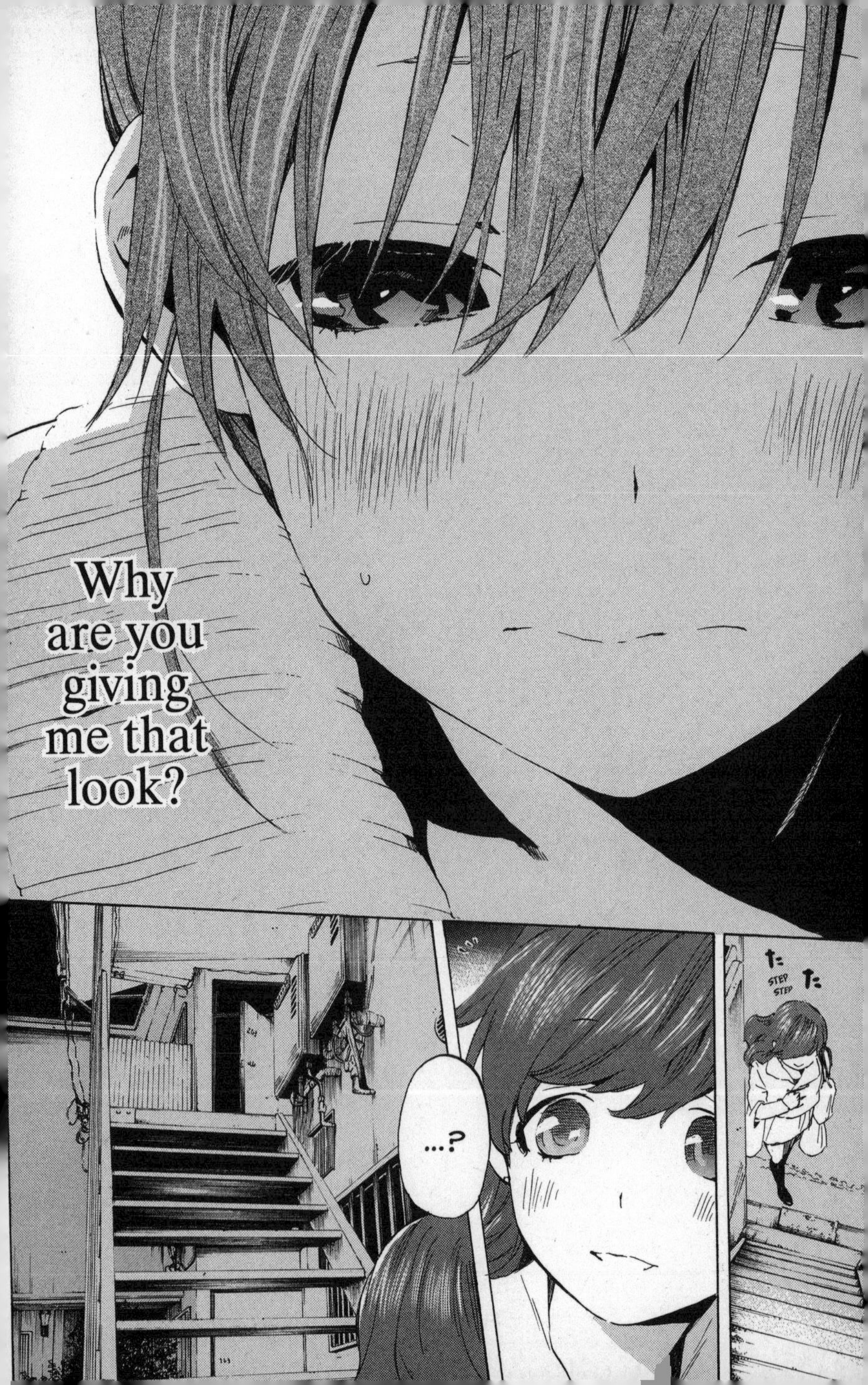
Why are you giving me that look?
た
STEP STEP
た
...?

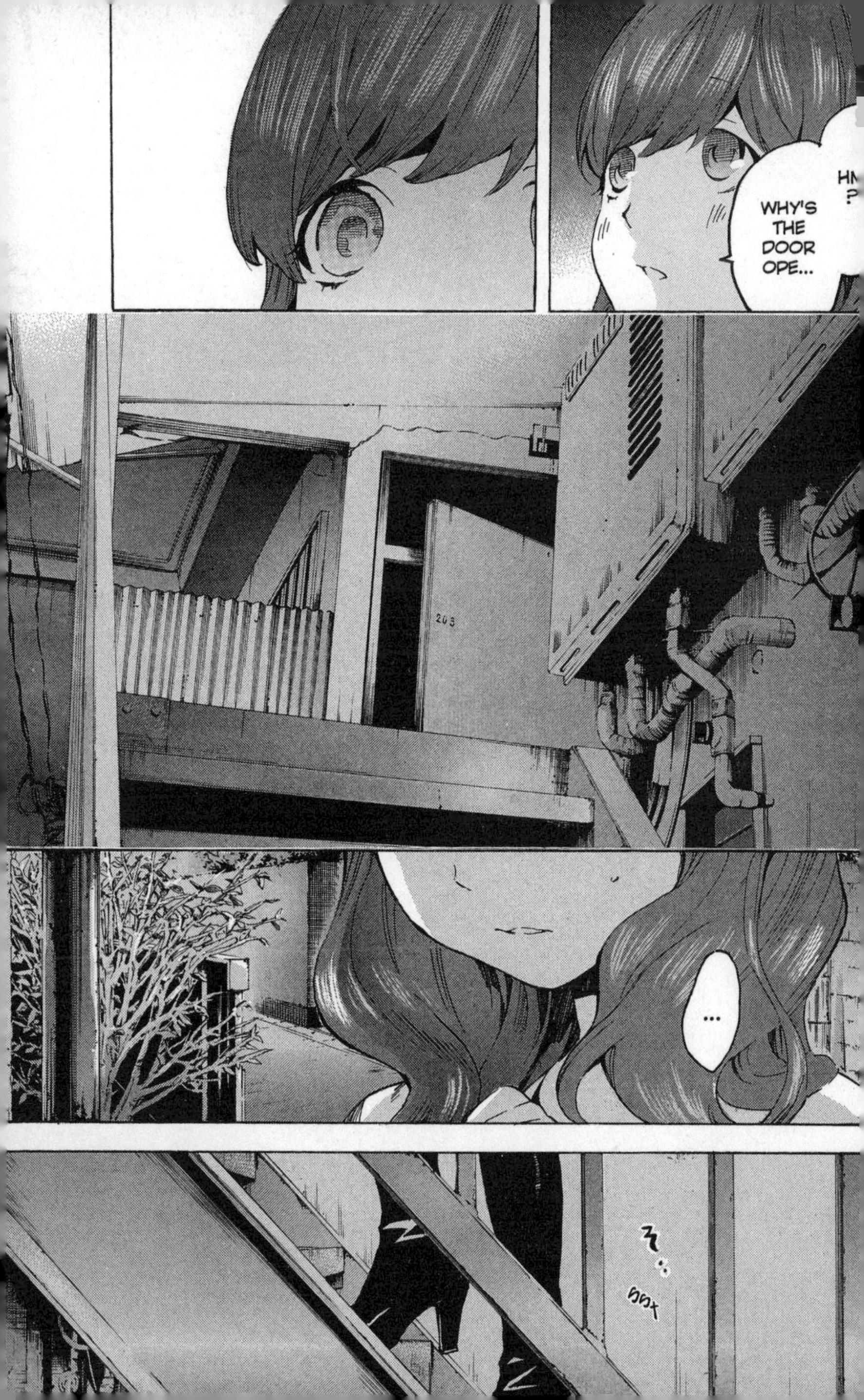
WHY'S THE DOOR OPE...
...

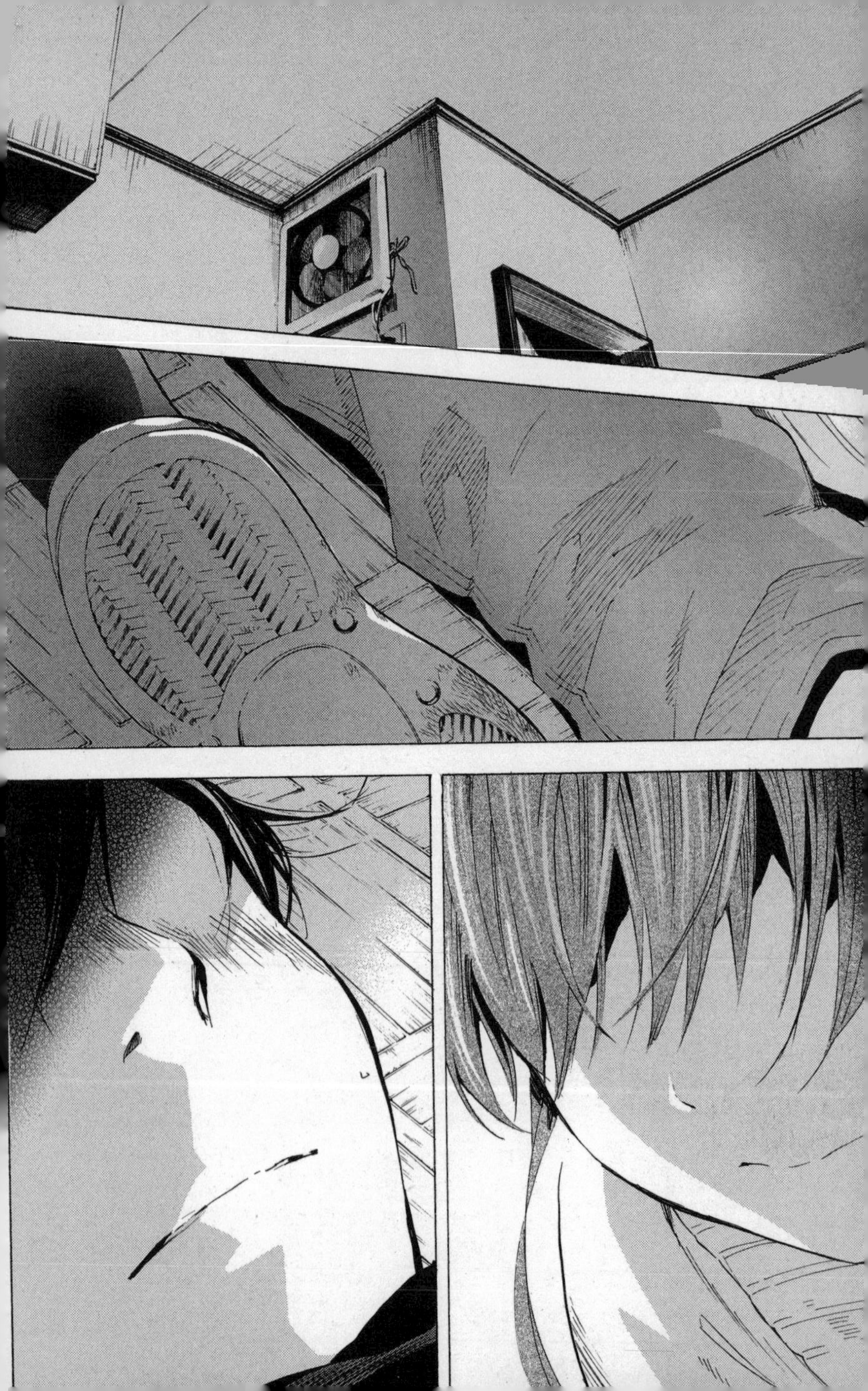

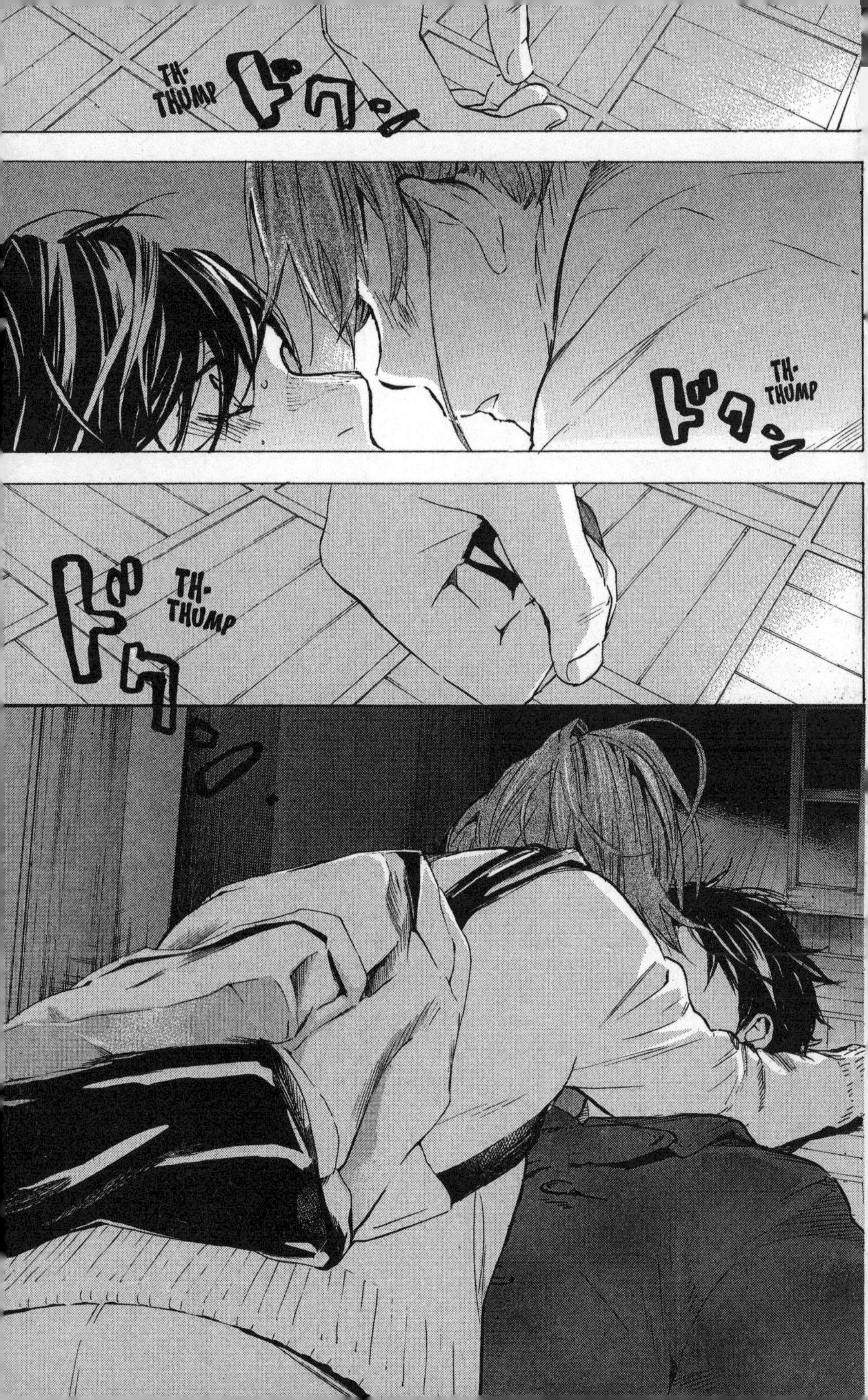
TH-THUMP
TH-THUMP
TH-THUMP

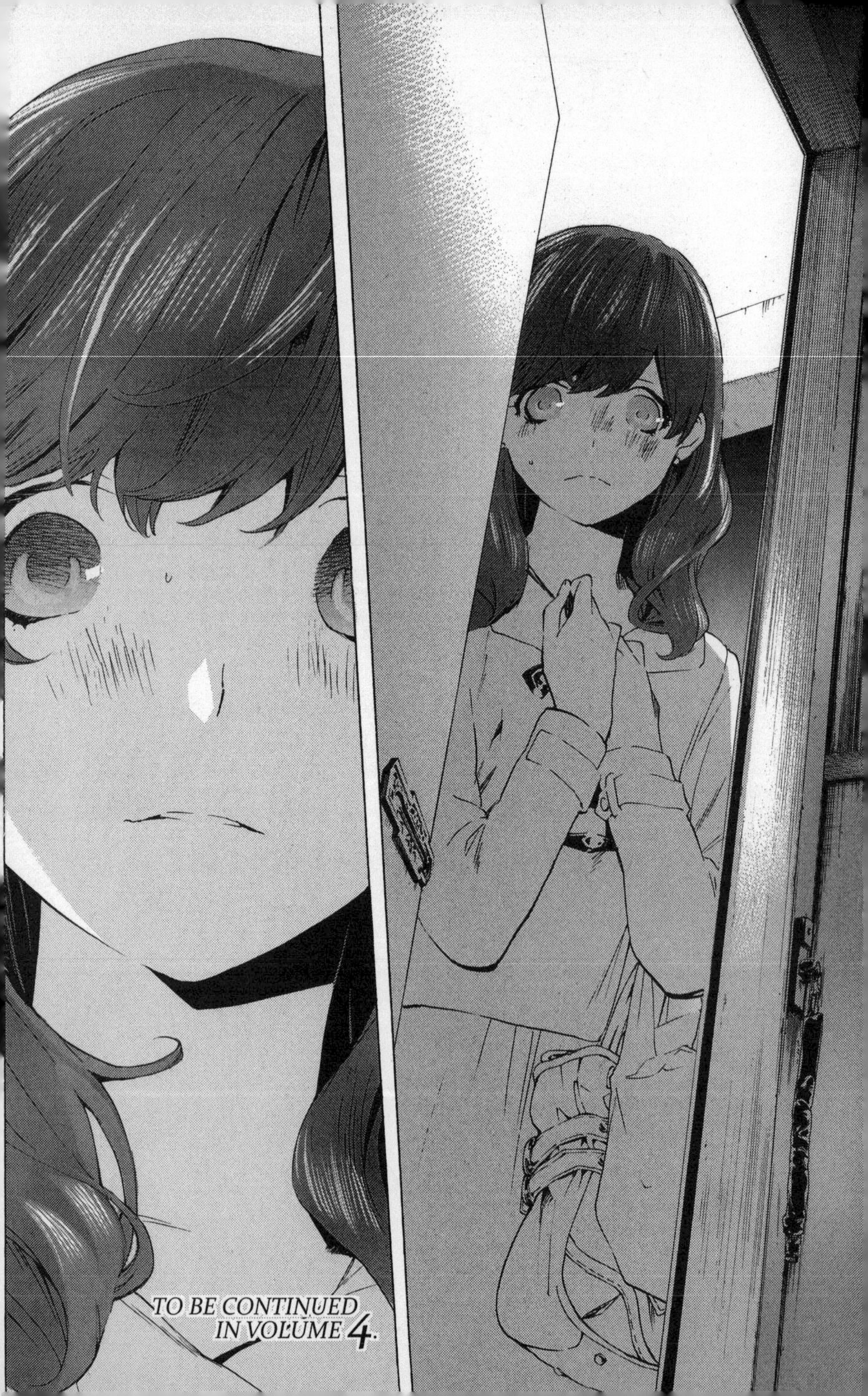
TO BE CONTINUED
IN VOLUME 4.

Forget Me Not

— TRANSLATION NOTES —

WOLF IN SHEEP'S CLOTHING page 62, panel 3

The original Japanese used the term "*rooru kyabetsu*," which translates to "rolled cabbage," an appetizer commonly known as stuffed cabbage that consists of meat stuffed or wrapped up in cooked cabbage leaves. In Japanese slang, a man (though this can also be used for women) who is aggressive when it comes to pursuing love interests is known as a carnivore, and its opposite is an herbivore. Therefore, meat wrapped in a vegetable à la stuffed cabbage describes a guy who looks soft and sensitive on the outside but who is actually a lady-killer. The opposite term is "*asupara-beicon*" (bacon-wrapped asparagus)—a guy who looks like a player, but is actually a sweet and sensitive guy.

COCONUT-HEAD page 67, panel 1

In the original Japanese, Serizawa uses "*onigiri*" to describe the funny shape of this guy's head. *Onigiri* is sushi rice formed into a ball or triangular shape that often has a filling (such as pickled plum, cooked salmon, or tuna) and may be wrapped in dried seaweed. To better get the image across to non-Japanese readers, coconut was used to describe his head instead.

ESORA AND LAZONA page 176, panel 1

Esora is the name of a real singer-songwriter and local musician in the Tokyo metropolitan scene. Lazona Kawasaki Plaza is a shopping mall designed by Spanish architect Richardo Bofil and is located in Kawasaki, Kanazawa Prefecture.

A Kodansha Comics Trade Paperback Original.

Forget Me Not volume 3 copyright © 2014 Mag Hsu & Nao Emoto
Original title "My Girls!: dedicated to those of you whom I love and hurt"
published in Taiwan 2011 by TITAN Publishing Co., Ltd.
English translation copyright © 2016 Mag Hsu & Nao Emoto

All rights reserved.

Published in the United States by Kodansha Comics,
an imprint of Kodansha USA Publishing, LLC, New York.

Publication rights for this English edition arranged through Kodansha Ltd.,
Tokyo.

First published in Japan in 2014 by Kodansha Ltd., Tokyo, as *Sore Demo
Boku Wa Kimi Ga Suki* volume 3.

ISBN 978-1-63236-313-8

Printed in the United States

www.kodanshacomics.com

9 8 7 6 5 4 3 2 1

Translation: Ko Ransom
Lettering: Evan Hayden
Editing: Ajani Oloye
Kodansha Comics Edition Cover Design: Phil Balsman